DOCUMENTS SU
TO ACCOM

INTERNATIONAL INTELLECTUAL PROPERTY

PROBLEMS, CASES, AND MATERIALS

Fourth Edition

■ ■ ■

Daniel C.K. Chow
Frank E. and Virginia H. Bazler Chair in Business Law
The Ohio State University Moritz College of Law

Edward Lee
Professor of Law and Co-Director of the Program in Intellectual Property Law,
Co-Director of the Center for Design, Law & Technology
Chicago-Kent College of Law

AMERICAN CASEBOOK SERIES®

American Casebook Series is a trademark registered in the U.S. Patent and Trademark Office.

© West, a Thomson business, 2006
© 2012 Thomson Reuters
© 2018 LEG, Inc. d/b/a West Academic
© 2021 LEG, Inc. d/b/a West Academic
      444 Cedar Street, Suite 700
      St. Paul, MN 55101
      1-877-888-1330

West, West Academic Publishing, and West Academic are trademarks of West Publishing Corporation, used under license.

Printed in the United States of America

ISBN: 978-1-63659-050-9

TABLE OF CONTENTS

DOCUMENTS SUPPLEMENT
TO ACCOMPANY

INTERNATIONAL
INTELLECTUAL
PROPERTY

PROBLEMS, CASES,
AND MATERIALS

Fourth Edition

AGREEMENT ON TRADE-RELATED ASPECTS OF INTELLECTUAL PROPERTY RIGHTS (TRIPS AGREEMENT)

(adopted in Marrakesh, Morocco on 15 April 1994, as amended through the Protocol of 6 December 2005 that entered into force on 23 January 2017)

PART VI.   TRANSITIONAL ARRANGEMENTS

PART VII.   INSTITUTIONAL   ARRANGEMENTS;   FINAL
                PROVISIONS

Annex and Appendix to the TRIPS Agreement

AGREEMENT ON TRADE-RELATED ASPECTS OF INTELLECTUAL PROPERTY RIGHTS (TRIPS Agreement)

Members,

Desiring to reduce distortions and impediments to international trade, and taking into account the need to promote effective and adequate protection of intellectual property rights, and to ensure that measures and procedures to enforce intellectual property rights do not themselves become barriers to legitimate trade;

Recognizing, to this end, the need for new rules and disciplines concerning:

(a)   the applicability of the basic principles of GATT 1994 and of relevant international intellectual property agreements or conventions;

(b)   the provision of adequate standards and principles concerning the availability, scope and use of trade-related intellectual property rights;

(c)   the provision of effective and appropriate means for the enforcement of trade-related intellectual property rights, taking into account differences in national legal systems;

(d)   the provision of effective and expeditious procedures for the multilateral prevention and settlement of disputes between governments; and

(e)   transitional arrangements aiming at the fullest participation in the results of the negotiations;

Recognizing the need for a multilateral framework of principles, rules and disciplines dealing with international trade in counterfeit goods;

Recognizing that intellectual property rights are private rights;

Recognizing the underlying public policy objectives of national systems for the protection of intellectual property, including developmental and technological objectives;

Recognizing also the special needs of the least-developed country Members in respect of maximum flexibility in the domestic implementation of laws and regulations in order to enable them to create a sound and viable technological base;

Emphasizing the importance of reducing tensions by reaching strengthened commitments to resolve disputes on trade-related intellectual property issues through multilateral procedures;

Desiring to establish a mutually supportive relationship between the WTO and the World Intellectual Property Organization (referred to in this Agreement as "WIPO") as well as other relevant international organizations;

Hereby agree as follows:

PART I

GENERAL PROVISIONS AND BASIC PRINCIPLES

Article 1

Nature and Scope of Obligations

1.   Members shall give effect to the provisions of this Agreement. Members may, but shall not be obliged to, implement in their law more extensive protection than is required by this Agreement, provided that such protection does not contravene the provisions of this Agreement. Members shall be free to determine the appropriate method of implementing the provisions of this Agreement within their own legal system and practice.

2.   For the purposes of this Agreement, the term "intellectual property" refers to all categories of intellectual property that are the subject of Sections 1 through 7 of Part II.

3.   Members shall accord the treatment provided for in this Agreement to the nationals of other Members.[1] In respect of the relevant intellectual property right, the nationals of other Members shall be understood as those natural or legal persons that would meet the criteria for eligibility for protection provided for in the Paris Convention (1967), the Berne Convention (1971), the Rome Convention and the Treaty on Intellectual Property in Respect of Integrated Circuits, were all Members of the WTO members of those conventions.[2] Any Member availing itself of the possibilities provided in paragraph 3 of Article 5 or paragraph 2 of

---

[1].   When "nationals" are referred to in this Agreement, they shall be deemed, in the case of a separate customs territory Member of the WTO, to mean persons, natural or legal, who are domiciled or who have a real and effective industrial or commercial establishment in that customs territory.

[2].   In this Agreement, "Paris Convention" refers to the Paris Convention for the Protection of Industrial Property; "Paris Convention (1967)" refers to the Stockholm Act of this Convention of 14 July 1967. "Berne Convention" refers to the Berne Convention for the Protection of Literary and Artistic Works; "Berne Convention (1971)" refers to the Paris Act of this Convention of 24 July 1971. "Rome Convention" refers to the International Convention for the Protection of Performers, Producers of Phonograms and Broadcasting Organizations, adopted at Rome on 26 October 1961. "Treaty on Intellectual Property in Respect of Integrated Circuits" (IPIC Treaty) refers to the Treaty on Intellectual Property in Respect of Integrated Circuits, adopted at Washington on 26 May 1989. "WTO Agreement" refers to the Agreement Establishing the WTO.

Article 6 of the Rome Convention shall make a notification as foreseen in those provisions to the Council for Trade-Related Aspects of Intellectual Property Rights (the "Council for TRIPS").

Article 2

Intellectual Property Conventions

1. In respect of Parts II, III and IV of this Agreement, Members shall comply with Articles 1 through 12, and Article 19, of the Paris Convention (1967).

2. Nothing in Parts I to IV of this Agreement shall derogate from existing obligations that Members may have to each other under the Paris Convention, the Berne Convention, the Rome Convention and the Treaty on Intellectual Property in Respect of Integrated Circuits.

Article 3

National Treatment

1. Each Member shall accord to the nationals of other Members treatment no less favourable than that it accords to its own nationals with regard to the protection[3] of intellectual property, subject to the exceptions already provided in, respectively, the Paris Convention (1967), the Berne Convention (1971), the Rome Convention or the Treaty on Intellectual Property in Respect of Integrated Circuits. In respect of performers, producers of phonograms and broadcasting organizations, this obligation only applies in respect of the rights provided under this Agreement. Any Member availing itself of the possibilities provided in Article 6 of the Berne Convention (1971) or paragraph 1(b) of Article 16 of the Rome Convention shall make a notification as foreseen in those provisions to the Council for TRIPS.

2. Members may avail themselves of the exceptions permitted under paragraph 1 in relation to judicial and administrative procedures, including the designation of an address for service or the appointment of an agent within the jurisdiction of a Member, only where such exceptions are necessary to secure compliance with laws and regulations which are not inconsistent with the provisions of this Agreement and where such practices are not applied in a manner which would constitute a disguised restriction on trade.

---

[3]. For the purposes of Articles 3 and 4, "protection" shall include matters affecting the availability, acquisition, scope, maintenance and enforcement of intellectual property rights as well as those matters affecting the use of intellectual property rights specifically addressed in this Agreement.

Article 4

Most-Favoured-Nation Treatment

With regard to the protection of intellectual property, any advantage, favour, privilege or immunity granted by a Member to the nationals of any other country shall be accorded immediately and unconditionally to the nationals of all other Members. Exempted from this obligation are any advantage, favour, privilege or immunity accorded by a Member:

(a) deriving from international agreements on judicial assistance or law enforcement of a general nature and not particularly confined to the protection of intellectual property;

(b) granted in accordance with the provisions of the Berne Convention (1971) or the Rome Convention authorizing that the treatment accorded be a function not of national treatment but of the treatment accorded in another country;

(c) in respect of the rights of performers, producers of phonograms and broadcasting organizations not provided under this Agreement;

(d) deriving from international agreements related to the protection of intellectual property which entered into force prior to the entry into force of the WTO Agreement, provided that such agreements are notified to the Council for TRIPS and do not constitute an arbitrary or unjustifiable discrimination against nationals of other Members.

Article 5

Multilateral Agreements on Acquisition or Maintenance of Protection

The obligations under Articles 3 and 4 do not apply to procedures provided in multilateral agreements concluded under the auspices of WIPO relating to the acquisition or maintenance of intellectual property rights.

Article 6

Exhaustion

For the purposes of dispute settlement under this Agreement, subject to the provisions of Articles 3 and 4 nothing in this Agreement shall be used to address the issue of the exhaustion of intellectual property rights.

Article 7

Objectives

The protection and enforcement of intellectual property rights should contribute to the promotion of technological innovation and to the transfer and dissemination of technology, to the mutual advantage of producers and users of technological knowledge and in a manner conducive to social and economic welfare, and to a balance of rights and obligations.

Article 8

Principles

1.   Members may, in formulating or amending their laws and regulations, adopt measures necessary to protect public health and nutrition, and to promote the public interest in sectors of vital importance to their socio-economic and technological development, provided that such measures are consistent with the provisions of this Agreement.

2.   Appropriate measures, provided that they are consistent with the provisions of this Agreement, may be needed to prevent the abuse of intellectual property rights by right holders or the resort to practices which unreasonably restrain trade or adversely affect the international transfer of technology.

PART II

STANDARDS CONCERNING THE AVAILABILITY, SCOPE AND USE OF INTELLECTUAL PROPERTY RIGHTS

SECTION 1: COPYRIGHT AND RELATED RIGHTS

Article 9

Relation to the Berne Convention

1.   Members shall comply with Articles 1 through 21 of the Berne Convention (1971) and the Appendix thereto. However, Members shall not have rights or obligations under this Agreement in respect of the rights conferred under Article 6*bis* of that Convention or of the rights derived therefrom.

2.   Copyright protection shall extend to expressions and not to ideas, procedures, methods of operation or mathematical concepts as such.

Article 10

Computer Programs and Compilations of Data

1.   Computer programs, whether in source or object code, shall be protected as literary works under the Berne Convention (1971).

2.   Compilations of data or other material, whether in machine readable or other form, which by reason of the selection or arrangement of their contents constitute intellectual creations shall be protected as such. Such protection, which shall not extend to the data or material itself, shall be without prejudice to any copyright subsisting in the data or material itself.

Article 11

Rental Rights

In respect of at least computer programs and cinematographic works, a Member shall provide authors and their successors in title the right to authorize or to prohibit the commercial rental to the public of originals or copies of their copyright works. A Member shall be excepted from this obligation in respect of cinematographic works unless such rental has led to widespread copying of such works which is materially impairing the exclusive right of reproduction conferred in that Member on authors and their successors in title. In respect of computer programs, this obligation does not apply to rentals where the program itself is not the essential object of the rental.

Article 12

Term of Protection

Whenever the term of protection of a work, other than a photographic work or a work of applied art, is calculated on a basis other than the life of a natural person, such term shall be no less than 50 years from the end of the calendar year of authorized publication, or, failing such authorized publication within 50 years from the making of the work, 50 years from the end of the calendar year of making.

Article 13

Limitations and Exceptions

Members shall confine limitations or exceptions to exclusive rights to certain special cases which do not conflict with a normal exploitation of the work and do not unreasonably prejudice the legitimate interests of the right holder.

Article 14

Protection of Performers, Producers of Phonograms (Sound Recordings) and Broadcasting Organizations

1. In respect of a fixation of their performance on a phonogram, performers shall have the possibility of preventing the following acts when undertaken without their authorization: the fixation of their unfixed performance and the reproduction of such fixation. Performers shall also have the possibility of preventing the following acts when undertaken without their authorization: the broadcasting by wireless means and the communication to the public of their live performance.

2. Producers of phonograms shall enjoy the right to authorize or prohibit the direct or indirect reproduction of their phonograms.

3. Broadcasting organizations shall have the right to prohibit the following acts when undertaken without their authorization: the fixation,

the reproduction of fixations, and the rebroadcasting by wireless means of broadcasts, as well as the communication to the public of television broadcasts of the same. Where Members do not grant such rights to broadcasting organizations, they shall provide owners of copyright in the subject matter of broadcasts with the possibility of preventing the above acts, subject to the provisions of the Berne Convention (1971).

4.   The provisions of Article 11 in respect of computer programs shall apply *mutatis mutandis* to producers of phonograms and any other right holders in phonograms as determined in a Member's law. If on 15 April 1994 a Member has in force a system of equitable remuneration of right holders in respect of the rental of phonograms, it may maintain such system provided that the commercial rental of phonograms is not giving rise to the material impairment of the exclusive rights of reproduction of right holders.

5.   The term of the protection available under this Agreement to performers and producers of phonograms shall last at least until the end of a period of 50 years computed from the end of the calendar year in which the fixation was made or the performance took place. The term of protection granted pursuant to paragraph 3 shall last for at least 20 years from the end of the calendar year in which the broadcast took place.

6.   Any Member may, in relation to the rights conferred under paragraphs 1, 2 and 3, provide for conditions, limitations, exceptions and reservations to the extent permitted by the Rome Convention. However, the provisions of Article 18 of the Berne Convention (1971) shall also apply, *mutatis mutandis*, to the rights of performers and producers of phonograms in phonograms.

SECTION 2: TRADEMARKS

Article 15

Protectable Subject Matter

1.   Any sign, or any combination of signs, capable of distinguishing the goods or services of one undertaking from those of other undertakings, shall be capable of constituting a trademark. Such signs, in particular words including personal names, letters, numerals, figurative elements and combinations of colours as well as any combination of such signs, shall be eligible for registration as trademarks. Where signs are not inherently capable of distinguishing the relevant goods or services, Members may make registrability depend on distinctiveness acquired through use. Members may require, as a condition of registration, that signs be visually perceptible.

2.   Paragraph 1 shall not be understood to prevent a Member from denying registration of a trademark on other grounds, provided that they do not derogate from the provisions of the Paris Convention (1967).

3.   Members may make registrability depend on use. However, actual use of a trademark shall not be a condition for filing an application for registration. An application shall not be refused solely on the ground that intended use has not taken place before the expiry of a period of three years from the date of application.

4.   The nature of the goods or services to which a trademark is to be applied shall in no case form an obstacle to registration of the trademark.

5.   Members shall publish each trademark either before it is registered or promptly after it is registered and shall afford a reasonable opportunity for petitions to cancel the registration. In addition, Members may afford an opportunity for the registration of a trademark to be opposed.

Article 16

Rights Conferred

1.   The owner of a registered trademark shall have the exclusive right to prevent all third parties not having the owner's consent from using in the course of trade identical or similar signs for goods or services which are identical or similar to those in respect of which the trademark is registered where such use would result in a likelihood of confusion. In case of the use of an identical sign for identical goods or services, a likelihood of confusion shall be presumed. The rights described above shall not prejudice any existing prior rights, nor shall they affect the possibility of Members making rights available on the basis of use.

2.   Article 6*bis* of the Paris Convention (1967) shall apply, *mutatis mutandis*, to services. In determining whether a trademark is well-known, Members shall take account of the knowledge of the trademark in the relevant sector of the public, including knowledge in the Member concerned which has been obtained as a result of the promotion of the trademark.

3.   Article 6*bis* of the Paris Convention (1967) shall apply, *mutatis mutandis*, to goods or services which are not similar to those in respect of which a trademark is registered, provided that use of that trademark in relation to those goods or services would indicate a connection between those goods or services and the owner of the registered trademark and provided that the interests of the owner of the registered trademark are likely to be damaged by such use.

Article 17

Exceptions

Members may provide limited exceptions to the rights conferred by a trademark, such as fair use of descriptive terms, provided that such exceptions take account of the legitimate interests of the owner of the trademark and of third parties.

Article 18

Term of Protection

Initial registration, and each renewal of registration, of a trademark shall be for a term of no less than seven years. The registration of a trademark shall be renewable indefinitely.

Article 19

Requirement of Use

1.   If use is required to maintain a registration, the registration may be cancelled only after an uninterrupted period of at least three years of non-use, unless valid reasons based on the existence of obstacles to such use are shown by the trademark owner. Circumstances arising independently of the will of the owner of the trademark which constitute an obstacle to the use of the trademark, such as import restrictions on or other government requirements for goods or services protected by the trademark, shall be recognized as valid reasons for non-use.

2.   When subject to the control of its owner, use of a trademark by another person shall be recognized as use of the trademark for the purpose of maintaining the registration.

Article 20

Other Requirements

The use of a trademark in the course of trade shall not be unjustifiably encumbered by special requirements, such as use with another trademark, use in a special form or use in a manner detrimental to its capability to distinguish the goods or services of one undertaking from those of other undertakings. This will not preclude a requirement prescribing the use of the trademark identifying the undertaking producing the goods or services along with, but without linking it to, the trademark distinguishing the specific goods or services in question of that undertaking.

Article 21

Licensing and Assignment

Members may determine conditions on the licensing and assignment of trademarks, it being understood that the compulsory licensing of trademarks shall not be permitted and that the owner of a registered trademark shall have the right to assign the trademark with or without the transfer of the business to which the trademark belongs.

SECTION 3: GEOGRAPHICAL INDICATIONS

Article 22

Protection of Geographical Indications

1.   Geographical indications are, for the purposes of this Agreement, indications which identify a good as originating in the territory of a Member, or a region or locality in that territory, where a given quality, reputation or other characteristic of the good is essentially attributable to its geographical origin.

2.   In respect of geographical indications, Members shall provide the legal means for interested parties to prevent:

   (a)   the use of any means in the designation or presentation of a good that indicates or suggests that the good in question originates in a geographical area other than the true place of origin in a manner which misleads the public as to the geographical origin of the good;

   (b)   any use which constitutes an act of unfair competition within the meaning of Article 10*bis* of the Paris Convention (1967).

3.   A Member shall, *ex officio* if its legislation so permits or at the request of an interested party, refuse or invalidate the registration of a trademark which contains or consists of a geographical indication with respect to goods not originating in the territory indicated, if use of the indication in the trademark for such goods in that Member is of such a nature as to mislead the public as to the true place of origin.

4.   The protection under paragraphs 1, 2 and 3 shall be applicable against a geographical indication which, although literally true as to the territory, region or locality in which the goods originate, falsely represents to the public that the goods originate in another territory.

Article 23

Additional Protection for Geographical Indications for Wines and Spirits

1.   Each Member shall provide the legal means for interested parties to prevent use of a geographical indication identifying wines for wines not originating in the place indicated by the geographical indication in question or identifying spirits for spirits not originating in the place indicated by the geographical indication in question, even where the true origin of the goods is indicated or the geographical indication is used in translation or accompanied by expressions such as "kind", "type", "style", "imitation" or the like.[4]

[4.]   Notwithstanding the first sentence of Article 42, Members may, with respect to these obligations, instead provide for enforcement by administrative action.

2.   The registration of a trademark for wines which contains or consists of a geographical indication identifying wines or for spirits which contains or consists of a geographical indication identifying spirits shall be refused or invalidated, *ex officio* if a Member's legislation so permits or at the request of an interested party, with respect to such wines or spirits not having this origin.

3.   In the case of homonymous geographical indications for wines, protection shall be accorded to each indication, subject to the provisions of paragraph 4 of Article 22. Each Member shall determine the practical conditions under which the homonymous indications in question will be differentiated from each other, taking into account the need to ensure equitable treatment of the producers concerned and that consumers are not misled.

4.   In order to facilitate the protection of geographical indications for wines, negotiations shall be undertaken in the Council for TRIPS concerning the establishment of a multilateral system of notification and registration of geographical indications for wines eligible for protection in those Members participating in the system.

Article 24

International Negotiations; Exceptions

1.   Members agree to enter into negotiations aimed at increasing the protection of individual geographical indications under Article 23. The provisions of paragraphs 4 through 8 below shall not be used by a Member to refuse to conduct negotiations or to conclude bilateral or multilateral agreements. In the context of such negotiations, Members shall be willing to consider the continued applicability of these provisions to individual geographical indications whose use was the subject of such negotiations.

2.   The Council for TRIPS shall keep under review the application of the provisions of this Section; the first such review shall take place within two years of the entry into force of the WTO Agreement. Any matter affecting the compliance with the obligations under these provisions may be drawn to the attention of the Council, which, at the request of a Member, shall consult with any Member or Members in respect of such matter in respect of which it has not been possible to find a satisfactory solution through bilateral or plurilateral consultations between the Members concerned. The Council shall take such action as may be agreed to facilitate the operation and further the objectives of this Section.

3.   In implementing this Section, a Member shall not diminish the protection of geographical indications that existed in that Member immediately prior to the date of entry into force of the WTO Agreement.

4.   Nothing in this Section shall require a Member to prevent continued and similar use of a particular geographical indication of another

Member identifying wines or spirits in connection with goods or services by any of its nationals or domiciliaries who have used that geographical indication in a continuous manner with regard to the same or related goods or services in the territory of that Member either (*a*) for at least 10 years preceding 15 April 1994 or (*b*) in good faith preceding that date.

5. Where a trademark has been applied for or registered in good faith, or where rights to a trademark have been acquired through use in good faith either:

(a) before the date of application of these provisions in that Member as defined in Part VI; or

(b) before the geographical indication is protected in its country of origin;

measures adopted to implement this Section shall not prejudice eligibility for or the validity of the registration of a trademark, or the right to use a trademark, on the basis that such a trademark is identical with, or similar to, a geographical indication.

6. Nothing in this Section shall require a Member to apply its provisions in respect of a geographical indication of any other Member with respect to goods or services for which the relevant indication is identical with the term customary in common language as the common name for such goods or services in the territory of that Member. Nothing in this Section shall require a Member to apply its provisions in respect of a geographical indication of any other Member with respect to products of the vine for which the relevant indication is identical with the customary name of a grape variety existing in the territory of that Member as of the date of entry into force of the WTO Agreement.

7. A Member may provide that any request made under this Section in connection with the use or registration of a trademark must be presented within five years after the adverse use of the protected indication has become generally known in that Member or after the date of registration of the trademark in that Member provided that the trademark has been published by that date, if such date is earlier than the date on which the adverse use became generally known in that Member, provided that the geographical indication is not used or registered in bad faith.

8. The provisions of this Section shall in no way prejudice the right of any person to use, in the course of trade, that person's name or the name of that person's predecessor in business, except where such name is used in such a manner as to mislead the public.

9. There shall be no obligation under this Agreement to protect geographical indications which are not or cease to be protected in their country of origin, or which have fallen into disuse in that country.

SECTION 4: INDUSTRIAL DESIGNS

Article 25

Requirements for Protection

1.   Members shall provide for the protection of independently created industrial designs that are new or original. Members may provide that designs are not new or original if they do not significantly differ from known designs or combinations of known design features. Members may provide that such protection shall not extend to designs dictated essentially by technical or functional considerations.

2.   Each Member shall ensure that requirements for securing protection for textile designs, in particular in regard to any cost, examination or publication, do not unreasonably impair the opportunity to seek and obtain such protection. Members shall be free to meet this obligation through industrial design law or through copyright law.

Article 26

Protection

1.   The owner of a protected industrial design shall have the right to prevent third parties not having the owner's consent from making, selling or importing articles bearing or embodying a design which is a copy, or substantially a copy, of the protected design, when such acts are undertaken for commercial purposes.

2.   Members may provide limited exceptions to the protection of industrial designs, provided that such exceptions do not unreasonably conflict with the normal exploitation of protected industrial designs and do not unreasonably prejudice the legitimate interests of the owner of the protected design, taking account of the legitimate interests of third parties.

3.   The duration of protection available shall amount to at least 10 years.

SECTION 5: PATENTS

Article 27

Patentable Subject Matter

1.   Subject to the provisions of paragraphs 2 and 3, patents shall be available for any inventions, whether products or processes, in all fields of technology, provided that they are new, involve an inventive step and are capable of industrial application.[5] Subject to paragraph 4 of Article 65, paragraph 8 of Article 70 and paragraph 3 of this Article, patents shall be available and patent rights enjoyable without discrimination as to the

---

[5]   For the purposes of this Article, the terms "inventive step" and "capable of industrial application" may be deemed by a Member to be synonymous with the terms "non-obvious" and "useful" respectively.

place of invention, the field of technology and whether products are imported or locally produced.

2.   Members may exclude from patentability inventions, the prevention within their territory of the commercial exploitation of which is necessary to protect *ordre public* or morality, including to protect human, animal or plant life or health or to avoid serious prejudice to the environment, provided that such exclusion is not made merely because the exploitation is prohibited by their law.

3.   Members may also exclude from patentability:

(a)   diagnostic, therapeutic and surgical methods for the treatment of humans or animals;

(b)   plants and animals other than micro-organisms, and essentially biological processes for the production of plants or animals other than non-biological and microbiological processes. However, Members shall provide for the protection of plant varieties either by patents or by an effective *sui generis* system or by any combination thereof. The provisions of this subparagraph shall be reviewed four years after the date of entry into force of the WTO Agreement.

Article 28

Rights Conferred

1.   A patent shall confer on its owner the following exclusive rights:

(a)   where the subject matter of a patent is a product, to prevent third parties not having the owner's consent from the acts of: making, using, offering for sale, selling, or importing[6] for these purposes that product;

(b)   where the subject matter of a patent is a process, to prevent third parties not having the owner's consent from the act of using the process, and from the acts of: using, offering for sale, selling, or importing for these purposes at least the product obtained directly by that process.

2.   Patent owners shall also have the right to assign, or transfer by succession, the patent and to conclude licensing contracts.

Article 29

Conditions on Patent Applicants

1.   Members shall require that an applicant for a patent shall disclose the invention in a manner sufficiently clear and complete for the invention to be carried out by a person skilled in the art and may require the

---

[6]   This right, like all other rights conferred under this Agreement in respect of the use, sale, importation or other distribution of goods, is subject to the provisions of Article 6.

applicant to indicate the best mode for carrying out the invention known to the inventor at the filing date or, where priority is claimed, at the priority date of the application.

2.   Members may require an applicant for a patent to provide information concerning the applicant's corresponding foreign applications and grants.

Article 30

Exceptions to Rights Conferred

Members may provide limited exceptions to the exclusive rights conferred by a patent, provided that such exceptions do not unreasonably conflict with a normal exploitation of the patent and do not unreasonably prejudice the legitimate interests of the patent owner, taking account of the legitimate interests of third parties.

Article 31

Other Use Without Authorization of the Right Holder

Where the law of a Member allows for other use[7] of the subject matter of a patent without the authorization of the right holder, including use by the government or third parties authorized by the government, the following provisions shall be respected:

(a)   authorization of such use shall be considered on its individual merits;

(b)   such use may only be permitted if, prior to such use, the proposed user has made efforts to obtain authorization from the right holder on reasonable commercial terms and conditions and that such efforts have not been successful within a reasonable period of time. This requirement may be waived by a Member in the case of a national emergency or other circumstances of extreme urgency or in cases of public non-commercial use. In situations of national emergency or other circumstances of extreme urgency, the right holder shall, nevertheless, be notified as soon as reasonably practicable. In the case of public noncommercial use, where the government or contractor, without making a patent search, knows or has demonstrable grounds to know that a valid patent is or will be used by or for the government, the right holder shall be informed promptly;

(c)   the scope and duration of such use shall be limited to the purpose for which it was authorized, and in the case of semiconductor technology shall only be for public non-commercial use or to

---

7.   "Other use" refers to use other than that allowed under Article 30.

remedy a practice determined after judicial or administrative process to be anti-competitive;

(d) such use shall be non-exclusive;

(e) such use shall be non-assignable, except with that part of the enterprise or goodwill which enjoys such use;

(f) any such use shall be authorized predominantly for the supply of the domestic market of the Member authorizing such use;

(g) authorization for such use shall be liable, subject to adequate protection of the legitimate interests of the persons so authorized, to be terminated if and when the circumstances which led to it cease to exist and are unlikely to recur. The competent authority shall have the authority to review, upon motivated request, the continued existence of these circumstances;

(h) the right holder shall be paid adequate remuneration in the circumstances of each case, taking into account the economic value of the authorization;

(i) the legal validity of any decision relating to the authorization of such use shall be subject to judicial review or other independent review by a distinct higher authority in that Member;

(j) any decision relating to the remuneration provided in respect of such use shall be subject to judicial review or other independent review by a distinct higher authority in that Member;

(k) Members are not obliged to apply the conditions set forth in subparagraphs (b) and (f) where such use is permitted to remedy a practice determined after judicial or administrative process to be anti-competitive. The need to correct anti-competitive practices may be taken into account in determining the amount of remuneration in such cases. Competent authorities shall have the authority to refuse termination of authorization if and when the conditions which led to such authorization are likely to recur;

(l) where such use is authorized to permit the exploitation of a patent ("the second patent") which cannot be exploited without infringing another patent ("the first patent"), the following additional conditions shall apply:

  (i) the invention claimed in the second patent shall involve an important technical advance of considerable economic significance in relation to the invention claimed in the first patent;

  (ii) the owner of the first patent shall be entitled to a cross-licence on reasonable terms to use the invention claimed in the second patent; and

(iii) the use authorized in respect of the first patent shall be non-assignable except with the assignment of the second patent.

Article 31*bis*

1.   The obligations of an exporting Member under Article 31(f) shall not apply with respect to the grant by it of a compulsory licence to the extent necessary for the purposes of production of a pharmaceutical product(s) and its export to an eligible importing Member(s) in accordance with the terms set out in paragraph 2 of the Annex to this Agreement.

2.   Where a compulsory licence is granted by an exporting Member under the system set out in this Article and the Annex to this Agreement, adequate remuneration pursuant to Article 31(h) shall be paid in that Member taking into account the economic value to the importing Member of the use that has been authorized in the exporting Member. Where a compulsory licence is granted for the same products in the eligible importing Member, the obligation of that Member under Article 31(h) shall not apply in respect of those products for which remuneration in accordance with the first sentence of this paragraph is paid in the exporting Member.

3.   With a view to harnessing economies of scale for the purposes of enhancing purchasing power for, and facilitating the local production of, pharmaceutical products: where a developing or least developed country WTO Member is a party to a regional trade agreement within the meaning of Article XXIV of the GATT 1994 and the Decision of 28 November 1979 on Differential and More Favourable Treatment Reciprocity and Fuller Participation of Developing Countries (L/4903), at least half of the current membership of which is made up of countries presently on the United Nations list of least developed countries, the obligation of that Member under Article 31(f) shall not apply to the extent necessary to enable a pharmaceutical product produced or imported under a compulsory licence in that Member to be exported to the markets of those other developing or least developed country parties to the regional trade agreement that share the health problem in question. It is understood that this will not prejudice the territorial nature of the patent rights in question.

4.   Members shall not challenge any measures taken in conformity with the provisions of this Article and the Annex to this Agreement under subparagraphs 1(b) and 1(c) of Article XXIII of GATT 1994.

5.   This Article and the Annex to this Agreement are without prejudice to the rights, obligations and flexibilities that Members have under the provisions of this Agreement other than paragraphs (f) and (h) of Article 31, including those reaffirmed by the Declaration on the TRIPS Agreement and Public Health (WT/MIN(01)/DEC/2), and to their interpretation. They are also without prejudice to the extent to which

pharmaceutical products produced under a compulsory licence can be exported under the provisions of Article 31(f).

Article 32

Revocation/Forfeiture

An opportunity for judicial review of any decision to revoke or forfeit a patent shall be available.

Article 33

Term of Protection

The term of protection available shall not end before the expiration of a period of twenty years counted from the filing date.[8]

Article 34

Process Patents: Burden of Proof

1.   For the purposes of civil proceedings in respect of the infringement of the rights of the owner referred to in paragraph 1(b) of Article 28, if the subject matter of a patent is a process for obtaining a product, the judicial authorities shall have the authority to order the defendant to prove that the process to obtain an identical product is different from the patented process. Therefore, Members shall provide, in at least one of the following circumstances, that any identical product when produced without the consent of the patent owner shall, in the absence of proof to the contrary, be deemed to have been obtained by the patented process:

(a)   if the product obtained by the patented process is new;

(b)   if there is a substantial likelihood that the identical product was made by the process and the owner of the patent has been unable through reasonable efforts to determine the process actually used.

2.   Any Member shall be free to provide that the burden of proof indicated in paragraph 1 shall be on the alleged infringer only if the condition referred to in subparagraph (a) is fulfilled or only if the condition referred to in subparagraph (b) is fulfilled.

3.   In the adduction of proof to the contrary, the legitimate interests of defendants in protecting their manufacturing and business secrets shall be taken into account.

[8.]   It is understood that those Members which do not have a system of original grant may provide that the term of protection shall be computed from the filing date in the system of original grant.

SECTION 6: LAYOUT-DESIGNS (TOPOGRAPHIES) OF INTEGRATED CIRCUITS

Article 35

Relation to the IPIC Treaty

Members agree to provide protection to the layout-designs (topographies) of integrated circuits (referred to in this Agreement as "layout-designs") in accordance with Articles 2 through 7 (other than paragraph 3 of Article 6), Article 12 and paragraph 3 of Article 16 of the Treaty on Intellectual Property in Respect of Integrated Circuits and, in addition, to comply with the following provisions.

Article 36

Scope of the Protection

Subject to the provisions of paragraph 1 of Article 37, Members shall consider unlawful the following acts if performed without the authorization of the right holder:[9] importing, selling, or otherwise distributing for commercial purposes a protected layout-design, an integrated circuit in which a protected layout-design is incorporated, or an article incorporating such an integrated circuit only in so far as it continues to contain an unlawfully reproduced layout-design.

Article 37

Acts Not Requiring the Authorization of the Right Holder

1.   Notwithstanding Article 36, no Member shall consider unlawful the performance of any of the acts referred to in that Article in respect of an integrated circuit incorporating an unlawfully reproduced layout-design or any article incorporating such an integrated circuit where the person performing or ordering such acts did not know and had no reasonable ground to know, when acquiring the integrated circuit or article incorporating such an integrated circuit, that it incorporated an unlawfully reproduced layout-design. Members shall provide that, after the time that such person has received sufficient notice that the layout-design was unlawfully reproduced, that person may perform any of the acts with respect to the stock on hand or ordered before such time, but shall be liable to pay to the right holder a sum equivalent to a reasonable royalty such as would be payable under a freely negotiated licence in respect of such a layout-design.

2.   The conditions set out in subparagraphs (a) through (k) of Article 31 shall apply *mutatis mutandis* in the event of any nonvoluntary licensing

---

[9]. The term "right holder" in this Section shall be understood as having the same meaning as the term "holder of the right" in the IPIC Treaty.

21

of a layout-design or of its use by or for the government without the authorization of the right holder.

Article 38

Term of Protection

1.   In Members requiring registration as a condition of protection, the term of protection of layout-designs shall not end before the expiration of a period of 10 years counted from the date of filing an application for registration or from the first commercial exploitation wherever in the world it occurs.

2.   In Members not requiring registration as a condition for protection, layout-designs shall be protected for a term of no less than 10 years from the date of the first commercial exploitation wherever in the world it occurs.

3.   Notwithstanding paragraphs 1 and 2, a Member may provide that protection shall lapse 15 years after the creation of the layout-design.

SECTION 7: PROTECTION OF UNDISCLOSED INFORMATION

Article 39

1.   In the course of ensuring effective protection against unfair competition as provided in Article 10*bis* of the Paris Convention (1967), Members shall protect undisclosed information in accordance with paragraph 2 and data submitted to governments or governmental agencies in accordance with paragraph 3.

2.   Natural and legal persons shall have the possibility of preventing information lawfully within their control from being disclosed to, acquired by, or used by others without their consent in a manner contrary to honest commercial practices[10] so long as such information:

(a)   is secret in the sense that it is not, as a body or in the precise configuration and assembly of its components, generally known among or readily accessible to persons within the circles that normally deal with the kind of information in question;

(b)   has commercial value because it is secret; and

(c)   has been subject to reasonable steps under the circumstances, by the person lawfully in control of the information, to keep it secret.

3.   Members, when requiring, as a condition of approving the marketing of pharmaceutical or of agricultural chemical products which utilize new chemical entities, the submission of undisclosed test or other

---

[10].   For the purpose of this provision, "a manner contrary to honest commercial practices" shall mean at least practices such as breach of contract, breach of confidence and inducement to breach, and includes the acquisition of undisclosed information by third parties who knew, or were grossly negligent in failing to know, that such practices were involved in the acquisition.

data, the origination of which involves a considerable effort, shall protect such data against unfair commercial use. In addition, Members shall protect such data against disclosure, except where necessary to protect the public, or unless steps are taken to ensure that the data are protected against unfair commercial use.

SECTION 8: CONTROL OF ANTI-COMPETITIVE PRACTICES IN CONTRACTUAL LICENCES

Article 40

1.   Members agree that some licensing practices or conditions pertaining to intellectual property rights which restrain competition may have adverse effects on trade and may impede the transfer and dissemination of technology.

2.   Nothing in this Agreement shall prevent Members from specifying in their legislation licensing practices or conditions that may in particular cases constitute an abuse of intellectual property rights having an adverse effect on competition in the relevant market. As provided above, a Member may adopt, consistently with the other provisions of this Agreement, appropriate measures to prevent or control such practices, which may include for example exclusive grantback conditions, conditions preventing challenges to validity and coercive package licensing, in the light of the relevant laws and regulations of that Member.

3.   Each Member shall enter, upon request, into consultations with any other Member which has cause to believe that an intellectual property right owner that is a national or domiciliary of the Member to which the request for consultations has been addressed is undertaking practices in violation of the requesting Member's laws and regulations on the subject matter of this Section, and which wishes to secure compliance with such legislation, without prejudice to any action under the law and to the full freedom of an ultimate decision of either Member. The Member addressed shall accord full and sympathetic consideration to, and shall afford adequate opportunity for, consultations with the requesting Member, and shall cooperate through supply of publicly available non-confidential information of relevance to the matter in question and of other information available to the Member, subject to domestic law and to the conclusion of mutually satisfactory agreements concerning the safeguarding of its confidentiality by the requesting Member.

4.   A Member whose nationals or domiciliaries are subject to proceedings in another Member concerning alleged violation of that other Member's laws and regulations on the subject matter of this Section shall, upon request, be granted an opportunity for consultations by the other Member under the same conditions as those foreseen in paragraph 3.

PART III

ENFORCEMENT OF INTELLECTUAL PROPERTY RIGHTS

SECTION 1: GENERAL OBLIGATIONS

Article 41

1.   Members shall ensure that enforcement procedures as specified in this Part are available under their law so as to permit effective action against any act of infringement of intellectual property rights covered by this Agreement, including expeditious remedies to prevent infringements and remedies which constitute a deterrent to further infringements. These procedures shall be applied in such a manner as to avoid the creation of barriers to legitimate trade and to provide for safeguards against their abuse.

2.   Procedures concerning the enforcement of intellectual property rights shall be fair and equitable. They shall not be unnecessarily complicated or costly, or entail unreasonable time-limits or unwarranted delays.

3.   Decisions on the merits of a case shall preferably be in writing and reasoned. They shall be made available at least to the parties to the proceeding without undue delay. Decisions on the merits of a case shall be based only on evidence in respect of which parties were offered the opportunity to be heard.

4.   Parties to a proceeding shall have an opportunity for review by a judicial authority of final administrative decisions and, subject to jurisdictional provisions in a Member's law concerning the importance of a case, of at least the legal aspects of initial judicial decisions on the merits of a case. However, there shall be no obligation to provide an opportunity for review of acquittals in criminal cases.

5.   It is understood that this Part does not create any obligation to put in place a judicial system for the enforcement of intellectual property rights distinct from that for the enforcement of law in general, nor does it affect the capacity of Members to enforce their law in general. Nothing in this Part creates any obligation with respect to the distribution of resources as between enforcement of intellectual property rights and the enforcement of law in general.

SECTION 2: CIVIL AND ADMINISTRATIVE PROCEDURES AND REMEDIES

Article 42

Fair and Equitable Procedures

Members shall make available to right holders[11] civil judicial procedures concerning the enforcement of any intellectual property right covered by this Agreement. Defendants shall have the right to written notice which is timely and contains sufficient detail, including the basis of the claims. Parties shall be allowed to be represented by independent legal counsel, and procedures shall not impose overly burdensome requirements concerning mandatory personal appearances. All parties to such procedures shall be duly entitled to substantiate their claims and to present all relevant evidence. The procedure shall provide a means to identify and protect confidential information, unless this would be contrary to existing constitutional requirements.

Article 43

Evidence

1.   The judicial authorities shall have the authority, where a party has presented reasonably available evidence sufficient to support its claims and has specified evidence relevant to substantiation of its claims which lies in the control of the opposing party, to order that this evidence be produced by the opposing party, subject in appropriate cases to conditions which ensure the protection of confidential information.

2.   In cases in which a party to a proceeding voluntarily and without good reason refuses access to, or otherwise does not provide necessary information within a reasonable period, or significantly impedes a procedure relating to an enforcement action, a Member may accord judicial authorities the authority to make preliminary and final determinations, affirmative or negative, on the basis of the information presented to them, including the complaint or the allegation presented by the party adversely affected by the denial of access to information, subject to providing the parties an opportunity to be heard on the allegations or evidence.

Article 44

Injunctions

1.   The judicial authorities shall have the authority to order a party to desist from an infringement, *inter alia* to prevent the entry into the channels of commerce in their jurisdiction of imported goods that involve the infringement of an intellectual property right, immediately after customs clearance of such goods. Members are not obliged to accord such

---

[11.] For the purpose of this Part, the term "right holder" includes federations and associations having legal standing to assert such rights.

authority in respect of protected subject matter acquired or ordered by a person prior to knowing or having reasonable grounds to know that dealing in such subject matter would entail the infringement of an intellectual property right.

2.   Notwithstanding the other provisions of this Part and provided that the provisions of Part II specifically addressing use by governments, or by third parties authorized by a government, without the authorization of the right holder are complied with, Members may limit the remedies available against such use to payment of remuneration in accordance with subparagraph (h) of Article 31. In other cases, the remedies under this Part shall apply or, where these remedies are inconsistent with a Member's law, declaratory judgments and adequate compensation shall be available.

Article 45

Damages

1.   The judicial authorities shall have the authority to order the infringer to pay the right holder damages adequate to compensate for the injury the right holder has suffered because of an infringement of that person's intellectual property right by an infringer who knowingly, or with reasonable grounds to know, engaged in infringing activity.

2.   The judicial authorities shall also have the authority to order the infringer to pay the right holder expenses, which may include appropriate attorney's fees. In appropriate cases, Members may authorize the judicial authorities to order recovery of profits and/or payment of pre-established damages even where the infringer did not knowingly, or with reasonable grounds to know, engage in infringing activity.

Article 46

Other Remedies

In order to create an effective deterrent to infringement, the judicial authorities shall have the authority to order that goods that they have found to be infringing be, without compensation of any sort, disposed of outside the channels of commerce in such a manner as to avoid any harm caused to the right holder, or, unless this would be contrary to existing constitutional requirements, destroyed. The judicial authorities shall also have the authority to order that materials and implements the predominant use of which has been in the creation of the infringing goods be, without compensation of any sort, disposed of outside the channels of commerce in such a manner as to minimize the risks of further infringements. In considering such requests, the need for proportionality between the seriousness of the infringement and the remedies ordered as well as the interests of third parties shall be taken into account. In regard to counterfeit trademark goods, the simple removal of the trademark unlawfully affixed shall not be sufficient, other than in exceptional cases, to permit release of the goods into the channels of commerce.

Article 47

Right of Information

Members may provide that the judicial authorities shall have the authority, unless this would be out of proportion to the seriousness of the infringement, to order the infringer to inform the right holder of the identity of third persons involved in the production and distribution of the infringing goods or services and of their channels of distribution.

Article 48

Indemnification of the Defendant

1.   The judicial authorities shall have the authority to order a party at whose request measures were taken and who has abused enforcement procedures to provide to a party wrongfully enjoined or restrained adequate compensation for the injury suffered because of such abuse. The judicial authorities shall also have the authority to order the applicant to pay the defendant expenses, which may include appropriate attorney's fees.

2.   In respect of the administration of any law pertaining to the protection or enforcement of intellectual property rights, Members shall only exempt both public authorities and officials from liability to appropriate remedial measures where actions are taken or intended in good faith in the course of the administration of that law.

Article 49

Administrative Procedures

To the extent that any civil remedy can be ordered as a result of administrative procedures on the merits of a case, such procedures shall conform to principles equivalent in substance to those set forth in this Section.

SECTION 3: PROVISIONAL MEASURES

Article 50

1.   The judicial authorities shall have the authority to order prompt and effective provisional measures:

(a) to prevent an infringement of any intellectual property right from occurring, and in particular to prevent the entry into the channels of commerce in their jurisdiction of goods, including imported goods immediately after customs clearance;

(b) to preserve relevant evidence in regard to the alleged infringement.

2.   The judicial authorities shall have the authority to adopt provisional measures *inaudita altera parte* where appropriate, in particular where any delay is likely to cause irreparable harm to the right holder, or where there is a demonstrable risk of evidence being destroyed.

3.   The judicial authorities shall have the authority to require the applicant to provide any reasonably available evidence in order to satisfy themselves with a sufficient degree of certainty that the applicant is the right holder and that the applicant's right is being infringed or that such infringement is imminent, and to order the applicant to provide a security or equivalent assurance sufficient to protect the defendant and to prevent abuse.

4.   Where provisional measures have been adopted *inaudita altera parte*, the parties affected shall be given notice, without delay after the execution of the measures at the latest. A review, including a right to be heard, shall take place upon request of the defendant with a view to deciding, within a reasonable period after the notification of the measures, whether these measures shall be modified, revoked or confirmed.

5.   The applicant may be required to supply other information necessary for the identification of the goods concerned by the authority that will execute the provisional measures.

6.   Without prejudice to paragraph 4, provisional measures taken on the basis of paragraphs 1 and 2 shall, upon request by the defendant, be revoked or otherwise cease to have effect, if proceedings leading to a decision on the merits of the case are not initiated within a reasonable period, to be determined by the judicial authority ordering the measures where a Member's law so permits or, in the absence of such a determination, not to exceed 20 working days or 31 calendar days, whichever is the longer.

7.   Where the provisional measures are revoked or where they lapse due to any act or omission by the applicant, or where it is subsequently found that there has been no infringement or threat of infringement of an intellectual property right, the judicial authorities shall have the authority to order the applicant, upon request of the defendant, to provide the defendant appropriate compensation for any injury caused by these measures.

8.   To the extent that any provisional measure can be ordered as a result of administrative procedures, such procedures shall conform to principles equivalent in substance to those set forth in this Section.

SECTION 4: SPECIAL REQUIREMENTS RELATED TO BORDER MEASURES[12]

Article 51

Suspension of Release by Customs Authorities

Members shall, in conformity with the provisions set out below, adopt procedures[13] to enable a right holder, who has valid grounds for suspecting that the importation of counterfeit trademark or pirated copyright goods[14] may take place, to lodge an application in writing with competent authorities, administrative or judicial, for the suspension by the customs authorities of the release into free circulation of such goods. Members may enable such an application to be made in respect of goods which involve other infringements of intellectual property rights, provided that the requirements of this Section are met. Members may also provide for corresponding procedures concerning the suspension by the customs authorities of the release of infringing goods destined for exportation from their territories.

Article 52

Application

Any right holder initiating the procedures under Article 51 shall be required to provide adequate evidence to satisfy the competent authorities that, under the laws of the country of importation, there is *prima facie* an infringement of the right holder's intellectual property right and to supply a sufficiently detailed description of the goods to make them readily recognizable by the customs authorities. The competent authorities shall inform the applicant within a reasonable period whether they have accepted the application and, where determined by the competent authorities, the period for which the customs authorities will take action.

---

[12] Where a Member has dismantled substantially all controls over movement of goods across its border with another Member with which it forms part of a customs union, it shall not be required to apply the provisions of this Section at that border.

[13] It is understood that there shall be no obligation to apply such procedures to imports of goods put on the market in another country by or with the consent of the right holder, or to goods in transit.

[14] For the purposes of this Agreement:

(a) "counterfeit trademark goods" shall mean any goods, including packaging, bearing without authorization a trademark which is identical to the trademark validly registered in respect of such goods, or which cannot be distinguished in its essential aspects from such a trademark, and which thereby infringes the rights of the owner of the trademark in question under the law of the country of importation;

(b) "pirated copyright goods" shall mean any goods which are copies made without the consent of the right holder or person duly authorized by the right holder in the country of production and which are made directly or indirectly from an article where the making of that copy would have constituted an infringement of a copyright or a related right under the law of the country of importation.

Article 53

Security or Equivalent Assurance

1.   The competent authorities shall have the authority to require an applicant to provide a security or equivalent assurance sufficient to protect the defendant and the competent authorities and to prevent abuse. Such security or equivalent assurance shall not unreasonably deter recourse to these procedures.

2.   Where pursuant to an application under this Section the release of goods involving industrial designs, patents, layout-designs or undisclosed information into free circulation has been suspended by customs authorities on the basis of a decision other than by a judicial or other independent authority, and the period provided for in Article 55 has expired without the granting of provisional relief by the duly empowered authority, and provided that all other conditions for importation have been complied with, the owner, importer, or consignee of such goods shall be entitled to their release on the posting of a security in an amount sufficient to protect the right holder for any infringement. Payment of such security shall not prejudice any other remedy available to the right holder, it being understood that the security shall be released if the right holder fails to pursue the right of action within a reasonable period of time.

Article 54

Notice of Suspension

The importer and the applicant shall be promptly notified of the suspension of the release of goods according to Article 51.

Article 55

Duration of Suspension

If, within a period not exceeding 10 working days after the applicant has been served notice of the suspension, the customs authorities have not been informed that proceedings leading to a decision on the merits of the case have been initiated by a party other than the defendant, or that the duly empowered authority has taken provisional measures prolonging the suspension of the release of the goods, the goods shall be released, provided that all other conditions for importation or exportation have been complied with; in appropriate cases, this time-limit may be extended by another 10 working days. If proceedings leading to a decision on the merits of the case have been initiated, a review, including a right to be heard, shall take place upon request of the defendant with a view to deciding, within a reasonable period, whether these measures shall be modified, revoked or confirmed. Notwithstanding the above, where the suspension of the release of goods is carried out or continued in accordance with a provisional judicial measure, the provisions of paragraph 6 of Article 50 shall apply.

Article 56

Indemnification of the Importer and of the Owner of the Goods

Relevant authorities shall have the authority to order the applicant to pay the importer, the consignee and the owner of the goods appropriate compensation for any injury caused to them through the wrongful detention of goods or through the detention of goods released pursuant to Article 55.

Article 57

Right of Inspection and Information

Without prejudice to the protection of confidential information, Members shall provide the competent authorities the authority to give the right holder sufficient opportunity to have any goods detained by the customs authorities inspected in order to substantiate the right holder's claims. The competent authorities shall also have authority to give the importer an equivalent opportunity to have any such goods inspected. Where a positive determination has been made on the merits of a case, Members may provide the competent authorities the authority to inform the right holder of the names and addresses of the consignor, the importer and the consignee and of the quantity of the goods in question.

Article 58

Ex Officio Action

Where Members require competent authorities to act upon their own initiative and to suspend the release of goods in respect of which they have acquired *prima facie* evidence that an intellectual property right is being infringed:

(a) the competent authorities may at any time seek from the right holder any information that may assist them to exercise these powers;

(b) the importer and the right holder shall be promptly notified of the suspension. Where the importer has lodged an appeal against the suspension with the competent authorities, the suspension shall be subject to the conditions, *mutatis mutandis*, set out at Article 55;

(c) Members shall only exempt both public authorities and officials from liability to appropriate remedial measures where actions are taken or intended in good faith.

Article 59

Remedies

Without prejudice to other rights of action open to the right holder and subject to the right of the defendant to seek review by a judicial authority, competent authorities shall have the authority to order the destruction or disposal of infringing goods in accordance with the principles set out in Article 46. In regard to counterfeit trademark goods, the authorities shall not allow the re-exportation of the infringing goods in an unaltered state or subject them to a different customs procedure, other than in exceptional circumstances.

Article 60

De Minimis Imports

Members may exclude from the application of the above provisions small quantities of goods of a non-commercial nature contained in travellers' personal luggage or sent in small consignments.

SECTION 5: CRIMINAL PROCEDURES

Article 61

Members shall provide for criminal procedures and penalties to be applied at least in cases of wilful trademark counterfeiting or copyright piracy on a commercial scale. Remedies available shall include imprisonment and/or monetary fines sufficient to provide a deterrent, consistently with the level of penalties applied for crimes of a corresponding gravity. In appropriate cases, remedies available shall also include the seizure, forfeiture and destruction of the infringing goods and of any materials and implements the predominant use of which has been in the commission of the offence. Members may provide for criminal procedures and penalties to be applied in other cases of infringement of intellectual property rights, in particular where they are committed wilfully and on a commercial scale.

PART IV

ACQUISITION AND MAINTENANCE OF INTELLECTUAL PROPERTY RIGHTS AND RELATED *INTER-PARTES* PROCEDURES

Article 62

1.   Members may require, as a condition of the acquisition or maintenance of the intellectual property rights provided for under Sections 2 through 6 of Part II, compliance with reasonable procedures and formalities. Such procedures and formalities shall be consistent with the provisions of this Agreement.

2.   Where the acquisition of an intellectual property right is subject to the right being granted or registered, Members shall ensure that the procedures for grant or registration, subject to compliance with the substantive conditions for acquisition of the right, permit the granting or registration of the right within a reasonable period of time so as to avoid unwarranted curtailment of the period of protection.

3.   Article 4 of the Paris Convention (1967) shall apply *mutatis mutandis* to service marks.

4.   Procedures concerning the acquisition or maintenance of intellectual property rights and, where a Member's law provides for such procedures, administrative revocation and *inter partes* procedures such as opposition, revocation and cancellation, shall be governed by the general principles set out in paragraphs 2 and 3 of Article 41.

5.   Final administrative decisions in any of the procedures referred to under paragraph 4 shall be subject to review by a judicial or quasi-judicial authority. However, there shall be no obligation to provide an opportunity for such review of decisions in cases of unsuccessful opposition or administrative revocation, provided that the grounds for such procedures can be the subject of invalidation procedures.

PART V

DISPUTE PREVENTION AND SETTLEMENT

Article 63

Transparency

1.   Laws and regulations, and final judicial decisions and administrative rulings of general application, made effective by a Member pertaining to the subject matter of this Agreement (the availability, scope, acquisition, enforcement and prevention of the abuse of intellectual property rights) shall be published, or where such publication is not practicable made publicly available, in a national language, in such a manner as to enable governments and right holders to become acquainted with them. Agreements concerning the subject matter of this Agreement which are in force between the government or a governmental agency of a Member and the government or a governmental agency of another Member shall also be published.

2.   Members shall notify the laws and regulations referred to in paragraph 1 to the Council for TRIPS in order to assist that Council in its review of the operation of this Agreement. The Council shall attempt to minimize the burden on Members in carrying out this obligation and may decide to waive the obligation to notify such laws and regulations directly to the Council if consultations with WIPO on the establishment of a common register containing these laws and regulations are successful. The

Council shall also consider in this connection any action required regarding notifications pursuant to the obligations under this Agreement stemming from the provisions of Article 6*ter* of the Paris Convention (1967).

3.   Each Member shall be prepared to supply, in response to a written request from another Member, information of the sort referred to in paragraph 1. A Member, having reason to believe that a specific judicial decision or administrative ruling or bilateral agreement in the area of intellectual property rights affects its rights under this Agreement, may also request in writing to be given access to or be informed in sufficient detail of such specific judicial decisions or administrative rulings or bilateral agreements.

4.   Nothing in paragraphs 1, 2 and 3 shall require Members to disclose confidential information which would impede law enforcement or otherwise be contrary to the public interest or would prejudice the legitimate commercial interests of particular enterprises, public or private.

Article 64

Dispute Settlement

1.   The provisions of Articles XXII and XXIII of GATT 1994 as elaborated and applied by the Dispute Settlement Understanding shall apply to consultations and the settlement of disputes under this Agreement except as otherwise specifically provided herein.

2.   Subparagraphs 1(b) and 1(c) of Article XXIII of GATT 1994 shall not apply to the settlement of disputes under this Agreement for a period of five years from the date of entry into force of the WTO Agreement.

3.   During the time period referred to in paragraph 2, the Council for TRIPS shall examine the scope and modalities for complaints of the type provided for under subparagraphs 1(b) and 1(c) of Article XXIII of GATT 1994 made pursuant to this Agreement, and submit its recommendations to the Ministerial Conference for approval. Any decision of the Ministerial Conference to approve such recommendations or to extend the period in paragraph 2 shall be made only by consensus, and approved recommendations shall be effective for all Members without further formal acceptance process.

PART VI

TRANSITIONAL ARRANGEMENTS

Article 65

Transitional Arrangements

1.   Subject to the provisions of paragraphs 2, 3 and 4, no Member shall be obliged to apply the provisions of this Agreement before the expiry

of a general period of one year following the date of entry into force of the WTO Agreement.

2.   A developing country Member is entitled to delay for a further period of four years the date of application, as defined in paragraph 1, of the provisions of this Agreement other than Articles 3, 4 and 5.

3.   Any other Member which is in the process of transformation from a centrally-planned into a market, free-enterprise economy and which is undertaking structural reform of its intellectual property system and facing special problems in the preparation and implementation of intellectual property laws and regulations, may also benefit from a period of delay as foreseen in paragraph 2.

4.   To the extent that a developing country Member is obliged by this Agreement to extend product patent protection to areas of technology not so protectable in its territory on the general date of application of this Agreement for that Member, as defined in paragraph 2, it may delay the application of the provisions on product patents of Section 5 of Part II to such areas of technology for an additional period of five years.

5.   A Member availing itself of a transitional period under paragraphs 1, 2, 3 or 4 shall ensure that any changes in its laws, regulations and practice made during that period do not result in a lesser degree of consistency with the provisions of this Agreement.

Article 66

Least-Developed Country Members

1.   In view of the special needs and requirements of least-developed country Members, their economic, financial and administrative constraints, and their need for flexibility to create a viable technological base, such Members shall not be required to apply the provisions of this Agreement, other than Articles 3, 4 and 5, for a period of 10 years from the date of application as defined under paragraph 1 of Article 65. The Council for TRIPS shall, upon duly motivated request by a least-developed country Member, accord extensions of this period.

2.   Developed country Members shall provide incentives to enterprises and institutions in their territories for the purpose of promoting and encouraging technology transfer to least-developed country Members in order to enable them to create a sound and viable technological base.

Article 67

Technical Cooperation

In order to facilitate the implementation of this Agreement, developed country Members shall provide, on request and on mutually agreed terms and conditions, technical and financial cooperation in favour of developing and least-developed country Members. Such cooperation shall include assistance in the preparation of laws and regulations on the protection and enforcement of intellectual property rights as well as on the prevention of their abuse, and shall include support regarding the establishment or reinforcement of domestic offices and agencies relevant to these matters, including the training of personnel.

PART VII
INSTITUTIONAL ARRANGEMENTS; FINAL PROVISIONS
Article 68
Council for Trade-Related Aspects of Intellectual Property Rights

The Council for TRIPS shall monitor the operation of this Agreement and, in particular, Members' compliance with their obligations hereunder, and shall afford Members the opportunity of consulting on matters relating to the trade-related aspects of intellectual property rights. It shall carry out such other responsibilities as assigned to it by the Members, and it shall, in particular, provide any assistance requested by them in the context of dispute settlement procedures. In carrying out its functions, the Council for TRIPS may consult with and seek information from any source it deems appropriate. In consultation with WIPO, the Council shall seek to establish, within one year of its first meeting, appropriate arrangements for cooperation with bodies of that Organization.

Article 69
International Cooperation

Members agree to cooperate with each other with a view to eliminating international trade in goods infringing intellectual property rights. For this purpose, they shall establish and notify contact points in their administrations and be ready to exchange information on trade in infringing goods. They shall, in particular, promote the exchange of information and cooperation between customs authorities with regard to trade in counterfeit trademark goods and pirated copyright goods.

Article 70
Protection of Existing Subject Matter

1. This Agreement does not give rise to obligations in respect of acts which occurred before the date of application of the Agreement for the Member in question.

2. Except as otherwise provided for in this Agreement, this Agreement gives rise to obligations in respect of all subject matter existing at the date of application of this Agreement for the Member in question, and which is protected in that Member on the said date, or which meets or comes subsequently to meet the criteria for protection under the terms of

this Agreement. In respect of this paragraph and paragraphs 3 and 4, copyright obligations with respect to existing works shall be solely determined under Article 18 of the Berne Convention (1971), and obligations with respect to the rights of producers of phonograms and performers in existing phonograms shall be determined solely under Article 18 of the Berne Convention (1971) as made applicable under paragraph 6 of Article 14 of this Agreement.

3.   There shall be no obligation to restore protection to subject matter which on the date of application of this Agreement for the Member in question has fallen into the public domain.

4.   In respect of any acts in respect of specific objects embodying protected subject matter which become infringing under the terms of legislation in conformity with this Agreement, and which were commenced, or in respect of which a significant investment was made, before the date of acceptance of the WTO Agreement by that Member, any Member may provide for a limitation of the remedies available to the right holder as to the continued performance of such acts after the date of application of this Agreement for that Member. In such cases the Member shall, however, at least provide for the payment of equitable remuneration.

5.   A Member is not obliged to apply the provisions of Article 11 and of paragraph 4 of Article 14 with respect to originals or copies purchased prior to the date of application of this Agreement for that Member.

6.   Members shall not be required to apply Article 31, or the requirement in paragraph 1 of Article 27 that patent rights shall be enjoyable without discrimination as to the field of technology, to use without the authorization of the right holder where authorization for such use was granted by the government before the date this Agreement became known.

7.   In the case of intellectual property rights for which protection is conditional upon registration, applications for protection which are pending on the date of application of this Agreement for the Member in question shall be permitted to be amended to claim any enhanced protection provided under the provisions of this Agreement. Such amendments shall not include new matter.

8.   Where a Member does not make available as of the date of entry into force of the WTO Agreement patent protection for pharmaceutical and agricultural chemical products commensurate with its obligations under Article 27, that Member shall:

(a)   notwithstanding the provisions of Part VI, provide as from the date of entry into force of the WTO Agreement a means by which applications for patents for such inventions can be filed;

(b) apply to these applications, as of the date of application of this Agreement, the criteria for patentability as laid down in this Agreement as if those criteria were being applied on the date of filing in that Member or, where priority is available and claimed, the priority date of the application; and

(c) provide patent protection in accordance with this Agreement as from the grant of the patent and for the remainder of the patent term, counted from the filing date in accordance with Article 33 of this Agreement, for those of these applications that meet the criteria for protection referred to in subparagraph (b).

9.   Where a product is the subject of a patent application in a Member in accordance with paragraph 8(a), exclusive marketing rights shall be granted, notwithstanding the provisions of Part VI, for a period of five years after obtaining marketing approval in that Member or until a product patent is granted or rejected in that Member, whichever period is shorter, provided that, subsequent to the entry into force of the WTO Agreement, a patent application has been filed and a patent granted for that product in another Member and marketing approval obtained in such other Member.

Article 71

Review and Amendment

1.   The Council for TRIPS shall review the implementation of this Agreement after the expiration of the transitional period referred to in paragraph 2 of Article 65. The Council shall, having regard to the experience gained in its implementation, review it two years after that date, and at identical intervals thereafter. The Council may also undertake reviews in the light of any relevant new developments which might warrant modification or amendment of this Agreement.

2.   Amendments merely serving the purpose of adjusting to higher levels of protection of intellectual property rights achieved, and in force, in other multilateral agreements and accepted under those agreements by all Members of the WTO may be referred to the Ministerial Conference for action in accordance with paragraph 6 of Article X of the WTO Agreement on the basis of a consensus proposal from the Council for TRIPS.

Article 72

Reservations

Reservations may not be entered in respect of any of the provisions of this Agreement without the consent of the other Members.

Article 73

Security Exceptions

Nothing in this Agreement shall be construed:

(a) to require a Member to furnish any information the disclosure of which it considers contrary to its essential security interests; or

(b) to prevent a Member from taking any action which it considers necessary for the protection of its essential security interests;

    (i) relating to fissionable materials or the materials from which they are derived;

    (ii) relating to the traffic in arms, ammunition and implements of war and to such traffic in other goods and materials as is carried on directly or indirectly for the purpose of supplying a military establishment;

    (iii) taken in time of war or other emergency in international relations; or

(c) to prevent a Member from taking any action in pursuance of its obligations under the United Nations Charter for the maintenance of international peace and security.

ANNEX TO THE TRIPS AGREEMENT

1. For the purposes of Article 31bis and this Annex:

(a) "pharmaceutical product" means any patented product, or product manufactured through a patented process, of the pharmaceutical sector needed to address the public health problems as recognized in paragraph 1 of the Declaration on the TRIPS Agreement and Public Health (WT/MIN(01)/DEC/2). It is understood that active ingredients necessary for its manufacture and diagnostic kits needed for its use would be included[1];

(b) "eligible importing Member" means any least-developed country Member, and any other Member that has made a notification[2] to the Council for TRIPS of its intention to use the system set out in Article 31bis and this Annex ("system") as an importer, it being understood that a Member may notify at any time that it will use the system in whole or in a limited way, for example only in the case of a national emergency or other circumstances of extreme urgency or in cases of public non-commercial use. It is noted that

---

[1] This subparagraph is without prejudice to subparagraph 1(b).

[2] It is understood that this notification does not need to be approved by a WTO body in order to use the system.

some Members will not use the system as importing Members[3] and that some other Members have stated that, if they use the system, it would be in no more than situations of national emergency or other circumstances of extreme urgency;

(c) "exporting Member" means a Member using the system to produce pharmaceutical products for, and export them to, an eligible importing Member.

(2) The terms referred to in paragraph 1 of Article 31bis are that:

(a) the eligible importing Member(s)[4] has made a notification[2] to the Council for TRIPS, that:

(i) specifies the names and expected quantities of the product(s) needed[5];

(ii) confirms that the eligible importing Member in question, other than a least developed country Member, has established that it has insufficient or no manufacturing capacities in the pharmaceutical sector for the product(s) in question in one of the ways set out in the Appendix to this Annex; and

(iii) confirms that, where a pharmaceutical product is patented in its territory, it has granted or intends to grant a compulsory licence in accordance with Articles 31 and 31bis of this Agreement and the provisions of this Annex[6];

(b) the compulsory licence issued by the exporting Member under the system shall contain the following conditions:

(i) only the amount necessary to meet the needs of the eligible importing Member(s) may be manufactured under the licence and the entirety of this production shall be exported to the Member(s) which has notified its needs to the Council for TRIPS;

(ii) products produced under the licence shall be clearly identified as being produced under the system through specific labelling or marking. Suppliers should distinguish such products through special packaging and/or special colouring/shaping of the products themselves, provided that such distinction is feasible and does not have a significant impact on price; and

[3] Australia, Canada, the European Communities with, for the purposes of Article 31bis and this Annex, its member States, Iceland, Japan, New Zealand, Norway, Switzerland, and the United States.

[4] Joint notifications providing the information required under this subparagraph may be made by the regional organizations referred to in paragraph 3 of Article 31bis on behalf of eligible importing Members using the system that are parties to them, with the agreement of those parties.

[5] The notification will be made available publicly by the WTO Secretariat through a page on the WTO website dedicated to the system.

[6] This subparagraph is without prejudice to Article 66.1 of this Agreement.

(iii) before shipment begins, the licensee shall post on a website[7] the following information:

— the quantities being supplied to each destination as referred to in indent (i) above; and

— the distinguishing features of the product(s) referred to in indent (ii) above;

(c)   the exporting Member shall notify[8] the Council for TRIPS of the grant of the licence, including the conditions attached to it.[9] The information provided shall include the name and address of the licensee, the product(s) for which the licence has been granted, the quantity(ies) for which it has been granted, the country(ies) to which the product(s) is (are) to be supplied and the duration of the licence. The notification shall also indicate the address of the website referred to in subparagraph (b)(iii) above.

3.   In order to ensure that the products imported under the system are used for the public health purposes underlying their importation, eligible importing Members shall take reasonable measures within their means, proportionate to their administrative capacities and to the risk of trade diversion to prevent re-exportation of the products that have actually been imported into their territories under the system. In the event that an eligible importing Member that is a developing country Member or a least-developed country Member experiences difficulty in implementing this provision, developed country Members shall provide, on request and on mutually agreed terms and conditions, technical and financial cooperation in order to facilitate its implementation.

4.   Members shall ensure the availability of effective legal means to prevent the importation into, and sale in, their territories of products produced under the system and diverted to their markets inconsistently with its provisions, using the means already required to be available under this Agreement. If any Member considers that such measures are proving insufficient for this purpose, the matter may be reviewed in the Council for TRIPS at the request of that Member.

5.   With a view to harnessing economies of scale for the purposes of enhancing purchasing power for, and facilitating the local production of, pharmaceutical products, it is recognized that the development of systems providing for the grant of regional patents to be applicable in the Members described in paragraph 3 of Article 31bis should be promoted. To this end,

---

7   The licensee may use for this purpose its own website or, with the assistance of the WTO Secretariat, the page on the WTO website dedicated to the system.

8   It is understood that this notification does not need to be approved by a WTO body in order to use the system.

9   The notification will be made available publicly by the WTO Secretariat through a page on the WTO website dedicated to the system.

developed country Members undertake to provide technical cooperation in accordance with Article 67 of this Agreement, including in conjunction with other relevant intergovernmental organizations.

6.   Members recognize the desirability of promoting the transfer of technology and capacity building in the pharmaceutical sector in order to overcome the problem faced by Members with insufficient or no manufacturing capacities in the pharmaceutical sector. To this end, eligible importing Members and exporting Members are encouraged to use the system in a way which would promote this objective. Members undertake to cooperate in paying special attention to the transfer of technology and capacity building in the pharmaceutical sector in the work to be undertaken pursuant to Article 66.2 of this Agreement, paragraph 7 of the Declaration on the TRIPS Agreement and Public Health and any other relevant work of the Council for TRIPS.

7.   The Council for TRIPS shall review annually the functioning of the system with a view to ensuring its effective operation and shall annually report on its operation to the General Council.

APPENDIX TO THE ANNEX TO THE TRIPS AGREEMENT

Assessment of Manufacturing Capacities in the Pharmaceutical Sector

Least-developed country Members are deemed to have insufficient or no manufacturing capacities in the pharmaceutical sector.

For other eligible importing Members insufficient or no manufacturing capacities for the product(s) in question may be established in either of the following ways:

(i)   the Member in question has established that it has no manufacturing capacity in the pharmaceutical sector;

or

(ii)   where the Member has some manufacturing capacity in this sector, it has examined this capacity and found that, excluding any capacity owned or controlled by the patent owner, it is currently insufficient for the purposes of meeting its needs. When it is established that such capacity has become sufficient to meet the Member's needs, the system shall no longer apply.

Notes:

1.   This subparagraph is without prejudice to subparagraph 1(b).

2.   It is understood that this notification does not need to be approved by a WTO body in order to use the system.

3.   Australia, Canada, the European Communities with, for the purposes of Article 31bis and this Annex, its member States,

Iceland, Japan, New Zealand, Norway, Switzerland, and the United States.

4.   Joint notifications providing the information required under this subparagraph may be made by the regional organizations referred to in paragraph 3 of Article 31bis on behalf of eligible importing Members using the system that are parties to them, with the agreement of those parties.

5.   The notification will be made available publicly by the WTO Secretariat through a page on the WTO website dedicated to the system.

6.   This subparagraph is without prejudice to Article 66.1 of this Agreement.

7.   The licensee may use for this purpose its own website or, with the assistance of the WTO Secretariat, the page on the WTO website dedicated to the system.

8.   It is understood that this notification does not need to be approved by a WTO body in order to use the system.

9.   The notification will be made available publicly by the WTO Secretariat through a page on the WTO website dedicated to the system.

ANNEX 2 TO THE AGREEMENT ESTABLISHING THE WTO— UNDERSTANDING ON RULES AND PROCEDURES GOVERNING THE SETTLEMENT OF DISPUTES

Members hereby *agree* as follows:

Article 1

Coverage and Application

1.   The rules and procedures of this Understanding shall apply to disputes brought pursuant to the consultation and dispute settlement provisions of the agreements listed in Appendix 1 to this Understanding (referred to in this Understanding as the "covered agreements"). The rules and procedures of this Understanding shall also apply to consultations and the settlement of disputes between Members concerning their rights and obligations under the provisions of the Agreement Establishing the World Trade Organization (referred to in this Understanding as the "WTO Agreement") and of this Understanding taken in isolation or in combination with any other covered agreement.

2.   The rules and procedures of this Understanding shall apply subject to such special or additional rules and procedures on dispute settlement contained in the covered agreements as are identified in Appendix 2 to this Understanding. To the extent that there is a difference between the rules and procedures of this Understanding and the special or additional rules and procedures set forth in Appendix 2, the special or additional rules and procedures in Appendix 2 shall prevail. In disputes involving rules and procedures under more than one covered agreement, if there is a conflict between special or additional rules and procedures of such agreements under review, and where the parties to the dispute cannot agree on rules and procedures within 20 days of the establishment of the panel, the Chairman of the Dispute Settlement Body provided for in paragraph 1 of Article 2 (referred to in this Understanding as the "DSB"), in consultation with the parties to the dispute, shall determine the rules and procedures to be followed within 10 days after a request by either Member. The Chairman shall be guided by the principle that special or

additional rules and procedures should be used where possible, and the rules and procedures set out in this Understanding should be used to the extent necessary to avoid conflict.

Article 2

Administration

1.   The Dispute Settlement Body is hereby established to administer these rules and procedures and, except as otherwise provided in a covered agreement, the consultation and dispute settlement provisions of the covered agreements. Accordingly, the DSB shall have the authority to establish panels, adopt panel and Appellate Body reports, maintain surveillance of implementation of rulings and recommendations, and authorize suspension of concessions and other obligations under the covered agreements. With respect to disputes arising under a covered agreement which is a Plurilateral Trade Agreement, the term "Member" as used herein shall refer only to those Members that are parties to the relevant Plurilateral Trade Agreement. Where the DSB administers the dispute settlement provisions of a Plurilateral Trade Agreement, only those Members that are parties to that Agreement may participate in decisions or actions taken by the DSB with respect to that dispute.

2.   The DSB shall inform the relevant WTO Councils and Committees of any developments in disputes related to provisions of the respective covered agreements.

3.   The DSB shall meet as often as necessary to carry out its functions within the time-frames provided in this Understanding.

4.   Where the rules and procedures of this Understanding provide for the DSB to take a decision, it shall do so by consensus.[1]

Article 3

General Provisions

1.   Members affirm their adherence to the principles for the management of disputes heretofore applied under Articles XXII and XXIII of GATT 1947, and the rules and procedures as further elaborated and modified herein.

2.   The dispute settlement system of the WTO is a central element in providing security and predictability to the multilateral trading system. The Members recognize that it serves to preserve the rights and obligations of Members under the covered agreements, and to clarify the existing provisions of those agreements in accordance with customary rules of interpretation of public international law. Recommendations and rulings

---

[1.]   The DSB shall be deemed to have decided by consensus on a matter submitted for its consideration, if no Member, present at the meeting of the DSB when the decision is taken, formally objects to the proposed decision.

of the DSB cannot add to or diminish the rights and obligations provided in the covered agreements.

3.   The prompt settlement of situations in which a Member considers that any benefits accruing to it directly or indirectly under the covered agreements are being impaired by measures taken by another Member is essential to the effective functioning of the WTO and the maintenance of a proper balance between the rights and obligations of Members.

4.   Recommendations or rulings made by the DSB shall be aimed at achieving a satisfactory settlement of the matter in accordance with the rights and obligations under this Understanding and under the covered agreements.

5.   All solutions to matters formally raised under the consultation and dispute settlement provisions of the covered agreements, including arbitration awards, shall be consistent with those agreements and shall not nullify or impair benefits accruing to any Member under those agreements, nor impede the attainment of any objective of those agreements.

6.   Mutually agreed solutions to matters formally raised under the consultation and dispute settlement provisions of the covered agreements shall be notified to the DSB and the relevant Councils and Committees, where any Member may raise any point relating thereto.

7.   Before bringing a case, a Member shall exercise its judgement as to whether action under these procedures would be fruitful. The aim of the dispute settlement mechanism is to secure a positive solution to a dispute. A solution mutually acceptable to the parties to a dispute and consistent with the covered agreements is clearly to be preferred. In the absence of a mutually agreed solution, the first objective of the dispute settlement mechanism is usually to secure the withdrawal of the measures concerned if these are found to be inconsistent with the provisions of any of the covered agreements. The provision of compensation should be resorted to only if the immediate withdrawal of the measure is impracticable and as a temporary measure pending the withdrawal of the measure which is inconsistent with a covered agreement. The last resort which this Understanding provides to the Member invoking the dispute settlement procedures is the possibility of suspending the application of concessions or other obligations under the covered agreements on a discriminatory basis vis-à-vis the other Member, subject to authorization by the DSB of such measures.

8.   In cases where there is an infringement of the obligations assumed under a covered agreement, the action is considered *prima facie* to constitute a case of nullification or impairment. This means that there is normally a presumption that a breach of the rules has an adverse impact on other Members parties to that covered agreement, and in such cases, it

shall be up to the Member against whom the complaint has been brought to rebut the charge.

9.   The provisions of this Understanding are without prejudice to the rights of Members to seek authoritative interpretation of provisions of a covered agreement through decision-making under the WTO Agreement or a covered agreement which is a Plurilateral Trade Agreement.

10.   It is understood that requests for conciliation and the use of the dispute settlement procedures should not be intended or considered as contentious acts and that, if a dispute arises, all Members will engage in these procedures in good faith in an effort to resolve the dispute. It is also understood that complaints and counter-complaints in regard to distinct matters should not be linked.

11.   This Understanding shall be applied only with respect to new requests for consultations under the consultation provisions of the covered agreements made on or after the date of entry into force of the WTO Agreement. With respect to disputes for which the request for consultations was made under GATT 1947 or under any other predecessor agreement to the covered agreements before the date of entry into force of the WTO Agreement, the relevant dispute settlement rules and procedures in effect immediately prior to the date of entry into force of the WTO Agreement shall continue to apply.[2]

12.   Notwithstanding paragraph 11, if a complaint based on any of the covered agreements is brought by a developing country Member against a developed country Member, the complaining party shall have the right to invoke, as an alternative to the provisions contained in Articles 4, 5, 6 and 12 of this Understanding, the corresponding provisions of the Decision of 5 April 1966 (BISD 14S/18), except that where the Panel considers that the time-frame provided for in paragraph 7 of that Decision is insufficient to provide its report and with the agreement of the complaining party, that time-frame may be extended. To the extent that there is a difference between the rules and procedures of Articles 4, 5, 6 and 12 and the corresponding rules and procedures of the Decision, the latter shall prevail.

Article 4

Consultations

1.   Members affirm their resolve to strengthen and improve the effectiveness of the consultation procedures employed by Members.

2.   Each Member undertakes to accord sympathetic consideration to and afford adequate opportunity for consultation regarding any representations made by another Member concerning measures affecting

---

[2.]   This paragraph shall also be applied to disputes on which panel reports have not been adopted or fully implemented.

the operation of any covered agreement taken within the territory of the former.[3]

3.   If a request for consultations is made pursuant to a covered agreement, the Member to which the request is made shall, unless otherwise mutually agreed, reply to the request within 10 days after the date of its receipt and shall enter into consultations in good faith within a period of no more than 30 days after the date of receipt of the request, with a view to reaching a mutually satisfactory solution. If the Member does not respond within 10 days after the date of receipt of the request, or does not enter into consultations within a period of no more than 30 days, or a period otherwise mutually agreed, after the date of receipt of the request, then the Member that requested the holding of consultations may proceed directly to request the establishment of a panel.

4.   All such requests for consultations shall be notified to the DSB and the relevant Councils and Committees by the Member which requests consultations. Any request for consultations shall be submitted in writing and shall give the reasons for the request, including identification of the measures at issue and an indication of the legal basis for the complaint.

5.   In the course of consultations in accordance with the provisions of a covered agreement, before resorting to further action under this Understanding, Members should attempt to obtain satisfactory adjustment of the matter.

6.   Consultations shall be confidential, and without prejudice to the rights of any Member in any further proceedings.

7.   If the consultations fail to settle a dispute within 60 days after the date of receipt of the request for consultations, the complaining party may request the establishment of a panel. The complaining party may request a panel during the 60-day period if the consulting parties jointly consider that consultations have failed to settle the dispute.

8.   In cases of urgency, including those which concern perishable goods, Members shall enter into consultations within a period of no more than 10 days after the date of receipt of the request. If the consultations have failed to settle the dispute within a period of 20 days after the date of receipt of the request, the complaining party may request the establishment of a panel.

9.   In cases of urgency, including those which concern perishable goods, the parties to the dispute, panels and the Appellate Body shall make every effort to accelerate the proceedings to the greatest extent possible.

[3.]   Where the provisions of any other covered agreement concerning measures taken by regional or local governments or authorities within the territory of a Member contain provisions different from the provisions of this paragraph, the provisions of such other covered agreement shall prevail.

10. During consultations Members should give special attention to the particular problems and interests of developing country Members.

11. Whenever a Member other than the consulting Members considers that it has a substantial trade interest in consultations being held pursuant to paragraph 1 of Article XXII of GATT 1994, paragraph 1 of Article XXII of GATS, or the corresponding provisions in other covered agreements[4], such Member may notify the consulting Members and the DSB, within 10 days after the date of the circulation of the request for consultations under said Article, of its desire to be joined in the consultations. Such Member shall be joined in the consultations, provided that the Member to which the request for consultations was addressed agrees that the claim of substantial interest is well-founded. In that event they shall so inform the DSB. If the request to be joined in the consultations is not accepted, the applicant Member shall be free to request consultations under paragraph 1 of Article XXII or paragraph 1 of Article XXIII of GATT 1994, paragraph 1 of Article XXII or paragraph 1 of Article XXIII of GATS, or the corresponding provisions in other covered agreements.

Article 5

Good Offices, Conciliation and Mediation

1.   Good offices, conciliation and mediation are procedures that are undertaken voluntarily if the parties to the dispute so agree.

2.   Proceedings involving good offices, conciliation and mediation, and in particular positions taken by the parties to the dispute during these proceedings, shall be confidential, and without prejudice to the rights of either party in any further proceedings under these procedures.

3.   Good offices, conciliation or mediation may be requested at any time by any party to a dispute. They may begin at any time and be terminated at any time. Once procedures for good offices, conciliation or mediation are terminated, a complaining party may then proceed with a request for the establishment of a panel.

4.   When good offices, conciliation or mediation are entered into within 60 days after the date of receipt of a request for consultations, the complaining party must allow a period of 60 days after the date of receipt

---

[4.] The corresponding consultation provisions in the covered agreements are listed hereunder: Agreement on Agriculture, Article 19; Agreement on the Application of Sanitary and Phytosanitary Measures, paragraph 1 of Article 11; Agreement on Textiles and Clothing, paragraph 4 of Article 8; Agreement on Technical Barriers to Trade, paragraph 1 of Article 14; Agreement on Trade-Related Investment Measures, Article 8; Agreement on Implementation of Article VI of GATT 1994, paragraph 2 of Article 17; Agreement on Implementation of Article VII of GATT 1994, paragraph 2 of Article 19; Agreement on Preshipment Inspection, Article 7; Agreement on Rules of Origin, Article 7; Agreement on Import Licensing Procedures, Article 6; Agreement on Subsidies and Countervailing Measures, Article 30; Agreement on Safeguards, Article 14; Agreement on Trade-Related Aspects of Intellectual Property Rights, Article 64.1; and any corresponding consultation provisions in Plurilateral Trade Agreements as determined by the competent bodies of each Agreement and as notified to the DSB.

of the request for consultations before requesting the establishment of a panel. The complaining party may request the establishment of a panel during the 60-day period if the parties to the dispute jointly consider that the good offices, conciliation or mediation process has failed to settle the dispute.

5.   If the parties to a dispute agree, procedures for good offices, conciliation or mediation may continue while the panel process proceeds.

6.   The Director-General may, acting in an *ex officio* capacity, offer good offices, conciliation or mediation with the view to assisting Members to settle a dispute.

Article 6

Establishment of Panels

1.   If the complaining party so requests, a panel shall be established at the latest at the DSB meeting following that at which the request first appears as an item on the DSB's agenda, unless at that meeting the DSB decides by consensus not to establish a panel.[5]

2.   The request for the establishment of a panel shall be made in writing. It shall indicate whether consultations were held, identify the specific measures at issue and provide a brief summary of the legal basis of the complaint sufficient to present the problem clearly. In case the applicant requests the establishment of a panel with other than standard terms of reference, the written request shall include the proposed text of special terms of reference.

Article 7

Terms of Reference of Panels

1.   Panels shall have the following terms of reference unless the parties to the dispute agree otherwise within 20 days from the establishment of the panel:

"To examine, in the light of the relevant provisions in (name of the covered agreement(s) cited by the parties to the dispute), the matter referred to the DSB by (name of party) in document . . . and to make such findings as will assist the DSB in making the recommendations or in giving the rulings provided for in that/ those agreement(s)."

2.   Panels shall address the relevant provisions in any covered agreement or agreements cited by the parties to the dispute.

[5.]   If the complaining party so requests, a meeting of the DSB shall be convened for this purpose within 15 days of the request, provided that at least 10 days' advance notice of the meeting is given.

3.   In establishing a panel, the DSB may authorize its Chairman to draw up the terms of reference of the panel in consultation with the parties to the dispute, subject to the provisions of paragraph 1. The terms of reference thus drawn up shall be circulated to all Members. If other than standard terms of reference are agreed upon, any Member may raise any point relating thereto in the DSB.

Article 8

Composition of Panels

1.   Panels shall be composed of well-qualified governmental and/or non-governmental individuals, including persons who have served on or presented a case to a panel, served as a representative of a Member or of a contracting party to GATT 1947 or as a representative to the Council or Committee of any covered agreement or its predecessor agreement, or in the Secretariat, taught or published on international trade law or policy, or served as a senior trade policy official of a Member.

2.   Panel members should be selected with a view to ensuring the independence of the members, a sufficiently diverse background and a wide spectrum of experience.

3.   Citizens of Members whose governments[6] are parties to the dispute or third parties as defined in paragraph 2 of Article 10 shall not serve on a panel concerned with that dispute, unless the parties to the dispute agree otherwise.

4.   To assist in the selection of panelists, the Secretariat shall maintain an indicative list of governmental and non-governmental individuals possessing the qualifications outlined in paragraph 1, from which panelists may be drawn as appropriate. That list shall include the roster of non-governmental panelists established on 30 November 1984 (BISD 31S/9), and other rosters and indicative lists established under any of the covered agreements, and shall retain the names of persons on those rosters and indicative lists at the time of entry into force of the WTO Agreement. Members may periodically suggest names of governmental and non-governmental individuals for inclusion on the indicative list, providing relevant information on their knowledge of international trade and of the sectors or subject matter of the covered agreements, and those names shall be added to the list upon approval by the DSB. For each of the individuals on the list, the list shall indicate specific areas of experience or expertise of the individuals in the sectors or subject matter of the covered agreements.

5.   Panels shall be composed of three panelists unless the parties to the dispute agree, within 10 days from the establishment of the panel, to a

---

[6]   In the case where customs unions or common markets are parties to a dispute, this provision applies to citizens of all member countries of the customs unions or common markets.

panel composed of five panelists. Members shall be informed promptly of the composition of the panel.

6.   The Secretariat shall propose nominations for the panel to the parties to the dispute. The parties to the dispute shall not oppose nominations except for compelling reasons.

7.   If there is no agreement on the panelists within 20 days after the date of the establishment of a panel, at the request of either party, the Director-General, in consultation with the Chairman of the DSB and the Chairman of the relevant Council or Committee, shall determine the composition of the panel by appointing the panelists whom the Director-General considers most appropriate in accordance with any relevant special or additional rules or procedures of the covered agreement or covered agreements which are at issue in the dispute, after consulting with the parties to the dispute. The Chairman of the DSB shall inform the Members of the composition of the panel thus formed no later than 10 days after the date the Chairman receives such a request.

8.   Members shall undertake, as a general rule, to permit their officials to serve as panelists.

9.   Panelists shall serve in their individual capacities and not as government representatives, nor as representatives of any organization. Members shall therefore not give them instructions nor seek to influence them as individuals with regard to matters before a panel.

10.   When a dispute is between a developing country Member and a developed country Member the panel shall, if the developing country Member so requests, include at least one panelist from a developing country Member.

11.   Panelists' expenses, including travel and subsistence allowance, shall be met from the WTO budget in accordance with criteria to be adopted by the General Council, based on recommendations of the Committee on Budget, Finance and Administration.

Article 9

Procedures for Multiple Complainants

1.   Where more than one Member requests the establishment of a panel related to the same matter, a single panel may be established to examine these complaints taking into account the rights of all Members concerned. A single panel should be established to examine such complaints whenever feasible.

2.   The single panel shall organize its examination and present its findings to the DSB in such a manner that the rights which the parties to the dispute would have enjoyed had separate panels examined the complaints are in no way impaired. If one of the parties to the dispute so

requests, the panel shall submit separate reports on the dispute concerned. The written submissions by each of the complainants shall be made available to the other complainants, and each complainant shall have the right to be present when any one of the other complainants presents its views to the panel.

3.   If more than one panel is established to examine the complaints related to the same matter, to the greatest extent possible the same persons shall serve as panelists on each of the separate panels and the timetable for the panel process in such disputes shall be harmonized.

Article 10

Third Parties

1.   The interests of the parties to a dispute and those of other Members under a covered agreement at issue in the dispute shall be fully taken into account during the panel process.

2.   Any Member having a substantial interest in a matter before a panel and having notified its interest to the DSB (referred to in this Understanding as a "third party") shall have an opportunity to be heard by the panel and to make written submissions to the panel. These submissions shall also be given to the parties to the dispute and shall be reflected in the panel report.

3.   Third parties shall receive the submissions of the parties to the dispute to the first meeting of the panel.

4.   If a third party considers that a measure already the subject of a panel proceeding nullifies or impairs benefits accruing to it under any covered agreement, that Member may have recourse to normal dispute settlement procedures under this Understanding. Such a dispute shall be referred to the original panel wherever possible.

Article 11

Function of Panels

The function of panels is to assist the DSB in discharging its responsibilities under this Understanding and the covered agreements. Accordingly, a panel should make an objective assessment of the matter before it, including an objective assessment of the facts of the case and the applicability of and conformity with the relevant covered agreements, and make such other findings as will assist the DSB in making the recommendations or in giving the rulings provided for in the covered agreements. Panels should consult regularly with the parties to the dispute and give them adequate opportunity to develop a mutually satisfactory solution.

Article 12

Panel Procedures

1.   Panels shall follow the Working Procedures in Appendix 3 unless the panel decides otherwise after consulting the parties to the dispute.

2.   Panel procedures should provide sufficient flexibility so as to ensure high-quality panel reports, while not unduly delaying the panel process.

3.   After consulting the parties to the dispute, the panelists shall, as soon as practicable and whenever possible within one week after the composition and terms of reference of the panel have been agreed upon, fix the timetable for the panel process, taking into account the provisions of paragraph 9 of Article 4, if relevant.

4.   In determining the timetable for the panel process, the panel shall provide sufficient time for the parties to the dispute to prepare their submissions.

5.   Panels should set precise deadlines for written submissions by the parties and the parties should respect those deadlines.

6.   Each party to the dispute shall deposit its written submissions with the Secretariat for immediate transmission to the panel and to the other party or parties to the dispute. The complaining party shall submit its first submission in advance of the responding party's first submission unless the panel decides, in fixing the timetable referred to in paragraph 3 and after consultations with the parties to the dispute, that the parties should submit their first submissions simultaneously. When there are sequential arrangements for the deposit of first submissions, the panel shall establish a firm time-period for receipt of the responding party's submission. Any subsequent written submissions shall be submitted simultaneously.

7.   Where the parties to the dispute have failed to develop a mutually satisfactory solution, the panel shall submit its findings in the form of a written report to the DSB. In such cases, the report of a panel shall set out the findings of fact, the applicability of relevant provisions and the basic rationale behind any findings and recommendations that it makes. Where a settlement of the matter among the parties to the dispute has been found, the report of the panel shall be confined to a brief description of the case and to reporting that a solution has been reached.

8.   In order to make the procedures more efficient, the period in which the panel shall conduct its examination, from the date that the composition and terms of reference of the panel have been agreed upon until the date the final report is issued to the parties to the dispute, shall, as a general rule, not exceed six months. In cases of urgency, including

those relating to perishable goods, the panel shall aim to issue its report to the parties to the dispute within three months.

9.   When the panel considers that it cannot issue its report within six months, or within three months in cases of urgency, it shall inform the DSB in writing of the reasons for the delay together with an estimate of the period within which it will issue its report. In no case should the period from the establishment of the panel to the circulation of the report to the Members exceed nine months.

10.   In the context of consultations involving a measure taken by a developing country Member, the parties may agree to extend the periods established in paragraphs 7 and 8 of Article 4. If, after the relevant period has elapsed, the consulting parties cannot agree that the consultations have concluded, the Chairman of the DSB shall decide, after consultation with the parties, whether to extend the relevant period and, if so, for how long. In addition, in examining a complaint against a developing country Member, the panel shall accord sufficient time for the developing country Member to prepare and present its argumentation. The provisions of paragraph 1 of Article 20 and paragraph 4 of Article 21 are not affected by any action pursuant to this paragraph.

11.   Where one or more of the parties is a developing country Member, the panel's report shall explicitly indicate the form in which account has been taken of relevant provisions on differential and more-favourable treatment for developing country Members that form part of the covered agreements which have been raised by the developing country Member in the course of the dispute settlement procedures.

12.   The panel may suspend its work at any time at the request of the complaining party for a period not to exceed 12 months. In the event of such a suspension, the time-frames set out in paragraphs 8 and 9 of this Article, paragraph 1 of Article 20, and paragraph 4 of Article 21 shall be extended by the amount of time that the work was suspended. If the work of the panel has been suspended for more than 12 months, the authority for establishment of the panel shall lapse.

Article 13

Right to Seek Information

1.   Each panel shall have the right to seek information and technical advice from any individual or body which it deems appropriate. However, before a panel seeks such information or advice from any individual or body within the jurisdiction of a Member it shall inform the authorities of that Member. A Member should respond promptly and fully to any request by a panel for such information as the panel considers necessary and appropriate. Confidential information which is provided shall not be

revealed without formal authorization from the individual, body, or authorities of the Member providing the information.

2.   Panels may seek information from any relevant source and may consult experts to obtain their opinion on certain aspects of the matter. With respect to a factual issue concerning a scientific or other technical matter raised by a party to a dispute, a panel may request an advisory report in writing from an expert review group. Rules for the establishment of such a group and its procedures are set forth in Appendix 4.

Article 14

Confidentiality

1.   Panel deliberations shall be confidential.

2.   The reports of panels shall be drafted without the presence of the parties to the dispute in the light of the information provided and the statements made.

3.   Opinions expressed in the panel report by individual panelists shall be anonymous.

Article 15

Interim Review Stage

1.   Following the consideration of rebuttal submissions and oral arguments, the panel shall issue the descriptive (factual and argument) sections of its draft report to the parties to the dispute. Within a period of time set by the panel, the parties shall submit their comments in writing.

2.   Following the expiration of the set period of time for receipt of comments from the parties to the dispute, the panel shall issue an interim report to the parties, including both the descriptive sections and the panel's findings and conclusions. Within a period of time set by the panel, a party may submit a written request for the panel to review precise aspects of the interim report prior to circulation of the final report to the Members. At the request of a party, the panel shall hold a further meeting with the parties on the issues identified in the written comments. If no comments are received from any party within the comment period, the interim report shall be considered the final panel report and circulated promptly to the Members.

3.   The findings of the final panel report shall include a discussion of the arguments made at the interim review stage. The interim review stage shall be conducted within the time-period set out in paragraph 8 of Article 12.

Article 16

Adoption of Panel Reports

1.   In order to provide sufficient time for the Members to consider panel reports, the reports shall not be considered for adoption by the DSB until 20 days after the date they have been circulated to the Members.

2.   Members having objections to a panel report shall give written reasons to explain their objections for circulation at least 10 days prior to the DSB meeting at which the panel report will be considered.

3.   The parties to a dispute shall have the right to participate fully in the consideration of the panel report by the DSB, and their views shall be fully recorded.

4.   Within 60 days after the date of circulation of a panel report to the Members, the report shall be adopted at a DSB meeting[7] unless a party to the dispute formally notifies the DSB of its decision to appeal or the DSB decides by consensus not to adopt the report. If a party has notified its decision to appeal, the report by the panel shall not be considered for adoption by the DSB until after completion of the appeal. This adoption procedure is without prejudice to the right of Members to express their views on a panel report.

Article 17

Appellate Review

Standing Appellate Body

1.   A standing Appellate Body shall be established by the DSB. The Appellate Body shall hear appeals from panel cases. It shall be composed of seven persons, three of whom shall serve on any one case. Persons serving on the Appellate Body shall serve in rotation. Such rotation shall be determined in the working procedures of the Appellate Body.

2.   The DSB shall appoint persons to serve on the Appellate Body for a four-year term, and each person may be reappointed once. However, the terms of three of the seven persons appointed immediately after the entry into force of the WTO Agreement shall expire at the end of two years, to be determined by lot. Vacancies shall be filled as they arise. A person appointed to replace a person whose term of office has not expired shall hold office for the remainder of the predecessor's term.

3.   The Appellate Body shall comprise persons of recognized authority, with demonstrated expertise in law, international trade and the subject matter of the covered agreements generally. They shall be unaffiliated with any government. The Appellate Body membership shall

---

[7]   If a meeting of the DSB is not scheduled within this period at a time that enables the requirements of paragraphs 1 and 4 of Article 16 to be met, a meeting of the DSB shall be held for this purpose.

be broadly representative of membership in the WTO. All persons serving on the Appellate Body shall be available at all times and on short notice, and shall stay abreast of dispute settlement activities and other relevant activities of the WTO. They shall not participate in the consideration of any disputes that would create a direct or indirect conflict of interest.

4.   Only parties to the dispute, not third parties, may appeal a panel report. Third parties which have notified the DSB of a substantial interest in the matter pursuant to paragraph 2 of Article 10 may make written submissions to, and be given an opportunity to be heard by, the Appellate Body.

5.   As a general rule, the proceedings shall not exceed 60 days from the date a party to the dispute formally notifies its decision to appeal to the date the Appellate Body circulates its report. In fixing its timetable the Appellate Body shall take into account the provisions of paragraph 9 of Article 4, if relevant. When the Appellate Body considers that it cannot provide its report within 60 days, it shall inform the DSB in writing of the reasons for the delay together with an estimate of the period within which it will submit its report. In no case shall the proceedings exceed 90 days.

6.   An appeal shall be limited to issues of law covered in the panel report and legal interpretations developed by the panel.

7.   The Appellate Body shall be provided with appropriate administrative and legal support as it requires.

8.   The expenses of persons serving on the Appellate Body, including travel and subsistence allowance, shall be met from the WTO budget in accordance with criteria to be adopted by the General Council, based on recommendations of the Committee on Budget, Finance and Administration.

Procedures for Appellate Review

9.   Working procedures shall be drawn up by the Appellate Body in consultation with the Chairman of the DSB and the Director-General, and communicated to the Members for their information.

10. The proceedings of the Appellate Body shall be confidential. The reports of the Appellate Body shall be drafted without the presence of the parties to the dispute and in the light of the information provided and the statements made.

11. Opinions expressed in the Appellate Body report by individuals serving on the Appellate Body shall be anonymous.

12. The Appellate Body shall address each of the issues raised in accordance with paragraph 6 during the appellate proceeding.

13. The Appellate Body may uphold, modify or reverse the legal findings and conclusions of the panel.

Adoption of Appellate Body Reports

14. An Appellate Body report shall be adopted by the DSB and unconditionally accepted by the parties to the dispute unless the DSB decides by consensus not to adopt the Appellate Body report within 30 days following its circulation to the Members.[8] This adoption procedure is without prejudice to the right of Members to express their views on an Appellate Body report.

Article 18

Communications with the Panel or Appellate Body

1. There shall be no *ex parte* communications with the panel or Appellate Body concerning matters under consideration by the panel or Appellate Body.

2. Written submissions to the panel or the Appellate Body shall be treated as confidential, but shall be made available to the parties to the dispute. Nothing in this Understanding shall preclude a party to a dispute from disclosing statements of its own positions to the public. Members shall treat as confidential information submitted by another Member to the panel or the Appellate Body which that Member has designated as confidential. A party to a dispute shall also, upon request of a Member, provide a non-confidential summary of the information contained in its written submissions that could be disclosed to the public.

Article 19

Panel and Appellate Body Recommendations

1. Where a panel or the Appellate Body concludes that a measure is inconsistent with a covered agreement, it shall recommend that the Member concerned[9] bring the measure into conformity with that agreement.[10] In addition to its recommendations, the panel or Appellate Body may suggest ways in which the Member concerned could implement the recommendations.

2. In accordance with paragraph 2 of Article 3, in their findings and recommendations, the panel and Appellate Body cannot add to or diminish the rights and obligations provided in the covered agreements.

---

[8]. If a meeting of the DSB is not scheduled during this period, such a meeting of the DSB shall be held for this purpose.

[9]. The "Member concerned" is the party to the dispute to which the panel or Appellate Body recommendations are directed.

[10]. With respect to recommendations in cases not involving a violation of GATT 1994 or any other covered agreement, see Article 26.

Article 20

Time-frame for DSB Decisions

Unless otherwise agreed to by the parties to the dispute, the period from the date of establishment of the panel by the DSB until the date the DSB considers the panel or appellate report for adoption shall as a general rule not exceed nine months where the panel report is not appealed or 12 months where the report is appealed. Where either the panel or the Appellate Body has acted, pursuant to paragraph 9 of Article 12 or paragraph 5 of Article 17, to extend the time for providing its report, the additional time taken shall be added to the above periods.

Article 21

Surveillance of Implementation of Recommendations and Rulings

1.   Prompt compliance with recommendations or rulings of the DSB is essential in order to ensure effective resolution of disputes to the benefit of all Members.

2.   Particular attention should be paid to matters affecting the interests of developing country Members with respect to measures which have been subject to dispute settlement.

3.   At a DSB meeting held within 30 days[11] after the date of adoption of the panel or Appellate Body report, the Member concerned shall inform the DSB of its intentions in respect of implementation of the recommendations and rulings of the DSB. If it is impracticable to comply immediately with the recommendations and rulings, the Member concerned shall have a reasonable period of time in which to do so. The reasonable period of time shall be:

(a)   the period of time proposed by the Member concerned, provided that such period is approved by the DSB; or, in the absence of such approval,

(b)   a period of time mutually agreed by the parties to the dispute within 45 days after the date of adoption of the recommendations and rulings; or, in the absence of such agreement,

(c)   a period of time determined through binding arbitration within 90 days after the date of adoption of the recommendations and rulings.[12] In such arbitration, a guideline for the arbitrator[13] should be that the reasonable period of time to implement panel

---

[11.] If a meeting of the DSB is not scheduled during this period, such a meeting of the DSB shall be held for this purpose.

[12.] If the parties cannot agree on an arbitrator within ten days after referring the matter to arbitration, the arbitrator shall be appointed by the Director-General within ten days, after consulting the parties.

[13.] The expression "arbitrator" shall be interpreted as referring either to an individual or a group.

or Appellate Body recommendations should not exceed 15 months from the date of adoption of a panel or Appellate Body report. However, that time may be shorter or longer, depending upon the particular circumstances.

4.   Except where the panel or the Appellate Body has extended, pursuant to paragraph 9 of Article 12 or paragraph 5 of Article 17, the time of providing its report, the period from the date of establishment of the panel by the DSB until the date of determination of the reasonable period of time shall not exceed 15 months unless the parties to the dispute agree otherwise. Where either the panel or the Appellate Body has acted to extend the time of providing its report, the additional time taken shall be added to the 15-month period; provided that unless the parties to the dispute agree that there are exceptional circumstances, the total time shall not exceed 18 months.

5.   Where there is disagreement as to the existence or consistency with a covered agreement of measures taken to comply with the recommendations and rulings such dispute shall be decided through recourse to these dispute settlement procedures, including wherever possible resort to the original panel. The panel shall circulate its report within 90 days after the date of referral of the matter to it. When the panel considers that it cannot provide its report within this time frame, it shall inform the DSB in writing of the reasons for the delay together with an estimate of the period within which it will submit its report.

6.   The DSB shall keep under surveillance the implementation of adopted recommendations or rulings. The issue of implementation of the recommendations or rulings may be raised at the DSB by any Member at any time following their adoption. Unless the DSB decides otherwise, the issue of implementation of the recommendations or rulings shall be placed on the agenda of the DSB meeting after six months following the date of establishment of the reasonable period of time pursuant to paragraph 3 and shall remain on the DSB's agenda until the issue is resolved. At least 10 days prior to each such DSB meeting, the Member concerned shall provide the DSB with a status report in writing of its progress in the implementation of the recommendations or rulings.

7.   If the matter is one which has been raised by a developing country Member, the DSB shall consider what further action it might take which would be appropriate to the circumstances.

8.   If the case is one brought by a developing country Member, in considering what appropriate action might be taken, the DSB shall take into account not only the trade coverage of measures complained of, but also their impact on the economy of developing country Members concerned.

Article 22

Compensation and the Suspension of Concessions

1.   Compensation and the suspension of concessions or other obligations are temporary measures available in the event that the recommendations and rulings are not implemented within a reasonable period of time. However, neither compensation nor the suspension of concessions or other obligations is preferred to full implementation of a recommendation to bring a measure into conformity with the covered agreements. Compensation is voluntary and, if granted, shall be consistent with the covered agreements.

2.   If the Member concerned fails to bring the measure found to be inconsistent with a covered agreement into compliance therewith or otherwise comply with the recommendations and rulings within the reasonable period of time determined pursuant to paragraph 3 of Article 21, such Member shall, if so requested, and no later than the expiry of the reasonable period of time, enter into negotiations with any party having invoked the dispute settlement procedures, with a view to developing mutually acceptable compensation. If no satisfactory compensation has been agreed within 20 days after the date of expiry of the reasonable period of time, any party having invoked the dispute settlement procedures may request authorization from the DSB to suspend the application to the Member concerned of concessions or other obligations under the covered agreements.

3.   In considering what concessions or other obligations to suspend, the complaining party shall apply the following principles and procedures:

(a)   the general principle is that the complaining party should first seek to suspend concessions or other obligations with respect to the same sector(s) as that in which the panel or Appellate Body has found a violation or other nullification or impairment;

(b)   if that party considers that it is not practicable or effective to suspend concessions or other obligations with respect to the same sector(s), it may seek to suspend concessions or other obligations in other sectors under the same agreement;

(c)   if that party considers that it is not practicable or effective to suspend concessions or other obligations with respect to other sectors under the same agreement, and that the circumstances are serious enough, it may seek to suspend concessions or other obligations under another covered agreement;

(d)   in applying the above principles, that party shall take into account:

(i) the trade in the sector or under the agreement under which the panel or Appellate Body has found a violation or other nullification or impairment, and the importance of such trade to that party;

(ii) the broader economic elements related to the nullification or impairment and the broader economic consequences of the suspension of concessions or other obligations;

(e) if that party decides to request authorization to suspend concessions or other obligations pursuant to subparagraphs (b) or (c), it shall state the reasons therefor in its request. At the same time as the request is forwarded to the DSB, it also shall be forwarded to the relevant Councils and also, in the case of a request pursuant to subparagraph (b), the relevant sectoral bodies;

(f) for purposes of this paragraph, "sector" means:

(i) with respect to goods, all goods;

(ii) with respect to services, a principal sector as identified in the current "Services Sectoral Classification List" which identifies such sectors;[14]

(iii) with respect to trade-related intellectual property rights, each of the categories of intellectual property rights covered in Section 1, or Section 2, or Section 3, or Section 4, or Section 5, or Section 6, or Section 7 of Part II, or the obligations under Part III, or Part IV of the Agreement on TRIPS;

(g) for purposes of this paragraph, "agreement" means:

(i) with respect to goods, the agreements listed in Annex 1A of the WTO Agreement, taken as a whole as well as the Plurilateral Trade Agreements in so far as the relevant parties to the dispute are parties to these agreements;

(ii) with respect to services, the GATS;

(iii) with respect to intellectual property rights, the Agreement on TRIPS.

4. The level of the suspension of concessions or other obligations authorized by the DSB shall be equivalent to the level of the nullification or impairment.

5. The DSB shall not authorize suspension of concessions or other obligations if a covered agreement prohibits such suspension.

---

[14] The list in document MTN. GNS/W/120 identifies eleven sectors.

6.   When the situation described in paragraph 2 occurs, the DSB, upon request, shall grant authorization to suspend concessions or other obligations within 30 days of the expiry of the reasonable period of time unless the DSB decides by consensus to reject the request. However, if the Member concerned objects to the level of suspension proposed, or claims that the principles and procedures set forth in paragraph 3 have not been followed where a complaining party has requested authorization to suspend concessions or other obligations pursuant to paragraph 3(b) or (c), the matter shall be referred to arbitration. Such arbitration shall be carried out by the original panel, if members are available, or by an arbitrator[15] appointed by the Director-General and shall be completed within 60 days after the date of expiry of the reasonable period of time. Concessions or other obligations shall not be suspended during the course of the arbitration.

7.   The arbitrator[16] acting pursuant to paragraph 6 shall not examine the nature of the concessions or other obligations to be suspended but shall determine whether the level of such suspension is equivalent to the level of nullification or impairment. The arbitrator may also determine if the proposed suspension of concessions or other obligations is allowed under the covered agreement. However, if the matter referred to arbitration includes a claim that the principles and procedures set forth in paragraph 3 have not been followed, the arbitrator shall examine that claim. In the event the arbitrator determines that those principles and procedures have not been followed, the complaining party shall apply them consistent with paragraph 3. The parties shall accept the arbitrator's decision as final and the parties concerned shall not seek a second arbitration. The DSB shall be informed promptly of the decision of the arbitrator and shall upon request, grant authorization to suspend concessions or other obligations where the request is consistent with the decision of the arbitrator, unless the DSB decides by consensus to reject the request.

8.   The suspension of concessions or other obligations shall be temporary and shall only be applied until such time as the measure found to be inconsistent with a covered agreement has been removed, or the Member that must implement recommendations or rulings provides a solution to the nullification or impairment of benefits, or a mutually satisfactory solution is reached. In accordance with paragraph 6 of Article 21, the DSB shall continue to keep under surveillance the implementation of adopted recommendations or rulings, including those cases where compensation has been provided or concessions or other obligations have

---

[15.] The expression "arbitrator" shall be interpreted as referring either to an individual or a group.

[16.] The expression "arbitrator" shall be interpreted as referring either to an individual or a group or to the members of the original panel when serving in the capacity of arbitrator.

been suspended but the recommendations to bring a measure into conformity with the covered agreements have not been implemented.

9.   The dispute settlement provisions of the covered agreements may be invoked in respect of measures affecting their observance taken by regional or local governments or authorities within the territory of a Member. When the DSB has ruled that a provision of a covered agreement has not been observed, the responsible Member shall take such reasonable measures as may be available to it to ensure its observance. The provisions of the covered agreements and this Understanding relating to compensation and suspension of concessions or other obligations apply in cases where it has not been possible to secure such observance.[17]

Article 23

Strengthening of the Multilateral System

1.   When Members seek the redress of a violation of obligations or other nullification or impairment of benefits under the covered agreements or an impediment to the attainment of any objective of the covered agreements, they shall have recourse to, and abide by, the rules and procedures of this Understanding.

2.   In such cases, Members shall:

(a)   not make a determination to the effect that a violation has occurred, that benefits have been nullified or impaired or that the attainment of any objective of the covered agreements has been impeded, except through recourse to dispute settlement in accordance with the rules and procedures of this Understanding, and shall make any such determination consistent with the findings contained in the panel or Appellate Body report adopted by the DSB or an arbitration award rendered under this Understanding;

(b)   follow the procedures set forth in Article 21 to determine the reasonable period of time for the Member concerned to implement the recommendations and rulings; and

(c)   follow the procedures set forth in Article 22 to determine the level of suspension of concessions or other obligations and obtain DSB authorization in accordance with those procedures before suspending concessions or other obligations under the covered agreements in response to the failure of the Member concerned to implement the recommendations and rulings within that reasonable period of time.

[17.] Where the provisions of any covered agreement concerning measures taken by regional or local governments or authorities within the territory of a Member contain provisions different from the provisions of this paragraph, the provisions of such covered agreement shall prevail.

Article 24

Special Procedures Involving
Least-Developed Country Members

1.   At all stages of the determination of the causes of a dispute and of dispute settlement procedures involving a least-developed country Member, particular consideration shall be given to the special situation of least-developed country Members. In this regard, Members shall exercise due restraint in raising matters under these procedures involving a least-developed country Member. If nullification or impairment is found to result from a measure taken by a least-developed country Member, complaining parties shall exercise due restraint in asking for compensation or seeking authorization to suspend the application of concessions or other obligations pursuant to these procedures.

2.   In dispute settlement cases involving a least-developed country Member, where a satisfactory solution has not been found in the course of consultations the Director-General or the Chairman of the DSB shall, upon request by a least-developed country Member offer their good offices, conciliation and mediation with a view to assisting the parties to settle the dispute, before a request for a panel is made. The Director-General or the Chairman of the DSB, in providing the above assistance, may consult any source which either deems appropriate.

Article 25

Arbitration

1.   Expeditious arbitration within the WTO as an alternative means of dispute settlement can facilitate the solution of certain disputes that concern issues that are clearly defined by both parties.

2.   Except as otherwise provided in this Understanding, resort to arbitration shall be subject to mutual agreement of the parties which shall agree on the procedures to be followed. Agreements to resort to arbitration shall be notified to all Members sufficiently in advance of the actual commencement of the arbitration process.

3.   Other Members may become party to an arbitration proceeding only upon the agreement of the parties which have agreed to have recourse to arbitration. The parties to the proceeding shall agree to abide by the arbitration award. Arbitration awards shall be notified to the DSB and the Council or Committee of any relevant agreement where any Member may raise any point relating thereto.

4.   Articles 21 and 22 of this Understanding shall apply *mutatis mutandis* to arbitration awards.

Article 26

1.   Non-Violation Complaints of the Type Described in Paragraph 1(b) of Article XXIII of GATT 1994

Where the provisions of paragraph 1(b) of Article XXIII of GATT 1994 are applicable to a covered agreement, a panel or the Appellate Body may only make rulings and recommendations where a party to the dispute considers that any benefit accruing to it directly or indirectly under the relevant covered agreement is being nullified or impaired or the attainment of any objective of that Agreement is being impeded as a result of the application by a Member of any measure, whether or not it conflicts with the provisions of that Agreement. Where and to the extent that such party considers and a panel or the Appellate Body determines that a case concerns a measure that does not conflict with the provisions of a covered agreement to which the provisions of paragraph 1(b) of Article XXIII of GATT 1994 are applicable, the procedures in this Understanding shall apply, subject to the following:

(a)   the complaining party shall present a detailed justification in support of any complaint relating to a measure which does not conflict with the relevant covered agreement;

(b)   where a measure has been found to nullify or impair benefits under, or impede the attainment of objectives, of the relevant covered agreement without violation thereof, there is no obligation to withdraw the measure. However, in such cases, the panel or the Appellate Body shall recommend that the Member concerned make a mutually satisfactory adjustment;

(c)   notwithstanding the provisions of Article 21, the arbitration provided for in paragraph 3 of Article 21, upon request of either party, may include a determination of the level of benefits which have been nullified or impaired, and may also suggest ways and means of reaching a mutually satisfactory adjustment; such suggestions shall not be binding upon the parties to the dispute;

(d)   notwithstanding the provisions of paragraph 1 of Article 22, compensation may be part of a mutually satisfactory adjustment as final settlement of the dispute.

2.   Complaints of the Type Described in Paragraph 1(c) of Article XXIII of GATT 1994

Where the provisions of paragraph 1(c) of Article XXIII of GATT 1994 are applicable to a covered agreement, a panel may only make rulings and recommendations where a party considers that any benefit accruing to it directly or indirectly under the relevant covered agreement is being nullified or impaired or the attainment of any objective of that Agreement is being impeded as a result of the existence of any situation other than those to which the provisions of paragraphs 1(a) and 1(b) of Article XXIII of GATT 1994 are applicable. Where and to the extent that such party considers and a panel determines that the matter is covered by this paragraph, the procedures of this Understanding shall apply only up to and including the point in the proceedings where the panel report has been circulated to the Members. The dispute settlement rules and procedures contained in the Decision of 12 April 1989 (BISD 36S/61-67) shall apply to consideration for adoption, and surveillance and implementation of recommendations and rulings. The following shall also apply:

(a) the complaining party shall present a detailed justification in support of any argument made with respect to issues covered under this paragraph;

(b) in cases involving matters covered by this paragraph, if a panel finds that cases also involve dispute settlement matters other than those covered by this paragraph, the panel shall circulate a report to the DSB addressing any such matters and a separate report on matters falling under this paragraph.

Article 27

Responsibilities of the Secretariat

1.   The Secretariat shall have the responsibility of assisting panels, especially on the legal, historical and procedural aspects of the matters dealt with, and of providing secretarial and technical support.

2.   While the Secretariat assists Members in respect of dispute settlement at their request, there may also be a need to provide additional legal advice and assistance in respect of dispute settlement to developing country Members. To this end, the Secretariat shall make available a qualified legal expert from the WTO technical cooperation services to any developing country Member which so requests. This expert shall assist the developing country Member in a manner ensuring the continued impartiality of the Secretariat.

3.   The Secretariat shall conduct special training courses for interested Members concerning these dispute settlement procedures and practices so as to enable Members' experts to be better informed in this regard.

APPENDIX 1

AGREEMENTS COVERED BY THE UNDERSTANDING

(A) Agreement Establishing the World Trade Organization

(B) Multilateral Trade Agreements

Annex 1A: Multilateral Agreements on Trade in Goods

Annex 1B: General Agreement on Trade in Services

Annex 1C: Agreement on Trade-Related Aspects of Intellectual Property Rights

Annex 2:   Understanding on Rules and Procedures Governing the Settlement of Disputes

(C) Plurilateral Trade Agreements

Annex 4:   Agreement on Trade in Civil Aircraft

Agreement on Government Procurement

International Dairy Agreement

International Bovine Meat Agreement

The applicability of this Understanding to the Plurilateral Trade Agreements shall be subject to the adoption of a decision by the parties to each agreement setting out the terms for the application of the Understanding to the individual agreement, including any special or additional rules or procedures for inclusion in Appendix 2, as notified to the DSB.

APPENDIX 2

SPECIAL OR ADDITIONAL RULES AND PROCEDURES CONTAINED IN THE COVERED AGREEMENTS

Agreement Rules and Procedures

Agreement on the Application of Sanitary and Phytosanitary Measures	11.2
Agreement on Textiles and Clothing	2.14, 2.21, 4.4, 5.2, 5.4, 5.6, 6.9, 6.10, 6.11, 8.1 through 8.12
Agreement on Technical Barriers to Trade	14.2 through 14.4, Annex 2
Agreement on Implementation of Article VI of GATT 1994	17.4 through 17.7
Agreement on Implementation of Article VII of GATT 1994	19.3 through 19.5, Annex II.2(f), 3, 9, 21
Agreement on Subsidies and Countervailing Measures	4.2 through 4.12, 6.6, 7.2 through 7.10, 8.5, footnote 35, 24.4, 27.7, Annex V
General Agreement on Trade in Services	XXII:3, XXIII:3
Annex on Financial Services	4

Annex on Air Transport   4
Services

Decision on Certain Dispute   1 through 5
Settlement Procedures for the
GATS

The list of rules and procedures in this Appendix includes provisions where only a part of the provision may be relevant in this context.

Any special or additional rules or procedures in the Plurilateral Trade Agreements as determined by the competent bodies of each agreement and as notified to the DSB.

APPENDIX 3

WORKING PROCEDURES

1.   In its proceedings the panel shall follow the relevant provisions of this Understanding. In addition, the following working procedures shall apply.

2.   The panel shall meet in closed session. The parties to the dispute, and interested parties, shall be present at the meetings only when invited by the panel to appear before it.

3.   The deliberations of the panel and the documents submitted to it shall be kept confidential. Nothing in this Understanding shall preclude a party to a dispute from disclosing statements of its own positions to the public. Members shall treat as confidential information submitted by another Member to the panel which that Member has designated as confidential. Where a party to a dispute submits a confidential version of its written submissions to the panel, it shall also, upon request of a Member, provide a non-confidential summary of the information contained in its submissions that could be disclosed to the public.

4.   Before the first substantive meeting of the panel with the parties, the parties to the dispute shall transmit to the panel written submissions in which they present the facts of the case and their arguments.

5.   At its first substantive meeting with the parties, the panel shall ask the party which has brought the complaint to present its case. Subsequently, and still at the same meeting, the party against which the complaint has been brought shall be asked to present its point of view.

6.   All third parties which have notified their interest in the dispute to the DSB shall be invited in writing to present their views during a session of the first substantive meeting of the panel set aside for that purpose. All such third parties may be present during the entirety of this session.

7. Formal rebuttals shall be made at a second substantive meeting of the panel. The party complained against shall have the right to take the floor first to be followed by the complaining party. The parties shall submit, prior to that meeting, written rebuttals to the panel.

8. The panel may at any time put questions to the parties and ask them for explanations either in the course of a meeting with the parties or in writing.

9. The parties to the dispute and any third party invited to present its views in accordance with Article 10 shall make available to the panel a written version of their oral statements.

10. In the interest of full transparency, the presentations, rebuttals and statements referred to in paragraphs 5 to 9 shall be made in the presence of the parties. Moreover, each party's written submissions, including any comments on the descriptive part of the report and responses to questions put by the panel, shall be made available to the other party or parties.

11. Any additional procedures specific to the panel.

12. Proposed timetable for panel work:

(a) Receipt of first written submissions of the parties:

    (1) complaining Party: _____ 3–6 weeks

    (2) Party complained against: _____ 2–3 weeks

(b) Date, time and place of first substantive meeting with the parties; third party session: _____ 1–2 weeks

(c) Receipt of written rebuttals of the parties: _____ 2–3 weeks

(d) Date, time and place of second substantive meeting with the parties: _____ 1–2 weeks

(e) Issuance of descriptive part of the report to the parties: _____ 2–4 weeks

(f) Receipt of comments by the parties on the descriptive part of the report: _____ 2 weeks

(g) Issuance of the interim report, including the findings and conclusions, to the parties: _____ 2–4 weeks

(h) Deadline for party to request review of part(s) of report: _____ 1 week

(i) Period of review by panel, including possible additional meeting with parties: _____ 2 weeks

(j) Issuance of final report to parties to dispute: _____ 2 weeks

(k) Circulation of the final report to the Members: _____ 3 weeks

The above calendar may be changed in the light of unforeseen developments. Additional meetings with the parties shall be scheduled if required.

APPENDIX 4

EXPERT REVIEW GROUPS

The following rules and procedures shall apply to expert review groups established in accordance with the provisions of paragraph 2 of Article 13.

1.   Expert review groups are under the panel's authority. Their terms of reference and detailed working procedures shall be decided by the panel, and they shall report to the panel.

2.   Participation in expert review groups shall be restricted to persons of professional standing and experience in the field in question.

3.   Citizens of parties to the dispute shall not serve on an expert review group without the joint agreement of the parties to the dispute, except in exceptional circumstances when the panel considers that the need for specialized scientific expertise cannot be fulfilled otherwise. Government officials of parties to the dispute shall not serve on an expert review group. Members of expert review groups shall serve in their individual capacities and not as government representatives, nor as representatives of any organization. Governments or organizations shall therefore not give them instructions with regard to matters before an expert review group.

4.   Expert review groups may consult and seek information and technical advice from any source they deem appropriate. Before an expert review group seeks such information or advice from a source within the jurisdiction of a Member, it shall inform the government of that Member. Any Member shall respond promptly and fully to any request by an expert review group for such information as the expert review group considers necessary and appropriate.

5.   The parties to a dispute shall have access to all relevant information provided to an expert review group, unless it is of a confidential nature. Confidential information provided to the expert review group shall not be released without formal authorization from the government, organization or person providing the information. Where such information is requested from the expert review group but release of such information by the expert review group is not authorized, a non-confidential summary of the information will be provided by the government, organization or person supplying the information.

6.   The expert review group shall submit a draft report to the parties to the dispute with a view to obtaining their comments, and taking them into account, as appropriate, in the final report, which shall also be issued

to the parties to the dispute when it is submitted to the panel. The final report of the expert review group shall be advisory only.

3

MEMBERS AND OBSERVERS OF THE WORLD TRADE ORGANIZATION

164 members as of 29 July 2016, with dates of membership.

Afghanistan	29 July 2016
Albania	8 September 2000
Angola	23 November 1996
Antigua and Barbuda	1 January 1995
Argentina	1 January 1995
Armenia	5 February 2003
Australia	1 January 1995
Austria	1 January 1995
Bahrain, Kingdom of	1 January 1995
Bangladesh	1 January 1995
Barbados	1 January 1995
Belgium	1 January 1995
Belize	1 January 1995
Benin	22 February 1996
Bolivia, Plurinational State of	12 September 1995
Botswana	31 May 1995
Brazil	1 January 1995
Brunei Darussalam	1 January 1995
Bulgaria	1 December 1996
Burkina Faso	3 June 1995
Burundi	23 July 1995
Cabo Verde	23 July 2008
Cambodia	13 October 2004
Cameroon	13 December 1995
Canada	1 January 1995
Central African Republic	31 May 1995
Chad	19 October 1996
Chile	1 January 1995
China	11 December 2001
Colombia	30 April 1995

Congo	27 March 1997
Costa Rica	1 January 1995
Côte d'Ivoire	1 January 1995
Croatia	30 November 2000
Cuba	20 April 1995
Cyprus	30 July 1995
Czech Republic	1 January 1995
Democratic Republic of the Congo	1 January 1997
Denmark	1 January 1995
Djibouti	31 May 1995
Dominica	1 January 1995
Dominican Republic	9 March 1995
Ecuador	21 January 1996
Egypt	30 June 1995
El Salvador	7 May 1995
Estonia	13 November 1999
European Union (formerly European Communities)	1 January 1995
Fiji	14 January 1996
Finland	1 January 1995
France	1 January 1995
Gabon	1 January 1995
Gambia	23 October 1996
Georgia	14 June 2000
Germany	1 January 1995
Ghana	1 January 1995
Greece	1 January 1995
Grenada	22 February 1996
Guatemala	21 July 1995
Guinea	25 October 1995
Guinea-Bissau	31 May 1995
Guyana	1 January 1995
Haiti	30 January 1996
Honduras	1 January 1995
Hong Kong, China	1 January 1995
Hungary	1 January 1995
Iceland	1 January 1995
India	1 January 1995
Indonesia	1 January 1995

Ireland	1 January 1995
Israel	21 April 1995
Italy	1 January 1995
Jamaica	9 March 1995
Japan	1 January 1995
Jordan	11 April 2000
Kazakhstan	30 November 2015
Kenya	1 January 1995
Korea, Republic of	1 January 1995
Kuwait, the State of	1 January 1995
Kyrgyz Republic	20 December 1998
Lao People's Democratic Republic	2 February 2013
Latvia	10 February 1999
Lesotho	31 May 1995
Liechtenstein	1 September 1995
Lithuania	31 May 2001
Luxembourg	1 January 1995
Macao, China	1 January 1995
Madagascar	17 November 1995
Malawi	31 May 1995
Malaysia	1 January 1995
Maldives	31 May 1995
Mali	31 May 1995
Malta	1 January 1995
Mauritania	31 May 1995
Mauritius	1 January 1995
Mexico	1 January 1995
Moldova, Republic of	26 July 2001
Mongolia	29 January 1997
Montenegro	12 April 2012
Morocco	1 January 1995
Mozambique	26 August 1995
Myanmar	1 January 1995
Namibia	1 January 1995
Nepal	23 April 2004
Netherlands	1 January 1995
New Zealand	1 January 1995
Nicaragua	3 September 1995
Niger	13 December 1996

Nigeria	1 January 1995
Norway	1 January 1995
Oman	9 November 2000
Pakistan	1 January 1995
Panama	6 September 1997
Papua New Guinea	9 June 1996
Paraguay	1 January 1995
Peru	1 January 1995
Philippines	1 January 1995
Poland	1 July 1995
Portugal	1 January 1995
Qatar	13 January 1996
Romania	1 January 1995
Russian Federation	22 August 2012
Rwanda	22 May 1996
Saint Kitts and Nevis	21 February 1996
Saint Lucia	1 January 1995
Saint Vincent & the Grenadines	1 January 1995
Samoa	10 May 2012
Saudi Arabia, Kingdom of	11 December 2005
Senegal	1 January 1995
Seychelles	26 April 2015
Sierra Leone	23 July 1995
Singapore	1 January 1995
Slovak Republic	1 January 1995
Slovenia	30 July 1995
Solomon Islands	26 July 1996
South Africa	1 January 1995
Spain	1 January 1995
Sri Lanka	1 January 1995
Suriname	1 January 1995
Swaziland	1 January 1995
Sweden	1 January 1995
Switzerland	1 July 1995
Chinese Taipei	1 January 2002
Tajikistan	2 March 2013
Tanzania	1 January 1995
Thailand	1 January 1995

The former Yugoslav Republic of Macedonia (FYROM)	4 April 2003
Togo	31 May 1995
Tonga	27 July 2007
Trinidad and Tobago	1 March 1995
Tunisia	29 March 1995
Turkey	26 March 1995
Uganda	1 January 1995
Ukraine	16 May 2008
United Arab Emirates	10 April 1996
United Kingdom	1 January 1995
United States of America	1 January 1995
Uruguay	1 January 1995
Vanuatu	24 August 2012
Venezuela, Bolivarian Republic of	1 January 1995
Viet Nam	11 January 2007
Yemen	26 June 2014
Zambia	1 January 1995
Zimbabwe	5 March 1995

Observer Governments

Algeria
Andorra
Azerbaijan
Bahamas
Belarus
Bhutan
Bosnia and Herzegovina
Comoros
Curaçao
Equatorial Guinea
Ethiopia
Holy See
Iran
Iraq
Lebanese Republic
Libya
Sao Tomé and Principe

Serbia
Somalia
South Sudan
Sudan
Syrian Arab Republic
Timor-Leste
Turkmenistan
Uzbekistan

Note: Observers must start accession negotiations within five years of becoming observers.

PART 1

COPYRIGHT AND NEIGHBORING RIGHTS

4

BERNE CONVENTION FOR THE PROTECTION OF LITERARY AND ARTISTIC WORKS

Paris Act of July 24, 1971, as amended on September 28, 1979

Berne Convention for the Protection of Literary and Artistic Works of September 9, 1886, completed at PARIS on May 4, 1896, revised at BERLIN on November 13, 1908, completed at BERNE on March 20, 1914, revised at ROME on June 2, 1928, at BRUSSELS on June 26, 1948, at STOCKHOLM on July 14, 1967, and at PARIS on July 24, 1971, and amended on September 28, 1979.

The countries of the Union, being equally animated by the desire to protect, in as effective and uniform a manner as possible, the rights of authors in their literary and artistic works,

Recognizing the importance of the work of the Revision Conference held at Stockholm in 1967,

Have resolved to revise the Act adopted by the Stockholm Conference, while maintaining without change Articles 1 to 20 and 22 to 26 of that Act.

Consequently, the undersigned Plenipotentiaries, having presented their full powers, recognized as in good and due form, have agreed as follows:

Article 1

The countries to which this Convention applies constitute a Union for the protection of the rights of authors in their literary and artistic works.

Article 2

(1) The expression "literary and artistic works" shall include every production in the literary, scientific and artistic domain, whatever may be the mode or form of its expression, such as books, pamphlets and other writings; lectures, addresses, sermons and other works of the same nature; dramatic or dramaticomusical works; choreographic works and entertainments in dumb show; musical compositions with or without words; cinematographic works to which are assimilated works expressed by a process analogous to cinematography; works of drawing, painting, architecture, sculpture, engraving and lithography; photographic works to which are assimilated works expressed by a process analogous to

photography; works of applied art; illustrations, maps, plans, sketches and three-dimensional works relative to geography, topography, architecture or science.

(2) It shall, however, be a matter for legislation in the countries of the Union to prescribe that works in general or any specified categories of works shall not be protected unless they have been fixed in some material form.

(3) Translations, adaptations, arrangements of music and other alterations of a literary or artistic work shall be protected as original works without prejudice to the copyright in the original work.

(4) It shall be a matter for legislation in the countries of the Union to determine the protection to be granted to official texts of a legislative, administrative and legal nature, and to official translations of such texts.

(5) Collections of literary or artistic works such as encyclopaedias and anthologies which, by reason of the selection and arrangement of their contents, constitute intellectual creations shall be protected as such, without prejudice to the copyright in each of the works forming part of such collections.

(6) The works mentioned in this Article shall enjoy protection in all countries of the Union. This protection shall operate for the benefit of the author and his successors in title.

(7) Subject to the provisions of Article 7(4) of this Convention, it shall be a matter for legislation in the countries of the Union to determine the extent of the application of their laws to works of applied art and industrial designs and models, as well as the conditions under which such works, designs and models shall be protected. Works protected in the country of origin solely as designs and models shall be entitled in another country of the Union only to such special protection as is granted in that country to designs and models; however, if no such special protection is granted in that country, such works shall be protected as artistic works.

(8) The protection of this Convention shall not apply to news of the day or to miscellaneous facts having the character of mere items of press information.

Article 2*bis*

(1) It shall be a matter for legislation in the countries of the Union to exclude, wholly or in part, from the protection provided by the preceding Article political speeches and speeches delivered in the course of legal proceedings.

(2) It shall also be a matter for legislation in the countries of the Union to determine the conditions under which lectures, addresses and other works of the same nature which are delivered in public may be

reproduced by the press, broadcast, communicated to the public by wire and made the subject of public communication as envisaged in Article 11*bis*(1) of this Convention, when such use is justified by the informatory purpose.

(3)   Nevertheless, the author shall enjoy the exclusive right of making a collection of his works mentioned in the preceding paragraphs.

Article 3

(1)   The protection of this Convention shall apply to:

(a)   authors who are nationals of one of the countries of the Union, for their works, whether published or not;

(b)   authors who are not nationals of one of the countries of the Union, for their works first published in one of those countries, or simultaneously in a country outside the Union and in a country of the Union.

(2)   Authors who are not nationals of one of the countries of the Union but who have their habitual residence in one of them shall, for the purposes of this Convention, be assimilated to nationals of that country.

(3)   The expression "published works" means works published with the consent of their authors, whatever may be the means of manufacture of the copies, provided that the availability of such copies has been such as to satisfy the reasonable requirements of the public, having regard to the nature of the work. The performance of a dramatic, dramaticomusical, cinematographic or musical work, the public recitation of a literary work, the communication by wire or the broadcasting of literary or artistic works, the exhibition of a work of art and the construction of a work of architecture shall not constitute publication.

(4)   A work shall be considered as having been published simultaneously in several countries if it has been published in two or more countries within thirty days of its first publication.

Article 4

The protection of this Convention shall apply, even if the conditions of Article 3 are not fulfilled, to:

(a)   authors of cinematographic works the maker of which has his headquarters or habitual residence in one of the countries of the Union;

(b)   authors of works of architecture erected in a country of the Union or of other artistic works incorporated in a building or other structure located in a country of the Union.

Article 5

(1) Authors shall enjoy, in respect of works for which they are protected under this Convention, in countries of the Union other than the country of origin, the rights which their respective laws do now or may hereafter grant to their nationals, as well as the rights specially granted by this Convention.

(2) The enjoyment and the exercise of these rights shall not be subject to any formality; such enjoyment and such exercise shall be independent of the existence of protection in the country of origin of the work. Consequently, apart from the provisions of this Convention, the extent of protection, as well as the means of redress afforded to the author to protect his rights, shall be governed exclusively by the laws of the country where protection is claimed.

(3) Protection in the country of origin is governed by domestic law. However, when the author is not a national of the country of origin of the work for which he is protected under this Convention, he shall enjoy in that country the same rights as national authors.

(4) The country of origin shall be considered to be:

(a) in the case of works first published in a country of the Union, that country; in the case of works published simultaneously in several countries of the Union which grant different terms of protection, the country whose legislation grants the shortest term of protection;

(b) in the case of works published simultaneously in a country outside the Union and in a country of the Union, the latter country;

(c) in the case of unpublished works or of works first published in a country outside the Union, without simultaneous publication in a country of the Union, the country of the Union of which the author is a national, provided that:

(i) when these are cinematographic works the maker of which has his headquarters or his habitual residence in a country of the Union, the country of origin shall be that country, and

(ii) when these are works of architecture erected in a country of the Union or other artistic works incorporated in a building or other structure located in a country of the Union, the country of origin shall be that country.

Article 6

(1) Where any country outside the Union fails to protect in an adequate manner the works of authors who are nationals of one of the countries of the Union, the latter country may restrict the protection given to the works of authors who are, at the date of the first publication thereof,

nationals of the other country and are not habitually resident in one of the countries of the Union. If the country of first publication avails itself of this right, the other countries of the Union shall not be required to grant to works thus subjected to special treatment a wider protection than that granted to them in the country of first publication.

(2) No restrictions introduced by virtue of the preceding paragraph shall affect the rights which an author may have acquired in respect of a work published in a country of the Union before such restrictions were put into force.

(3) The countries of the Union which restrict the grant of copyright in accordance with this Article shall give notice thereof to the Director General of the World Intellectual Property Organization (hereinafter designated as "the Director General") by a written declaration specifying the countries in regard to which protection is restricted, and the restrictions to which rights of authors who are nationals of those countries are subjected. The Director General shall immediately communicate this declaration to all the countries of the Union.

Article 6*bis*

(1) Independently of the author's economic rights, and even after the transfer of the said rights, the author shall have the right to claim authorship of the work and to object to any distortion, mutilation or other modification of, or other derogatory action in relation to, the said work, which would be prejudicial to his honor or reputation.

(2) The rights granted to the author in accordance with the preceding paragraph shall, after his death, be maintained, at least until the expiry of the economic rights, and shall be exercisable by the persons or institutions authorized by the legislation of the country where protection is claimed. However, those countries whose legislation, at the moment of their ratification of or accession to this Act, does not provide for the protection after the death of the author of all the rights set out in the preceding paragraph may provide that some of these rights may, after his death, cease to be maintained.

(3) The means of redress for safeguarding the rights granted by this Article shall be governed by the legislation of the country where protection is claimed.

Article 7

(1) The term of protection granted by this Convention shall be the life of the author and fifty years after his death.

(2) However, in the case of cinematographic works, the countries of the Union may provide that the term of protection shall expire fifty years after the work has been made available to the public with the consent of

the author, or, failing such an event within fifty years from the making of such a work, fifty years after the making.

(3) In the case of anonymous or pseudonymous works, the term of protection granted by this Convention shall expire fifty years after the work has been lawfully made available to the public. However, when the pseudonym adopted by the author leaves no doubt as to his identity, the term of protection shall be that provided in paragraph (1). If the author of an anonymous or pseudonymous work discloses his identity during the above-mentioned period, the term of protection applicable shall be that provided in paragraph (1). The countries of the Union shall not be required to protect anonymous or pseudonymous works in respect of which it is reasonable to presume that their author has been dead for fifty years.

(4) It shall be a matter for legislation in the countries of the Union to determine the term of protection of photographic works and that of works of applied art in so far as they are protected as artistic works; however, this term shall last at least until the end of a period of twenty-five years from the making of such a work.

(5) The term of protection subsequent to the death of the author and the terms provided by paragraphs (2), (3) and (4) shall run from the date of death or of the event referred to in those paragraphs, but such terms shall always be deemed to begin on the first of January of the year following the death or such event.

(6) The countries of the Union may grant a term of protection in excess of those provided by the preceding paragraphs.

(7) Those countries of the Union bound by the Rome Act of this Convention which grant, in their national legislation in force at the time of signature of the present Act, shorter terms of protection than those provided for in the preceding paragraphs shall have the right to maintain such terms when ratifying or acceding to the present Act.

(8) In any case, the term shall be governed by the legislation of the country where protection is claimed; however, unless the legislation of that country otherwise provides, the term shall not exceed the term fixed in the country of origin of the work.

Article 7*bis*

The provisions of the preceding Article shall also apply in the case of a work of joint authorship, provided that the terms measured from the death of the author shall be calculated from the death of the last surviving author.

Article 8

Authors of literary and artistic works protected by this Convention shall enjoy the exclusive right of making and of authorizing the translation of their works throughout the term of protection of their rights in the original works.

Article 9

(1) Authors of literary and artistic works protected by this Convention shall have the exclusive right of authorizing the reproduction of these works, in any manner or form.

(2) It shall be a matter for legislation in the countries of the Union to permit the reproduction of such works in certain special cases, provided that such reproduction does not conflict with a normal exploitation of the work and does not unreasonably prejudice the legitimate interests of the author.

(3) Any sound or visual recording shall be considered as a reproduction for the purposes of this Convention.

Article 10

(1) It shall be permissible to make quotations from a work which has already been lawfully made available to the public, provided that their making is compatible with fair practice, and their extent does not exceed that justified by the purpose, including quotations from newspaper articles and periodicals in the form of press summaries.

(2) It shall be a matter for legislation in the countries of the Union, and for special agreements existing or to be concluded between them, to permit the utilization, to the extent justified by the purpose, of literary or artistic works by way of illustration in publications, broadcasts or sound or visual recordings for teaching, provided such utilization is compatible with fair practice.

(3) Where use is made of works in accordance with the preceding paragraphs of this Article, mention shall be made of the source, and of the name of the author if it appears thereon.

Article 10*bis*

(1) It shall be a matter for legislation in the countries of the Union to permit the reproduction by the press, the broadcasting or the communication to the public by wire of articles published in newspapers or periodicals on current economic, political or religious topics, and of broadcast works of the same character, in cases in which the reproduction, broadcasting or such communication thereof is not expressly reserved. Nevertheless, the source must always be clearly indicated; the legal consequences of a breach of this obligation shall be determined by the legislation of the country where protection is claimed.

(2) It shall also be a matter for legislation in the countries of the Union to determine the conditions under which, for the purpose of reporting current events by means of photography, cinematography,

broadcasting or communication to the public by wire, literary or artistic works seen or heard in the course of the event may, to the extent justified by the informatory purpose, be reproduced and made available to the public.

Article 11

(1) Authors of dramatic, dramatico-musical and musical works shall enjoy the exclusive right of authorizing:

(i)   the public performance of their works, including such public performance by any means or process;

(ii)   any communication to the public of the performance of their works.

(2) Authors of dramatic or dramatico-musical works shall enjoy, during the full term of their rights in the original works, the same rights with respect to translations thereof.

Article 11*bis*

(1) Authors of literary and artistic works shall enjoy the exclusive right of authorizing:

(i)   the broadcasting of their works or the communication thereof to the public by any other means of wireless diffusion of signs, sounds or images;

(ii)   any communication to the public by wire or by rebroadcasting of the broadcast of the work, when this communication is made by an organization other than the original one;

(iii) the public communication by loudspeaker or any other analogous instrument transmitting, by signs, sounds or images, the broadcast of the work.

(2) It shall be a matter for legislation in the countries of the Union to determine the conditions under which the rights mentioned in the preceding paragraph may be exercised, but these conditions shall apply only in the countries where they have been prescribed. They shall not in any circumstances be prejudicial to the moral rights of the author, nor to his right to obtain equitable remuneration which, in the absence of agreement, shall be fixed by competent authority.

(3) In the absence of any contrary stipulation, permission granted in accordance with paragraph (1) of this Article shall not imply permission to record, by means of instruments recording sounds or images, the work broadcast. It shall, however, be a matter for legislation in the countries of the Union to determine the regulations for ephemeral recordings made by a broadcasting organization by means of its own facilities and used for its own broadcasts. The preservation of these recordings in official archives

may, on the ground of their exceptional documentary character, be authorized by such legislation.

Article 11*ter*

(1) Authors of literary works shall enjoy the exclusive right of authorizing:

   (i)   the public recitation of their works, including such public recitation by any means or process;

   (ii) any communication to the public of the recitation of their works.

(2) Authors of literary works shall enjoy, during the full term of their rights in the original works, the same rights with respect to translations thereof.

Article 12

Authors of literary or artistic works shall enjoy the exclusive right of authorizing adaptations, arrangements and other alterations of their works.

Article 13

(1) Each country of the Union may impose for itself reservations and conditions on the exclusive right granted to the author of a musical work and to the author of any words, the recording of which together with the musical work has already been authorized by the latter, to authorize the sound recording of that musical work, together with such words, if any; but all such reservations and conditions shall apply only in the countries which have imposed them and shall not, in any circumstances, be prejudicial to the rights of these authors to obtain equitable remuneration which, in the absence of agreement, shall be fixed by competent authority.

(2) Recordings of musical works made in a country of the Union in accordance with Article 13(3) of the Conventions signed at Rome on June 2, 1928, and at Brussels on June 26, 1948, may be reproduced in that country without the permission of the author of the musical work until a date two years after that country becomes bound by this Act.

(3) Recordings made in accordance with paragraphs (1) and (2) of this Article and imported without permission from the parties concerned into a country where they are treated as infringing recordings shall be liable to seizure.

Article 14

(1) Authors of literary or artistic works shall have the exclusive right of authorizing:

   (i)   the cinematographic adaptation and reproduction of these works, and the distribution of the works thus adapted or reproduced;

(ii)   the public performance and communication to the public by wire of the works thus adapted or reproduced.

(2)   The adaptation into any other artistic form of a cinematographic production derived from literary or artistic works shall, without prejudice to the authorization of the author of the cinematographic production, remain subject to the authorization of the authors of the original works.

(3)   The provisions of Article 13(1) shall not apply.

Article 14*bis*

(1)   Without prejudice to the copyright in any work which may have been adapted or reproduced, a cinematographic work shall be protected as an original work. The owner of copyright in a cinematographic work shall enjoy the same rights as the author of an original work, including the rights referred to in the preceding Article.

(2)

(a)   Ownership of copyright in a cinematographic work shall be a matter for legislation in the country where protection is claimed.

(b)   However, in the countries of the Union which, by legislation, include among the owners of copyright in a cinematographic work authors who have brought contributions to the making of the work, such authors, if they have undertaken to bring such contributions, may not, in the absence of any contrary or special stipulation, object to the reproduction, distribution, public performance, communication to the public by wire, broadcasting or any other communication to the public, or to the subtitling or dubbing of texts, of the work.

(c)   The question whether or not the form of the undertaking referred to above should, for the application of the preceding subparagraph *(b)*, be in a written agreement or a written act of the same effect shall be a matter for the legislation of the country where the maker of the cinematographic work has his headquarters or habitual residence. However, it shall be a matter for the legislation of the country of the Union where protection is claimed to provide that the said undertaking shall be in a written agreement or a written act of the same effect. The countries whose legislation so provides shall notify the Director General by means of a written declaration, which will be immediately communicated by him to all the other countries of the Union.

(d)   By "contrary or special stipulation" is meant any restrictive condition which is relevant to the aforesaid undertaking.

(3)   Unless the national legislation provides to the contrary, the provisions of paragraph (2)*(b)* above shall not be applicable to authors of

scenarios, dialogues and musical works created for the making of the cinematographic work, or to the principal director thereof. However, those countries of the Union whose legislation does not contain rules providing for the application of the said paragraph (2)*(b)* to such director shall notify the Director General by means of a written declaration, which will be immediately communicated by him to all the other countries of the Union.

Article 14*ter*

(1) The author, or after his death the persons or institutions authorized by national legislation, shall, with respect to original works of art and original manuscripts of writers and composers, enjoy the inalienable right to an interest in any sale of the work subsequent to the first transfer by the author of the work.

(2) The protection provided by the preceding paragraph may be claimed in a country of the Union only if legislation in the country to which the author belongs so permits, and to the extent permitted by the country where this protection is claimed.

(3) The procedure for collection and the amounts shall be matters for determination by national legislation.

Article 15

(1) In order that the author of a literary or artistic work protected by this Convention shall, in the absence of proof to the contrary, be regarded as such, and consequently be entitled to institute infringement proceedings in the countries of the Union, it shall be sufficient for his name to appear on the work in the usual manner. This paragraph shall be applicable even if this name is a pseudonym, where the pseudonym adopted by the author leaves no doubt as to his identity.

(2) The person or body corporate whose name appears on a cinematographic work in the usual manner shall, in the absence of proof to the contrary, be presumed to be the maker of the said work.

(3) In the case of anonymous and pseudonymous works, other than those referred to in paragraph (1) above, the publisher whose name appears on the work shall, in the absence of proof to the contrary, be deemed to represent the author, and in this capacity he shall be entitled to protect and enforce the author's rights. The provisions of this paragraph shall cease to apply when the author reveals his identity and establishes his claim to authorship of the work.

(4)

(a) In the case of unpublished works where the identity of the author is unknown, but where there is every ground to presume that he is a national of a country of the Union, it shall be a matter for legislation in that country to designate the competent authority

which shall represent the author and shall be entitled to protect and enforce his rights in the countries of the Union.

(b) Countries of the Union which make such designation under the terms of this provision shall notify the Director General by means of a written declaration giving full information concerning the authority thus designated. The Director General shall at once communicate this declaration to all other countries of the Union.

Article 16

(1) Infringing copies of a work shall be liable to seizure in any country of the Union where the work enjoys legal protection.

(2) The provisions of the preceding paragraph shall also apply to reproductions coming from a country where the work is not protected, or has ceased to be protected.

(3) The seizure shall take place in accordance with the legislation of each country.

Article 17

The provisions of this Convention cannot in any way affect the right of the Government of each country of the Union to permit, to control, or to prohibit, by legislation or regulation, the circulation, presentation, or exhibition of any work or production in regard to which the competent authority may find it necessary to exercise that right.

Article 18

(1) This Convention shall apply to all works which, at the moment of its coming into force, have not yet fallen into the public domain in the country of origin through the expiry of the term of protection.

(2) If, however, through the expiry of the term of protection which was previously granted, a work has fallen into the public domain of the country where protection is claimed, that work shall not be protected anew.

(3) The application of this principle shall be subject to any provisions contained in special conventions to that effect existing or to be concluded between countries of the Union. In the absence of such provisions, the respective countries shall determine, each in so far as it is concerned, the conditions of application of this principle.

(4) The preceding provisions shall also apply in the case of new accessions to the Union and to cases in which protection is extended by the application of Article 7 or by the abandonment of reservations.

Article 19

The provisions of this Convention shall not preclude the making of a claim to the benefit of any greater protection which may be granted by legislation in a country of the Union.

Article 20

The Governments of the countries of the Union reserve the right to enter into special agreements among themselves, in so far as such agreements grant to authors more extensive rights than those granted by the Convention, or contain other provisions not contrary to this Convention. The provisions of existing agreements which satisfy these conditions shall remain applicable.

Article 21

(1) Special provisions regarding developing countries are included in the Appendix.

(2) Subject to the provisions of Article 28(1)*(b)*, the Appendix forms an integral part of this Act.

Article 22

(1)

(a) The Union shall have an Assembly consisting of those countries of the Union which are bound by Articles 22 to 26.

(b) The Government of each country shall be represented by one delegate, who may be assisted by alternate delegates, advisors, and experts.

(c) The expenses of each delegation shall be borne by the Government which has appointed it.

(2)

(a) The Assembly shall:

  (i)   deal with all matters concerning the maintenance and development of the Union and the implementation of this Convention;

  (ii) give directions concerning the preparation for conferences of revision to the International Bureau of Intellectual Property (hereinafter designated as "the International Bureau") referred to in the Convention Establishing the World Intellectual Property Organization (hereinafter designated as "the Organization"), due account being taken of any comments made by those countries of the Union which are not bound by Articles 22 to 26;

(iii)   review and approve the reports and activities of the Director General of the Organization concerning the Union, and give him all necessary instructions concerning matters within the competence of the Union;

(iv)   elect the members of the Executive Committee of the Assembly;

(v)   review and approve the reports and activities of its Executive Committee, and give instructions to such Committee;

(vi)   determine the program and adopt the biennial budget of the Union, and approve its final accounts;

(vii)   adopt the financial regulations of the Union;

(viii)   establish such committees of experts and working groups as may be necessary for the work of the Union;

(ix)   determine which countries not members of the Union and which intergovernmental and international non-governmental organizations shall be admitted to its meetings as observers;

(x)   adopt amendments to Articles 22 to 26;

(xi)   take any other appropriate action designed to further the objectives of the Union;

(xii)   exercise such other functions as are appropriate under this Convention;

(xiii)   subject to its acceptance, exercise such rights as are given to it in the Convention establishing the Organization.

(b)   With respect to matters which are of interest also to other Unions administered by the Organization, the Assembly shall make its decisions after having heard the advice of the Coordination Committee of the Organization.

(3)

(a)   Each country member of the Assembly shall have one vote.

(b)   One-half of the countries members of the Assembly shall constitute a quorum.

(c)   Notwithstanding the provisions of subparagraph (b), if, in any session, the number of countries represented is less than one-half but equal to or more than one-third of the countries members of the Assembly, the Assembly may make decisions but, with the exception of decisions concerning its own procedure, all such decisions shall take effect only if the following conditions are fulfilled. The International Bureau shall communicate the said decisions to the countries members of the Assembly which were not represented and shall invite them to express in writing their vote or abstention within a period of three months from the date of the communication. If, at the expiration of this period, the number of countries having thus expressed their vote or abstention attains the number of countries which was lacking for attaining the quorum in the session itself, such decisions shall take effect provided that at the same time the required majority still obtains.

(d) Subject to the provisions of Article 26(2), the decisions of the Assembly shall require two-thirds of the votes cast.

(e) Abstentions shall not be considered as votes.

(f) A delegate may represent, and vote in the name of, one country only.

(g) Countries of the Union not members of the Assembly shall be admitted to its meetings as observers.

(4)

(a) The Assembly shall meet once in every second calendar year in ordinary session upon convocation by the Director General and, in the absence of exceptional circumstances, during the same period and at the same place as the General Assembly of the Organization.

(b) The Assembly shall meet in extraordinary session upon convocation by the Director General, at the request of the Executive Committee or at the request of one-fourth of the countries members of the Assembly.

(5) The Assembly shall adopt its own rules of procedure.

Article 23

(1) The Assembly shall have an Executive Committee.

(2)

(a) The Executive Committee shall consist of countries elected by the Assembly from among countries members of the Assembly. Furthermore, the country on whose territory the Organization has its headquarters shall, subject to the provisions of Article 25(7)*(b)*, have an ex officio seat on the Committee.

(b) The Government of each country member of the Executive Committee shall be represented by one delegate, who may be assisted by alternate delegates, advisors, and experts.

(c) The expenses of each delegation shall be borne by the Government which has appointed it.

(3) The number of countries members of the Executive Committee shall correspond to one-fourth of the number of countries members of the Assembly. In establishing the number of seats to be filled, remainders after division by four shall be disregarded.

(4) In electing the members of the Executive Committee, the Assembly shall have due regard to an equitable geographical distribution and to the need for countries party to the Special Agreements which might be established in relation with the Union to be among the countries constituting the Executive Committee.

(5)

(a) Each member of the Executive Committee shall serve from the close of the session of the Assembly which elected it to the close of the next ordinary session of the Assembly.

(b) Members of the Executive Committee may be re-elected, but not more than two-thirds of them.

(c) The Assembly shall establish the details of the rules governing the election and possible reelection of the members of the Executive Committee.

(6)

(a) The Executive Committee shall:

  (i)   prepare the draft agenda of the Assembly;

  (ii) submit proposals to the Assembly respecting the draft program and biennial budget of the Union prepared by the Director General;

  (iii) [*deleted*]

  (iv) submit, with appropriate comments, to the Assembly the periodical reports of the Director General and the yearly audit reports on the accounts;

  (v)   in accordance with the decisions of the Assembly and having regard to circumstances arising between two ordinary sessions of the Assembly, take all necessary measures to ensure the execution of the program of the Union by the Director General;

  (vi) perform such other functions as are allocated to it under this Convention.

(b) With respect to matters which are of interest also to other Unions administered by the Organization, the Executive Committee shall

make its decisions after having heard the advice of the Coordination Committee of the Organization.

(7)

(a) The Executive Committee shall meet once a year in ordinary session upon convocation by the Director General, preferably during the same period and at the same place as the Coordination Committee of the Organization.

(b) The Executive Committee shall meet in extraordinary session upon convocation by the Director General, either on his own initiative, or at the request of its Chairman or one-fourth of its members.

(8)

(a) Each country member of the Executive Committee shall have one vote.

(b) One-half of the members of the Executive Committee shall constitute a quorum.

(c) Decisions shall be made by a simple majority of the votes cast.

(d) Abstentions shall not be considered as votes.

(e) A delegate may represent, and vote in the name of, one country only.

(9) Countries of the Union not members of the Executive Committee shall be admitted to its meetings as observers.

(10) The Executive Committee shall adopt its own rules of procedure.

Article 24

(1)

(a) The administrative tasks with respect to the Union shall be performed by the International Bureau, which is a continuation of the Bureau of the Union united with the Bureau of the Union established by the International Convention for the Protection of Industrial Property.

(b) In particular, the International Bureau shall provide the secretariat of the various organs of the Union.

(c) The Director General of the Organization shall be the chief executive of the Union and shall represent the Union.

(2) The International Bureau shall assemble and publish information concerning the protection of copyright. Each country of the Union shall promptly communicate to the International Bureau all new laws and official texts concerning the protection of copyright.

(3)   The International Bureau shall publish a monthly periodical.

(4)   The International Bureau shall, on request, furnish information to any country of the Union on matters concerning the protection of copyright.

(5)   The International Bureau shall conduct studies, and shall provide services, designed to facilitate the protection of copyright.

(6)   The Director General and any staff member designated by him shall participate, without the right to vote, in all meetings of the Assembly, the Executive Committee and any other committee of experts or working group. The Director General, or a staff member designated by him, shall be ex officio secretary of these bodies.

(7)

(a)   The International Bureau shall, in accordance with the directions of the Assembly and in cooperation with the Executive Committee, make the preparations for the conferences of revision of the provisions of the Convention other than Articles 22 to 26.

(b)   The International Bureau may consult with intergovernmental and international non-governmental organizations concerning preparations for conferences of revision.

(c)   The Director General and persons designated by him shall take part, without the right to vote, in the discussions at these conferences.

(8)   The International Bureau shall carry out any other tasks assigned to it.

Article 25

(1)

(a)   The Union shall have a budget.

(b)   The budget of the Union shall include the income and expenses proper to the Union, its contribution to the budget of expenses common to the Unions, and, where applicable, the sum made available to the budget of the Conference of the Organization.

(c)   Expenses not attributable exclusively to the Union but also to one or more other Unions administered by the Organization shall be considered as expenses common to the Unions. The share of the Union in such common expenses shall be in proportion to the interest the Union has in them.

(2)   The budget of the Union shall be established with due regard to the requirements of coordination with the budgets of the other Unions administered by the Organization.

(3) The budget of the Union shall be financed from the following sources:

    (i)   contributions of the countries of the Union;

    (ii) fees and charges due for services performed by the International Bureau in relation to the Union;

    (iii) sale of, or royalties on, the publications of the International Bureau concerning the Union;

    (iv) gifts, bequests, and subventions;

    (v) rents, interests, and other miscellaneous income.

(4)

(a) For the purpose of establishing its contribution towards the budget, each country of the Union shall belong to a class, and shall pay its annual contributions on the basis of a number of units fixed as follows:

Class I	25
Class II	20
Class III	15
Class IV	10
Class V	5
Class VI	3
Class VII	1

(b) Unless it has already done so, each country shall indicate, concurrently with depositing its instrument of ratification or accession, the class to which it wishes to belong. Any country may change class. If it chooses a lower class, the country must announce it to the Assembly at one of its ordinary sessions. Any such change shall take effect at the beginning of the calendar year following the session.

(c) The annual contribution of each country shall be an amount in the same proportion to the total sum to be contributed to the annual budget of the Union by all countries as the number of its units is to the total of the units of all contributing countries.

(d) Contributions shall become due on the first of January of each year.

(e) A country which is in arrears in the payment of its contributions shall have no vote in any of the organs of the Union of which it is a member if the amount of its arrears equals or exceeds the amount of the contributions due from it for the preceding two full

years. However, any organ of the Union may allow such a country to continue to exercise its vote in that organ if, and as long as, it is satisfied that the delay in payment is due to exceptional and unavoidable circumstances.

(f)   If the budget is not adopted before the beginning of a new financial period, it shall be at the same level as the budget of the previous year, in accordance with the financial regulations.

(5)   The amount of the fees and charges due for services rendered by the International Bureau in relation to the Union shall be established, and shall be reported to the Assembly and the Executive Committee, by the Director General.

(6)

(a)   The Union shall have a working capital fund which shall be constituted by a single payment made by each country of the Union. If the fund becomes insufficient, an increase shall be decided by the Assembly.

(b)   The amount of the initial payment of each country to the said fund or of its participation in the increase thereof shall be a proportion of the contribution of that country for the year in which the fund is established or the increase decided.

(c)   The proportion and the terms of payment shall be fixed by the Assembly on the proposal of the Director General and after it has heard the advice of the Coordination Committee of the Organization.

(7)

(a)   In the headquarters agreement concluded with the country on the territory of which the Organization has its headquarters, it shall be provided that, whenever the working capital fund is insufficient, such country shall grant advances. The amount of these advances and the conditions on which they are granted shall be the subject of separate agreements, in each case, between such country and the Organization. As long as it remains under the obligation to grant advances, such country shall have an ex officio seat on the Executive Committee.

(b)   The country referred to in subparagraph (a) and the Organization shall each have the right to denounce the obligation to grant advances, by written notification. Denunciation shall take effect three years after the end of the year in which it has been notified.

(8)   The auditing of the accounts shall be effected by one or more of the countries of the Union or by external auditors, as provided in the

financial regulations. They shall be designated, with their agreement, by the Assembly.

Article 26

(1) Proposals for the amendment of Articles 22, 23, 24, 25, and the present Article, may be initiated by any country member of the Assembly, by the Executive Committee, or by the Director General. Such proposals shall be communicated by the Director General to the member countries of the Assembly at least six months in advance of their consideration by the Assembly.

(2) Amendments to the Articles referred to in paragraph (1) shall be adopted by the Assembly. Adoption shall require three-fourths of the votes cast, provided that any amendment of Article 22, and of the present paragraph, shall require four-fifths of the votes cast.

(3) Any amendment to the Articles referred to in paragraph (1) shall enter into force one month after written notifications of acceptance, effected in accordance with their respective constitutional processes, have been received by the Director General from three-fourths of the countries members of the Assembly at the time it adopted the amendment. Any amendment to the said Articles thus accepted shall bind all the countries which are members of the Assembly at the time the amendment enters into force, or which become members thereof at a subsequent date, provided that any amendment increasing the financial obligations of countries of the Union shall bind only those countries which have notified their acceptance of such amendment.

Article 27

(1) This Convention shall be submitted to revision with a view to the introduction of amendments designed to improve the system of the Union.

(2) For this purpose, conferences shall be held successively in one of the countries of the Union among the delegates of the said countries.

(3) Subject to the provisions of Article 26 which apply to the amendment of Articles 22 to 26, any revision of this Act, including the Appendix, shall require the unanimity of the votes cast.

Article 28

(1)

(a) Any country of the Union which has signed this Act may ratify it, and, if it has not signed it, may accede to it. Instruments of ratification or accession shall be deposited with the Director General.

(b) Any country of the Union may declare in its instrument of ratification or accession that its ratification or accession shall not apply to Articles 1 to 21 and the Appendix, provided that, if such country has previously made a declaration under Article VI(1) of the Appendix, then it may declare in the said instrument only that its ratification or accession shall not apply to Articles 1 to 20.

(c) Any country of the Union which, in accordance with subparagraph *(b)*, has excluded provisions therein referred to from the effects of its ratification or accession may at any later time declare that it extends the effects of its ratification or accession to those provisions. Such declaration shall be deposited with the Director General.

(2)

(a) Articles 1 to 21 and the Appendix shall enter into force three months after both of the following two conditions are fulfilled:

(i) at least five countries of the Union have ratified or acceded to this Act without making a declaration under paragraph (1)*(b)*,

(ii) France, Spain, the United Kingdom of Great Britain and Northern Ireland, and the United States of America, have become bound by the Universal Copyright Convention as revised at Paris on July 24, 1971.

(b) The entry into force referred to in subparagraph *(a)* shall apply to those countries of the Union which, at least three months before the said entry into force, have deposited instruments of ratification or accession not containing a declaration under paragraph (1)*(b)*.

(c) With respect to any country of the Union not covered by subparagraph *(b)* and which ratifies or accedes to this Act without making a declaration under paragraph (1)*(b)*, Articles 1 to 21 and the Appendix shall enter into force three months after the date on which the Director General has notified the deposit of the relevant instrument of ratification or accession, unless a subsequent date has been indicated in the instrument deposited. In the latter case, Articles 1 to 21 and the Appendix shall enter into force with respect to that country on the date thus indicated.

(d) The provisions of subparagraphs *(a)* to *(c)* do not affect the application of Article VI of the Appendix.

(3) With respect to any country of the Union which ratifies or accedes to this Act with or without a declaration made under paragraph (1)*(b)*, Articles 22 to 38 shall enter into force three months after the date on which the Director General has notified the deposit of the relevant instrument of ratification or accession, unless a subsequent date has been indicated in

the instrument deposited. In the latter case, Articles 22 to 38 shall enter into force with respect to that country on the date thus indicated.

Article 29

(1) Any country outside the Union may accede to this Act and thereby become party to this Convention and a member of the Union. Instruments of accession shall be deposited with the Director General.

(2)

(a) Subject to subparagraph *(b)*, this Convention shall enter into force with respect to any country outside the Union three months after the date on which the Director General has notified the deposit of its instrument of accession, unless a subsequent date has been indicated in the instrument deposited. In the latter case, this Convention shall enter into force with respect to that country on the date thus indicated.

(b) If the entry into force according to subparagraph *(a)* precedes the entry into force of Articles 1 to 21 and the Appendix according to Article 28(2)*(a)*, the said country shall, in the meantime, be bound, instead of by Articles 1 to 21 and the Appendix, by Articles 1 to 20 of the Brussels Act of this Convention.

Article 29*bis*

Ratification of or accession to this Act by any country not bound by Articles 22 to 38 of the Stockholm Act of this Convention shall, for the sole purposes of Article 14(2) of the Convention establishing the Organization, amount to ratification of or accession to the said Stockholm Act with the limitation set forth in Article 28(1)*(b)*(i) thereof.

Article 30

(1) Subject to the exceptions permitted by paragraph (2) of this Article, by Article 28(1)*(b)*, by Article 33(2), and by the Appendix, ratification or accession shall automatically entail acceptance of all the provisions and admission to all the advantages of this Convention.

(2)

(a) Any country of the Union ratifying or acceding to this Act may, subject to Article V(2) of the Appendix, retain the benefit of the reservations it has previously formulated on condition that it makes a declaration to that effect at the time of the deposit of its instrument of ratification or accession.

(b) Any country outside the Union may declare, in acceding to this Convention and subject to Article V(2) of the Appendix, that it intends to substitute, temporarily at least, for Article 8 of this Act concerning the right of translation, the provisions of Article 5 of the Union Convention of 1886, as completed at Paris in 1896, on the clear understanding that the said provisions are applicable only to translations into a language in general use in the said country. Subject to Article I(6)*(b)* of the Appendix, any country has the right to apply, in relation to the right of translation of works whose country of origin is a country availing itself of such a reservation, a protection which is equivalent to the protection granted by the latter country.

(c) Any country may withdraw such reservations at any time by notification addressed to the Director General.

Article 31

(1) Any country may declare in its instrument of ratification or accession, or may inform the Director General by written notification at any time thereafter, that this Convention shall be applicable to all or part of those territories, designated in the declaration or notification, for the external relations of which it is responsible.

(2) Any country which has made such a declaration or given such a notification may, at any time, notify the Director General that this Convention shall cease to be applicable to all or part of such territories.

(3)

(a) Any declaration made under paragraph (1) shall take effect on the same date as the ratification or accession in which it was included, and any notification given under that paragraph shall take effect three months after its notification by the Director General.

(b) Any notification given under paragraph (2) shall take effect twelve months after its receipt by the Director General.

(4) This Article shall in no way be understood as implying the recognition or tacit acceptance by a country of the Union of the factual situation concerning a territory to which this Convention is made applicable by another country of the Union by virtue of a declaration under paragraph (1).

Article 32

(1) This Act shall, as regards relations between the countries of the Union, and to the extent that it applies, replace the Berne Convention of September 9, 1886, and the subsequent Acts of revision. The Acts previously in force shall continue to be applicable, in their entirety or to the extent that this Act does not replace them by virtue of the preceding sentence, in relations with countries of the Union which do not ratify or accede to this Act.

(2) Countries outside the Union which become party to this Act shall, subject to paragraph (3), apply it with respect to any country of the Union

not bound by this Act or which, although bound by this Act, has made a declaration pursuant to Article 28(1)*(b)*. Such countries recognize that the said country of the Union, in its relations with them:

(i) may apply the provisions of the most recent Act by which it is bound, and

(ii) subject to Article I(6) of the Appendix, has the right to adapt the protection to the level provided for by this Act.

(3) Any country which has availed itself of any of the faculties provided for in the Appendix may apply the provisions of the Appendix relating to the faculty or faculties of which it has availed itself in its relations with any other country of the Union which is not bound by this Act, provided that the latter country has accepted the application of the said provisions.

Article 33

(1) Any dispute between two or more countries of the Union concerning the interpretation or application of this Convention, not settled by negotiation, may, by any one of the countries concerned, be brought before the International Court of Justice by application in conformity with the Statute of the Court, unless the countries concerned agree on some other method of settlement. The country bringing the dispute before the Court shall inform the International Bureau; the International Bureau shall bring the matter to the attention of the other countries of the Union.

(2) Each country may, at the time it signs this Act or deposits its instrument of ratification or accession, declare that it does not consider itself bound by the provisions of paragraph (1). With regard to any dispute between such country and any other country of the Union, the provisions of paragraph (1) shall not apply.

(3) Any country having made a declaration in accordance with the provisions of paragraph (2) may, at any time, withdraw its declaration by notification addressed to the Director General.

Article 34

(1) Subject to Article 29*bis* no country may ratify or accede to earlier Acts of this Convention once Articles 1 to 21 and the Appendix have entered into force.

(2) Once Articles 1 to 21 and the Appendix have entered into force, no country may make a declaration under Article 5 of the Protocol Regarding Developing Countries attached to the Stockholm Act.

Article 35

(1) This Convention shall remain in force without limitation as to time.

(2) Any country may denounce this Act by notification addressed to the Director General. Such denunciation shall constitute also denunciation of all earlier Acts and shall affect only the country making it, the Convention remaining in full force and effect as regards the other countries of the Union.

(3) Denunciation shall take effect one year after the day on which the Director General has received the notification.

(4) The right of denunciation provided by this Article shall not be exercised by any country before the expiration of five years from the date upon which it becomes a member of the Union.

Article 36

(1) Any country party to this Convention undertakes to adopt, in accordance with its constitution, the measures necessary to ensure the application of this Convention.

(2) It is understood that, at the time a country becomes bound by this Convention, it will be in a position under its domestic law to give effect to the provisions of this Convention.

Article 37

(1)

(a) This Act shall be signed in a single copy in the French and English languages and, subject to paragraph (2), shall be deposited with the Director General.

(b) Official texts shall be established by the Director General, after consultation with the interested Governments, in the Arabic, German, Italian, Portuguese and Spanish languages, and such other languages as the Assembly may designate.

(c) In case of differences of opinion on the interpretation of the various texts, the French text shall prevail.

(2) This Act shall remain open for signature until January 31, 1972. Until that date, the copy referred to in paragraph (1)(a) shall be deposited with the Government of the French Republic.

(3) The Director General shall certify and transmit two copies of the signed text of this Act to the Governments of all countries of the Union and, on request, to the Government of any other country.

(4) The Director General shall register this Act with the Secretariat of the United Nations.

(5) The Director General shall notify the Governments of all countries of the Union of signatures, deposits of instruments of ratification or accession and any declarations included in such instruments or made

pursuant to Articles 28(1)*(c)*, 30(2)*(a)* and *(b)*, and 33(2), entry into force of any provisions of this Act, notifications of denunciation, and notifications pursuant to Articles 30(2)*(c)*, 31(1) and (2), 33(3), and 38(1), as well as the Appendix.

Article 38

(1)   Countries of the Union which have not ratified or acceded to this Act and which are not bound by Articles 22 to 26 of the Stockholm Act of this Convention may, until April 26, 1975, exercise, if they so desire, the rights provided under the said Articles as if they were bound by them. Any country desiring to exercise such rights shall give written notification to this effect to the Director General; this notification shall be effective on the date of its receipt. Such countries shall be deemed to be members of the Assembly until the said date.

(2)   As long as all the countries of the Union have not become Members of the Organization, the International Bureau of the Organization shall also function as the Bureau of the Union, and the Director General as the Director of the said Bureau.

(3)   Once all the countries of the Union have become Members of the Organization, the rights, obligations, and property, of the Bureau of the Union shall devolve on the International Bureau of the Organization.

APPENDIX

[SPECIAL PROVISIONS REGARDING DEVELOPING COUNTRIES]

Article I

(1)   Any country regarded as a developing country in conformity with the established practice of the General Assembly of the United Nations which ratifies or accedes to this Act, of which this Appendix forms an integral part, and which, having regard to its economic situation and its social or cultural needs, does not consider itself immediately in a position to make provision for the protection of all the rights as provided for in this Act, may, by a notification deposited with the Director General at the time of depositing its instrument of ratification or accession or, subject to Article V(1)*(c)*, at any time thereafter, declare that it will avail itself of the faculty provided for in Article II, or of the faculty provided for in Article III, or of both of those faculties. It may, instead of availing itself of the faculty provided for in Article II, make a declaration according to Article V(1)*(a)*.

(2)

(a)   Any declaration under paragraph (1) notified before the expiration of the period of ten years from the entry into force of Articles 1 to 21 and this Appendix according to Article 28(2) shall be effective until the expiration of the said period. Any such declaration may

be renewed in whole or in part for periods of ten years each by a notification deposited with the Director General not more than fifteen months and not less than three months before the expiration of the ten-year period then running.

(b)   Any declaration under paragraph (1) notified after the expiration of the period of ten years from the entry into force of Articles 1 to 21 and this Appendix according to Article 28(2) shall be effective until the expiration of the ten-year period then running. Any such declaration may be renewed as provided for in the second sentence of subparagraph *(a)*.

(3)   Any country of the Union which has ceased to be regarded as a developing country as referred to in paragraph (1) shall no longer be entitled to renew its declaration as provided in paragraph (2), and, whether or not it formally withdraws its declaration, such country shall be precluded from availing itself of the faculties referred to in paragraph (1) from the expiration of the ten-year period then running or from the expiration of a period of three years after it has ceased to be regarded as a developing country, whichever period expires later.

(4)   Where, at the time when the declaration made under paragraph (1) or (2) ceases to be effective, there are copies in stock which were made under a license granted by virtue of this Appendix, such copies may continue to be distributed until their stock is exhausted.

(5)   Any country which is bound by the provisions of this Act and which has deposited a declaration or a notification in accordance with Article 31(1) with respect to the application of this Act to a particular territory, the situation of which can be regarded as analogous to that of the countries referred to in paragraph (1), may, in respect of such territory, make the declaration referred to in paragraph (1) and the notification of renewal referred to in paragraph (2). As long as such declaration or notification remains in effect, the provisions of this Appendix shall be applicable to the territory in respect of which it was made.

(6)

(a)   The fact that a country avails itself of any of the faculties referred to in paragraph (1) does not permit another country to give less protection to works of which the country of origin is the former country than it is obliged to grant under Articles 1 to 20.

(b)   The right to apply reciprocal treatment provided for in Article 30(2)*(b)*, second sentence, shall not, until the date on which the period applicable under Article I(3) expires, be exercised in respect of works the country of origin of which is a country which has made a declaration according to Article V(1)*(a)*.

Article II

(1) Any country which has declared that it will avail itself of the faculty provided for in this Article shall be entitled, so far as works published in printed or analogous forms of reproduction are concerned, to substitute for the exclusive right of translation provided for in Article 8 a system of non-exclusive and nontransferable licenses, granted by the competent authority under the following conditions and subject to Article IV.

(2)

(a) Subject to paragraph (3), if, after the expiration of a period of three years, or of any longer period determined by the national legislation of the said country, commencing on the date of the first publication of the work, a translation of such work has not been published in a language in general use in that country by the owner of the right of translation, or with his authorization, any national of such country may obtain a license to make a translation of the work in the said language and publish the translation in printed or analogous forms of reproduction.

(b) A license under the conditions provided for in this Article may also be granted if all the editions of the translation published in the language concerned are out of print.

(3)

(a) In the case of translations into a language which is not in general use in one or more developed countries which are members of the Union, a period of one year shall be substituted for the period of three years referred to in paragraph (2)(a).

(b) Any country referred to in paragraph (1) may, with the unanimous agreement of the developed countries which are members of the Union and in which the same language is in general use, substitute, in the case of translations into that language, for the period of three years referred to in paragraph (2)(a) a shorter period as determined by such agreement but not less than one year. However, the provisions of the foregoing sentence shall not apply where the language in question is English, French or Spanish. The Director General shall be notified of any such agreement by the Governments which have concluded it.

(4)

(a) No license obtainable after three years shall be granted under this Article until a further period of six months has elapsed, and no license obtainable after one year shall be granted under this Article until a further period of nine months has elapsed

    (i)   from the date on which the applicant complies with the requirements mentioned in Article IV(1), or

    (ii) where the identity or the address of the owner of the right of translation is unknown, from the date on which the applicant sends, as provided for in Article IV(2), copies of his application submitted to the authority competent to grant the license.

  (b) If, during the said period of six or nine months, a translation in the language in respect of which the application was made is published by the owner of the right of translation or with his authorization, no license under this Article shall be granted.

(5) Any license under this Article shall be granted only for the purpose of teaching, scholarship or research.

(6) If a translation of a work is published by the owner of the right of translation or with his authorization at a price reasonably related to that normally charged in the country for comparable works, any license granted under this Article shall terminate if such translation is in the same language and with substantially the same content as the translation published under the license. Any copies already made before the license terminates may continue to be distributed until their stock is exhausted.

(7) For works which are composed mainly of illustrations, a license to make and publish a translation of the text and to reproduce and publish the illustrations may be granted only if the conditions of Article III are also fulfilled.

(8) No license shall be granted under this Article when the author has withdrawn from circulation all copies of his work.

(9)

  (a) A license to make a translation of a work which has been published in printed or analogous forms of reproduction may also be granted to any broadcasting organization having its headquarters in a country referred to in paragraph (1), upon an application made to the competent authority of that country by the said organization, provided that all of the following conditions are met:

    (i)   the translation is made from a copy made and acquired in accordance with the laws of the said country;

    (ii) the translation is only for use in broadcasts intended exclusively for teaching or for the dissemination of the results of specialized technical or scientific research to experts in a particular profession;

(iii) the translation is used exclusively for the purposes referred to in condition (ii) through broadcasts made lawfully and intended for recipients on the territory of the said country, including broadcasts made through the medium of sound or visual recordings lawfully and exclusively made for the purpose of such broadcasts;

(iv) all uses made of the translation are without any commercial purpose.

(b) Sound or visual recordings of a translation which was made by a broadcasting organization under a license granted by virtue of this paragraph may, for the purposes and subject to the conditions referred to in subparagraph *(a)* and with the agreement of that organization, also be used by any other broadcasting organization having its headquarters in the country whose competent authority granted the license in question.

(c) Provided that all of the criteria and conditions set out in subparagraph *(a)* are met, a license may also be granted to a broadcasting organization to translate any text incorporated in an audiovisual fixation where such fixation was itself prepared and published for the sole purpose of being used in connection with systematic instructional activities.

(d) Subject to subparagraphs *(a)* to *(c)*, the provisions of the preceding paragraphs shall apply to the grant and exercise of any license granted under this paragraph.

Article III

(1) Any country which has declared that it will avail itself of the faculty provided for in this Article shall be entitled to substitute for the exclusive right of reproduction provided for in Article 9 a system of nonexclusive and non-transferable licenses, granted by the competent authority under the following conditions and subject to Article IV.

(2)

(a) If, in relation to a work to which this Article applies by virtue of paragraph (7), after the expiration of

(i) the relevant period specified in paragraph (3), commencing on the date of first publication of a particular edition of the work, or

(ii) any longer period determined by national legislation of the country referred to in paragraph (1), commencing on the same date, copies of such edition have not been distributed in that country to the general public or in connection with systematic instructional activities, by the owner of the right of reproduction or with his authorization, at a price reasonably related to that normally charged in the country for comparable works, any national of such country may obtain a license to reproduce and publish such edition at that or a lower price for use in connection with systematic instructional activities.

(b) A license to reproduce and publish an edition which has been distributed as described in subparagraph *(a)* may also be granted under the conditions provided for in this Article if, after the expiration of the applicable period, no authorized copies of that edition have been on sale for a period of six months in the country concerned to the general public or in connection with systematic instructional activities at a price reasonably related to that normally charged in the country for comparable works.

(3) The period referred to in paragraph *(2)(a)(i)* shall be five years, except that

(i)   for works of the natural and physical sciences, including mathematics, and of technology, the period shall be three years;

(ii) for works of fiction, poetry, drama and music, and for art books, the period shall be seven years.

(4)

(a) No license obtainable after three years shall be granted under this Article until a period of six months has elapsed

(i)   from the date on which the applicant complies with the requirements mentioned in Article IV(1), or

(ii) where the identity or the address of the owner of the right of reproduction is unknown, from the date on which the applicant sends, as provided for in Article IV(2), copies of his application submitted to the authority competent to grant the license.

(b) Where licenses are obtainable after other periods and Article IV(2) is applicable, no license shall be granted until a period of three months has elapsed from the date of the dispatch of the copies of the application.

(c) If, during the period of six or three months referred to in subparagraphs *(a)* and *(b)*, a distribution as described in paragraph *(2)(a)* has taken place, no license shall be granted under this Article.

(d) No license shall be granted if the author has withdrawn from circulation all copies of the edition for the reproduction and publication of which the license has been applied for.

(5) A license to reproduce and publish a translation of a work shall not be granted under this Article in the following cases:

(i)   where the translation was not published by the owner of the right of translation or with his authorization, or

(ii) where the translation is not in a language in general use in the country in which the license is applied for.

(6) If copies of an edition of a work are distributed in the country referred to in paragraph (1) to the general public or in connection with systematic instructional activities, by the owner of the right of reproduction or with his authorization, at a price reasonably related to that normally charged in the country for comparable works, any license granted under this Article shall terminate if such edition is in the same language and with substantially the same content as the edition which was published under the said license. Any copies already made before the license terminates may continue to be distributed until their stock is exhausted.

(7)

(a) Subject to subparagraph *(b)*, the works to which this Article applies shall be limited to works published in printed or analogous forms of reproduction.

(b) This Article shall also apply to the reproduction in audio-visual form of lawfully made audiovisual fixations including any protected works incorporated therein and to the translation of any incorporated text into a language in general use in the country in which the license is applied for, always provided that the audio-visual fixations in question were prepared and published for the sole purpose of being used in connection with systematic instructional activities.

Article IV

(1) A license under Article II or Article III may be granted only if the applicant, in accordance with the procedure of the country concerned, establishes either that he has requested, and has been denied, authorization by the owner of the right to make and publish the translation or to reproduce and publish the edition, as the case may be, or that, after due diligence on his part, he was unable to find the owner of the right. At the same time as making the request, the applicant shall inform any national or international information center referred to in paragraph (2).

(2) If the owner of the right cannot be found, the applicant for a license shall send, by registered airmail, copies of his application, submitted to the authority competent to grant the license, to the publisher whose name appears on the work and to any national or international information center which may have been designated, in a notification to that effect deposited with the Director General, by the Government of the country in which the publisher is believed to have his principal place of business.

(3) The name of the author shall be indicated on all copies of the translation or reproduction published under a license granted under Article II or Article III. The title of the work shall appear on all such copies. In the case of a translation, the original title of the work shall appear in any case on all the said copies.

(4)

(a) No license granted under Article II or Article III shall extend to the export of copies, and any such license shall be valid only for publication of the translation or of the reproduction, as the case may be, in the territory of the country in which it has been applied for.

(b) For the purposes of subparagraph (a), the notion of export shall include the sending of copies from any territory to the country which, in respect of that territory, has made a declaration under Article I(5).

(c) Where a governmental or other public entity of a country which has granted a license to make a translation under Article II into a language other than English, French or Spanish sends copies of a translation published under such license to another country, such sending of copies shall not, for the purposes of subparagraph (a), be considered to constitute export if all of the following conditions are met:

(i) the recipients are individuals who are nationals of the country whose competent authority has granted the license, or organizations grouping such individuals;

(ii) the copies are to be used only for the purpose of teaching, scholarship or research;

(iii) the sending of the copies and their subsequent distribution to recipients is without any commercial purpose; and

(iv) the country to which the copies have been sent has agreed with the country whose competent authority has granted the license to allow the receipt, or distribution, or both, and the Director General has been notified of the agreement by the

Government of the country in which the license has been granted.

(5)   All copies published under a license granted by virtue of Article II or Article III shall bear a notice in the appropriate language stating that the copies are available for distribution only in the country or territory to which the said license applies.

(6)

(a)   Due provision shall be made at the national level to ensure

(i)   that the license provides, in favour of the owner of the right of translation or of reproduction, as the case may be, for just compensation that is consistent with standards of royalties normally operating on licenses freely negotiated between persons in the two countries concerned, and

(ii)   payment and transmittal of the compensation: should national currency regulations intervene, the competent authority shall make all efforts, by the use of international machinery, to ensure transmittal in internationally convertible currency or its equivalent.

(b)   Due provision shall be made by national legislation to ensure a correct translation of the work, or an accurate reproduction of the particular edition, as the case may be.

Article V

(1)

(a)   Any country entitled to make a declaration that it will avail itself of the faculty provided for in Article II may, instead, at the time of ratifying or acceding to this Act:

(i)   if it is a country to which Article 30(2)*(a)* applies, make a declaration under that provision as far as the right of translation is concerned;

(ii)   if it is a country to which Article 30(2)*(a)* does not apply, and even if it is not a country outside the Union, make a declaration as provided for in Article 30(2)*(b)*, first sentence.

(b)   In the case of a country which ceases to be regarded as a developing country as referred to in Article I(1), a declaration made according to this paragraph shall be effective until the date on which the period applicable under Article I(3) expires.

(c)   Any country which has made a declaration according to this paragraph may not subsequently avail itself of the faculty provided for in Article II even if it withdraws the said declaration.

(2) Subject to paragraph (3), any country which has availed itself of the faculty provided for in Article II may not subsequently make a declaration according to paragraph (1).

(3) Any country which has ceased to be regarded as a developing country as referred to in Article I(1) may, not later than two years prior to the expiration of the period applicable under Article I(3), make a declaration to the effect provided for in Article 30(2)*(b)*, first sentence, notwithstanding the fact that it is not a country outside the Union. Such declaration shall take effect at the date on which the period applicable under Article I(3) expires.

Article VI

(1) Any country of the Union may declare, as from the date of this Act, and at any time before becoming bound by Articles 1 to 21 and this Appendix:

    (i)   if it is a country which, were it bound by Articles 1 to 21 and this Appendix, would be entitled to avail itself of the faculties referred to in Article I(1), that it will apply the provisions of Article II or of Article III or of both to works whose country of origin is a country which, pursuant to (ii) below, admits the application of those Articles to such works, or which is bound by Articles 1 to 21 and this Appendix; such declaration may, instead of referring to Article II, refer to Article V;

    (ii)   that it admits the application of this Appendix to works of which it is the country of origin by countries which have made a declaration under (i) above or a notification under Article I.

(2) Any declaration made under paragraph (1) shall be in writing and shall be deposited with the Director General. The declaration shall become effective from the date of its deposit.

5

PARTIES TO THE BERNE CONVENTION FOR THE PROTECTION OF LITERARY AND ARTISTIC WORKS

Status on October 1, 2020

State	Date on which State became party to the Convention	Latest Act[1] of the Convention to which State is party and date on which State became party to that Act	
Afghanistan	June 2, 2018	Paris:	June 2, 2018
Albania	March 6, 1994	Paris:	March 6, 1994
Algeria	April 19, 1998	Paris:	April 19, 1998[2, 3]
Andorra	June 2, 2004	Paris:	June 2, 2004
Antigua and Barbuda	March 17, 2000	Paris:	March 17, 2000
Argentina	June 10, 1967	Paris:	Article 1 to 21: February 19, 2000
			Article 22 to 38: October 8, 1980
Armenia	October 19, 2000	Paris:	October 19, 2000
Australia	April 14, 1928	Paris:	March 1, 1978
Austria	October 1, 1920	Paris:	August 21, 1982
Azerbaijan	June 4, 1999	Paris:	June 4, 1999
Bahamas	July 10, 1973	Brussels:	July 10, 1973
		Paris:	Article 22 to 38: January 8, 1972[2]

[1.] "Paris" means the Berne Convention for the Protection of Literary and Artistic Works as revised at Paris on July 24, 1971 (Paris Act); "Stockholm" means the said Convention as revised at Stockholm on July 14, 1967 (Stockholm Act); "Brussels" means the said Convention as revised at Brussels on June 26, 1948 (Brussels Act); "Rome" means the said Convention as revised at Rome on June 2, 1928 (Rome Act); "Berlin" means the said Convention as revised at Berlin on November 13, 1908 (Berlin Act).

[2.] With the declaration provided for in Article 33(2) relating to the International Court of Justice.

State	Date on which State became party to the Convention	Latest Act[1] of the Convention to which State is party and date on which State became party to that Act	
Bahrain	March 2, 1997	Paris:	March 2, 1997
Bangladesh	May 4, 1999	Paris:	May 4, 1999[3]
Barbados	July 30, 1983	Paris:	July 30, 1983
Belarus	December 12, 1997	Paris:	December 12, 1997
Belgium	December 5, 1887	Paris:	September 29, 1999
Belize	June 17, 2000	Paris:	June 17, 2000
Benin	January 3, 1961[4]	Paris:	March 12, 1975
Bhutan	November 25, 2004	Paris:	November 25, 2004
Bolivia (Plurinational State of)	November 4, 1993	Paris:	November 4, 1993
Bosnia and Herzegovina	March 1, 1992	Paris:	March 1, 1992[5]
Botswana	April 15, 1998	Paris:	April 15, 1998
Brazil	February 9, 1922	Paris:	April 20, 1975
Brunei Darussalam	August 30, 2006	Paris:	August 30, 2006
Bulgaria	December 5, 1921	Paris:	December 4, 1974
Burkina Faso	August 19, 1963[6]	Paris:	January 24, 1976
Burundi	April 12, 2016	Paris:	April 12, 2016
Cabo Verde	July 7, 1997	Paris:	July 7, 1997
Cameroon	September 21, 1964[4]	Paris:	Article 1 to 21: October 10, 1974

[3.] Pursuant to Article I of the Appendix of the Paris Act, this State availed itself of the faculties provided for in Articles II and III of the Appendix. The relevant declaration is effective until October 10, 2024.

[4.] Date on which the declaration of continued adherence was sent, after the accession of the State to independence.

[5.] Subject to the reservation concerning the right of translation.

[6.] Burkina Faso, which had acceded to the Berne Convention (Brussels Act) as from August 19, 1963, denounced the said Convention as from September 20, 1970. Later on, Burkina Faso acceded again to the Berne Convention (Paris Act); this accession took effect on January 24, 1976.

State	Date on which State became party to the Convention	Latest Act[1] of the Convention to which State is party and date on which State became party to that Act	
			Article 22 to 38: November 10, 1973
Canada	April 10, 1928	Paris:	June 26, 1998
Central African Republic	September 3, 1977	Paris:	September 3, 1977
Chad	November 25, 1971	Brussels:	November 25, 1971[7, 8]
		Stockholm:	Article 22 to 38: November 25, 1971
Chile	June 5, 1970	Paris:	July 10, 1975
China	October 15, 1992	Paris:	October 15, 1992[9]
Colombia	March 7, 1988	Paris:	March 7, 1988
Comoros	April 17, 2005	Paris:	April 17, 2005
Congo	May 8, 1962[4]	Paris:	December 5, 1975
Cook Islands	August 3, 2017	Paris:	August 3, 2017[19]
Costa Rica	June 10, 1978	Paris:	June 10, 1978
Côte d'Ivoire	January 1, 1962	Paris:	Article 1 to 21: October 10, 1974 Article 22 to 38: May 4, 1974
Croatia	October 8, 1991	Paris:	October 8, 1991
Cuba	February 20, 1997	Paris:	February 20, 1997[2, 3]
Cyprus	February 24, 1964[4]	Paris:	July 27, 1983[5]
Czech Republic	January 1, 1993	Paris:	January 1, 1993
Democratic People's	April 28, 2003	Paris:	April 28, 2003[2]

[7.] This State deposited its instrument of ratification of (or of accession to) the Stockholm Act in its entirety; however, Articles 1 to 21 (substantive clauses) of the said Act have not entered into force.

[8.] In accordance with the provision of Article 29 of the Stockholm Act applicable to the States outside the Union which accede to the said Act, this State is bound by Articles 1 to 20 of the Brussels Act.

[9.] The Paris Act applies also to Hong Kong, China with effect from July 1, 1997, and to Macao, China with effect from December 20, 1999.

State	Date on which State became party to the Convention	Latest Act[1] of the Convention to which State is party and date on which State became party to that Act	
Republic of Korea			
Democratic Republic of the Congo	October 8, 1963[4]	Paris:	January 31, 1975
Denmark	July 1, 1903	Paris:	June 30, 1979
Djibouti	May 13, 2002	Paris:	May 13, 2002
Dominica	August 7, 1999	Paris:	August 7, 1999
Dominican Republic	December 24, 1997	Paris:	December 24, 1997
Ecuador	October 9, 1991	Paris:	October 9, 1999
Egypt	June 7, 1977	Paris:	June 7, 1977[2]
El Salvador	February 19, 1994	Paris:	February 19, 1994
Equatorial Guinea	June 26, 1997	Paris:	June 26, 1997
Estonia	October 26, 1994[10]	Paris:	October 26, 1994
Eswatini	December 14, 1998	Paris:	December 14, 1998
Fiji	December 1, 1971[4]	Brussels:	December 1, 1971
		Stockholm:	Article 22 to 38: March 15, 1972
Finland	April 1, 1928	Paris:	November 1, 1986
France	December 5, 1887	Paris:	Articles 1 to 21: October 10, 1974
			Article 22 to 38: December 15, 1972
Gabon	March 26, 1962	Paris:	June 10, 1975
Gambia	March 7, 1993	Paris:	March 7, 1993
Georgia	May 16, 1995	Paris:	May 16, 1995

---

10. Estonia acceded to the Berne Convention (Berlin Act, 1908) with effect from June 9, 1927. It lost its independence on August 6, 1940, and regained it on August 20, 1991.

State	Date on which State became party to the Convention	Latest Act[1] of the Convention to which State is party and date on which State became party to that Act	
Germany	December 5, 1887	Paris:	Article 1 to 21: October 10, 1974[11] Article 22 to 38: January 22, 1974
Ghana	October 11, 1991	Paris:	October 11, 1991
Greece	November 9, 1920	Paris:	March 8, 1976
Grenada	September 22, 1998	Paris:	September 22, 1998
Guatemala	July 28, 1997	Paris:	July 28, 1997[2]
Guinea	November 20, 1980	Paris:	November 20, 1980
Guinea-Bissau	July 22, 1991	Paris:	July 22, 1991
Guyana	October 25, 1994	Paris:	October 25, 1994
Haiti	January 11, 1996	Paris:	January 11, 1996
Holy See	September 12, 1935	Paris:	April 24, 1975
Honduras	January 25, 1990	Paris:	January 25, 1990
Hungary	February 14, 1922	Paris:	Article 1 to 21: October 10, 1974 Article 22 to 38: December 15, 1972
Iceland	September 7, 1947	Paris:	Article 1 to 21: August 25, 1999 Article 22 to 38: December 28, 1984

11. This State has declared that it admits the application of the Appendix of the Paris Act to works of which it is the State of origin by States which have made a declaration under Article VI(1)(i) of the Appendix or a notification under Article I of the Appendix. The declarations took effect on October 18, 1973, for Germany, on March 8, 1974, for Norway and on September 27, 1971, for the United Kingdom.

State	Date on which State became party to the Convention	Latest Act[1] of the Convention to which State is party and date on which State became party to that Act	
India	April 1, 1928	Paris:	Article 1 to 21: May 6, 1984[12, 13]
			Article 22 to 38: January 10, 1975[2]
Indonesia	September 5, 1997	Paris:	September 5, 1997[2]
Ireland	October 5, 1927	Paris:	March 2, 2005
Israel	March 24, 1950	Paris:	January 1, 2004[2]
Italy	December 5, 1887	Paris:	November 14, 1979
Jamaica	January 1, 1994	Paris:	January 1, 1994
Japan	July 15, 1899	Paris:	April 24, 1975
Jordan	July 28, 1999	Paris:	July 28, 1999[2]
Kazakhstan	April 12, 1999	Paris:	April 12, 1999
Kenya	June 11, 1993	Paris:	June 11, 1993
Kiribati	January 2, 2018	Paris:	January 2, 2018
Kuwait	December 2, 2014	Paris:	December 2, 2014[3]
Kyrgyzstan	July 8, 1999	Paris:	July 8, 1999
Lao People's Democratic Republic	March 14, 2012	Paris:	March 14, 2012
Latvia	August 11, 1995[14]	Paris:	August 11, 1995
Lebanon	September 30, 1947	Rome:	September 30, 1947
Lesotho	September 28, 1989	Paris:	September 28, 1989[2]

[12.] This State declared that its ratification shall not apply to the provisions of Article 14*bis*(2)(b) of the Paris Act (presumption of legitimation for some authors who have brought contributions to the making of the cinematographic work).

[13.] This State notified the designation of the competent authority provided by Article 15(4) of the Paris Act.

[14.] Latvia acceded to the Berne Convention (Rome Act, 1928) with effect from May 15, 1937. It lost its independence on July 21, 1940, and regained it on August 21, 1991.

State	Date on which State became party to the Convention	Latest Act[1] of the Convention to which State is party and date on which State became party to that Act	
Liberia	March 8, 1989	Paris:	March 8, 1989[2]
Libya	September 28, 1976	Paris:	September 28, 1976[2]
Liechtenstein	July 30, 1931	Paris:	September 23, 1999
Lithuania	December 14, 1994	Paris:	December 14, 1994[2]
Luxembourg	June 20, 1888		April 20, 1975
Madagascar	January 1, 1966	Brussels:	January 1, 1966
Malawi	October 12, 1991	Paris:	October 12, 1991
Malaysia	October 1, 1990	Paris:	October 1, 1990
Mali	March 19, 1962[4]	Paris:	December 5, 1977
Malta	September 21, 1964	Rome:	September 21, 1964
		Paris:	Article 22 to 38: December 12, 1977[2]
Mauritania	February 6, 1973	Paris:	September 21, 1964
Mauritius	May 10, 1989	Paris:	May 10, 1989[2]
Mexico	June 11, 1967	Paris:	December 17, 1974
Micronesia (Federated States of)	October 7, 2003	Paris:	October 7, 2003
Monaco	May 30, 1889	Paris:	November 23, 1974
Mongolia	March 12, 1998	Paris:	March 12, 1998[2]
Montenegro	June 3, 2006	Paris:	June 3, 2006
Morocco	June 16, 1917	Paris:	May 17, 1987
Mozambique	November 22, 2013	Paris:	November 22, 2013
Namibia	March 21, 1990	Paris:	December 24, 1993
Nauru	May 11, 2020	Paris:	May 11, 2020

State	Date on which State became party to the Convention	Latest Act[1] of the Convention to which State is party and date on which State became party to that Act	
Nepal	January 11, 2006	Paris:	January 11, 2006[2]
Netherlands	November 1, 1912	Paris:	Article 1 to 21: January 30, 1986[15]
			Article 22 to 38: January 10, 1975[16]
New Zealand	April 24, 1928	Rome:	December 4, 1947[17]
Nicaragua	August 23, 2000	Paris:	August 23, 2000
Niger	May 2, 1962[4]	Paris:	May 21, 1975
Nigeria	September 14, 1993	Paris:	September 14, 1993
Niue	September 24, 2016	Paris:	September 24, 2016
North Macedonia	September 8, 1991	Paris:	September 8, 1991
Norway	April 13, 1896	Paris:	Article 1 to 21: October 11, 1995[11]
			Article 22 to 38: June 13, 1974
Oman	July 14, 1999	Paris:	July 14, 1999[2]
Pakistan	July 5, 1948	Rome:	July 5, 1948[7]
		Stockholm:	Article 22 to 38: January 29 or February 26, 1970
Panama	June 8, 1996	Paris:	June 8, 1996
Paraguay	January 2, 1992	Paris:	January 2, 1992
Peru	August 20, 1988	Paris:	August 20, 1988
Philippines	August 1, 1951	Paris:	Article 1 to 21: June 18, 1997

[15.] Ratification for the Kingdom in Europe.

[16.] Ratification for the Kingdom in Europe. Articles 22 to 38 of the Paris Act apply also to the Netherlands Antilles and Aruba. The Netherlands Antilles ceased to exist on October 10, 2010. As from that date, Articles 22 to 38 continue to apply to Curaçao and Sint Maarten. Articles 22 to 38 also continue to apply to the islands of Bonaire, Sint Eustatius and Saba which, with effect from October 10, 2010, have become part of the territory of the Kingdom of the Netherlands in Europe.

[17.] The accession by New Zealand to the Paris Act shall extend to Tokelau.

State	Date on which State became party to the Convention	Latest Act[1] of the Convention to which State is party and date on which State became party to that Act	
Poland	January 28, 1920	Paris:	Article 22 to 38: August 4, 1980 Article 1 to 21: October 22, 1994 Article 22 to 38: August 4, 1990
Portugal	March 29, 1911	Paris:	January 12, 1979[18]
Qatar	July 5, 2000	Paris:	July 5, 2000
Republic of Korea	August 21, 1996	Paris:	August 21, 1996
Republic of Moldova	November 2, 1995	Paris:	November 2, 1995
Romania	January 1, 1927	Paris:	September 9, 1998
Russian Federation	March 13, 1995	Paris:	March 13, 1995
Rwanda	March 1, 1984	Paris:	March 1, 1984
Saint Kitts and Nevis	April 9, 1995	Paris:	April 9, 1995
Saint Lucia	August 24, 1993	Paris:	August 24, 1993[2]
Saint Vincent and the Grenadines	August 29, 1995	Paris:	August 29, 1995
Samoa	July 21, 2006	Paris:	July 21, 2006
San Marino	September 2, 2020	Paris:	September 2, 2020
Sao Tome and Principe	June 14, 2016	Paris:	June 14, 2016
Saudi Arabia	March 11, 2004	Paris:	March 11, 2004
Senegal	August 25, 1962	Paris:	August 12, 1975

[18.] Pursuant to the provisions of Article 14*bis*(2)(c) of the Paris Act, this State has made a declaration to the effect that the undertaking by authors to bring contributions to the making of a cinematographic work must be in a written agreement. This declaration was received on November 5, 1986.

State	Date on which State became party to the Convention	Latest Act[1] of the Convention to which State is party and date on which State became party to that Act	
Serbia[19]	April 27, 1992	Paris:	April 27, 1992[5]
Singapore	December 21, 1998	Paris:	December 21, 1998
Slovakia	January 1, 1993	Paris:	January 1, 1993
Slovenia	June 25, 1991	Paris:	June 25, 1991[5]
Solomon Islands	July 4, 2019	Paris:	July 4, 2019
South Africa	October 3, 1928	Brussels:	August 1, 1951
		Paris:	Article 22 to 38: March 24, 1975[2]
Spain	December 5, 1887	Paris:	Article 1 to 21: October 10, 1974
		Paris:	Article 22 to 38: February 19, 1974
Sri Lanka	July 20, 1959[4]	Rome:	July 20, 1959
		Paris:	Article 22 to 38: September 23, 1978
Sudan	December 28, 2000	Paris:	December 28, 2000
Suriname	February 23, 1977	Paris:	February 23, 1977
Sweden	August 1, 1904	Paris:	Article 1 to 21: October 10, 1974
			Article 22 to 38: September 20, 1973
Switzerland	December 5, 1887	Paris:	September 25, 1993
Syrian Arab Republic	June 11, 2004	Paris:	June 11, 2004
Tajikistan	March 9, 2000	Paris:	March 9, 2000
Thailand	July 17, 1931	Paris:	Article 1 to 21: September 2, 1995[20]

---

[19]. Serbia is the continuing State from Serbia and Montenegro as from June 3, 2006.

[20]. Pursuant to Article I of the Appendix of the Paris Act, this State availed itself of the faculty provided for in Article II of the said Appendix. The relevant declaration is effective until October 10, 2024.

State	Date on which State became party to the Convention	Latest Act[1] of the Convention to which State is party and date on which State became party to that Act	
			Article 22 to 38: December 29, 1980[2]
Togo	April 30, 1975	Paris:	April 30, 1975
Tonga	June 14, 2001	Paris:	June 14, 2001
Trinidad and Tobago	August 16, 1988	Paris:	August 16, 1988
Tunisia	December 5, 1887	Paris:	August 16, 1975[2]
Turkey	January 1, 1952	Paris:	January 1, 1996[2]
Turkmenistan	May 29, 2016	Paris:	May 29, 2016[2]
Tuvalu	June 2, 2017	Paris:	June 2, 2017
Ukraine	October 25, 1995	Paris:	October 25, 1995
United Arab Emirates	July 14, 2004	Paris:	July 14, 2004[3]
United Kingdom	December 5, 1887	Paris:	January 2, 1990[11, 21, 22]
United Republic of Tanzania	July 25, 1994	Paris:	July 25, 1994[2]
United States of America	March 1, 1989	Paris:	March 1, 1989
Uruguay	July 10, 1967	Paris:	December 28, 1979
Uzbekistan	April 19, 2005	Paris:	April 19, 2005[13]
Vanuatu	December 27, 2012	Paris:	December 27, 2012
Venezuela (Bolivarian Republic of)	December 30, 1982	Paris:	December 30, 1982[2]
Viet Nam	October 26, 2004	Paris:	October 26, 2004[2, 3]
Yemen	July 14, 2008	Paris:	July 14, 2008[3]

[21.] The United Kingdom extended the application of the Paris Act to the Isle of Man with effect from March 18, 1996, to the territory of the Bailiwick of Jersey with effect from January 31, 2014, and to the territory of the Bailiwick of Guernsey with effect from November 21, 2014.

[22.] The United Kingdom extended the application of the Convention to the territory of Gibraltar with effect from January 1, 2021.

State	Date on which State became party to the Convention	Latest Act[1] of the Convention to which State is party and date on which State became party to that Act	
Zambia	January 2, 1992	Paris:	January 2, 1992
Zimbabwe	April 18, 1980	Rome:	April 18, 1980
		Paris:	Article 22 to 38: December 30, 1981

Total: 179 States

6

WIPO COPYRIGHT TREATY

(adopted in Geneva on December 20, 1996)

CONTENTS

Preamble

The Contracting Parties,

Desiring to develop and maintain the protection of the rights of authors in their literary and artistic works in a manner as effective and uniform as possible,

Recognizing the need to introduce new international rules and clarify the interpretation of certain existing rules in order to provide adequate solutions to the questions raised by new economic, social, cultural and technological developments,

Recognizing the profound impact of the development and convergence of information and communication technologies on the creation and use of literary and artistic works,

Emphasizing the outstanding significance of copyright protection as an incentive for literary and artistic creation,

Recognizing the need to maintain a balance between the rights of authors and the larger public interest, particularly education, research and access to information, as reflected in the Berne Convention,

Have agreed as follows:

Article 1

Relation to the Berne Convention

(1) This Treaty is a special agreement within the meaning of Article 20 of the Berne Convention for the Protection of Literary and Artistic Works, as regards Contracting Parties that are countries of the Union established by that Convention. This Treaty shall not have any connection with treaties other than the Berne Convention, nor shall it prejudice any rights and obligations under any other treaties.

(2) Nothing in this Treaty shall derogate from existing obligations that Contracting Parties have to each other under the Berne Convention for the Protection of Literary and Artistic Works.

(3) Hereinafter, "Berne Convention" shall refer to the Paris Act of July 24, 1971, of the Berne Convention for the Protection of Literary and Artistic Works.

(4) Contracting Parties shall comply with Articles 1 to 21 and the Appendix of the Berne Convention.

Article 2

Scope of Copyright Protection

Copyright protection extends to expressions and not to ideas, procedures, methods of operation or mathematical concepts as such.

Article 3

Application of Articles 2 to 6 of the Berne Convention

Contracting Parties shall apply *mutatis mutandis* the provisions of Articles 2 to 6 of the Berne Convention in respect of the protection provided for in this Treaty.

Article 4

Computer Programs

Computer programs are protected as literary works within the meaning of Article 2 of the Berne Convention. Such protection applies to computer programs, whatever may be the mode or form of their expression.

Article 5

Compilations of Data (Databases)

Compilations of data or other material, in any form, which by reason of the selection or arrangement of their contents constitute intellectual creations, are protected as such. This protection does not extend to the data or the material itself and is without prejudice to any copyright subsisting in the data or material contained in the compilation.

Article 6

Right of Distribution

(1) Authors of literary and artistic works shall enjoy the exclusive right of authorizing the making available to the public of the original and copies of their works through sale or other transfer of ownership.

(2) Nothing in this Treaty shall affect the freedom of Contracting Parties to determine the conditions, if any, under which the exhaustion of the right in paragraph (1) applies after the first sale or other transfer of ownership of the original or a copy of the work with the authorization of the author.

Article 7

Right of Rental

(1) Authors of

(i) computer programs;

(ii) cinematographic works; and

(iii) works embodied in phonograms, as determined in the national law of Contracting Parties,

shall enjoy the exclusive right of authorizing commercial rental to the public of the originals or copies of their works.

(2) Paragraph (1) shall not apply

(i) in the case of computer programs, where the program itself is not the essential object of the rental; and

(ii) in the case of cinematographic works, unless such commercial rental has led to widespread copying of such works materially impairing the exclusive right of reproduction.

(3) Notwithstanding the provisions of paragraph (1), a Contracting Party that, on April 15, 1994, had and continues to have in force a system of equitable remuneration of authors for the rental of copies of their works embodied in phonograms may maintain that system provided that the commercial rental of works embodied in phonograms is not giving rise to the material impairment of the exclusive right of reproduction of authors.

Article 8

Right of Communication to the Public

Without prejudice to the provisions of Articles 11(1)(ii), 11*bis*(1)(i) and (ii), 11*ter*(1)(ii), 14(1)(ii) and 14*bis*(1) of the Berne Convention, authors of literary and artistic works shall enjoy the exclusive right of authorizing any communication to the public of their works, by wire or wireless means, including the making available to the public of their works in such a way that members of the public may access these works from a place and at a time individually chosen by them.

Article 9

Duration of the Protection of Photographic Works

In respect of photographic works, the Contracting Parties shall not apply the provisions of Article 7(4) of the Berne Convention.

Article 10

Limitations and Exceptions

(1) Contracting Parties may, in their national legislation, provide for limitations of or exceptions to the rights granted to authors of literary and artistic works under this Treaty in certain special cases that do not conflict with a normal exploitation of the work and do not unreasonably prejudice the legitimate interests of the author.

(2) Contracting Parties shall, when applying the Berne Convention, confine any limitations of or exceptions to rights provided for therein to certain special cases that do not conflict with a normal exploitation of the work and do not unreasonably prejudice the legitimate interests of the author.

Article 11

Obligations concerning Technological Measures

Contracting Parties shall provide adequate legal protection and effective legal remedies against the circumvention of effective technological measures that are used by authors in connection with the exercise of their rights under this Treaty or the Berne Convention and that restrict acts, in respect of their works, which are not authorized by the authors concerned or permitted by law.

Article 12

Obligations concerning Rights Management Information

(1) Contracting Parties shall provide adequate and effective legal remedies against any person knowingly performing any of the following acts knowing, or with respect to civil remedies having reasonable grounds to know, that it will induce, enable, facilitate or conceal an infringement of any right covered by this Treaty or the Berne Convention:

(i) to remove or alter any electronic rights management information without authority;

(ii) to distribute, import for distribution, broadcast or communicate to the public, without authority, works or copies of works knowing that electronic rights management information has been removed or altered without authority.

(2) As used in this Article, "rights management information" means information which identifies the work, the author of the work, the owner of any right in the work, or information about the terms and conditions of use of the work, and any numbers or codes that represent such information, when any of these items of information is attached to a copy of a work or appears in connection with the communication of a work to the public.

Article 13

Application in Time

Contracting Parties shall apply the provisions of Article 18 of the Berne Convention to all protection provided for in this Treaty.

Article 14

Provisions on Enforcement of Rights

(1) Contracting Parties undertake to adopt, in accordance with their legal systems, the measures necessary to ensure the application of this Treaty.

(2) Contracting Parties shall ensure that enforcement procedures are available under their law so as to permit effective action against any act of infringement of rights covered by this Treaty, including expeditious

remedies to prevent infringements and remedies which constitute a deterrent to further infringements.

Article 15

Assembly

(1)*(a)* The Contracting Parties shall have an Assembly.

(b) Each Contracting Party shall be represented by one delegate who may be assisted by alternate delegates, advisors and experts.

(c) The expenses of each delegation shall be borne by the Contracting Party that has appointed the delegation. The Assembly may ask the World Intellectual Property Organization (hereinafter referred to as "WIPO") to grant financial assistance to facilitate the participation of delegations of Contracting Parties that are regarded as developing countries in conformity with the established practice of the General Assembly of the United Nations or that are countries in transition to a market economy.

(2)*(a)* The Assembly shall deal with matters concerning the maintenance and development of this Treaty and the application and operation of this Treaty.

(b) The Assembly shall perform the function allocated to it under Article 17(2) in respect of the admission of certain intergovernmental organizations to become party to this Treaty.

(c) The Assembly shall decide the convocation of any diplomatic conference for the revision of this Treaty and give the necessary instructions to the Director General of WIPO for the preparation of such diplomatic conference.

(3)*(a)* Each Contracting Party that is a State shall have one vote and shall vote only in its own name.

(b) Any Contracting Party that is an intergovernmental organization may participate in the vote, in place of its Member States, with a number of votes equal to the number of its Member States which are party to this Treaty. No such intergovernmental organization shall participate in the vote if any one of its Member States exercises its right to vote and *vice versa*.

(4) The Assembly shall meet in ordinary session once every two years upon convocation by the Director General of WIPO.

(5) The Assembly shall establish its own rules of procedure, including the convocation of extraordinary sessions, the requirements of a quorum and, subject to the provisions of this Treaty, the required majority for various kinds of decisions.

Article 16

International Bureau

The International Bureau of WIPO shall perform the administrative tasks concerning the Treaty.

Article 17

Eligibility for Becoming Party to the Treaty

(1)   Any Member State of WIPO may become party to this Treaty.

(2)   The Assembly may decide to admit any intergovernmental organization to become party to this Treaty which declares that it is competent in respect of, and has its own legislation binding on all its Member States on, matters covered by this Treaty and that it has been duly authorized, in accordance with its internal procedures, to become party to this Treaty.

(3)   The European Community, having made the declaration referred to in the preceding paragraph in the Diplomatic Conference that has adopted this Treaty, may become party to this Treaty.

Article 18

Rights and Obligations under the Treaty

Subject to any specific provisions to the contrary in this Treaty, each Contracting Party shall enjoy all of the rights and assume all of the obligations under this Treaty.

Article 19

Signature of the Treaty

This Treaty shall be open for signature until December 31, 1997, by any Member State of WIPO and by the European Community.

Article 20

Entry into Force of the Treaty

This Treaty shall enter into force three months after 30 instruments of ratification or accession by States have been deposited with the Director General of WIPO.

Article 21

Effective Date of Becoming Party to the Treaty

This Treaty shall bind:

(i)   the 30 States referred to in Article 20, from the date on which this Treaty has entered into force;

(ii) each other State, from the expiration of three months from the date on which the State has deposited its instrument with the Director General of WIPO;

(iii) the European Community, from the expiration of three months after the deposit of its instrument of ratification or accession if such instrument has been deposited after the entry into force of this Treaty according to Article 20, or, three months after the entry into force of this Treaty if such instrument has been deposited before the entry into force of this Treaty;

(iv) any other intergovernmental organization that is admitted to become party to this Treaty, from the expiration of three months after the deposit of its instrument of accession.

Article 22

No Reservations to the Treaty

No reservation to this Treaty shall be admitted.

Article 23

Denunciation of the Treaty

This Treaty may be denounced by any Contracting Party by notification addressed to the Director General of WIPO. Any denunciation shall take effect one year from the date on which the Director General of WIPO received the notification.

Article 24

Languages of the Treaty

(1) This Treaty is signed in a single original in English, Arabic, Chinese, French, Russian and Spanish languages, the versions in all these languages being equally authentic.

(2) An official text in any language other than those referred to in paragraph (1) shall be established by the Director General of WIPO on the request of an interested party, after consultation with all the interested parties. For the purposes of this paragraph, "interested party" means any Member State of WIPO whose official language, or one of whose official languages, is involved and the European Community, and any other intergovernmental organization that may become party to this Treaty, if one of its official languages is involved.

Article 25

Depositary

The Director General of WIPO is the depositary of this Treaty.

*Entry into force: March 6, 2002.

Source: International Bureau of WIPO.

Note: The agreed statements of the Diplomatic Conference that adopted the Treaty (WIPO Diplomatic Conference on Certain Copyright and Neighboring Rights Questions) concerning certain provisions of the WCT are reproduced in endnotes below.

Agreed statement concerning Article 1(4): The reproduction right, as set out in Article 9 of the Berne Convention, and the exceptions permitted thereunder, fully apply in the digital environment, in particular to the use of works in digital form. It is understood that the storage of a protected work in digital form in an electronic medium constitutes a reproduction within the meaning of Article 9 of the Berne Convention.

Agreed statement concerning Article 3: It is understood that, in applying Article 3 of this Treaty, the expression "country of the Union" in Articles 2 to 6 of the Berne Convention will be read as if it were a reference to a Contracting Party to this Treaty, in the application of those Berne Articles in respect of protection provided for in this Treaty. It is also understood that the expression "country outside the Union" in those Articles in the Berne Convention will, in the same circumstances, be read as if it were a reference to a country that is not a Contracting Party to this Treaty, and that "this Convention" in Articles 2(8), 2*bis*(2), 3, 4 and 5 of the Berne Convention will be read as if it were a reference to the Berne Convention and this Treaty. Finally, it is understood that a reference in Articles 3 to 6 of the Berne Convention to a "national of one of the countries of the Union" will, when these Articles are applied to this Treaty, mean, in regard to an intergovernmental organization that is a Contracting Party to this Treaty, a national of one of the countries that is member of that organization.

Agreed statement concerning Article 4: The scope of protection for computer programs under Article 4 of this Treaty, read with Article 2, is consistent with Article 2 of the Berne Convention and on a par with the relevant provisions of the TRIPS Agreement.

Agreed statement concerning Article 5: The scope of protection for compilations of data (databases) under Article 5 of this Treaty, read with Article 2, is consistent with Article 2 of the Berne Convention and on a par with the relevant provisions of the TRIPS Agreement.

Agreed statement concerning Articles 6 and 7: As used in these Articles, the expressions "copies" and "original and copies," being subject to the right of distribution and the right of rental under the said Articles, refer exclusively to fixed copies that can be put into circulation as tangible objects.

Agreed statement concerning Articles 6 and 7: As used in these Articles, the expressions "copies" and "original and copies," being subject to the right of distribution and the right of rental under the said Articles, refer exclusively to fixed copies that can be put into circulation as tangible objects.

Agreed statement concerning Article 7: It is understood that the obligation under Article 7(1) does not require a Contracting Party to provide an exclusive right of commercial rental to authors who, under that Contracting Party's law, are not granted rights in respect of phonograms. It is understood that this obligation is consistent with Article 14(4) of the TRIPS Agreement.

Agreed statement concerning Article 8: It is understood that the mere provision of physical facilities for enabling or making a communication does not in itself amount to communication within the meaning of this Treaty or the Berne Convention. It is further understood that nothing in Article 8 precludes a Contracting Party from applying Article 11*bis*(2).

Agreed statement concerning Article 10: It is understood that the provisions of Article 10 permit Contracting Parties to carry forward and appropriately extend into the digital environment limitations and exceptions in their national laws which have been considered acceptable under the Berne Convention. Similarly, these provisions should be understood to permit Contracting Parties to devise new exceptions and limitations that are appropriate in the digital network environment. It is also understood that Article 10(2) neither reduces nor extends the scope of applicability of the limitations and exceptions permitted by the Berne Convention.

Agreed statement concerning Article 12: It is understood that the reference to "infringement of any right covered by this Treaty or the Berne Convention" includes both exclusive rights and rights of remuneration. It is further understood that Contracting Parties will not rely on this Article to devise or implement rights management systems that would have the effect of imposing formalities which are not permitted under the Berne Convention or this Treaty, prohibiting the free movement of goods or impeding the enjoyment of rights under this Treaty.

7

PARTIES TO THE WIPO COPYRIGHT TREATY

Status on February 9, 2021

State	Date on which State became party to the Treaty
Afghanistan	February 9, 2021
Albania	August 6, 2005
Algeria	January 31, 2014
Argentina	March 6, 2002
Armenia	March 6, 2005
Australia	July 26, 2007
Austria	March 14, 2010
Azerbaijan	April 11, 2006
Bahrain	December 15, 2005
Barbados	December 13, 2019
Belarus	March 6, 2002
Belgium	August 30, 2006
Belize	February 9, 2019
Benin	April 16, 2006
Bosnia and Herzegovina	November 25, 2009
Botswana	January 27, 2005
Brunei Darussalam	May 2, 2017
Bulgaria	March 6, 2002
Burkina Faso	March 6, 2002
Burundi	April 12, 2016
Cabo Verde	May 22, 2019
Canada	August 13, 2014
Chile	March 6, 2002

State	Date on which State became party to the Treaty
China[1,2]	June 9, 2007
Colombia	March 6, 2002
Cook Islands	June 19, 2019
Costa Rica	March 6, 2002
Croatia	March 6, 2002
Cyprus	November 4, 2003
Czech Republic	March 6, 2002
Denmark[3]	March 14, 2010
Dominican Republic	January 10, 2006
Ecuador	March 6, 2002
El Salvador	March 6, 2002
Estonia	March 14, 2010
European Union	March 14, 2010
Finland	March 14, 2010
France	March 14, 2010
Gabon	March 6, 2002
Georgia	March 6, 2002
Germany	March 14, 2010
Ghana	November 18, 2006
Greece	March 14, 2010
Guatemala	February 4, 2003
Guinea	May 25, 2002
Honduras	May 20, 2002
Hungary	March 6, 2002
India	December 25, 2018
Indonesia	March 6, 2002
Ireland	March 14, 2010
Italy	March 14, 2010
Jamaica	June 12, 2002
Japan	March 6, 2002
Jordan	April 27, 2004
Kazakhstan	November 12, 2004

---

[1]. In accordance with the Basic Law of Hong Kong, China, the Government of the People's Republic of China has decided that the Treaty will apply to Hong Kong, China with effect from October 1, 2008.

[2]. In accordance with the Basic Law of the Macao Special Administrative Region of the People's Republic of China (PRC), the Government of the PRC decides that the Treaty shall apply to the Macao Special Administrative Region. The declaration took effect on November 6, 2013.

[3]. Applicable to the Faroe Islands as of April 30, 2018.

State	Date on which State became party to the Treaty
Kyrgyzstan	March 6, 2002
Latvia	March 6, 2002
Liechtenstein	April 30, 2007
Lithuania	March 6, 2002
Luxembourg	March 14, 2010
Madagascar	February 24, 2015
Malaysia	December 27, 2012
Mali	April 24, 2002
Malta	March 14, 2010
Mexico	March 6, 2002
Mongolia	October 25, 2002
Montenegro	June 3, 2006
Morocco	July 20, 2011
Nauru	August 11, 2020
Netherlands	March 14, 2010
New Zealand[4]	March 17, 2019
Nicaragua	March 6, 2003
Nigeria	January 4, 2018
North Macedonia	February 4, 2004
Oman	September 20, 2005
Panama	March 6, 2002
Paraguay	March 6, 2002
Peru	March 6, 2002
Philippines	October 4, 2002
Poland	March 23, 2004
Portugal	March 14, 2010
Qatar	October 28, 2005
Republic of Korea	June 24, 2004
Republic of Moldova	March 6, 2002
Romania	March 6, 2002
Russian Federation	February 5, 2009
Saint Lucia	March 6, 2002
San Marino	September 2, 2020
Sao Tome and Principe	April 27, 2020
Senegal	May 18, 2002

---

4. The accession by New Zealand shall extend to Tokelau.

State	Date on which State became party to the Treaty
Serbia[5]	June 13, 2003
Singapore	April 17, 2005
Slovakia	March 6, 2002
Slovenia	March 6, 2002
Spain	March 14, 2010
Sweden	March 14, 2010
Switzerland	July 1, 2008
Tajikistan	April 5, 2009
Togo	May 21, 2003
Trinidad and Tobago	November 28, 2008
Turkey	November 28, 2008
Ukraine	March 6, 2002
United Arab Emirates	July 14, 2004
United Kingdom[6]	March 14, 2010
United States of America	March 6, 2002
Uruguay	June 5, 2009
Uzbekistan	July 17, 2019
Vanuatu	August 6, 2020

Total: 109 States

---

[5] Serbia is the continuing State from Serbia and Montenegro as from June 3, 2006.

[6] The United Kingdom extended the application of the Treaty to the territories of the Bailiwick of Guernsey and the Isle of Man with effect from January 1, 2021.

8

WIPO PERFORMANCES AND PHONOGRAMS TREATY

(adopted in Geneva on December 20, 1996)

TABLE OF CONTENTS

TABLE OF CONTENTS

Preamble

The Contracting Parties,

Desiring to develop and maintain the protection of the rights of performers and producers of phonograms in a manner as effective and uniform as possible,

Recognizing the need to introduce new international rules in order to provide adequate solutions to the questions raised by economic, social, cultural and technological developments,

Recognizing the profound impact of the development and convergence of information and communication technologies on the production and use of performances and phonograms,

Recognizing the need to maintain a balance between the rights of performers and producers of phonograms and the larger public interest, particularly education, research and access to information,

Have agreed as follows:

Chapter I
General Provisions
Article 1
Relation to Other Conventions

(1) Nothing in this Treaty shall derogate from existing obligations that Contracting Parties have to each other under the International Convention for the Protection of Performers, Producers of Phonograms and Broadcasting Organizations done in Rome, October 26, 1961 (hereinafter the "Rome Convention").

(2) Protection granted under this Treaty shall leave intact and shall in no way affect the protection of copyright in literary and artistic works. Consequently, no provision of this Treaty may be interpreted as prejudicing such protection.

(3) This Treaty shall not have any connection with, nor shall it prejudice any rights and obligations under, any other treaties.

Article 2
Definitions

For the purposes of this Treaty:

(a) "performers" are actors, singers, musicians, dancers, and other persons who act, sing, deliver, declaim, play in, interpret, or otherwise perform literary or artistic works or expressions of folklore;

(b) "phonogram" means the fixation of the sounds of a performance or of other sounds, or of a representation of sounds, other than in the form of a fixation incorporated in a cinematographic or other audiovisual work;

(c) "fixation" means the embodiment of sounds, or of the representations thereof, from which they can be perceived, reproduced or communicated through a device;

(d) "producer of a phonogram" means the person, or the legal entity, who or which takes the initiative and has the responsibility for the first fixation of the sounds of a performance or other sounds, or the representations of sounds;

(e) "publication" of a fixed performance or a phonogram means the offering of copies of the fixed performance or the phonogram to the public, with the consent of the rightholder, and provided that copies are offered to the public in reasonable quantity;

(f) "broadcasting" means the transmission by wireless means for public reception of sounds or of images and sounds or of the representations thereof; such transmission by satellite is also "broadcasting"; transmission of encrypted signals is "broadcasting" where the means for decrypting are provided to the public by the broadcasting organization or with its consent;

(g) "communication to the public" of a performance or a phonogram means the transmission to the public by any medium, otherwise than by broadcasting, of sounds of a performance or the sounds or the representations of sounds fixed in a phonogram. For the purposes of Article 15, "communication to the public" includes making the sounds or representations of sounds fixed in a phonogram audible to the public.

Article 3

Beneficiaries of Protection under this Treaty

(1) Contracting Parties shall accord the protection provided under this Treaty to the performers and producers of phonograms who are nationals of other Contracting Parties.

(2) The nationals of other Contracting Parties shall be understood to be those performers or producers of phonograms who would meet the criteria for eligibility for protection provided under the Rome Convention, were all the Contracting Parties to this Treaty Contracting States of that Convention. In respect of these criteria of eligibility, Contracting Parties shall apply the relevant definitions in Article 2 of this Treaty.

(3) Any Contracting Party availing itself of the possibilities provided in Article 5(3) of the Rome Convention or, for the purposes of Article 5 of the same Convention, Article 17 thereof shall make a notification as foreseen in those provisions to the Director General of the World Intellectual Property Organization (WIPO).

Article 4

National Treatment

(1) Each Contracting Party shall accord to nationals of other Contracting Parties, as defined in Article 3(2), the treatment it accords to its own nationals with regard to the exclusive rights specifically granted in this Treaty, and to the right to equitable remuneration provided for in Article 15 of this Treaty.

(2) The obligation provided for in paragraph (1) does not apply to the extent that another Contracting Party makes use of the reservations permitted by Article 15(3) of this Treaty.

Chapter II

Rights of Performers

Article 5

Moral Rights of Performers

(1)   Independently of a performer's economic rights, and even after the transfer of those rights, the performer shall, as regards his live aural performances or performances fixed in phonograms, have the right to claim to be identified as the performer of his performances, except where omission is dictated by the manner of the use of the performance, and to object to any distortion, mutilation or other modification of his performances that would be prejudicial to his reputation.

(2)   The rights granted to a performer in accordance with paragraph (1) shall, after his death, be maintained, at least until the expiry of the economic rights, and shall be exercisable by the persons or institutions authorized by the legislation of the Contracting Party where protection is claimed. However, those Contracting Parties whose legislation, at the moment of their ratification of or accession to this Treaty, does not provide for protection after the death of the performer of all rights set out in the preceding paragraph may provide that some of these rights will, after his death, cease to be maintained.

(3)   The means of redress for safeguarding the rights granted under this Article shall be governed by the legislation of the Contracting Party where protection is claimed.

Article 6

Economic Rights of Performers in their Unfixed Performances

Performers shall enjoy the exclusive right of authorizing, as regards their performances:

(i)   the broadcasting and communication to the public of their unfixed performances except where the performance is already a broadcast performance; and

(ii)   the fixation of their unfixed performances.

Article 7

Right of Reproduction

Performers shall enjoy the exclusive right of authorizing the direct or indirect reproduction of their performances fixed in phonograms, in any manner or form.

Article 8

Right of Distribution

(1) Performers shall enjoy the exclusive right of authorizing the making available to the public of the original and copies of their performances fixed in phonograms through sale or other transfer of ownership.

(2) Nothing in this Treaty shall affect the freedom of Contracting Parties to determine the conditions, if any, under which the exhaustion of the right in paragraph (1) applies after the first sale or other transfer of ownership of the original or a copy of the fixed performance with the authorization of the performer.

Article 9

Right of Rental

(1) Performers shall enjoy the exclusive right of authorizing the commercial rental to the public of the original and copies of their performances fixed in phonograms as determined in the national law of Contracting Parties, even after distribution of them by, or pursuant to, authorization by the performer.

(2) Notwithstanding the provisions of paragraph (1), a Contracting Party that, on April 15, 1994, had and continues to have in force a system of equitable remuneration of performers for the rental of copies of their performances fixed in phonograms, may maintain that system provided that the commercial rental of phonograms is not giving rise to the material impairment of the exclusive right of reproduction of performers.

Article 10

Right of Making Available of Fixed Performances

Performers shall enjoy the exclusive right of authorizing the making available to the public of their performances fixed in phonograms, by wire or wireless means, in such a way that members of the public may access them from a place and at a time individually chosen by them.

Chapter III

Rights of Producers of Phonograms

Article 11

Right of Reproduction

Producers of phonograms shall enjoy the exclusive right of authorizing the direct or indirect reproduction of their phonograms, in any manner or form.

Article 12

Right of Distribution

(1) Producers of phonograms shall enjoy the exclusive right of authorizing the making available to the public of the original and copies of their phonograms through sale or other transfer of ownership.

(2) Nothing in this Treaty shall affect the freedom of Contracting Parties to determine the conditions, if any, under which the exhaustion of the right in paragraph (1) applies after the first sale or other transfer of ownership of the original or a copy of the phonogram with the authorization of the producer of the phonogram.

Article 13

Right of Rental

(1) Producers of phonograms shall enjoy the exclusive right of authorizing the commercial rental to the public of the original and copies of their phonograms, even after distribution of them, by or pursuant to, authorization by the producer.

(2) Notwithstanding the provisions of paragraph (1), a Contracting Party that, on April 15, 1994, had and continues to have in force a system of equitable remuneration of producers of phonograms for the rental of copies of their phonograms, may maintain that system provided that the commercial rental of phonograms is not giving rise to the material impairment of the exclusive rights of reproduction of producers of phonograms.

Article 14

Right of Making Available of Phonograms

Producers of phonograms shall enjoy the exclusive right of authorizing the making available to the public of their phonograms, by wire or wireless means, in such a way that members of the public may access them from a place and at a time individually chosen by them.

Chapter IV

Common Provisions

Article 15

Right to Remuneration for Broadcasting
and Communication to the Public

(1) Performers and producers of phonograms shall enjoy the right to a single equitable remuneration for the direct or indirect use of phonograms published for commercial purposes for broadcasting or for any communication to the public.

(2)   Contracting Parties may establish in their national legislation that the single equitable remuneration shall be claimed from the user by the performer or by the producer of a phonogram or by both. Contracting Parties may enact national legislation that, in the absence of an agreement between the performer and the producer of a phonogram, sets the terms according to which performers and producers of phonograms shall share the single equitable remuneration.

(3)   Any Contracting Party may, in a notification deposited with the Director General of WIPO, declare that it will apply the provisions of paragraph (1) only in respect of certain uses, or that it will limit their application in some other way, or that it will not apply these provisions at all.

(4)   For the purposes of this Article, phonograms made available to the public by wire or wireless means in such a way that members of the public may access them from a place and at a time individually chosen by them shall be considered as if they had been published for commercial purposes.

Article 16

Limitations and Exceptions

(1)   Contracting Parties may, in their national legislation, provide for the same kinds of limitations or exceptions with regard to the protection of performers and producers of phonograms as they provide for, in their national legislation, in connection with the protection of copyright in literary and artistic works.

(2)   Contracting Parties shall confine any limitations of or exceptions to rights provided for in this Treaty to certain special cases which do not conflict with a normal exploitation of the performance or phonogram and do not unreasonably prejudice the legitimate interests of the performer or of the producer of the phonogram.

Article 17

Term of Protection

(1)   The term of protection to be granted to performers under this Treaty shall last, at least, until the end of a period of 50 years computed from the end of the year in which the performance was fixed in a phonogram.

(2)   The term of protection to be granted to producers of phonograms under this Treaty shall last, at least, until the end of a period of 50 years computed from the end of the year in which the phonogram was published, or failing such publication within 50 years from fixation of the phonogram, 50 years from the end of the year in which the fixation was made.

Article 18

Obligations concerning Technological Measures

Contracting Parties shall provide adequate legal protection and effective legal remedies against the circumvention of effective technological measures that are used by performers or producers of phonograms in connection with the exercise of their rights under this Treaty and that restrict acts, in respect of their performances or phonograms, which are not authorized by the performers or the producers of phonograms concerned or permitted by law.

Article 19

Obligations concerning Rights Management Information

(1) Contracting Parties shall provide adequate and effective legal remedies against any person knowingly performing any of the following acts knowing, or with respect to civil remedies having reasonable grounds to know, that it will induce, enable, facilitate or conceal an infringement of any right covered by this Treaty:

(i)   to remove or alter any electronic rights management information without authority;

(ii) to distribute, import for distribution, broadcast, communicate or make available to the public, without authority, performances, copies of fixed performances or phonograms knowing that electronic rights management information has been removed or altered without authority.

(2) As used in this Article, "rights management information" means information which identifies the performer, the performance of the performer, the producer of the phonogram, the phonogram, the owner of any right in the performance or phonogram, or information about the terms and conditions of use of the performance or phonogram, and any numbers or codes that represent such information, when any of these items of information is attached to a copy of a fixed performance or a phonogram or appears in connection with the communication or making available of a fixed performance or a phonogram to the public.

Article 20

Formalities

The enjoyment and exercise of the rights provided for in this Treaty shall not be subject to any formality.

Article 21

Reservations

Subject to the provisions of Article 15(3), no reservations to this Treaty shall be permitted.

Article 22

Application in Time

(1) Contracting Parties shall apply the provisions of Article 18 of the Berne Convention, *mutatis mutandis*, to the rights of performers and producers of phonograms provided for in this Treaty.

(2) Notwithstanding paragraph (1), a Contracting Party may limit the application of Article 5 of this Treaty to performances which occurred after the entry into force of this Treaty for that Party.

Article 23

Provisions on Enforcement of Rights

(1) Contracting Parties undertake to adopt, in accordance with their legal systems, the measures necessary to ensure the application of this Treaty.

(2) Contracting Parties shall ensure that enforcement procedures are available under their law so as to permit effective action against any act of infringement of rights covered by this Treaty, including expeditious remedies to prevent infringements and remedies which constitute a deterrent to further infringements.

Chapter V

Administrative and Final Clauses

Article 24

Assembly

(1)*(a)*   The Contracting Parties shall have an Assembly.

(b) Each Contracting Party shall be represented by one delegate who may be assisted by alternate delegates, advisors and experts.

(c) The expenses of each delegation shall be borne by the Contracting Party that has appointed the delegation. The Assembly may ask WIPO to grant financial assistance to facilitate the participation of delegations of Contracting Parties that are regarded as developing countries in conformity with the established practice of the General Assembly of the United Nations or that are countries in transition to a market economy.

(2)*(a)*   The Assembly shall deal with matters concerning the maintenance and development of this Treaty and the application and operation of this Treaty.

(b)   The Assembly shall perform the function allocated to it under Article 26(2) in respect of the admission of certain intergovernmental organizations to become party to this Treaty.

(c)   The Assembly shall decide the convocation of any diplomatic conference for the revision of this Treaty and give the necessary instructions to the Director General of WIPO for the preparation of such diplomatic conference.

(3)*(a)*   Each Contracting Party that is a State shall have one vote and shall vote only in its own name.

(b)   Any Contracting Party that is an intergovernmental organization may participate in the vote, in place of its Member States, with a number of votes equal to the number of its Member States which are party to this Treaty. No such intergovernmental organization shall participate in the vote if any one of its Member States exercises its right to vote and vice versa.

(4)   The Assembly shall meet in ordinary session once every two years upon convocation by the Director General of WIPO.

(5)   The Assembly shall establish its own rules of procedure, including the convocation of extraordinary sessions, the requirements of a quorum and, subject to the provisions of this Treaty, the required majority for various kinds of decisions.

Article 25

International Bureau

The International Bureau of WIPO shall perform the administrative tasks concerning the Treaty.

Article 26

Eligibility for Becoming Party to the Treaty

(1)   Any Member State of WIPO may become party to this Treaty.

(2)   The Assembly may decide to admit any intergovernmental organization to become party to this Treaty which declares that it is competent in respect of, and has its own legislation binding on all its Member States on, matters covered by this Treaty and that it has been duly authorized, in accordance with its internal procedures, to become party to this Treaty.

(3) The European Community, having made the declaration referred to in the preceding paragraph in the Diplomatic Conference that has adopted this Treaty, may become party to this Treaty.

Article 27

Rights and Obligations under the Treaty

Subject to any specific provisions to the contrary in this Treaty, each Contracting Party shall enjoy all of the rights and assume all of the obligations under this Treaty.

Article 28

Signature of the Treaty

This Treaty shall be open for signature until December 31, 1997, by any Member State of WIPO and by the European Community.

Article 29

Entry into Force of the Treaty

This Treaty shall enter into force three months after 30 instruments of ratification or accession by States have been deposited with the Director General of WIPO.

Article 30

Effective Date of Becoming Party to the Treaty

This Treaty shall bind

(i)   the 30 States referred to in Article 29, from the date on which this Treaty has entered into force;

(ii) each other State from the expiration of three months from the date on which the State has deposited its instrument with the Director General of WIPO;

(iii) the European Community, from the expiration of three months after the deposit of its instrument of ratification or accession if such instrument has been deposited after the entry into force of this Treaty according to Article 29, or, three months after the entry into force of this Treaty if such instrument has been deposited before the entry into force of this Treaty;

(iv) any other intergovernmental organization that is admitted to become party to this Treaty, from the expiration of three months after the deposit of its instrument of accession.

Article 31

Denunciation of the Treaty

This Treaty may be denounced by any Contracting Party by notification addressed to the Director General of WIPO. Any denunciation shall take effect one year from the date on which the Director General of WIPO received the notification.

Article 32

Languages of the Treaty

(1) This Treaty is signed in a single original in English, Arabic, Chinese, French, Russian and Spanish languages, the versions in all these languages being equally authentic.

(2) An official text in any language other than those referred to in paragraph (1) shall be established by the Director General of WIPO on the request of an interested party, after consultation with all the interested parties. For the purposes of this paragraph, "interested party" means any Member State of WIPO whose official language, or one of whose official languages, is involved and the European Community, and any other intergovernmental organization that may become party to this Treaty, if one of its official languages is involved.

Article 33

Depositary

The Director General of WIPO is the depositary of this Treaty.

Entry into force: May 20, 2002.

Source: International Bureau of WIPO.

Note: The agreed statements of the Diplomatic Conference that adopted the Treaty (WIPO Diplomatic Conference on Certain Copyright and Neighboring Rights Questions) concerning certain provisions of the WPPT, are reproduced in endnotes below.

1. *Agreed statement concerning Article 1(2):* It is understood that Article 1(2) clarifies the relationship between rights in phonograms under this Treaty and copyright in works embodied in the phonograms. In cases where authorization is needed from both the author of a work embodied in the phonogram and a performer or producer owning rights in the phonogram, the need for the authorization of the author does not cease to exist because the authorization of the performer or producer is also required, and vice versa.

It is further understood that nothing in Article 1(2) precludes a Contracting Party from providing exclusive rights to a performer or producer of phonograms beyond those required to be provided under this Treaty.

2.   *Agreed statement concerning Article 2*(b)*:* It is understood that the definition of phonogram provided in Article 2*(b)* does not suggest that rights in the phonogram are in any way affected through their incorporation into a cinematographic or other audiovisual work.

3.   *Agreed statement concerning Articles 2*(e)*, 8, 9, 12, and 13:* As used in these Articles, the expressions "copies" and "original and copies," being subject to the right of distribution and the right of rental under the said Articles, refer exclusively to fixed copies that can be put into circulation as tangible objects.

4.   *Agreed statement concerning Article 3(2):* For the application of Article 3(2), it is understood that fixation means the finalization of the master tape ("bande-m'ere").

5.   *Agreed statement concerning Article 3:* It is understood that the reference in Articles 5*(a)* and 16*(a)(iv)* of the Rome Convention to "national of another Contracting State" will, when applied to this Treaty, mean, in regard to an intergovernmental organization that is a Contracting Party to this Treaty, a national of one of the countries that is a member of that organization.

6.   *Agreed statement concerning Articles 7, 11 and 16:* The reproduction right, as set out in Articles 7 and 11, and the exceptions permitted thereunder through Article 16, fully apply in the digital environment, in particular to the use of performances and phonograms in digital form. It is understood that the storage of a protected performance or phonogram in digital form in an electronic medium constitutes a reproduction within the meaning of these Articles.

7.   *Agreed statement concerning Articles 2*(e)*, 8, 9, 12, and 13:* As used in these Articles, the expressions "copies" and "original and copies," being subject to the right of distribution and the right of rental under the said Articles, refer exclusively to fixed copies that can be put into circulation as tangible objects.

8.   *Agreed statement concerning Articles 2*(e)*, 8, 9, 12, and 13:* As used in these Articles, the expressions "copies" and "original and copies," being subject to the right of distribution and the right of rental under the said Articles, refer exclusively to fixed copies that can be put into circulation as tangible objects.

9.   *Agreed statement concerning Articles 7, 11 and 16:* The reproduction right, as set out in Articles 7 and 11, and the exceptions permitted thereunder through Article 16, fully apply in the digital environment, in particular to the use of performances and phonograms in digital form. It is understood that the storage of a protected performance

or phonogram in digital form in an electronic medium constitutes a reproduction within the meaning of these Articles.

10. *Agreed statement concerning Articles 2*(e)*, 8, 9, 12, and 13:* As used in these Articles, the expressions "copies" and "original and copies," being subject to the right of distribution and the right of rental under the said Articles, refer exclusively to fixed copies that can be put into circulation as tangible objects.

11. *Agreed statement concerning Articles 2*(e)*, 8, 9, 12, and 13:* As used in these Articles, the expressions "copies" and "original and copies," being subject to the right of distribution and the right of rental under the said Articles, refer exclusively to fixed copies that can be put into circulation as tangible objects.

12. *Agreed statement concerning Article 15:* It is understood that Article 15 does not represent a complete resolution of the level of rights of broadcasting and communication to the public that should be enjoyed by performers and phonogram producers in the digital age. Delegations were unable to achieve consensus on differing proposals for aspects of exclusivity to be provided in certain circumstances or for rights to be provided without the possibility of reservations, and have therefore left the issue to future resolution.

13. *Agreed statement concerning Article 15:* It is understood that Article 15 does not prevent the granting of the right conferred by this Article to performers of folklore and producers of phonograms recording folklore where such phonograms have not been published for commercial gain.

14. *Agreed statement concerning Articles 7, 11 and 16:* The reproduction right, as set out in Articles 7 and 11, and the exceptions permitted thereunder through Article 16, fully apply in the digital environment, in particular to the use of performances and phonograms in digital form. It is understood that the storage of a protected performance or phonogram in digital form in an electronic medium constitutes a reproduction within the meaning of these Articles.

15. *Agreed statement concerning Article 16:* The agreed statement concerning Article 10 (on Limitations and Exceptions) of the WIPO Copyright Treaty is applicable *mutatis mutandis* also to Article 16 (on Limitations and Exceptions) of the WIPO Performances and Phonograms Treaty. [The text of the agreed statement concerning Article 10 of the WCT reads as follows: "It is understood that the provisions of Article 10 permit Contracting Parties to carry forward and appropriately extend into the digital environment limitations and exceptions in their national laws which have been considered acceptable under the Berne Convention. Similarly, these provisions should be understood to permit Contracting Parties to devise new exceptions and limitations that are appropriate in

the digital network environment. It is also understood that Article 10(2) neither reduces nor extends the scope of applicability of the limitations and exceptions permitted by the Berne Convention."]

16. *Agreed statement concerning Article 19:* The agreed statement concerning Article 12 (on Obligations concerning Rights Management Information) of the WIPO Copyright Treaty is applicable *mutatis mutandis* also to Article 19 (on Obligations concerning Rights Management Information) of the WIPO Performances and Phonograms Treaty. [The text of the agreed statement concerning Article 12 of the WCT reads as follows: "It is understood that the reference to 'infringement of any right covered by this Treaty or the Berne Convention' includes both exclusive rights and rights of remuneration. It is further understood that Contracting Parties will not rely on this Article to devise or implement rights management systems that would have the effect of imposing formalities which are not permitted under the Berne Convention or this Treaty, prohibiting the free movement of goods or impeding the enjoyment of rights under this Treaty."]

9

PARTIES TO THE WIPO PERFORMANCES AND PHONOGRAMS TREATY

Status on February 9, 2021

State	Date on which State became party to the Treaty
Afghanistan	February 9, 2021
Albania	May 20, 2002
Algeria	January 31, 2014
Argentina	May 20, 2002
Armenia	March 6, 2005
Australia[1,2]	July 26, 2007
Austria	March 14, 2010
Azerbaijan	April 11, 2006
Bahrain	December 15, 2005
Barbados	December 13, 2019
Belarus	May 20, 2002
Belgium	August 30, 2006[2]
Belize	February 9, 2019
Benin	April 16, 2006
Bosnia and Herzegovina	November 25, 2009
Botswana	January 27, 2005
Brunei Darussalam	May 2, 2017
Bulgaria	May 20, 2002
Burkina Faso	May 20, 2002
Cabo Verde	May 22, 2019

[1.] Pursuant to Article 15(3), Australia will not apply the provisions of Article 15(1) in respect of:

(a) the use of phonograms for (i) radio broadcasting, and (ii) radio communication to the public within the meaning of the first sentence of Article 2(g), and

(b) the communication to the public of phonograms by way of making the sounds of the phonograms audible to the public by means of the operation of equipment to receive a broadcast or other transmission of the phonograms.

[2.] In accordance with Article 3(3) of the Treaty, this State has declared that it will not apply the criterion of publication concerning the protection of phonograms.

State	Date on which State became party to the Treaty
Canada[3, 4, 5]	August 13, 2014
Chile[6]	May 20, 2002
China[7, 8, 9]	June 9, 2007
Colombia	May 20, 2002
Cook Islands	June 19, 2019
Costa Rica	May 20, 2002
Croatia	May 20, 2002
Cyprus	December 2, 2005
Czech Republic	May 20, 2002
Denmark[2, 10]	March 14, 2010
Dominican Republic	January 10, 2006
Ecuador	May 20, 2002
El Salvador	May 20, 2002
Estonia	March 14, 2010
European Union	March 14, 2010
Finland[11]	March 14, 2010
France[2]	March 14, 2010

[3.] Pursuant to Article 3(3) of the Treaty, Canada will not apply the criterion of fixation with regard to exclusive rights of producers of phonograms.

[4.] Pursuant to Article 3(3) of the Treaty, Canada will not apply the criterion of publication with regard to the remuneration right of Article 15(1) of the Treaty.

[5.] Pursuant to Article 15(3) of the Treaty, Canada will not apply Article 15(1) of the Treaty with regard to the retransmission of phonograms.

[6.] Pursuant to Article 15, paragraph 3 of the Treaty, the Republic of Chile will apply the provisions of Article 15, paragraph 1 of the Treaty only in respect of direct uses of phonograms published for commercial purposes for broadcasting or for any communication to the public. Pursuant to Article 15, paragraph 3 of the Treaty, as regards phonograms the producer or performer of which is a national of another Contracting Party which has made a declaration under Article 15, paragraph 3 of the Treaty, the Republic of Chile will apply, notwithstanding the provisions of the preceding declaration, the provisions of Article 15, paragraph 1 of the Treaty to the extent that Party grants the protection provided for by the provisions of Article 15, paragraph 1 of the Treaty.

[7.] Pursuant to Article 15(3) of the Treaty, the People's Republic of China will not apply the provisions of Article 15(1).

[8.] In accordance with the Basic Law of Hong Kong, China, the Government of the People's Republic of China has decided that the Treaty will apply to Hong Kong, China, with effect from October 1, 2008. Hong Kong, China, does not consider itself bound by Article 15(1) of the Treaty with regard to the right of the performers. With respect to the right of the producers of phonograms stipulated in Article 15(1) of the Treaty, relevant laws of Hong Kong, China shall apply.

[9.] In accordance with the Basic Law of the Macao, China, the Government of the People's Republic of China decides that the Treaty shall apply to Macao, China. Macao, China, shall not be bound by Article 15(1) of the Treaty with regard to the right of producers of phonograms. With respect to the right of performers stipulated in Article 15(1) of the Treaty, relevant laws of Macao, China, shall apply.

[10.] Applicable to the Faroe Islands as of April 30, 2018.

[11.] Pursuant to Article 3(3) of the Treaty the Republic of Finland, availing itself of the possibilities provided in Article 5(3) of the Rome Convention, declares that it will not apply the criterion of publication.

State	Date on which State became party to the Treaty
Gabon	May 20, 2002
Georgia	May 20, 2002
Germany[24]	March 14, 2010
Ghana	February 16, 2013
Greece	March 14, 2010
Guatemala	January 8, 2003
Guinea	May 25, 2002
Honduras	May 20, 2002
Hungary	May 20, 2002
India[12, 13]	December 25, 2019
Indonesia	February 15, 2005
Ireland	March 14, 2010
Italy	March 14, 2010
Jamaica	June 12, 2002
Japan	October 9, 2002[2, 14]
Jordan	May 24, 2004
Kazakhstan	November 12, 2004
Kyrgyzstan	August 15, 2002
Latvia	May 20, 2002
Liechtenstein	April 30, 2007
Lithuania	May 20, 2002
Luxembourg	March 14, 2010
Madagascar	February 24, 2015
Malaysia	December 27, 2012
Mali	May 20, 2002
Malta	March 14, 2010
Mexico	May 20, 2002

[12.] In accordance with Article 3(3) of the Treaty, the Republic of India availing itself of the possibilities provided in Article 5(3) of the Rome Convention, will not apply the criterion of fixation while granting national treatment to phonograms producers.

[13.] In accordance with Article 15(3) of the Treaty, the Republic of India will not apply the provisions of Article 15(1) relating to a single equitable remuneration for performers and producers of phonograms.

[14.] Pursuant to Article 15(3) Japan will apply, as regards phonograms the producer of which is a national of another Contracting Party, the provisions of Article 15(1) to the extent that Contracting Party grants the protection provided for by these provisions; Japan will apply the provisions of Article 15(1) in respect of the direct or indirect use of the phonograms published for commercial purposes for broadcasting, cablecasting or "automatic public transmission of unfixed information"; and in respect of the direct or indirect use of phonograms made available to the public, by wire or wireless means, in such a way that members of the public may access them from a place and at a time individually chosen by them for broadcasting, cablecasting (wire diffusion) or "automatic public transmission of unfixed information".

State	Date on which State became party to the Treaty
Mongolia	October 25, 2002
Montenegro	June 3, 2006
Morocco	July 20, 2011
Netherlands	March 14, 2010
New Zealand[15, 16]	March 17, 2019
Nicaragua	March 6, 2003
Nigeria	January 4, 2018
North Macedonia	March 20, 2005[2, 17]
Oman	September 20, 2005
Panama	May 20, 2002
Paraguay	May 20, 2002
Peru	July 18, 2002
Philippines	October 4, 2002
Poland	October 21, 2003
Portugal	March 14, 2010
Qatar	October 28, 2005
Republic of Korea	March 18, 2009[2, 18, 19]
Republic of Moldova	May 20, 2002
Romania	May 20, 2002
Russian Federation[20]	February 5, 2009

[15.] In accordance with Article 15(3) of the Treaty, the provision of Article 15(1) will not be applied in New Zealand.

[16.] The accession by New Zealand shall extend to Tokelau.

[17.] Pursuant to Article 15(3) of the WPPT, the Republic of Macedonia does not apply the provision on single equitable remuneration for the performers and for the phonogram producers for direct or indirect use of phonograms published for commercial purposes for broadcasting or for any other communication to the public, in relation to the expressed reservation of the then former Yugoslav Republic of Macedonia on Article 16 (1)(a)(i) of the Rome Convention.

[18.] In accordance with Article 15(3) of the Treaty, the Republic of Korea will apply the provision of Article 15(1) thereof in respect of the use of phonograms published for commercial purposes for broadcasting or transmission by wire. Transmission by wire does not include transmission over the Internet.

[19.] In accordance with 15(3) of the Treaty, as regards phonograms the producer or performer of which is a national of another Contracting Party which has made a declaration under Article 15(3) thereof, the Republic of Korea will apply the provisions of Article 15(1) thereof to the extent to which, and to the term for which, the other Contracting Party grants protection to phonograms the producer or performer of which is a national of the Republic of Korea under the provisions of Article 15(1) thereof.

[20.] In accordance with Article 15(3) of the WPPT, the Russian Federation shall not apply the provisions of Article 15(1) of the said Treaty in relation to phonograms, the producer of which is not a citizen or legal person of another Contracting Party; shall limit the protection granted, in accordance with Article 15(1) of the WPPT, in relation to phonograms, the producer of which is a citizen or legal person of another Contracting Party, within the scope and on the conditions provided for by this Contracting Party for phonograms first recorded by a citizen or legal person of the Russian Federation; and In accordance with Article 3(3) of the WPPT, the Russian Federation notifies that when it acceded to the International Convention for the Protection of Performers, Producers of Phonograms and Broadcasting Organisations (Rome Convention) of

State	Date on which State became party to the Treaty
Saint Lucia	May 20, 2002
Saint Vincent and the Grenadines	February 12, 2011
San Marino	September 2, 2020
Sao Tome and Principe	April 27, 2020
Senegal	May 20, 2002
Serbia[21]	June 13, 2003
Singapore	April 17, 2005[22]
Slovakia	May 20, 2002
Slovenia	May 20, 2002
Spain	March 14, 2010
Sweden[23]	March 14, 2010
Switzerland	July 1, 2008[24]
Tajikistan	August 24, 2011
Togo	May 21, 2003
Trinidad and Tobago	November 28, 2008
Turkey	November 28, 2008
Ukraine	May 20, 2002
United Arab Emirates	June 9, 2005
United Kingdom[25]	March 14, 2010
United States of America	May 20, 2002[26]

October 26, 1961, the Russian Federation in accordance with Article 5(3) of the Rome Convention, declared that it shall not apply the fixation criterion provided for in Article 5(1)(b) of the Rome Convention.

[21]. Serbia is the continuing State from Serbia and Montenegro as from June 3, 2006.

[22]. Pursuant to Article 15(3), Singapore will limit the provisions of Article 15(1) in the following ways: (i) Producers of phonograms have the exclusive right to make available to the public a sound recording by means of, or as part of, a digital audio transmission; and (ii) Performers can bring an action of unauthorized communication of a live performance to the public (on a network or otherwise) in such a way that the recording may be accessed by any person from a place and at a time chosen by him. In this context, "communication" includes broadcasting, inclusion in a cable programme service and the making available of the live performance in such a way that the performance may be accessed by any person from a place and at a time chosen by him.

[23]. In accordance with Article 3(3) of WPPT, the Kingdom of Sweden has declared that it will not apply the criterion of publication, with the exception of the reproduction right for phonogram producers.

[24]. In accordance with Article 3(3) of the Treaty, this State has declared that it will not apply the criterion of fixation concerning the protection of phonograms.

[25]. The United Kingdom extended the application of the Treaty to the territories of the Bailiwick of Guernsey and the Isle of Man with effect from January 1, 2021.

[26]. Pursuant to Article 15(3) of the WIPO Performances and Phonograms Treaty, the United States will apply the provisions of Article 15(1) of the WIPO Performances and Phonograms Treaty

State	Date on which State became party to the Treaty
Uruguay	August 28, 2008
Uzbekistan	July 17, 2019
Vanuatu	August 6, 2020

Total: 108 States

---

only in respect of certain acts of broadcasting and communication to the public by digital means for which a direct or indirect fee is charged for reception, and for other retransmissions and digital phonorecord deliveries, as provided under the United States law.

10

ROME CONVENTION INTERNATIONAL CONVENTION FOR THE PROTECTION OF PERFORMERS, PRODUCERS OF PHONOGRAMS AND BROADCASTING ORGANIZATIONS

Done at Rome on October 26, 1961

The Contracting States, moved by the desire to protect the rights of performers, producers of phonograms, and broadcasting organisations,

Have agreed as follows:

Article 1

Protection granted under this Convention shall leave intact and shall in no way affect the protection of copyright in literary and artistic works. Consequently, no provision of this Convention may be interpreted as prejudicing such protection.

Article 2

1. For the purposes of this Convention, national treatment shall mean the treatment accorded by the domestic law of the Contracting State in which protection is claimed:

   (a) to performers who are its nationals, as regards performances taking place, broadcast, or first fixed, on its territory;

   (b) to producers of phonograms who are its nationals, as regards phonograms first fixed or first published on its territory;

   (c) to broadcasting organisations which have their headquarters on its territory, as regards broadcasts transmitted from transmitters situated on its territory.

2. National treatment shall be subject to the protection specifically guaranteed, and the limitations specifically provided for, in this Convention.

Article 3

For the purposes of this Convention:

(a) "performers" means actors, singers, musicians, dancers, and other persons who act, sing, deliver, declaim, play in, or otherwise perform literary or artistic works;

(b) "phonogram" means any exclusively aural fixation of sounds of a performance or of other sounds;

(c) "producer of phonograms" means the person who, or the legal entity which, first fixes the sounds of a performance or other sounds;

(d) "publication" means the offering of copies of a phonogram to the public in reasonable quantity;

(e) "reproduction" means the making of a copy or copies of a fixation;

(f) "broadcasting" means the transmission by wireless means for public reception of sounds or of images and sounds;

(g) "rebroadcasting" means the simultaneous broadcasting by one broadcasting organisation of the broadcast of another broadcasting organisation.

Article 4

Each Contracting State shall grant national treatment to performers if any of the following conditions is met:

(a) the performance takes place in another Contracting State;

(b) the performance is incorporated in a phonogram which is protected under Article 5 of this Convention;

(c) the performance, not being fixed on a phonogram, is carried by a broadcast which is protected by Article 6 of this Convention.

Article 5

1. Each Contracting State shall grant national treatment to producers of phonograms if any of the following conditions is met:

(a) the producer of the phonogram is a national of another Contracting State (criterion of nationality);

(b) the first fixation of the sound was made in another Contracting State (criterion of fixation);

(c) the phonogram was first published in another Contracting State (criterion of publication).

2. If a phonogram was first published in a non-contracting State but if it was also published, within thirty days of its first publication, in a

Contracting State (simultaneous publication), it shall be considered as first published in the Contracting State.

3. By means of a notification deposited with the Secretary-General of the United Nations, any Contracting State may declare that it will not apply the criterion of publication or, alternatively, the criterion of fixation. Such notification may be deposited at the time of ratification, acceptance or accession, or at any time thereafter; in the last case, it shall become effective six months after it has been deposited.

Article 6

1. Each Contracting State shall grant national treatment to broadcasting organisations if either of the following conditions is met:

   (a) the headquarters of the broadcasting organisation is situated in another Contracting State;

   (b) the broadcast was transmitted from a transmitter situated in another Contracting State.

2. By means of a notification deposited with the Secretary-General of the United Nations, any Contracting State may declare that it will protect broadcasts only if the headquarters of the broadcasting organisation is situated in another Contracting State and the broadcast was transmitted from a transmitter situated in the same Contracting State. Such notification may be deposited at the time of ratification, acceptance or accession, or at any time thereafter; in the last case, it shall become effective six months after it has been deposited.

Article 7

1. The protection provided for performers by this Convention shall include the possibility of preventing:

   (a) the broadcasting and the communication to the public, without their consent, of their performance, except where the performance used in the broadcasting or the public communication is itself already a broadcast performance or is made from a fixation;

   (b) the fixation, without their consent, of their unfixed performance;

   (c) the reproduction, without their consent, of a fixation of their performance:

      (i) if the original fixation itself was made without their consent;

      (ii) if the reproduction is made for purposes different from those for which the performers gave their consent;

      (iii) if the original fixation was made in accordance with the provisions of Article 15, and the reproduction is made for purposes different from those referred to in those provisions.

2.

(1) If broadcasting was consented to by the performers, it shall be a matter for the domestic law of the Contracting State where protection is claimed to regulate the protection against rebroadcasting, fixation for broadcasting purposes and the reproduction of such fixation for broadcasting purposes.

(2) The terms and conditions governing the use by broadcasting organisations of fixations made for broadcasting purposes shall be determined in accordance with the domestic law of the Contracting State where protection is claimed.

(3) However, the domestic law referred to in sub-paragraphs (1) and (2) of this paragraph shall not operate to deprive performers of the ability to control, by contract, their relations with broadcasting organisations.

Article 8

Any Contracting State may, by its domestic laws and regulations, specify the manner in which performers will be represented in connection with the exercise of their rights if several of them participate in the same performance.

Article 9

Any Contracting State may, by its domestic laws and regulations, extend the protection provided for in this Convention to artists who do not perform literary or artistic works.

Article 10

Producers of phonograms shall enjoy the right to authorize or prohibit the direct or indirect reproduction of their phonograms.

Article 11

If, as a condition of protecting the rights of producers of phonograms, or of performers, or both, in relation to phonograms, a Contracting State, under its domestic law, requires compliance with formalities, these shall be considered as fulfilled if all the copies in commerce of the published phonogram or their containers bear a notice consisting of the symbol (P), accompanied by the year date of the first publication, placed in such a manner as to give reasonable notice of claim of protection; and if the copies or their containers do not identify the producer or the licensee of the producer (by carrying his name, trade mark or other appropriate designation), the notice shall also include the name of the owner of the rights of the producer; and, furthermore, if the copies or their containers do not identify the principal performers, the notice shall also include the name of the person who, in the country in which the fixation was effected, owns the rights of such performers.

Article 12

If a phonogram published for commercial purposes, or a reproduction of such phonogram, is used directly for broadcasting or for any communication to the public, a single equitable remuneration shall be paid by the user to the performers, or to the producers of the phonograms, or to both. Domestic law may, in the absence of agreement between these parties, lay down the conditions as to the sharing of this remuneration.

Article 13

Broadcasting organisations shall enjoy the right to authorize or prohibit:

(a) the rebroadcasting of their broadcasts;

(b) the fixation of their broadcasts;

(c) the reproduction:

> (i) of fixations, made without their consent, of their broadcasts;
>
> (ii) of fixations, made in accordance with the provisions of Article 15, of their broadcasts, if the reproduction is made for purposes different from those referred to in those provisions;

(d) the communication to the public of their television broadcasts if such communication is made in places accessible to the public against payment of an entrance fee; it shall be a matter for the domestic law of the State where protection of this right is claimed to determine the conditions under which it may be exercised.

Article 14

The term of protection to be granted under this Convention shall last at least until the end of a period of twenty years computed from the end of the year in which:

(a) the fixation was made—for phonograms and for performances incorporated therein;

(b) the performance took place—for performances not incorporated in phonograms;

(c) the broadcast took place—for broadcasts.

Article 15

1. Any Contracting State may, in its domestic laws and regulations, provide for exceptions to the protection guaranteed by this Convention as regards:

(a) private use;

(b) use of short excerpts in connection with the reporting of current events;

(c) ephemeral fixation by a broadcasting organisation by means of its own facilities and for its own broadcasts;

(d) use solely for the purposes of teaching or scientific research.

2.   Irrespective of paragraph 1 of this Article, any Contracting State may, in its domestic laws and regulations, provide for the same kinds of limitations with regard to the protection of performers, producers of phonograms and broadcasting organisations, as it provides for, in its domestic laws and regulations, in connection with the protection of copyright in literary and artistic works. However, compulsory licences may be provided for only to the extent to which they are compatible with this Convention.

Article 16

1.   Any State, upon becoming party to this Convention, shall be bound by all the obligations and shall enjoy all the benefits thereof. However, a State may at any time, in a notification deposited with the Secretary-General of the United Nations, declare that:

(a) as regards Article 12:

   (i)   it will not apply the provisions of that Article;

   (ii) it will not apply the provisions of that Article in respect of certain uses;

   (iii) as regards phonograms the producer of which is not a national of another Contracting State, it will not apply that Article;

   (iv) as regards phonograms the producer of which is a national of another Contracting State, it will limit the protection provided for by that Article to the extent to which, and to the term for which, the latter State grants protection to phonograms first fixed by a national of the State making the declaration; however, the fact that the Contracting State of which the producer is a national does not grant the protection to the same beneficiary or beneficiaries as the State making the declaration shall not be considered as a difference in the extent of the protection;

(b) as regards Article 13, it will not apply item *(d)* of that Article; if a Contracting State makes such a declaration, the other Contracting States shall not be obliged to grant the right referred to in Article 13, item *(d)*, to broadcasting organisations whose headquarters are in that State.

2.   If the notification referred to in paragraph 1 of this Article is made after the date of the deposit of the instrument of ratification, acceptance or

accession, the declaration will become effective six months after it has been deposited.

Article 17

Any State which, on October 26, 1961, grants protection to producers of phonograms solely on the basis of the criterion of fixation may, by a notification deposited with the Secretary-General of the United Nations at the time of ratification, acceptance or accession, declare that it will apply, for the purposes of Article 5, the criterion of fixation alone and, for the purposes of paragraph 1(a)(iii) and (iv) of Article 16, the criterion of fixation instead of the criterion of nationality.

Article 18

Any State which has deposited a notification under paragraph 3 of Article 5, paragraph 2 of Article 6, paragraph 1 of Article 16 or Article 17, may, by a further notification deposited with the Secretary-General of the United Nations, reduce its scope or withdraw it.

Article 19

Notwithstanding anything in this Convention, once a performer has consented to the incorporation of his performance in a visual or audio-visual fixation, Article 7 shall have no further application.

Article 20

1. This Convention shall not prejudice rights acquired in any Contracting State before the date of coming into force of this Convention for that State.

2. No Contracting State shall be bound to apply the provisions of this Convention to performances or broadcasts which took place, or to phonograms which were fixed, before the date of coming into force of this Convention for that State.

Article 21

The protection provided for in this Convention shall not prejudice any protection otherwise secured to performers, producers of phonograms and broadcasting organisations.

Article 22

Contracting States reserve the right to enter into special agreements among themselves in so far as such agreements grant to performers, producers of phonograms or broadcasting organisations more extensive rights than those granted by this Convention or contain other provisions not contrary to this Convention.

Article 23

This Convention shall be deposited with the Secretary-General of the United Nations. It shall be open until June 30, 1962, for signature by any State invited to the Diplomatic Conference on the International Protection of Performers, Producers of Phonograms and Broadcasting Organisations which is a party to the Universal Copyright Convention or a member of the International Union for the Protection of Literary and Artistic Works.

Article 24

1.   This Convention shall be subject to ratification or acceptance by the signatory States.

2.   This Convention shall be open for accession by any State invited to the Conference referred to in Article 23, and by any State Member of the United Nations, provided that in either case such State is a party to the Universal Copyright Convention or a member of the International Union for the Protection of Literary and Artistic Works.

3.   Ratification, acceptance or accession shall be effected by the deposit of an instrument to that effect with the Secretary-General of the United Nations.

Article 25

1.   This Convention shall come into force three months after the date of deposit of the sixth instrument of ratification, acceptance or accession.

2.   Subsequently, this Convention shall come into force in respect of each State three months after the date of deposit of its instrument of ratification, acceptance or accession.

Article 26

1.   Each Contracting State undertakes to adopt, in accordance with its Constitution, the measures necessary to ensure the application of this Convention.

2.   At the time of deposit of its instrument of ratification, acceptance or accession, each State must be in a position under its domestic law to give effect to the terms of this Convention.

Article 27

1.   Any State may, at the time of ratification, acceptance or accession, or at any time thereafter, declare by notification addressed to the Secretary-General of the United Nations that this Convention shall extend to all or any of the territories for whose international relations it is responsible, provided that the Universal Copyright Convention or the International Convention for the Protection of Literary and Artistic Works applies to the territory or territories concerned. This notification shall take effect three months after the date of its receipt.

2. The notifications referred to in paragraph 3 of Article 5, paragraph 2 of Article 6, paragraph 1 of Article 16 and Articles 17 and 18, may be extended to cover all or any of the territories referred to in paragraph 1 of this Article.

Article 28

1. Any Contracting State may denounce this Convention, on its own behalf or on behalf of all or any of the territories referred to in Article 27.

2. The denunciation shall be effected by a notification addressed to the Secretary-General of the United Nations and shall take effect twelve months after the date of receipt of the notification.

3. The right of denunciation shall not be exercised by a Contracting State before the expiry of a period of five years from the date on which the Convention came into force with respect to that State.

4. A Contracting State shall cease to be a party to this Convention from that time when it is neither a party to the Universal Copyright Convention nor a member of the International Union for the Protection of Literary and Artistic Works.

5. This Convention shall cease to apply to any territory referred to in Article 27 from that time when neither the Universal Copyright Convention nor the International Convention for the Protection of Literary and Artistic Works applies to that territory.

Article 29

1. After this Convention has been in force for five years, any Contracting State may, by notification addressed to the Secretary-General of the United Nations, request that a conference be convened for the purpose of revising the Convention. The Secretary-General shall notify all Contracting States of this request. If, within a period of six months following the date of notification by the Secretary-General of the United Nations, not less than one half of the Contracting States notify him of their concurrence with the request, the Secretary-General shall inform the Director-General of the International Labor Office, the Director-General of the United Nations Educational, Scientific and Cultural Organization and the Director of the Bureau of the International Union for the Protection of Literary and Artistic Works, who shall convene a revision conference in co-operation with the Intergovernmental Committee provided for in Article 32.

2. The adoption of any revision of this Convention shall require an affirmative vote by two-thirds of the States attending the revision conference, provided that this majority includes two-thirds of the States which, at the time of the revision conference, are parties to the Convention.

3.   In the event of adoption of a Convention revising this Convention in whole or in part, and unless the revising Convention provides otherwise:

(a) this Convention shall cease to be open to ratification, acceptance or accession as from the date of entry into force of the revising Convention;

(b) this Convention shall remain in force as regards relations between or with Contracting States which have not become parties to the revising Convention.

Article 30

Any dispute which may arise between two or more Contracting States concerning the interpretation or application of this Convention and which is not settled by negotiation shall, at the request of any one of the parties to the dispute, be referred to the International Court of Justice for decision, unless they agree to another mode of settlement.

Article 31

Without prejudice to the provisions of paragraph 3 of Article 5, paragraph 2 of Article 6, paragraph 1 of Article 16 and Article 17, no reservation may be made to this Convention.

Article 32

1.   An Intergovernmental Committee is hereby established with the following duties:

(a) to study questions concerning the application and operation of this Convention; and

(b) to collect proposals and to prepare documentation for possible revision of this Convention.

2.   The Committee shall consist of representatives of the Contracting States, chosen with due regard to equitable geographical distribution. The number of members shall be six if there are twelve Contracting States or less, nine if there are thirteen to eighteen Contracting States and twelve if there are more than eighteen Contracting States.

3.   The Committee shall be constituted twelve months after the Convention comes into force by an election organized among the Contracting States, each of which shall have one vote, by the Director-General of the International Labor Office, the Director-General of the United Nations Educational, Scientific and Cultural Organization and the Director of the Bureau of the International Union for the Protection of Literary and Artistic Works, in accordance with rules previously approved by a majority of all Contracting States.

4.   The Committee shall elect its Chairman and officers. It shall establish its own rules of procedure. These rules shall in particular provide

for the future operation of the Committee and for a method of selecting its members for the future in such a way as to ensure rotation among the various Contracting States.

5. Officials of the International Labor Office, the United Nations Educational, Scientific and Cultural Organization and the Bureau of the International Union for the Protection of Literary and Artistic Works, designated by the Directors-General and the Director thereof, shall constitute the Secretariat of the Committee.

6. Meetings of the Committee, which shall be convened whenever a majority of its members deems it necessary, shall be held successively at the headquarters of the International Labor Office, the United Nations Educational, Scientific and Cultural Organization and the Bureau of the International Union for the Protection of Literary and Artistic Works.

7. Expenses of members of the Committee shall be borne by their respective Governments.

Article 33

1. The present Convention is drawn up in English, French and Spanish, the three texts being equally authentic.

2. In addition, official texts of the present Convention shall be drawn up in German, Italian and Portuguese.

Article 34

1. The Secretary-General of the United Nations shall notify the States invited to the Conference referred to in Article 23 and every State Member of the United Nations, as well as the Director-General of the International Labor Office, the Director-General of the United Nations Educational, Scientific and Cultural Organization and the Director of the Bureau of the International Union for the Protection of Literary and Artistic Works:

(a) of the deposit of each instrument of ratification, acceptance or accession;

(b) of the date of entry into force of the Convention;

(c) of all notifications, declarations or communications provided for in this Convention;

(d) if any of the situations referred to in paragraphs 4 and 5 of Article 28 arise.

2. The Secretary-General of the United Nations shall also notify the Director-General of the International Labor Office, the Director-General of the United Nations Educational, Scientific and Cultural Organization and the Director of the Bureau of the International Union for the Protection of Literary and Artistic Works of the requests communicated to him in

accordance with Article 29, as well as of any communication received from the Contracting States concerning the revision of the Convention.

IN FAITH WHEREOF, the undersigned, being duly authorised thereto, have signed this Convention.

DONE at Rome, this twenty-sixth day of October 1961, in a single copy in the English, French and Spanish languages. Certified true copies shall be delivered by the Secretary-General of the United Nations to all the States invited to the Conference referred to in Article 23 and to every State Member of the United Nations, as well as to the Director-General of the International Labor Office, the Director-General of the United Nations Educational, Scientific and Cultural Organization and the Director of the Bureau of the International Union for the Protection of Literary and Artistic Works.

11

PARTIES TO THE ROME CONVENTION

Status on September 15, 2020

State	Date on which State became party to the Treaty
Albania	September 1, 2000
Algeria	April 22, 2007
Andorra	May 25, 2004
Argentina	March 2, 1992
Armenia	January 31, 2003
Australia[1]	September 30, 1992

[1.] The instruments of ratification or accession, or subsequent notifications, deposited with the Secretary-General of the United Nations by the following States contain declarations made under the articles mentioned hereafter (with reference to publication in *Le Droit d'auteur* (Copyright) for the years 1962 to 1964, in *Copyright* for the years 1965 to 1994, in *Industrial Property and Copyright* until May 1998 and, in *Intellectual Property Laws and Treaties* from June 1998 until December 2001):

Australia, Articles 5(3) (concerning Article 5(1)(c)), 6(2), 16(1)(a)(i) and 16(1)(b) [1992, p. 301];

Austria, Article 16(1)(a)(iii) and (iv) and 1(b) [1973, p. 67];

Belarus, Articles 5(3) (concerning Article 5(1)(b)), 6(2), 16(1)(a)(iii) and (iv);

Belgium, Articles 5(3) (concerning Article 5(1)(c)), 6(2), 16(1)(a)(iii) and (iv) [1999, p. 119];

Bulgaria, Article 16(1)(a)(iii) and (iv) [1995, p. 262];

Canada, Article 5(3) (concerning Articles 5(1)(b) and (c)), 6(2) (concerning Article 6(1)) and 16(1)(a)(iv) [1998, p. 42]

Congo, Articles 5(3) (concerning Article 5(1)(c)) and 16(1)(a)(i) [1964, p. 127];

Croatia, Articles 5(3) (concerning Article 5(1)(b)) and 16(1)(a)(iii) and (iv) [2000, p.14];

Czech Republic, Article 16(1)(a)(iii) and (iv) [1964, p. 110];

Denmark, Articles 5(3) (concerning Article 5(1)(c)), 6(2), 16(1)(a)(ii) and (iv) [1965, p. 214];

Estonia, Articles 5(3) (concerning Article 5(1)(c)), and 6(2), and as from October 9, 2003, Article 16(1)(a)(iv);

Fiji, Articles 5(3) (concerning Article 5(1)(b)), 6(2) and 16(1)(a)(i) [1972, pp. 88 and 178];

Finland, Articles 16(1)(a)(i), (ii) and (iv) and 17 [1983, p. 287 and 1994, p. 152];

France, Articles 5(3) (concerning Article 5(1)(c)) and 16(1)(a)(iii) and (iv) [1987, p. 184];

Germany, Articles 5(3) (concerning Article 5(1)(b)) and 16(1)(a)(iv) [1966, p. 237];

Iceland, Articles 5(3) (concerning Article 5(1)(b)), 6(2) and 16(1)(a)(i), (ii), (iii) and (iv) [1994, p. 152];

Ireland, Articles 5(3) (concerning Article 5(1)(b)), 6(2) and 16(1)(a)(ii) [1979, p. 218];

Israel, Articles 5(3) (concerning Article 5(1)(b)), 6(2) (concerning Article 6(1)) and 16(1)(a)(iii), (iv) and 16(1)(b);

Italy, Articles 6(2), 16(1)(a)(ii), (iii) and (iv), 16(1)(b) and 17 [1975, p. 44];

Japan, Articles 5(3) (concerning Article 5(1)(c)) and 16(1)(a)(ii) and (iv) [1989, p. 288];

Latvia, Article 16(1)(a)(iii) [1999, p. 76];

Lesotho, Article 16(1)(a)(ii) and (1)(b) [1990, p. 95];

State	Date on which State became party to the Treaty
Austria[1]	June 9, 1973
Azerbaijan	October 5, 2005
Bahrain	January 18, 2006
Barbados	September 18, 1983
Belarus[1]	May 27, 2003
Belgium[1]	October 2, 1999
Belize	February 9, 2019
Bolivia (Plurinational State of)	November 24, 1993
Bosnia and Herzegovina	May 19, 2009
Brazil	September 29, 1965
Bulgaria[1]	August 31, 1995
Burkina Faso	January 14, 1988
Cabo Verde	July 3, 1997
Canada[1]	June 4, 1998

Liechtenstein, Article 5(3) (concerning Article 5(1)(b)) and Article 16(1)(a)(iii) and (iv) [1999, p. 119];

Lithuania, Article 16(1)(a)(iii) [1999, p. 76];

Luxembourg, Articles 5(3) (concerning Article 5(1)(c)), 16(1)(a)(i) and 16(1)(b) [1976, p. 24];

Monaco, Articles 5(3) (concerning Article 5(1)(c)), 16(1)(a)(i) and 16(1)(b) [1985, p. 422];

Netherlands, Article 16(1)(a)(iii) and (iv) [1993, p. 253];

Niger, Articles 5(3) (concerning Article 5(1)(c)) and 16(1)(a)(i) [1963, p. 155];

Nigeria, Articles 5(3) (concerning Article 5(1)(c)), 6(2) and 16(1)(a)(ii), (iii) and (iv) [1993, p. 253];

North Macedonia, Articles 5(3) (concerning Article 5(1)(c)) and 16(1)(a)(i) [1998, p. 42];

Norway, Articles 6(2) and 16(1)(a)(iii) and (iv) [1978, p. 133; in respect of 16(1)(a)(ii) modified: 1989, p. 288];

Poland, Articles 5(3) (concerning Article 5(1)(c)), 6(2), 16(1)(a)(i), (iii) and (iv) and 16(1)(b) [1997 p. 170];

Republic of Korea, Articles 5(3), 6(2), 16(1)(a)(ii), (iii) and (iv) and 16(1)(b);

Republic of Moldova, Articles 5(3) (concerning Article 5(1)(b)), 6(2), 16(1)(a)(ii), (iii) and (iv) [1996, p. 40];

Romania, Articles 5(3), 6(2), 16(1)(a)(iii) and (iv) [1998, p. 54];

Russian Federation, Articles 5(3) (concerning Article 5(1)(b)), 6(2) and 16(1)(a)(iii) and (iv);

Saint Lucia, Articles 5(3) (concerning Article 5(1)(c)) and 16(1)(a)(iii);

Slovakia, Article 16(1)(a)(iii) and (iv) [1964, p. 110];

Slovenia, Articles 5(3) (concerning Article 5(1)(c)) and 16(1)(a)(i) [1996, p. 318];

Spain, Articles 5(3) (concerning Article 5(1)(c)), 6(2) and 16(1)(a)(iii) and (iv) [1991, p. 221];

Sweden, Article 16(1)(a)(iv) [1962, p. 211; 1986, p. 382];

Switzerland, Articles 5(3) (concerning Article 5(1)(b)) and 16(1)(a)(iii) and (iv) [1993, p. 254];

United Kingdom, Articles 5(3) (concerning Article 5(1)(b)), 6(2) and 16(1)(a)(ii), (iii) and (iv) [1963, p. 244]; the same declarations were made for Gibraltar and Bermuda [1967, p. 36; 1970, p. 108].

State	Date on which State became party to the Treaty
Chile	September 5, 1974
Colombia	September 17, 1976
Congo[1]	May 18, 1964
Costa Rica	September 9, 1971
Croatia[1]	April 20, 2000
Cyprus	June 17, 2009
Czech Republic[1]	January 1, 1993
Denmark[1]	September 23, 1965
Dominica	November 9, 1999
Dominican Republic	January 27, 1987
Ecuador	May 18, 1964
El Salvador	June 29, 1979
Estonia[1]	April 28, 2000
Fiji[1]	April 11, 1972
Finland[1]	October 21, 1983
France[1]	July 3, 1987
Georgia	August 14, 2004
Germany[1]	October 21, 1966
Greece	January 6, 1993
Guatemala	January 14, 1977
Honduras	February 16, 1990
Hungary	February 10, 1995
Iceland[1]	June 15, 1994
Ireland[1]	September 19, 1979
Israel[1]	December 30, 2002
Italy[1]	April 8, 1975
Jamaica	January 27, 1994
Japan[1]	October 26, 1989
Kazakhstan	June 30, 2012
Kyrgyzstan	August 13, 2003
Latvia[1]	August 20, 1999
Lebanon	August 12, 1997
Lesotho[1]	January 26, 1990
Liberia	December 16, 2005
Liechtenstein[1]	October 12, 1999
Lithuania[1]	July 22, 1999
Luxembourg[1]	February 25, 1976
Mexico	May 18, 1964

State	Date on which State became party to the Treaty
Monaco[1]	December 6, 1985
Montenegro[2]	June 3, 2006
Netherlands[1, 3]	October 7, 1993
Nicaragua	August 10, 2000
Niger[1]	May 18, 1964
Nigeria[1]	October 29, 1993
North Macedonia[1]	March 2, 1998
Norway[1]	July 10, 1978
Panama	September 2, 1983
Paraguay	February 26, 1970
Peru	August 7, 1985
Philippines	September 25, 1984
Poland[1]	June 13, 1997
Portugal	July 17, 2002
Qatar	September 23, 2017
Republic of Korea[1]	March 18, 2009
Republic of Moldova[1]	December 5, 1995
Romania[1]	October 22, 1998
Russian Federation[1]	May 26, 2003
Saint Lucia[1]	August 17, 1996
Serbia	June 10, 2003
Slovakia[1]	January 1, 1993
Slovenia[1]	October 9, 1996
Spain[1]	November 14, 1991
Sweden[1]	May 18, 1964
Switzerland[1]	September 24, 1993
Syrian Arab Republic	May 13, 2006
Tajikistan	May 19, 2008
Togo	June 10, 2003
Trinidad and Tobago	March 9, 2020
Turkey	April 8, 2004
Turkmenistan	November 30, 2020
Ukraine	June 12, 2002

[2.] Deposited declaration on October 23, 2006, with effect from June 3, 2006, the date of State succession.

[3.] Accession for the Kingdom in Europe.

State	Date on which State became party to the Treaty
United Arab Emirates	January 14, 2005
United Kingdom[1, 4]	May 18, 1964
Uruguay	July 4, 1977
Venezuela (Bolivarian Republic of)	January 30, 1996
Viet Nam[5]	March 1, 2007

Total Contracting Parties: 96

[4.]   The United Kingdom extended the application of the Rome Convention to the Isle of Man with effect from July 28, 1999.

[5.]   This State has declared that in accordance with Articles 16(1)(a)(i) and 16(1)(b), it will not apply the provisions of Articles 12 and 13(d).

12

EU DATABASE DIRECTIVE (96/9/EC)

THE EUROPEAN PARLIAMENT AND THE COUNCIL OF THE EUROPEAN UNION,

Having regard to the Treaty establishing the European Community, and in particular Article 57 (2), 66 and 100a thereof,

Having regard to the proposal from the Commission (1),

Having regard to the opinion of the Economic and Social Committee (2),

Acting in accordance with the procedure laid down in Article 189b of the Treaty (3),

(1) Whereas databases are at present not sufficiently protected in all Member States by existing legislation; whereas such protection, where it exists, has different attributes;

(2) Whereas such differences in the legal protection of databases offered by the legislation of the Member States have direct negative effects on the functioning of the internal market as regards databases and in particular on the freedom of natural and legal persons to provide on-line database goods and services on the basis of harmonized legal arrangements throughout the Community; whereas such differences could well become more pronounced as Member States introduce new legislation in this field, which is now taking on an increasingly international dimension;

(3) Whereas existing differences distorting the functioning of the internal market need to be removed and new ones prevented from arising, while differences not adversely affecting the functioning of the internal market or the development of an information market within the Community need not be removed or prevented from arising;

(4) Whereas copyright protection for databases exists in varying forms in the Member States according to legislation or case-law, and whereas, if differences in legislation in the scope and conditions of protection remain between the Member States, such unharmonized intellectual property rights can have the effect of preventing the free movement of goods or services within the Community;

(5) Whereas copyright remains an appropriate form of exclusive right for authors who have created databases;

(6)   Whereas, nevertheless, in the absence of a harmonized system of unfair-competition legislation or of case-law, other measures are required in addition to prevent the unauthorized extraction and/or reutilization of the contents of a database;

(7)   Whereas the making of databases requires the investment of considerable human, technical and financial resources while such databases can be copied or accessed at a fraction of the cost needed to design them independently;

(8)   Whereas the unauthorized extraction and/or re-utilization of the contents of a database constitute acts which can have serious economic and technical consequences;

(9)   Whereas databases are a vital tool in the development of an information market within the Community; whereas this tool will also be of use in many other fields;

(10) Whereas the exponential growth, in the Community and worldwide, in the amount of information generated and processed annually in all sectors of commerce and industry calls for investment in all the Member States in advanced information processing systems;

(11) Whereas there is at present a very great imbalance in the level of investment in the database sector both as between the Member States and between the Community and the world's largest database-producing third countries;

(12) Whereas such an investment in modern information storage and processing systems will not take place within the Community unless a stable and uniform legal protection regime is introduced for the protection of the rights of makers of databases;

(13) Whereas this Directive protects collections, sometimes called 'compilations', of works, data or other materials which are arranged, stored and accessed by means which include electronic, electromagnetic or electro-optical processes or analogous processes;

(14) Whereas protection under this Directive should be extended to cover non-electronic databases;

(15) Whereas the criteria used to determine whether a database should be protected by copyright should be defined to the fact that the selection or the arrangement of the contents of the database is the author's own intellectual creation; whereas such protection should cover the structure of the database;

(16) Whereas no criterion other than originality in the sense of the author's intellectual creation should be applied to determine the eligibility of the database for copyright protection, and in particular no aesthetic or qualitative criteria should be applied;

(17) Whereas the term 'database' should be understood to include literary, artistic, musical or other collections of works or collections of other material such as texts, sound, images, numbers, facts, and data; whereas it should cover collections of independent works, data or other materials which are systematically or methodically arranged and can be individually accessed; whereas this means that a recording or an audiovisual, cinematographic, literary or musical work as such does not fall within the scope of this Directive;

(18) Whereas this Directive is without prejudice to the freedom of authors to decide whether, or in what manner, they will allow their works to be included in a database, in particular whether or not the authorization given is exclusive; whereas the protection of databases by the sui generis right is without prejudice to existing rights over their contents, and whereas in particular where an author or the holder of a related right permits some of his works or subject matter to be included in a database pursuant to a non-exclusive agreement, a third party may make use of those works or subject matter subject to the required consent of the author or of the holder of the related right without the sui generis right of the maker of the database being invoked to prevent him doing so, on condition that those works or subject matter are neither extracted from the database nor re-utilized on the basis thereof;

(19) Whereas, as a rule, the compilation of several recordings of musical performances on a CD does not come within the scope of this Directive, both because, as a compilation, it does not meet the conditions for copyright protection and because it does not represent a substantial enough investment to be eligible under the sui generis right;

(20) Whereas protection under this Directive may also apply to the materials necessary for the operation or consultation of certain databases such as thesaurus and indexation systems;

(21) Whereas the protection provided for in this Directive relates to databases in which works, data or other materials have been arranged systematically or methodically; whereas it is not necessary for those materials to have been physically stored in an organized manner;

(22) Whereas electronic databases within the meaning of this Directive may also include devices such as CD-ROM and CD-i;

(23) Whereas the term 'database' should not be taken to extend to computer programs used in the making or operation of a database, which are protected by Council Directive 91/250/EEC of 14 May 1991 on the legal protection of computer programs (1);

(24) Whereas the rental and lending of databases in the field of copyright and related rights are governed exclusively by Council Directive

92/100/EEC of 19 November 1992 on rental right and lending right and on certain rights related to copyright in the field of intellectual property (2);

(25) Whereas the term of copyright is already governed by Council Directive 93/98/EEC of 29 October 1993 harmonizing the term of protection of copyright and certain related rights (3);

(26) Whereas works protected by copyright and subject matter protected by related rights, which are incorporated into a database, remain nevertheless protected by the respective exclusive rights and may not be incorporated into, or extracted from, the database without the permission of the right holder or his successors in title;

(27) Whereas copyright in such works and related rights in subject matter thus incorporated into a database are in no way affected by the existence of a separate right in the selection or arrangement of these works and subject matter in a database;

(28) Whereas the moral rights of the natural person who created the database belong to the author and should be exercised according to the legislation of the Member States and the provisions of the Berne Convention for the Protection of Literary and Artistic Works; whereas such moral rights remain outside the scope of this Directive;

(29) Whereas the arrangements applicable to databases created by employees are left to the discretion of the Member States; whereas, therefore nothing in this Directive prevents Member States from stipulating in their legislation that where a database is created by an employee in the execution of his duties or following the instructions given by his employer, the employer exclusively shall be entitled to exercise all economic rights in the database so created, unless otherwise provided by contract;

(30) Whereas the author's exclusive rights should include the right to determine the way in which his work is exploited and by whom, and in particular to control the distribution of his work to unauthorized persons;

(31) Whereas the copyright protection of databases includes making databases available by means other than the distribution of copies;

(32) Whereas Member States are required to ensure that their national provisions are at least materially equivalent in the case of such acts subject to restrictions as are provided for by this Directive;

(33) Whereas the question of exhaustion of the right of distribution does not arise in the case of on-line databases, which come within the field of provision of services; whereas this also applies with regard to a material copy of such a database made by the user of such a service with the consent of the right holder; whereas, unlike CD-ROM or CD-i, where the intellectual property is incorporated in a material medium, namely an item

of goods, every on-line service is in fact an act which will have to be subject to authorization where the copyright so provides;

(34) Whereas, nevertheless, once the rightholder has chosen to make available a copy of the database to a user, whether by an on-line service or by other means of distribution, that lawful user must be able to access and use the database for the purposes and in the way set out in the agreement with the rightholder, even if such access and use necessitate performance of otherwise restricted acts;

(35) Whereas a list should be drawn up of exceptions to restricted acts, taking into account the fact that copyright as covered by this Directive applies only to the selection or arrangements of the contents of a database; whereas Member States should be given the option of providing for such exceptions in certain cases; whereas, however, this option should be exercised in accordance with the Berne Convention and to the extent that the exceptions relate to the structure of the database; whereas a distinction should be drawn between exceptions for private use and exceptions for reproduction for private purposes, which concerns provisions under national legislation of some Member States on levies on blank media or recording equipment;

(36) Whereas the term 'scientific research' within the meaning of this Directive covers both the natural sciences and the human sciences;

(37) Whereas Article 10 (1) of the Berne Convention is not affected by this Directive;

(38) Whereas the increasing use of digital recording technology exposes the database maker to the risk that the contents of his database may be copied and rearranged electronically, without his authorization, to produce a database of identical content which, however, does not infringe any copyright in the arrangement of his database;

(39) Whereas, in addition to aiming to protect the copyright in the original selection or arrangement of the contents of a database, this Directive seeks to safeguard the position of makers of databases against misappropriation of the results of the financial and professional investment made in obtaining and collection the contents by protecting the whole or substantial parts of a database against certain acts by a user or competitor;

(40) Whereas the object of this sui generis right is to ensure protection of any investment in obtaining, verifying or presenting the contents of a database for the limited duration of the right; whereas such investment may consist in the deployment of financial resources and/or the expending of time, effort and energy;

(41) Whereas the objective of the sui generis right is to give the maker of a database the option of preventing the unauthorized extraction and/or

re-utilization of all or a substantial part of the contents of that database; whereas the maker of a database is the person who takes the initiative and the risk of investing; whereas this excludes subcontractors in particular from the definition of maker;

(42) Whereas the special right to prevent unauthorized extraction and/or re-utilization relates to acts by the user which go beyond his legitimate rights and thereby harm the investment; whereas the right to prohibit extraction and/or re-utilization of all or a substantial part of the contents relates not only to the manufacture of a parasitical competing product but also to any user who, through his acts, causes significant detriment, evaluated qualitatively or quantitatively, to the investment;

(43) Whereas, in the case of on-line transmission, the right to prohibit re-utilization is not exhausted either as regards the database or as regards a material copy of the database or of part thereof made by the addressee of the transmission with the consent of the right holder;

(44) Whereas, when on-screen display of the contents of a database necessitates the permanent or temporary transfer of all or a substantial part of such contents to another medium, that act should be subject to authorization by the rightholder;

(45) Whereas the right to prevent unauthorized extraction and/or re-utilization does not in any way constitute an extension of copyright protection to mere facts or data;

(46) Whereas the existence of a right to prevent the unauthorized extraction and/or re-utilization of the whole or a substantial part of works, data or materials from a database should not give rise to the creation of a new right in the works, data or materials themselves;

(47) Whereas, in the interests of competition between suppliers of information products and services, protection by the sui generis right must not be afforded in such a way as to facilitate abuses of a dominant position, in particular as regards the creation and distribution of new products and services which have an intellectual, documentary, technical, economic or commercial added value; whereas, therefore, the provisions of this Directive are without prejudice to the application of Community or national competition rules;

(48) Whereas the objective of this Directive, which is to afford an appropriate and uniform level of protection of databases as a means to secure the remuneration of the maker of the database, is different from the aim of Directive 95/46/EC of the European Parliament and of the Council of 24 October 1995 on the protection of individuals with regard to the processing of personal data and on the free movement of such data (1), which is to guarantee free circulation of personal data on the basis of harmonized rules designed to protect fundamental rights, notably the right

to privacy which is recognized in Article 8 of the European Convention for the Protection of Human Rights and Fundamental Freedoms; whereas the provisions of this Directive are without prejudice to data protection legislation;

(49) Whereas, notwithstanding the right to prevent extraction and/or re-utilization of all or a substantial part of a database, it should be laid down that the maker of a database or rightholder may not prevent a lawful user of the database from extracting and re-utilizing insubstantial parts; whereas, however, that user may not unreasonably prejudice either the legitimate interests of the holder of the sui generis right or the holder of copyright or a related right in respect of the works or subject matter contained in the database;

(50) Whereas the Member States should be given the option of providing for exceptions to the right to prevent the unauthorized extraction and/or re-utilization of a substantial part of the contents of a database in the case of extraction for private purposes, for the purposes of illustration for teaching or scientific research, or where extraction and/or re-utilization are/is carried out in the interests of public security or for the purposes of an administrative or judicial procedure; whereas such operations must not prejudice the exclusive rights of the maker to exploit the database and their purpose must not be commercial;

(51) Whereas the Member States, where they avail themselves of the option to permit a lawful user of a database to extract a substantial part of the contents for the purposes of illustration for teaching or scientific research, may limit that permission to certain categories of teaching or scientific research institution;

(52) Whereas those Member States which have specific rules providing for a right comparable to the sui generic right provided for in this Directive should be permitted to retain, as far as the new right is concerned, the exceptions traditionally specified by such rules;

(53) Whereas the burden of proof regarding the date of completion of the making of a database lies with the maker of the database;

(54) Whereas the burden of proof that the criteria exist for concluding that a substantial modification of the contents of a database is to be regarded as a substantial new investment lies with the maker of the database resulting from such investment;

(55) Whereas a substantial new investment involving a new term of protection may include a substantial verification of the contents of the database;

(56) Whereas the right to prevent unauthorized extraction and/or re-utilization in respect of a database should apply to databases whose makers are nationals or habitual residents of third countries or to those

produced by legal persons not established in a Member State, within the meaning of the Treaty, only if such third countries offer comparable protection to databases produced by nationals of a Member State or persons who have their habitual residence in the territory of the Community;

(57) Whereas, in addition to remedies provided under the legislation of the Member States for infringements of copyright or other rights, Member States should provide for appropriate remedies against unauthorized extraction and/or re-utilization of the contents of a database;

(58) Whereas, in addition to the protection given under this Directive to the structure of the database by copyright, and to its contents against unauthorized extraction and/or re-utilization under the sui generis right, other legal provisions in the Member States relevant to the supply of database goods and services continue to apply;

(59) Whereas this Directive is without prejudice to the application to databases composed of audiovisual works of any rules recognized by a Member State's legislation concerning the broadcasting of audiovisual programmes;

(60) Whereas some Member States currently protect under copyright arrangements databases which do not meet the criteria for eligibility for copyright protection laid down in this Directive; whereas, even if the databases concerned are eligible for protection under the right laid down in this Directive to prevent unauthorized extraction and/or reutilization of their contents, the term of protection under that right is considerably shorter than that which they enjoy under the national arrangements currently in force; whereas harmonization of the criteria for determining whether a database is to be protected by copyright may not have the effect of reducing the term of protection currently enjoyed by the rightholders concerned; whereas a derogation should be laid down to that effect; whereas the effects of such derogation must be confined to the territories of the Member States concerned,

HAVE ADOPTED THIS DIRECTIVE:

CHAPTER I

SCOPE

Article 1

Scope

1.   This Directive concerns the legal protection of databases in any form.

2.   For the purposes of this Directive, 'database' shall mean a collection of independent works, data or other materials arranged in a systematic or methodical way and individually accessible by electronic or other means.

3.   Protection under this Directive shall not apply to computer programs used in the making or operation of databases accessible by electronic means.

Article 2

Limitations on the scope

This Directive shall apply without prejudice to Community provisions relating to:

(a)   the legal protection of computer programs;

(b)   rental right, lending right and certain rights related to copyright in the field of intellectual property;

(c)   the term of protection of copyright and certain related rights.

CHAPTER II

COPYRIGHT

Article 3

Object of protection

1.   In accordance with this Directive, databases which, by reason of the selection or arrangement of their contents, constitute the author's own intellectual creation shall be protected as such by copyright. No other criteria shall be applied to determine their eligibility for that protection.

2.   The copyright protection of databases provided for by this Directive shall not extend to their contents and shall be without prejudice to any rights subsisting in those contents themselves.

Article 4

Database authorship

1.   The author of a database shall be the natural person or group of natural persons who created the base or, where the legislation of the Member States so permits, the legal person designated as the rightholder by that legislation.

2.   Where collective works are recognized by the legislation of a Member State, the economic rights shall be owned by the person holding the copyright.

3.   In respect of a database created by a group of natural persons jointly, the exclusive rights shall be owned jointly.

Article 5

Restricted acts

In respect of the expression of the database which is protectable by copyright, the author of a database shall have the exclusive right to carry out or to authorize:

(a) temporary or permanent reproduction by any means and in any form, in whole or in part;

(b) translation, adaptation, arrangement and any other alteration;

(c) any form of distribution to the public of the database or of copies thereof. The first sale in the Community of a copy of the database by the rightholder or with his consent shall exhaust the right to control resale of that copy within the Community;

(d) any communication, display or performance to the public;

(e) any reproduction, distribution, communication, display or performance to the public of the results of the acts referred to in (b).

Article 6

Exceptions to restricted acts

1.   The performance by the lawful user of a database or of a copy thereof of any of the acts listed in Article 5 which is necessary for the purposes of access to the contents of the databases and normal use of the contents by the lawful user shall not require the authorization of the author of the database. Where the lawful user is authorized to use only part of the database, this provision shall apply only to that part.

2.   Member States shall have the option of providing for limitations on the rights set out in Article 5 in the following cases:

(a) in the case of reproduction for private purposes of a non-electronic database;

(b) where there is use for the sole purpose of illustration for teaching or scientific research, as long as the source is indicated and to the extent justified by the non-commercial purpose to be achieved;

(c) where there is use for the purposes of public security of for the purposes of an administrative or judicial procedure;

(d) where other exceptions to copyright which are traditionally authorized under national law are involved, without prejudice to points (a), (b) and (c).

3.   In accordance with the Berne Convention for the protection of Literary and Artistic Works, this Article may not be interpreted in such a way as to allow its application to be used in a manner which unreasonably

prejudices the rightholder's legitimate interests or conflicts with normal exploitation of the database.

CHAPTER III

SUI GENERIS RIGHT

Article 7

Object of protection

1.   Member States shall provide for a right for the maker of a database which shows that there has been qualitatively and/or quantitatively a substantial investment in either the obtaining, verification or presentation of the contents to prevent extraction and/or re-utilization of the whole or of a substantial part, evaluated qualitatively and/or quantitatively, of the contents of that database.

2.   For the purposes of this Chapter:

(a) 'extraction' shall mean the permanent or temporary transfer of all or a substantial part of the contents of a database to another medium by any means or in any form;

(b) 're-utilization' shall mean any form of making available to the public all or a substantial part of the contents of a database by the distribution of copies, by renting, by on-line or other forms of transmission. The first sale of a copy of a database within the Community by the rightholder or with his consent shall exhaust the right to control resale of that copy within the Community; Public lending is not an act of extraction or re-utilization.

3.   The right referred to in paragraph 1 may be transferred, assigned or granted under contractual licence.

4.   The right provided for in paragraph 1 shall apply irrespective of the eligibility of that database for protection by copyright or by other rights. Moreover, it shall apply irrespective of eligibility of the contents of that database for protection by copyright or by other rights. Protection of databases under the right provided for in paragraph 1 shall be without prejudice to rights existing in respect of their contents.

5.   The repeated and systematic extraction and/or re-utilization of insubstantial parts of the contents of the database implying acts which conflict with a normal exploitation of that database or which unreasonably prejudice the legitimate interests of the maker of the database shall not be permitted.

Article 8

Rights and obligations of lawful users

1.   The maker of a database which is made available to the public in whatever manner may not prevent a lawful user of the database from extracting and/or re-utilizing insubstantial parts of its contents, evaluated qualitatively and/or quantitatively, for any purposes whatsoever. Where the lawful user is authorized to extract and/or re-utilize only part of the database, this paragraph shall apply only to that part.

2.   A lawful user of a database which is made available to the public in whatever manner may not perform acts which conflict with normal exploitation of the database or unreasonably prejudice the legitimate interests of the maker of the database.

3.   A lawful user of a database which is made available to the public in any manner may not cause prejudice to the holder of a copyright or related right in respect of the works or subject matter contained in the database.

Article 9

Exceptions to the sui generis right

Member States may stipulate that lawful users of a database which is made available to the public in whatever manner may, without the authorization of its maker, extract or re-utilize a substantial part of its contents:

(a)   in the case of extraction for private purposes of the contents of a non-electronic database;

(b)   in the case of extraction for the purposes of illustration for teaching or scientific research, as long as the source is indicated and to the extent justified by the non-commercial purpose to be achieved;

(c)   in the case of extraction and/or re-utilization for the purposes of public security or an administrative or judicial procedure.

Article 10

Term of protection

1.   The right provided for in Article 7 shall run from the date of completion of the making of the database. It shall expire fifteen years from the first of January of the year following the date of completion.

2.   In the case of a database which is made available to the public in whatever manner before expiry of the period provided for in paragraph 1, the term of protection by that right shall expire fifteen years from the first

of January of the year following the date when the database was first made available to the public.

3.   Any substantial change, evaluated qualitatively or quantitatively, to the contents of a database, including any substantial change resulting from the accumulation of successive additions, deletions or alterations, which would result in the database being considered to be a substantial new investment, evaluated qualitatively or quantitatively, shall qualify the database resulting from that investment for its own term of protection.

Article 11

Beneficiaries of protection under the sui generis right

1.   The right provided for in Article 7 shall apply to database whose makers or rightholders are nationals of a Member State or who have their habitual residence in the territory of the Community.

2.   Paragraph 1 shall also apply to companies and firms formed in accordance with the law of a Member State and having their registered office, central administration or principal place of business within the Community; however, where such a company or firm has only its registered office in the territory of the Community, its operations must be genuinely linked on an ongoing basis with the economy of a Member State.

3.   Agreements extending the right provided for in Article 7 to databases made in third countries and falling outside the provisions of paragraphs 1 and 2 shall be concluded by the Council acting on a proposal from the Commission. The term of any protection extended to databases by virtue of that procedure shall not exceed that available pursuant to Article 10.

CHAPTER IV

COMMON PROVISIONS

Article 12

Remedies

Member States shall provide appropriate remedies in respect of infringements of the rights provided for in this Directive.

Article 13

Continued application of other legal provisions

This Directive shall be without prejudice to provisions concerning in particular copyright, rights related to copyright or any other rights or obligations subsisting in the data, works or other materials incorporated into a database, patent rights, trade marks, design rights, the protection of national treasures, laws on restrictive practices and unfair competition, trade secrets, security, confidentiality, data protection and privacy, access to public documents, and the law of contract.

Article 14

Application over time

1.   Protection pursuant to this Directive as regards copyright shall also be available in respect of databases created prior to the date referred to Article 16(1) which on that date fulfil the requirements laid down in this Directive as regards copyright protection of databases.

2.   Notwithstanding paragraph 1, where a database protected under copyright arrangements in a Member State on the date of publication of this Directive does not fulfil the eligibility criteria for copyright protection laid down in Article 3(1), this Directive shall not result in any curtailing in that Member State of the remaining term of protection afforded under those arrangements.

3.   Protection pursuant to the provisions of this Directive as regards the right provided for in Article 7 shall also be available in respect of databases the making of which was completed not more than fifteen years prior to the date referred to in Article 16(1) and which on that date fulfil the requirements laid down in Article 7.

4.   The protection provided for in paragraphs 1 and 3 shall be without prejudice to any acts concluded and rights acquired before the date referred to in those paragraphs.

5.   In the case of a database the making of which was completed not more than fifteen years prior to the date referred to in Article 16(1), the term of protection by the right provided for in Article 7 shall expire fifteen years from the first of January following that date.

Article 15

Binding nature of certain provisions

Any contractual provision contrary to Articles 6(1) and 8 shall be null and void.

Article 16

Final provisions

1.   Member States shall bring into force the laws, regulations and administrative provisions necessary to comply with this Directive before 1 January 1998.

When Member States adopt these provisions, they shall contain a reference to this Directive or shall be accompanied by such reference on the occasion of their official publication. The methods of making such reference shall be laid down by Member States.

2.   Member States shall communicate to the Commission the text of the provisions of domestic law which they adopt in the field governed by this Directive.

3.   Not later than at the end of the third year after the date referred to in paragraph 1, and every three years thereafter, the Commission shall submit to the European Parliament, the Council and the Economic and Social Committee a report on the application of this Directive, in which, inter alia, on the basis of specific information supplied by the Member States, it shall examine in particular the application of the sui generis right, including Articles 8 and 9, and shall verify especially whether the application of this right has led to abuse of a dominant position or other interference with free competition which would justify appropriate measures being taken, including the establishment of non-voluntary licensing arrangements. Where necessary, it shall submit proposals for adjustment of this Directive in line with developments in the area of databases.

Article 17

This Directive is addressed to the Member States.

Done at Strasbourg, 11 March 1996.

For the European Parliament The President K. HAENSCH

For the Council The President L. DINI

13

EU DIRECTIVE ON THE TERM OF PROTECTION OF COPYRIGHT AND CERTAIN RELATED RIGHTS

DIRECTIVE 2006/116/EC OF THE EUROPEAN PARLIAMENT AND OF THE COUNCIL

of 12 December 2006

on the term of protection of copyright and certain related rights, as amended by

DIRECTIVE 2011/77/EU of the European Parliament and of the Council of 27 September 2011

(consolidated text)

THE EUROPEAN PARLIAMENT AND THE COUNCIL OF THE EUROPEAN UNION,

Having regard to the Treaty establishing the European Community, and in particular Articles 47(2), 55 and 95 thereof,

Having regard to the proposal from the Commission,

Having regard to the opinion of the European Economic and Social Committee[1],

Acting in accordance with the procedure laid down in Article 251 of the Treaty[2],

Whereas:

(1) Council Directive 93/98/EEC of 29 October 1993 harmonising the term of protection of copyright and certain related rights[3] has been substantially amended[4]. In the interests of clarity and rationality the said Directive should be codified.

---

[1] Opinion of 26 October 2006 (not yet published in the Official Journal).

[2] Opinion of the European Parliament of 12 October 2006 (not yet published in the Official Journal) and Council Decision of 30 November 2006.

[3] OJ L 290, 24.11.1993, p. 9. Directive as amended by Directive 2001/29/EC of the European Parliament and of the Council (OJ L 167, 22.6.2001, p. 10).

[4] See Annex I, Part A.

(2)   The Berne Convention for the protection of literary and artistic works and the International Convention for the protection of performers, producers of phonograms and broadcasting organisations (Rome Convention) lay down only minimum terms of protection of the rights they refer to, leaving the Contracting States free to grant longer terms. Certain Member States have exercised this entitlement. In addition, some Member States have not yet become party to the Rome Convention.

(3)   There are consequently differences between the national laws governing the terms of protection of copyright and related rights, which are liable to impede the free movement of goods and freedom to provide services and to distort competition in the common market. Therefore, with a view to the smooth operation of the internal market, the laws of the Member States should be harmonised so as to make terms of protection identical throughout the Community.

(4)   It is important to lay down not only the terms of protection as such, but also certain implementing arrangements, such as the date from which each term of protection is calculated.

(5)   The provisions of this Directive should not affect the application by the Member States of the provisions of Article 14*bis*(2)(b), (c) and (d) and (3) of the Berne Convention.

(6)   The minimum term of protection laid down by the Berne Convention, namely the life of the author and 50 years after his death, was intended to provide protection for the author and the first two generations of his descendants. The average lifespan in the Community has grown longer, to the point where this term is no longer sufficient to cover two generations.

(7)   Certain Member States have granted a term longer than 50 years after the death of the author in order to offset the effects of the world wars on the exploitation of authors' works.

(8)   For the protection of related rights certain Member States have introduced a term of 50 years after lawful publication or lawful communication to the public.

(9)   The Diplomatic Conference held in December 1996, under the auspices of the World Intellectual Property Organization (WIPO), led to the adoption of the WIPO Performances and Phonograms Treaty, which deals with the protection of performers and producers of phonograms. This Treaty took the form of a substantial up-date of the international protection of related rights.

(10) Due regard for established rights is one of the general principles of law protected by the Community legal order. Therefore, the terms of protection of copyright and related rights established by Community law cannot have the effect of reducing the protection enjoyed by rightholders in

the Community before the entry into force of Directive 93/98/EEC. In order to keep the effects of transitional measures to a minimum and to allow the internal market to function smoothly, those terms of protection should be applied for long periods.

(11) The level of protection of copyright and related rights should be high, since those rights are fundamental to intellectual creation. Their protection ensures the maintenance and development of creativity in the interest of authors, cultural industries, consumers and society as a whole.

(12) In order to establish a high level of protection which at the same time meets the requirements of the internal market and the need to establish a legal environment conducive to the harmonious development of literary and artistic creation in the Community, the term of protection for copyright should be harmonised at 70 years after the death of the author or 70 years after the work is lawfully made available to the public, and for related rights at 50 years after the event which sets the term running.

(13) Collections are protected according to Article 2(5) of the Berne Convention when, by reason of the selection and arrangement of their content, they constitute intellectual creations. Those works are protected as such, without prejudice to the copyright in each of the works forming part of such collections. Consequently, specific terms of protection may apply to works included in collections.

(14) In all cases where one or more physical persons are identified as authors, the term of protection should be calculated after their death. The question of authorship of the whole or a part of a work is a question of fact which the national courts may have to decide.

(15) Terms of protection should be calculated from the first day of January of the year following the relevant event, as they are in the Berne and Rome Conventions.

(16) The protection of photographs in the Member States is the subject of varying regimes. A photographic work within the meaning of the Berne Convention is to be considered original if it is the author's own intellectual creation reflecting his personality, no other criteria such as merit or purpose being taken into account. The protection of other photographs should be left to national law.

(17) In order to avoid differences in the term of protection as regards related rights it is necessary to provide the same starting point for the calculation of the term throughout the Community. The performance, fixation, transmission, lawful publication, and lawful communication to the public, that is to say the means of making a subject of a related right perceptible in all appropriate ways to persons in general, should be taken into account for the calculation of the term of protection regardless of the

country where this performance, fixation, transmission, lawful publication, or lawful communication to the public takes place.

(18) The rights of broadcasting organisations in their broadcasts, whether these broadcasts are transmitted by wire or over the air, including by cable or satellite, should not be perpetual. It is therefore necessary to have the term of protection running from the first transmission of a particular broadcast only. This provision is understood to avoid a new term running in cases where a broadcast is identical to a previous one.

(19) The Member States should remain free to maintain or introduce other rights related to copyright in particular in relation to the protection of critical and scientific publications. In order to ensure transparency at Community level, it is however necessary for Member States which introduce new related rights to notify the Commission.

(20) It should be made clear that this Directive does not apply to moral rights.

(21) For works whose country of origin within the meaning of the Berne Convention is a third country and whose author is not a Community national, comparison of terms of protection should be applied, provided that the term accorded in the Community does not exceed the term laid down in this Directive.

(22) Where a rightholder who is not a Community national qualifies for protection under an international agreement, the term of protection of related rights should be the same as that laid down in this Directive. However, this term should not exceed that fixed in the third country of which the rightholder is a national.

(23) Comparison of terms should not result in Member States being brought into conflict with their international obligations.

(24) Member States should remain free to adopt provisions on the interpretation, adaptation and further execution of contracts on the exploitation of protected works and other subject matter which were concluded before the extension of the term of protection resulting from this Directive.

(25) Respect of acquired rights and legitimate expectations is part of the Community legal order. Member States may provide in particular that in certain circumstances the copyright and related rights which are revived pursuant to this Directive may not give rise to payments by persons who undertook in good faith the exploitation of the works at the time when such works lay within the public domain.

(26) This Directive should be without prejudice to the obligations of the Member States relating to the time-limits for transposition into

national law and application of the Directives, as set out in Part B of Annex I,

HAVE ADOPTED THIS DIRECTIVE:

Article 1

Duration of authors' rights

1.   The rights of an author of a literary or artistic work within the meaning of Article 2 of the Berne Convention shall run for the life of the author and for 70 years after his death, irrespective of the date when the work is lawfully made available to the public.

2.   In the case of a work of joint authorship, the term referred to in paragraph 1 shall be calculated from the death of the last surviving author.

3.   In the case of anonymous or pseudonymous works, the term of protection shall run for 70 years after the work is lawfully made available to the public. However, when the pseudonym adopted by the author leaves no doubt as to his identity, or if the author discloses his identity during the period referred to in the first sentence, the term of protection applicable shall be that laid down in paragraph 1.

4.   Where a Member State provides for particular provisions on copyright in respect of collective works or for a legal person to be designated as the rightholder, the term of protection shall be calculated according to the provisions of paragraph 3, except if the natural persons who have created the work are identified as such in the versions of the work which are made available to the public. This paragraph is without prejudice to the rights of identified authors whose identifiable contributions are included in such works, to which contributions paragraph 1 or 2 shall apply.

5.   Where a work is published in volumes, parts, instalments, issues or episodes and the term of protection runs from the time when the work was lawfully made available to the public, the term of protection shall run for each such item separately.

6.   In the case of works for which the term of protection is not calculated from the death of the author or authors and which have not been lawfully made available to the public within 70 years from their creation, the protection shall terminate.

7.   The term of protection of a musical composition with words shall expire 70 years after the death of the last of the following persons to survive, whether or not those persons are designated as co-authors: the author of the lyrics and the composer of the musical composition, provided that both contributions were specifically created for the respective musical composition with words.

Article 2

Cinematographic or audiovisual works

1.   The principal director of a cinematographic or audiovisual work shall be considered as its author or one of its authors. Member States shall be free to designate other co-authors.

2.   The term of protection of cinematographic or audiovisual works shall expire 70 years after the death of the last of the following persons to survive, whether or not these persons are designated as co-authors: the principal director, the author of the screenplay, the author of the dialogue and the composer of music specifically created for use in the cinematographic or audiovisual work.

Article 3

Duration of related rights

1.   The rights of performers shall expire 50 years after the date of the performance. However,

—   if a fixation of the performance otherwise than in a phonogram is lawfully published or lawfully communicated to the public within this period, the rights shall expire 50 years from the date of the first such publication or the first such communication to the public, whichever is the earlier,

—   if a fixation of the performance in a phonogram is lawfully published or lawfully communicated to the public within this period, the rights shall expire 70 years from the date of the first such publication or the first such communication to the public, whichever is the earlier.

2.   The rights of producers of phonograms shall expire 50 years after the fixation is made. However, if the phonogram has been lawfully published within this period, the said rights shall expire 70 years from the date of the first lawful publication. If no lawful publication has taken place within the period mentioned in the first sentence, and if the phonogram has been lawfully communicated to the public within this period, the said rights shall expire 70 years from the date of the first lawful communication to the public.

However, this paragraph shall not have the effect of protecting anew the rights of producers of phonograms where, through the expiry of the term of protection granted them pursuant to Article 3(2) of Directive 93/98/EEC in its version before amendment by Directive 2001/29/EEC, they were no longer protected on 22 December 2002.

2a.   If, 50 years after the phonogram was lawfully published or, failing such publication, 50 years after it was lawfully communicated to the public, the phonogram producer does not offer copies of the phonogram for sale in

sufficient quantity or does not make it available to the public, by wire or
wireless means, in such a way that members of the public may access it
from a place and at a time individually chosen by them, the performer may
terminate the contract by which the performer has transferred or assigned
his rights in the fixation of his performance to a phonogram producer
(hereinafter a "contract on transfer or assignment"). The right to terminate
the contract on transfer or assignment may be exercised if the producer,
within a year from the notification by the performer of his intention to
terminate the contract on transfer or assignment pursuant to the previous
sentence, fails to carry out both of the acts of exploitation referred to in that
sentence. This right to terminate may not be waived by the performer.
Where a phonogram contains the fixation of the performances of a plurality
of performers, they may terminate their contracts on transfer or
assignment in accordance with applicable national law. If the contract on
transfer or assignment is terminated pursuant to this paragraph, the
rights of the phonogram producer in the phonogram shall expire.

2b. Where a contract on transfer or assignment gives the performer a
right to claim a non-recurring remuneration, the performer shall have the
right to obtain an annual supplementary remuneration from the
phonogram producer for each full year immediately following the 50th year
after the phonogram was lawfully published or, failing such publication,
the 50th year after it was lawfully communicated to the public. The right
to obtain such annual supplementary remuneration may not be waived by
the performer.

2c. The overall amount to be set aside by a phonogram producer for
payment of the annual supplementary remuneration referred to in
paragraph 2b shall correspond to 20% of the revenue which the phonogram
producer has derived, during the year preceding that for which the said
remuneration is paid, from the reproduction, distribution and making
available of the phonogram in question, following the 50th year after it was
lawfully published or, failing such publication, the 50th year after it was
lawfully communicated to the public.

Member States shall ensure that phonogram producers are required
on request to provide to performers who are entitled to the annual
supplementary remuneration referred to in paragraph 2b any information
which may be necessary in order to secure payment of that remuneration.

2d. Member States shall ensure that the right to obtain an annual
supplementary remuneration as referred to in paragraph 2b is
administered by collecting societies.

2e. Where a performer is entitled to recurring payments, neither
advance payments nor any contractually defined deductions shall be
deducted from the payments made to the performer following the 50th year

after the phonogram was lawfully published or, failing such publication, the 50th year after it was lawfully communicated to the public.

3.   The rights of producers of the first fixation of a film shall expire 50 years after the fixation is made. However, if the film is lawfully published or lawfully communicated to the public during this period, the rights shall expire 50 years from the date of the first such publication or the first such communication to the public, whichever is the earlier. The term 'film' shall designate a cinematographic or audiovisual work or moving images, whether or not accompanied by sound.

4.   The rights of broadcasting organisations shall expire 50 years after the first transmission of a broadcast, whether this broadcast is transmitted by wire or over the air, including by cable or satellite.

Article 4

Protection of previously unpublished works

Any person who, after the expiry of copyright protection, for the first time lawfully publishes or lawfully communicates to the public a previously unpublished work, shall benefit from a protection equivalent to the economic rights of the author. The term of protection of such rights shall be 25 years from the time when the work was first lawfully published or lawfully communicated to the public.

Article 5

Critical and scientific publications

Member States may protect critical and scientific publications of works which have come into the public domain. The maximum term of protection of such rights shall be 30 years from the time when the publication was first lawfully published.

Article 6

Protection of photographs

Photographs which are original in the sense that they are the author's own intellectual creation shall be protected in accordance with Article 1. No other criteria shall be applied to determine their eligibility for protection. Member States may provide for the protection of other photographs.

Article 7

Protection vis-à-vis third countries

1.   Where the country of origin of a work, within the meaning of the Berne Convention, is a third country, and the author of the work is not a Community national, the term of protection granted by the Member States

shall expire on the date of expiry of the protection granted in the country of origin of the work, but may not exceed the term laid down in Article 1.

2.   The terms of protection laid down in Article 3 shall also apply in the case of rightholders who are not Community nationals, provided Member States grant them protection. However, without prejudice to the international obligations of the Member States, the term of protection granted by Member States shall expire no later than the date of expiry of the protection granted in the country of which the rightholder is a national and may not exceed the term laid down in Article 3.

3.   Member States which, on 29 October 1993, in particular pursuant to their international obligations, granted a longer term of protection than that which would result from the provisions of paragraphs 1 and 2 may maintain this protection until the conclusion of international agreements on the term of protection of copyright or related rights.

Article 8

Calculation of terms

The terms laid down in this Directive shall be calculated from the first day of January of the year following the event which gives rise to them.

Article 9

Moral rights

This Directive shall be without prejudice to the provisions of the Member States regulating moral rights.

Article 10

Application in time

1.   Where a term of protection which is longer than the corresponding term provided for by this Directive was already running in a Member State on 1 July 1995, this Directive shall not have the effect of shortening that term of protection in that Member State.

2.   The terms of protection provided for in this Directive shall apply to all works and subject matter which were protected in at least one Member State on the date referred to in paragraph 1, pursuant to national provisions on copyright or related rights, or which meet the criteria for protection under [Council Directive 92/100/EEC of 19 November 1992 on rental right and lending right and on certain rights related to copyright in the field of intellectual property].[5]

3.   This Directive shall be without prejudice to any acts of exploitation performed before the date referred to in paragraph 1. Member

---

[5].   OJ L 346, 27.11.1992, p. 61. Directive as last amended by Directive 2001/29/EC.

States shall adopt the necessary provisions to protect in particular
acquired rights of third parties.

4.   Member States need not apply the provisions of Article 2(1) to
cinematographic or audiovisual works created before 1 July 1994.

5.   Article 3(1) to (2e) in the version thereof in force on 31 October
2011 shall apply to fixations of performances and phonograms in regard to
which the performer and the phonogram producer are still protected, by
virtue of those provisions in the version thereof in force on 30 October 2011,
as at 1 November 2013 and to fixations of performances and phonograms
which come into being after that date.

6.   Article 1(7) shall apply to musical compositions with words of
which at least the musical composition or the lyrics are protected in at least
one Member State on 1 November 2013, and to musical compositions with
words which come into being after that date.

The first subparagraph of this paragraph shall be without prejudice to
any acts of exploitation performed before 1 November 2013. Member States
shall adopt the necessary provisions to protect, in particular, acquired
rights of third parties.

Article 10a

Transitional measures

1.   In the absence of clear contractual indications to the contrary, a
contract on transfer or assignment concluded before 1 November 2013 shall
be deemed to continue to produce its effects beyond the moment at which,
by virtue of Article 3(1) in the version thereof in force on 30 October 2011,
the performer would no longer be protected.

2.   Member States may provide that contracts on transfer or
assignment which entitle a performer to recurring payments and which are
concluded before 1 November 2013 can be modified following the 50th year
after the phonogram was lawfully published or, failing such publication,
the 50th year after it was lawfully communicated to the public.

Article 11

Notification and communication

1.   Member States shall immediately notify the Commission of any
governmental plan to grant new related rights, including the basic reasons
for their introduction and the term of protection envisaged.

2.   Member States shall communicate to the Commission the texts of
the provisions of internal law which they adopt in the field governed by this
Directive.

Article 12

Repeal

Directive 93/98/EEC is hereby repealed, without prejudice to the obligations of the Member States relating to the time-limits for transposition into national law, as set out in Part B of Annex I, of the Directives, and their application.

References made to the repealed Directive shall be construed as being made to this Directive and should be read in accordance with the correlation table in Annex II.

Article 13

Entry into force

This Directive shall enter into force on the twentieth day following that of its publication in the *Official Journal of the European Union.*

Article 14

Addressees

This Directive is addressed to the Member States.

Done at Strasbourg, the 12 December 2006.

For the European Parliament

The President

J. BORRELL FONTELLES

For the Council

The President

M. PEKKARINEN

ANNEX I

PART A

Repealed Directive with its amendment

Council Directive 93/98/EEC (OJ L 290, 24.11.1993, p. 9)	Article 11(2) only
Directive 2001/29/EC of the European Parliament and of the Council (OJ L 167, 22.6.2001, p. 10)	

PART B

List of time-limits for transposition into national law and application

(referred to in Article 12)

Directive	Time-limit for transposition	Date of application
93/98/EEC	1 July 1995 (Articles 1 to 11)	19 November 1993 (Article 12) 1 July 1997 at the latest as regards Article 2(1) (Article 10(5))
2001/29/EC	22 December 2002	

ANNEX II

Correlation Table

Directive 93/98/EEC	This Directive
Articles 1 to 9	Articles 1 to 9
Article 10(1) to (4)	Article 10(1) to (4)
Article 10(5)	—
Article 11	—
Article 12	Article 11(1)
Article 13(1), first subparagraph	—
Article 13(1), second subparagraph	—
Article 13(1), third subparagraph	Article 11(2)
Article 13(2)	—
—	Article 12
—	Article 13
Article 14	Article 14
—	Annex I
—	Annex II

14

CONVENTION FOR THE PROTECTION OF PRODUCERS OF PHONOGRAMS AGAINST UNAUTHORIZED DUPLICATION OF THEIR PHONOGRAMS

of October 29, 1971

The Contracting States,

concerned at the widespread and increasing unauthorized duplication of phonograms and the damage this is occasioning to the interests of authors, performers and producers of phonograms;

convinced that the protection of producers of phonograms against such acts will also benefit the performers whose performances, and the authors whose works, are recorded on the said phonograms;

recognizing the value of the work undertaken in this field by the United Nations Educational, Scientific and Cultural Organization and the World Intellectual Property Organization;

anxious not to impair in any way international agreements already in force and in particular in no way to prejudice wider acceptance of the Rome Convention of October 26, 1961, which affords protection to performers and to broadcasting organizations as well as to producers of phonograms;

have agreed as follows:

Article 1

For the purposes of this Convention:

(a) "phonogram" means any exclusively aural fixation of sounds of a performance or of other sounds;

(b) "producer of phonograms" means the person who, or the legal entity which, first fixes the sounds of a performance or other sounds;

(c) "duplicate" means an article which contains sounds taken directly or indirectly from a phonogram and which embodies all or a substantial part of the sounds fixed in that phonogram;

(d) "distribution to the public" means any act by which duplicates of a phonogram are offered, directly or indirectly, to the general public or any section thereof.

Article 2

Each Contracting State shall protect producers of phonograms who are nationals of other Contracting States against the making of duplicates without the consent of the producer and against the importation of such duplicates, provided that any such making or importation is for the purpose of distribution to the public, and against the distribution of such duplicates to the public.

Article 3

The means by which this Convention is implemented shall be a matter for the domestic law of each Contracting State and shall include one or more of the following: protection by means of the grant of a copyright or other specific right; protection by means of the law relating to unfair competition; protection by means of penal sanctions.

Article 4

The duration of the protection given shall be a matter for the domestic law of each Contracting State. However, if the domestic law prescribes a specific duration for the protection, that duration shall not be less than twenty years from the end either of the year in which the sounds embodied in the phonogram were first fixed or of the year in which the phonogram was first published.

Article 5

If, as a condition of protecting the producers of phonograms, a Contracting State, under its domestic law, requires compliance with formalities, these shall be considered as fulfilled if all the authorized duplicates of the phonogram distributed to the public or their containers bear a notice consisting of the symbol (P), accompanied by the year date of the first publication, placed in such manner as to give reasonable notice of claim of protection; and, if the duplicates or their containers do not identify the producer, his successor in title or the exclusive licensee (by carrying his name, trademark or other appropriate designation), the notice shall also include the name of the producer, his successor in title or the exclusive licensee.

Article 6

Any Contracting State which affords protection by means of copyright or other specific right, or protection by means of penal sanctions, may in its domestic law provide, with regard to the protection of producers of phonograms, the same kinds of limitations as are permitted with respect to the protection of authors of literary and artistic works. However, no compulsory licenses may be permitted unless all of the following conditions are met:

(a) the duplication is for use solely for the purpose of teaching or scientific research;

(b) the license shall be valid for duplication only within the territory of the Contracting State whose competent authority has granted the license and shall not extend to the export of duplicates;

(c) the duplication made under the license gives rise to an equitable remuneration fixed by the said authority taking into account, inter alia, the number of duplicates which will be made.

Article 7

(1) This Convention shall in no way be interpreted to limit or prejudice the protection otherwise secured to authors, to performers, to producers of phonograms or to broadcasting organizations under any domestic law or international agreement.

(2) It shall be a matter for the domestic law of each Contracting State to determine the extent, if any, to which performers whose performances are fixed in a phonogram are entitled to enjoy protection and the conditions for enjoying any such protection.

(3) No Contracting State shall be required to apply the provisions of this Convention to any phonogram fixed before this Convention entered into force with respect to that State.

(4) Any Contracting State which, on October 29, 1971, affords protection to producers of phonograms solely on the basis of the place of first fixation may, by a notification deposited with the Director General of the World Intellectual Property Organization, declare that it will apply this criterion instead of the criterion of the nationality of the producer.

Article 8

(1) The International Bureau of the World Intellectual Property Organization shall assemble and publish information concerning the protection of phonograms. Each Contracting State shall promptly communicate to the International Bureau all new laws and official texts on this subject.

(2) The International Bureau shall, on request, furnish information to any Contracting State on matters concerning this Convention, and shall conduct studies and provide services designed to facilitate the protection provided for therein.

(3) The International Bureau shall exercise the functions enumerated in paragraphs (1) and (2) above in cooperation, for matters within their respective competence, with the United Nations Educational,

Scientific and Cultural Organization and the International Labor Organisation.

Article 9

(1) This Convention shall be deposited with the Secretary-General of the United Nations. It shall be open until April 30, 1972, for signature by any State that is a member of the United Nations, any of the Specialized Agencies brought into relationship with the United Nations, or the International Atomic Energy Agency, or is a party to the Statute of the International Court of Justice.

(2) This Convention shall be subject to ratification or acceptance by the signatory States. It shall be open for accession by any State referred to in paragraph (1) of this Article.

(3) Instruments of ratification, acceptance or accession shall be deposited with the Secretary-General of the United Nations.

(4) It is understood that, at the time a State becomes bound by this Convention, it will be in a position in accordance with its domestic law to give effect to the provisions of the Convention.

Article 10

No reservations to this Convention are permitted.

Article 11

(1) This Convention shall enter into force three months after deposit of the fifth instrument of ratification, acceptance or accession.

(2) For each State ratifying, accepting or acceding to this Convention after the deposit of the fifth instrument of ratification, acceptance or accession, the Convention shall enter into force three months after the date on which the Director General of the World Intellectual Property Organization informs the States, in accordance with Article 13, paragraph (4), of the deposit of its instrument.

(3) Any State may, at the time of ratification, acceptance or accession or at any later date, declare by notification addressed to the Secretary-General of the United Nations that this Convention shall apply to all or any one of the territories for whose international affairs it is responsible. This notification will take effect three months after the date on which it is received.

(4) However, the preceding paragraph may in no way be understood as implying the recognition or tacit acceptance by a Contracting State of the factual situation concerning a territory to which this Convention is made applicable by another Contracting State by virtue of the said paragraph.

Article 12

(1) Any Contracting State may denounce this Convention, on its own behalf or on behalf of any of the territories referred to in Article 11, paragraph (3), by written notification addressed to the Secretary-General of the United Nations.

(2) Denunciation shall take effect twelve months after the date on which the Secretary-General of the United Nations has received the notification.

Article 13

(1) This Convention shall be signed in a single copy in English, French, Russian and Spanish, the four texts being equally authentic.

(2) Official texts shall be established by the Director General of the World Intellectual Property Organization, after consultation with the interested Governments, in the Arabic, Dutch, German, Italian and Portuguese languages.

(3) The Secretary-General of the United Nations shall notify the Director General of the World Intellectual Property Organization, the Director-General of the United Nations Educational, Scientific and Cultural Organization and the Director-General of the International Labor Office of:

(a) signatures to this Convention;

(b) the deposit of instruments of ratification, acceptance or accession;

(c) the date of entry into force of this Convention;

(d) any declaration notified pursuant to Article 11, paragraph (3);

(e) the receipt of notifications of denunciation.

(4) The Director General of the World Intellectual Property Organization shall inform the States referred to in Article 9, paragraph (1), of the notifications received pursuant to the preceding paragraph and of any declarations made under Article 7, paragraph (4). He shall also notify the Director-General of the United Nations Educational, Scientific and Cultural Organization and the Director-General of the International Labor Office of such declarations.

(5) The Secretary-General of the United Nations shall transmit two certified copies of this Convention to the States referred to in Article 9, paragraph (1).

15

PARTIES TO THE GENEVA PHONOGRAMS CONVENTION

Status on September 15, 2019

State	Date on which State became party to the Convention
Albania	June 26, 2001
Argentina	June 30, 1973
Armenia	January 31, 2003
Australia	June 22, 1974
Austria	August 21, 1982
Azerbaijan	September 1, 2001
Barbados	July 29, 1983
Belarus	April 17, 2003
Bosnia and Herzegovina	May 25, 2009
Brazil	November 28, 1975
Bulgaria	September 6, 1995
Burkina Faso	January 30, 1988
Chile	March 24, 1977
China[1]	April 30, 1993
Colombia	May 16, 1994
Costa Rica	June 17, 1982
Croatia	April 20, 2000
Cyprus	September 30, 1993
Czech Republic	January 1, 1993
Democratic Republic of the Congo	November 29, 1977
Denmark	March 24, 1977
Ecuador	September 14, 1974
Egypt	April 23, 1978
El Salvador	February 9, 1979

[1.] The Phonograms Convention applies also to Hong Kong, China with effect from July 1, 1997.

State	Date on which State became party to the Convention
Estonia	May 28, 2000
Fiji	April 18, 1973
Finland[2]	April 18, 1973
France	April 18, 1973
Germany	May 18, 1974
Ghana	February 10, 2017
Greece	February 9, 1994
Guatemala	February 1, 1977
Holy See	July 18, 1977
Honduras	March 6, 1990
Hungary	May 28, 1975
India	February 12, 1975
Israel	May 1, 1978
Italy[2]	March 24, 1977
Jamaica	January 11, 1994
Japan	October 14, 1978
Kazakhstan	August 3, 2001
Kenya	April 21, 1976
Kyrgyzstan	October 12, 2002
Latvia	August 23, 1997
Liberia	December 16, 2005
Liechtenstein	October 12, 1999
Lithuania	January 27, 2000
Luxembourg	March 8, 1976
Mexico	December 21, 1973
Monaco	December 2, 1974
Montenegro[3]	June 3, 2006
Netherlands[4]	October 12, 1993
New Zealand	August 13, 1976
Nicaragua	August 10, 2000
North Macedonia	March 2, 1998
Norway	August 1, 1978

[2]   This State has declared, in accordance with Article 7(4) of the Convention, that it will apply the criterion according to which it affords protection to producers of phonograms solely on the basis of the place of first fixation instead of the criterion of the nationality of the producer.

[3]   Deposited declaration on October 23, 2006, with effect June 3, 2006, the date of State succession.

[4]   Accession for the Kingdom in Europe.

State	Date on which State became party to the Convention
Panama	June 29, 1974
Paraguay	February 13, 1979
Peru	August 24, 1985
Republic of Korea	October 10, 1987
Republic of Moldova	July 17, 2000
Romania	October 1, 1998
Russian Federation	March 13, 1995
Saint Lucia	April 2, 2001
Serbia	June 10, 2003
Slovakia	January 1, 1993
Slovenia	October 15, 1996
Spain	August 24, 1974
Sweden	April 18, 1973
Switzerland	September 30, 1993
Tajikistan	February 26, 2013
Togo	June 10, 2003
Trinidad and Tobago	October 1, 1988
Ukraine	February 18, 2000
United Kingdom	April 18, 1973
United States of America	March 10, 1974
Uruguay	January 18, 1983
Uzbekistan	April 25, 2019
Venezuela (Bolivarian Republic of)	November 18, 1982
Viet Nam	July 6, 2005

(Total: 80 States)

PART 2

PATENTS

16

PARIS CONVENTION FOR THE PROTECTION OF INDUSTRIAL PROPERTY

of March 20, 1883,

as revised at Brussels on December 14, 1900, at Washington on June 2, 1911, at The Hague on November 6, 1925, at London on June 2, 1934, at Lisbon on October 31, 1958, and at Stockholm on July 14, 1967, and as amended on September 28, 1979

Article 1

[Establishment of the Union; Scope of Industrial Property][2]

(1) The countries to which this Convention applies constitute a Union for the protection of industrial property.

(2) The protection of industrial property has as its object patents, utility models, industrial designs, trademarks, service marks, trade names, indications of source or appellations of origin, and the repression of unfair competition.

(3) Industrial property shall be understood in the broadest sense and shall apply not only to industry and commerce proper, but likewise to agricultural and extractive industries and to all manufactured or natural products, for example, wines, grain, tobacco leaf, fruit, cattle, minerals, mineral waters, beer, flowers, and flour.

(4) Patents shall include the various kinds of industrial patents recognized by the laws of the countries of the Union, such as patents of importation, patents of improvement, patents and certificates of addition, etc.

Article 2

[National Treatment for Nationals of Countries of the Union]

(1) Nationals of any country of the Union shall, as regards the protection of industrial property, enjoy in all the other countries of the Union the advantages that their respective laws now grant, or may hereafter grant, to nationals; all without prejudice to the rights specially provided for by this Convention. Consequently, they shall have the same

---

[2] Articles have been given titles to facilitate their identification. There are no titles in the signed (French) text.

protection as the latter, and the same legal remedy against any infringement of their rights, provided that the conditions and formalities imposed upon nationals are complied with.

(2) However, no requirement as to domicile or establishment in the country where protection is claimed may be imposed upon nationals of countries of the Union for the enjoyment of any industrial property rights.

(3) The provisions of the laws of each of the countries of the Union relating to judicial and administrative procedure and to jurisdiction, and to the designation of an address for service or the appointment of an agent, which may be required by the laws on industrial property are expressly reserved.

Article 3

[Same Treatment for Certain Categories of Persons as for Nationals of Countries of the Union]

Nationals of countries outside the Union who are domiciled or who have real and effective industrial or commercial establishments in the territory of one of the countries of the Union shall be treated in the same manner as nationals of the countries of the Union.

Article 4

[A to I. *Patents, Utility Models, Industrial Designs, Marks, Inventors' Certificates:* Right of Priority. G. *Patents:* Division of the Application]

A.—

(1) Any person who has duly filed an application for a patent, or for the registration of a utility model, or of an industrial design, or of a trademark, in one of the countries of the Union, or his successor in title, shall enjoy, for the purpose of filing in the other countries, a right of priority during the periods hereinafter fixed.

(2) Any filing that is equivalent to a regular national filing under the domestic legislation of any country of the Union or under bilateral or multilateral treaties concluded between countries of the Union shall be recognized as giving rise to the right of priority.

(3) By a regular national filing is meant any filing that is adequate to establish the date on which the application was filed in the country concerned, whatever may be the subsequent fate of the application.

B.—Consequently, any subsequent filing in any of the other countries of the Union before the expiration of the periods referred to above shall not be invalidated by reason of any acts accomplished in the interval, in particular, another filing, the publication or exploitation of the invention, the putting on sale of copies of the design, or the use of the mark, and such acts cannot give rise to any third-party right or any right of personal possession. Rights acquired by third parties before the date of the first application that serves as the basis for the right of priority are reserved in accordance with the domestic legislation of each country of the Union

C.—

(1) The periods of priority referred to above shall be twelve months for patents and utility models, and six months for industrial designs and trademarks.

(2) These periods shall start from the date of filing of the first application; the day of filing shall not be included in the period.

(3) If the last day of the period is an official holiday, or a day when the Office is not open for the filing of applications in the country where protection is claimed, the period shall be extended until the first following working day.

(4) A subsequent application concerning the same subject as a previous first application within the meaning of paragraph (2), above, filed in the same country of the Union shall be considered as the first application, of which the filing date shall be the starting point of the period of priority, if, at the time of filing the subsequent application, the said previous application has been withdrawn, abandoned, or refused, without having been laid open to public inspection and without leaving any rights outstanding, and if it has not yet served as a basis for claiming a right of priority. The previous application may not thereafter serve as a basis for claiming a right of priority.

D.—

(1) Any person desiring to take advantage of the priority of a previous filing shall be required to make a declaration indicating the date of such filing and the country in which it was made. Each country shall determine the latest date on which such declaration must be made.

(2) These particulars shall be mentioned in the publications issued by the competent authority, and in particular in the patents and the specifications relating thereto.

(3) The countries of the Union may require any person making a declaration of priority to produce a copy of the application (description, drawings, etc.) previously filed. The copy, certified as correct by the authority which received such application, shall not require any authentication, and may in any case be filed, without fee, at any time within three months of the filing of the subsequent application. They may require it to be accompanied by a certificate from the same authority showing the date of filing, and by a translation.

(4) No other formalities may be required for the declaration of priority at the time of filing the application. Each country of the Union shall determine the consequences of failure to comply with the formalities prescribed by this Article, but such consequences shall in no case go beyond the loss of the right of priority.

(5) Subsequently, further proof may be required. Any person who avails himself of the priority of a previous application shall be required to specify the number of that application; this number shall be published as provided for by paragraph (2), above.

E.—

(1) Where an industrial design is filed in a country by virtue of a right of priority based on the filing of a utility model, the period of priority shall be the same as that fixed for industrial designs

(2) Furthermore, it is permissible to file a utility model in a country by virtue of a right of priority based on the filing of a patent application, and vice versa.

F.—No country of the Union may refuse a priority or a patent application on the ground that the applicant claims multiple priorities, even if they originate in different countries, or on the ground that an application claiming one or more priorities contains one or more elements that were not included in the application or applications whose priority is claimed, provided that, in both cases, there is unity of invention within the meaning of the law of the country.

With respect to the elements not included in the application or applications whose priority is claimed, the filing of the subsequent application shall give rise to a right of priority under ordinary conditions.

G.—

(1) If the examination reveals that an application for a patent contains more than one invention, the applicant may divide the application into a certain number of divisional applications and preserve as the date of each the date of the initial application and the benefit of the right of priority, if any.

(2) The applicant may also, on his own initiative, divide a patent application and preserve as the date of each divisional application the date of the initial application and the benefit of the right of priority, if any. Each country of the Union shall have the right to determine the conditions under which such division shall be authorized.

H.—Priority may not be refused on the ground that certain elements of the invention for which priority is claimed do not appear among the claims formulated in the application in the country of origin, provided that the application documents as a whole specifically disclose such elements.

I.—

(1) Applications for inventors' certificates filed in a country in which applicants have the right to apply at their own option either for a patent or for an inventor's certificate shall give rise to the right of priority provided for by this Article, under the same conditions and with the same effects as applications for patents.

(2) In a country in which applicants have the right to apply at their own option either for a patent or for an inventor's certificate, an applicant for an inventor's certificate shall, in accordance with the provisions of this Article relating to patent applications, enjoy a right of priority based on an application for a patent, a utility model, or an inventor's certificate.

Article 4*bis*

[*Patents:* Independence of Patents Obtained for
the Same Invention in Different Countries]

(1) Patents applied for in the various countries of the Union by nationals of countries of the Union shall be independent of patents obtained for the same invention in other countries, whether members of the Union or not.

(2) The foregoing provision is to be understood in an unrestricted sense, in particular, in the sense that patents applied for during the period of priority are independent, both as regards the grounds for nullity and forfeiture, and as regards their normal duration.

(3) The provision shall apply to all patents existing at the time when it comes into effect.

(4) Similarly, it shall apply, in the case of the accession of new countries, to patents in existence on either side at the time of accession.

(5) Patents obtained with the benefit of priority shall, in the various countries of the Union, have a duration equal to that which they would have, had they been applied for or granted without the benefit of priority.

Article 4*ter*

[*Patents:* Mention of the Inventor in the Patent]

The inventor shall have the right to be mentioned as such in the patent.

Article 4*quater*

[*Patents:* Patentability in Case of Restrictions of Sale by Law]

The grant of a patent shall not be refused and a patent shall not be invalidated on the ground that the sale of the patented product or of a product obtained by means of a patented process is subject to restrictions or limitations resulting from the domestic law.

Article 5

[A. *Patents:* Importation of Articles; Failure to
Work or Insufficient Working; Compulsory Licenses.
B. *Industrial Designs:* Failure to Work; Importation of Articles.
C. *Marks:* Failure to Use; Different Forms; Use by Co-proprietors.
D. *Patents, Utility Models, Marks, Industrial Designs:* Marking]

A.—

(1) Importation by the patentee into the country where the patent has been granted of articles manufactured in any of the countries of the Union shall not entail forfeiture of the patent.

(2) Each country of the Union shall have the right to take legislative measures providing for the grant of compulsory licenses to prevent the abuses which might result from the exercise of the exclusive rights conferred by the patent, for example, failure to work.

(3) Forfeiture of the patent shall not be provided for except in cases where the grant of compulsory licenses would not have been sufficient to prevent the said abuses. No proceedings for the forfeiture or revocation of a patent may be instituted before the expiration of two years from the grant of the first compulsory license.

(4) A compulsory license may not be applied for on the ground of failure to work or insufficient working before the expiration of a period of four years from the date of filing of the patent application or three years from the date of the grant of the patent, whichever period expires last; it shall be refused if the patentee justifies his inaction by legitimate reasons. Such a compulsory license shall be non-exclusive and shall not be transferable, even in the form of the grant of a sub-license, except with that part of the enterprise or goodwill which exploits such license.

(5) The foregoing provisions shall be applicable, mutatis mutandis, to utility models.

B.—The protection of industrial designs shall not, under any circumstance, be subject to any forfeiture, either by reason of failure to work or by reason of the importation of articles corresponding to those which are protected.

C.—

(1) If, in any country, use of the registered mark is compulsory, the registration may be cancelled only after a reasonable period, and then only if the person concerned does not justify his inaction.

(2) Use of a trademark by the proprietor in a form differing in elements which do not alter the distinctive character of the mark in the form in which it was registered in one of the countries of the Union shall

not entail invalidation of the registration and shall not diminish the protection granted to the mark.

(3)   Concurrent use of the same mark on identical or similar goods by industrial or commercial establishments considered as co-proprietors of the mark according to the provisions of the domestic law of the country where protection is claimed shall not prevent registration or diminish in any way the protection granted to the said mark in any country of the Union, provided that such use does not result in misleading the public and is not contrary to the public interest.

D.—No indication or mention of the patent, of the utility model, of the registration of the trademark, or of the deposit of the industrial design, shall be required upon the goods as a condition of recognition of the right to protection.

Article 5*bis*

[*All Industrial Property Rights:* Period of Grace for the Payment
of Fees for the Maintenance of Rights; *Patents:* Restoration]

(1)   A period of grace of not less than six months shall be allowed for the payment of the fees prescribed for the maintenance of industrial property rights, subject, if the domestic legislation so provides, to the payment of a surcharge.

(2)   The countries of the Union shall have the right to provide for the restoration of patents which have lapsed by reason of non-payment of fees.

Article 5*ter*

[*Patents:* Patented Devices Forming Part
of Vessels, Aircraft, or Land Vehicles]

In any country of the Union the following shall not be considered as infringements of the rights of a patentee:

1.   the use on board vessels of other countries of the Union of devices forming the subject of his patent in the body of the vessel, in the machinery, tackle, gear and other accessories, when such vessels temporarily or accidentally enter the waters of the said country, provided that such devices are used there exclusively for the needs of the vessel;

2.   the use of devices forming the subject of the patent in the construction or operation of aircraft or land vehicles of other countries of the Union, or of accessories of such aircraft or land vehicles, when those aircraft or land vehicles temporarily or accidentally enter the said country.

Article 5*quater*

[*Patents:* Importation of Products Manufactured by
a Process Patented in the Importing Country]

When a product is imported into a country of the Union where there exists a patent protecting a process of manufacture of the said product, the patentee shall have all the rights, with regard to the imported product, that are accorded to him by the legislation of the country of importation, on the basis of the process patent, with respect to products manufactured in that country.

Article 5*quinquies*

[*Industrial Designs*]

Industrial designs shall be protected in all the countries of the Union.

Article 6

[*Marks:* Conditions of Registration; Independence of
Protection of Same Mark in Different Countries]

(1) The conditions for the filing and registration of trademarks shall be determined in each country of the Union by its domestic legislation.

(2) However, an application for the registration of a mark filed by a national of a country of the Union in any country of the Union may not be refused, nor may a registration be invalidated, on the ground that filing, registration, or renewal, has not been effected in the country of origin.

(3) A mark duly registered in a country of the Union shall be regarded as independent of marks registered in the other countries of the Union, including the country of origin.

Article 6*bis*

[*Marks:* Well-Known Marks]

(1) The countries of the Union undertake, ex officio if their legislation so permits, or at the request of an interested party, to refuse or to cancel the registration, and to prohibit the use, of a trademark which constitutes a reproduction, an imitation, or a translation, liable to create confusion, of a mark considered by the competent authority of the country of registration or use to be well known in that country as being already the mark of a person entitled to the benefits of this Convention and used for identical or similar goods. These provisions shall also apply when the essential part of the mark constitutes a reproduction of any such well-known mark or an imitation liable to create confusion therewith.

(2) A period of at least five years from the date of registration shall be allowed for requesting the cancellation of such a mark. The countries of

the Union may provide for a period within which the prohibition of use must be requested.

(3)   No time limit shall be fixed for requesting the cancellation or the prohibition of the use of marks registered or used in bad faith.

Article 6*ter*

[*Marks:* Prohibitions concerning State Emblems, Official Hallmarks, and Emblems of Intergovernmental Organizations]

(1)

(a)   The countries of the Union agree to refuse or to invalidate the registration, and to prohibit by appropriate measures the use, without authorization by the competent authorities, either as trademarks or as elements of trademarks, of armorial bearings, flags, and other State emblems, of the countries of the Union, official signs and hallmarks indicating control and warranty adopted by them, and any imitation from a heraldic point of view.

(b)   The provisions of subparagraph (a), above, shall apply equally to armorial bearings, flags, other emblems, abbreviations, and names, of international intergovernmental organizations of which one or more countries of the Union are members, with the exception of armorial bearings, flags, other emblems, abbreviations, and names, that are already the subject of international agreements in force, intended to ensure their protection.

(c)   No country of the Union shall be required to apply the provisions of subparagraph (b), above, to the prejudice of the owners of rights acquired in good faith before the entry into force, in that country, of this Convention. The countries of the Union shall not be required to apply the said provisions when the use or registration referred to in subparagraph (a), above, is not of such a nature as to suggest to the public that a connection exists between the organization concerned and the armorial bearings, flags, emblems, abbreviations, and names, or if such use or registration is probably not of such a nature as to mislead the public as to the existence of a connection between the user and the organization.

(2)   Prohibition of the use of official signs and hallmarks indicating control and warranty shall apply solely in cases where the marks in which they are incorporated are intended to be used on goods of the same or a similar kind.

(3)

(a)   For the application of these provisions, the countries of the Union agree to communicate reciprocally, through the intermediary of the International Bureau, the list of State emblems, and official signs and hallmarks indicating control and warranty, which they desire, or may hereafter desire, to place wholly or within certain limits under the protection of this Article, and all subsequent modifications of such list. Each country of the Union shall in due course make available to the public the lists so communicated. Nevertheless such communication is not obligatory in respect of flags of States.

(b) The provisions of subparagraph *(b)* of paragraph (1) of this Article shall apply only to such armorial bearings, flags, other emblems, abbreviations, and names, of international intergovernmental organizations as the latter have communicated to the countries of the Union through the intermediary of the International Bureau.

(4) Any country of the Union may, within a period of twelve months from the receipt of the notification, transmit its objections, if any, through the intermediary of the International Bureau, to the country or international intergovernmental organization concerned.

(5) In the case of State flags, the measures prescribed by paragraph (1), above, shall apply solely to marks registered after November 6, 1925.

(6) In the case of State emblems other than flags, and of official signs and hallmarks of the countries of the Union, and in the case of armorial bearings, flags, other emblems, abbreviations, and names, of international intergovernmental organizations, these provisions shall apply only to marks registered more than two months after receipt of the communication provided for in paragraph (3), above.

(7) In cases of bad faith, the countries shall have the right to cancel even those marks incorporating State emblems, signs, and hallmarks, which were registered before November 6, 1925.

(8) Nationals of any country who are authorized to make use of the State emblems, signs, and hallmarks, of their country may use them even if they are similar to those of another country.

(9) The countries of the Union undertake to prohibit the unauthorized use in trade of the State armorial bearings of the other countries of the Union, when the use is of such a nature as to be misleading as to the origin of the goods.

(10) The above provisions shall not prevent the countries from exercising the right given in paragraph (3) of Article 6quinquies, Section B, to refuse or to invalidate the registration of marks incorporating, without authorization, armorial bearings, flags, other State emblems, or official signs and hallmarks adopted by a country of the Union, as well as the distinctive signs of international intergovernmental organizations referred to in paragraph (1), above.

Article 6*quater*

[*Marks:* Assignment of Marks]

(1) When, in accordance with the law of a country of the Union, the assignment of a mark is valid only if it takes place at the same time as the transfer of the business or goodwill to which the mark belongs, it shall suffice for the recognition of such validity that the portion of the business or goodwill located in that country be transferred to the assignee, together with the exclusive right to manufacture in the said country, or to sell therein, the goods bearing the mark assigned.

(2) The foregoing provision does not impose upon the countries of the Union any obligation to regard as valid the assignment of any mark the use of which by the assignee would, in fact, be of such a nature as to mislead the public, particularly as regards the origin, nature, or essential qualities, of the goods to which the mark is applied.

Article 6*quinquies*

[*Marks:* Protection of Marks Registered in One Country
of the Union in the Other Countries of the Union]

A.—

(1) Every trademark duly registered in the country of origin shall be accepted for filing and protected as is in the other countries of the Union, subject to the reservations indicated in this Article. Such countries may, before proceeding to final registration, require the production of a certificate of registration in the country of origin, issued by the competent authority. No authentication shall be required for this certificate.

(2) Shall be considered the country of origin the country of the Union where the applicant has a real and effective industrial or commercial establishment, or, if he has no such establishment within the Union, the country of the Union where he has his domicile, or, if he has no domicile within the Union but is a national of a country of the Union, the country of which he is a national.

B.—Trademarks covered by this Article may be neither denied registration nor invalidated except in the following cases:

1. when they are of such a nature as to infringe rights acquired by third parties in the country where protection is claimed;

2. when they are devoid of any distinctive character, or consist exclusively of signs or indications which may serve, in trade, to designate the kind, quality, quantity, intended purpose, value, place of origin, of the goods, or the time of production, or have become customary in the current language or in the bona fide and established practices of the trade of the country where protection is claimed;

3. when they are contrary to morality or public order and, in particular, of such a nature as to deceive the public. It is understood that a mark may not be considered contrary to public order for the sole reason that it does not conform to a provision of the legislation on marks, except if such provision itself relates to public order.

This provision is subject, however, to the application of Article 10*bis*.

C.—

(1) In determining whether a mark is eligible for protection, all the factual circumstances must be taken into consideration, particularly the length of time the mark has been in use.

(2) No trademark shall be refused in the other countries of the Union for the sole reason that it differs from the mark protected in the country of origin only in respect of elements that do not alter its distinctive character and do not affect its identity in the form in which it has been registered in the said country of origin.

D.—No person may benefit from the provisions of this Article if the mark for which he claims protection is not registered in the country of origin.

E.—However, in no case shall the renewal of the registration of the mark in the country of origin involve an obligation to renew the registration in the other countries of the Union in which the mark has been registered.

F.—The benefit of priority shall remain unaffected for applications for the registration of marks filed within the period fixed by Article 4, even if registration in the country of origin is effected after the expiration of such period.

Article 6*sexies*

[*Marks:* Service Marks]

The countries of the Union undertake to protect service marks. They shall not be required to provide for the registration of such marks.

Article 6*septies*

[*Marks:* Registration in the Name of the Agent or Representative of the Proprietor Without the Latter's Authorization]

(1) If the agent or representative of the person who is the proprietor of a mark in one of the countries of the Union applies, without such proprietor's authorization, for the registration of the mark in his own name, in one or more countries of the Union, the proprietor shall be entitled to oppose the registration applied for or demand its cancellation or, if the law of the country so allows, the assignment in his favor of the said registration, unless such agent or representative justifies his action.

(2) The proprietor of the mark shall, subject to the provisions of paragraph (1), above, be entitled to oppose the use of his mark by his agent or representative if he has not authorized such use.

(3) Domestic legislation may provide an equitable time limit within which the proprietor of a mark must exercise the rights provided for in this Article.

Article 7

[*Marks:* Nature of the Goods to which the Mark is Applied]

The nature of the goods to which a trademark is to be applied shall in no case form an obstacle to the registration of the mark.

Article 7*bis*

[*Marks:* Collective Marks]

(1) The countries of the Union undertake to accept for filing and to protect collective marks belonging to associations the existence of which is not contrary to the law of the country of origin, even if such associations do not possess an industrial or commercial establishment.

(2) Each country shall be the judge of the particular conditions under which a collective mark shall be protected and may refuse protection if the mark is contrary to the public interest.

(3) Nevertheless, the protection of these marks shall not be refused to any association the existence of which is not contrary to the law of the country of origin, on the ground that such association is not established in the country where protection is sought or is not constituted according to the law of the latter country.

Article 8

[*Trade Names*]

A trade name shall be protected in all the countries of the Union without the obligation of filing or registration, whether or not it forms part of a trademark.

Article 9

[*Marks, Trade Names:* Seizure, on Importation, etc., of
Goods Unlawfully Bearing a Mark or Trade Name]

(1) All goods unlawfully bearing a trademark or trade name shall be seized on importation into those countries of the Union where such mark or trade name is entitled to legal protection.

(2) Seizure shall likewise be effected in the country where the unlawful affixation occurred or in the country into which the goods were imported.

(3) Seizure shall take place at the request of the public prosecutor, or any other competent authority, or any interested party, whether a natural person or a legal entity, in conformity with the domestic legislation of each country.

(4) The authorities shall not be bound to effect seizure of goods in transit.

(5) If the legislation of a country does not permit seizure on importation, seizure shall be replaced by prohibition of importation or by seizure inside the country.

(6) If the legislation of a country permits neither seizure on importation nor prohibition of importation nor seizure inside the country, then, until such time as the legislation is modified accordingly, these measures shall be replaced by the actions and remedies available in such cases to nationals under the law of such country.

Article 10

[False Indications: Seizure, on Importation, etc.,
of Goods Bearing False Indications as to their
Source or the Identity of the Producer]

(1) The provisions of the preceding Article shall apply in cases of direct or indirect use of a false indication of the source of the goods or the identity of the producer, manufacturer, or merchant.

(2) Any producer, manufacturer, or merchant, whether a natural person or a legal entity, engaged in the production or manufacture of or trade in such goods and established either in the locality falsely indicated as the source, or in the region where such locality is situated, or in the country falsely indicated, or in the country where the false indication of source is used, shall in any case be deemed an interested party.

Article 10*bis*

[*Unfair Competition*]

(1) The countries of the Union are bound to assure to nationals of such countries effective protection against unfair competition.

(2) Any act of competition contrary to honest practices in industrial or commercial matters constitutes an act of unfair competition.

(3) The following in particular shall be prohibited:

1. all acts of such a nature as to create confusion by any means whatever with the establishment, the goods, or the industrial or commercial activities, of a competitor;

2.   false allegations in the course of trade of such a nature as to discredit the establishment, the goods, or the industrial or commercial activities, of a competitor;

3.   indications or allegations the use of which in the course of trade is liable to mislead the public as to the nature, the manufacturing process, the characteristics, the suitability for their purpose, or the quantity, of the goods.

Article 10*ter*

[Marks, Trade Names, False Indications, Unfair Competition: Remedies, Right to Sue]

(1)   The countries of the Union undertake to assure to nationals of the other countries of the Union appropriate legal remedies effectively to repress all the acts referred to in Articles 9, 10, and 10*bis*.

(2)   They undertake, further, to provide measures to permit federations and associations representing interested industrialists, producers, or merchants, provided that the existence of such federations and associations is not contrary to the laws of their countries, to take action in the courts or before the administrative authorities, with a view to the repression of the acts referred to in Articles 9, 10, and 10bis, in so far as the law of the country in which protection is claimed allows such action by federations and associations of that country.

Article 11

[Inventions, Utility Models, Industrial Designs, Marks: Temporary Protection at Certain International Exhibitions]

(1)   The countries of the Union shall, in conformity with their domestic legislation, grant temporary protection to patentable inventions, utility models, industrial designs, and trademarks, in respect of goods exhibited at official or officially recognized international exhibitions held in the territory of any of them.

(2)   Such temporary protection shall not extend the periods provided by Article 4. If, later, the right of priority is invoked, the authorities of any country may provide that the period shall start from the date of introduction of the goods into the exhibition.

(3)   Each country may require, as proof of the identity of the article exhibited and of the date of its introduction, such documentary evidence as it considers necessary.

Article 12

[Special National Industrial Property Services]

(1)   Each country of the Union undertakes to establish a special industrial property service and a central office for the communication to the public of patents, utility models, industrial designs, and trademarks.

(2)   This service shall publish an official periodical journal. It shall publish regularly:

(*a*)   the names of the proprietors of patents granted, with a brief designation of the inventions patented;

(*b*)   the reproductions of registered trademarks.

Article 13

[Assembly of the Union]

(1)

(*a*)   The Union shall have an Assembly consisting of those countries of the Union which are bound by Articles 13 to 17.

(*b*)   The Government of each country shall be represented by one delegate, who may be assisted by alternate delegates, advisors, and experts.

(*c*)   The expenses of each delegation shall be borne by the Government which has appointed it.

(2)

(*a*)   The Assembly shall:

   (i)   deal with all matters concerning the maintenance and development of the Union and the implementation of this Convention;

   (ii)   give directions concerning the preparation for conferences of revision to the International Bureau of Intellectual Property (hereinafter designated as "the International Bureau") referred to in the Convention establishing the World Intellectual Property Organization (hereinafter designated as "the Organization"), due account being taken of any comments made by those countries of the Union which are not hound by Articles 13 to 17;

   (iii) review and approve the reports and activities of the Director General of the Organization concerning the Union, and give him all necessary instructions concerning matters within the competence of the Union;

(iv)   elect the members of the Executive Committee of the Assembly;

(v)   review and approve the reports and activities of its Executive Committee, and give instructions to such Committee;

(vi)   determine the program and adopt the biennial budget of the Union, and approve its final accounts;

(vii) adopt the financial regulations of the Union;

(viii) establish such committees of experts and working groups as it deems appropriate to achieve the objectives of the Union;

(ix)   determine which countries not members of the Union and which intergovernmental and international nongovernmental organizations shall be admitted to its meetings as observers;

(x)   adopt amendments to Articles 13 to 17;

(xi)   take any other appropriate action designed to further the objectives of the Union;

(xii) perform such other functions as are appropriate under this Convention;

(xiii) subject to its acceptance, exercise such rights as are given to it in the Convention establishing the Organization.

(b) With respect to matters which are of interest also to other Unions administered by the Organization, the Assembly shall make its decisions after having heard the advice of the Coordination Committee of the Organization.

(3)

(a) Subject to the provisions of subparagraph (b), a delegate may represent one country only.

(b) Countries of the Union grouped under the terms of a special agreement in a common office possessing for each of them the character of a special national service of industrial property as referred to in Article 12 may be jointly represented during discussions by one of their number.

(4)

(a) Each country member of the Assembly shall have one vote.

(b) One-half of the countries members of the Assembly shall constitute a quorum.

(c) Notwithstanding the provisions of subparagraph *(b)*, if, in any session, the number of countries represented is less than one-half but equal to or more than one-third of the countries members of the Assembly, the Assembly may make decisions but, with the exception of decisions concerning its own procedure, all such decisions shall take effect only if the conditions, set forth hereinafter are fulfilled. The International Bureau shall communicate the said decisions to the countries members of the Assembly which were not represented and shall invite them to express in writing their vote or abstention within a period of three months from the date of the communication. If, at the expiration of this period, the number of countries having thus expressed their vote or abstention attains the number of countries which was lacking for attaining the quorum in the session itself, such decisions shall take effect provided that at the same time the required majority still obtains.

(d) Subject to the provisions of Article 17(2), the decisions of the Assembly shall require two-thirds of the votes cast.

(e) Abstentions shall not be considered as votes.

(5)

(a) Subject to the provisions of subparagraph *(b)*, a delegate may vote in the name of one country only.

(b) The countries of the Union referred to in paragraph (3)*(b)* shall, as a general rule, endeavor to send their own delegations to the sessions of the Assembly. If, however, for exceptional reasons, any such country cannot send its own delegation, it may give to the delegation of another such country the power to vote in its name, provided that each delegation may vote by proxy for one country only. Such power to vote shall be granted in a document signed by the Head of State or the competent Minister.

(6) Countries of the Union not members of the Assembly shall be admitted to the meetings of the latter as observers.

(7)

(a) The Assembly shall meet once in every second calendar year in ordinary session upon convocation by the Director General and, in the absence of exceptional circumstances, during the same period and at the same place as the General Assembly of the Organization.

(b) The Assembly shall meet in extraordinary session upon convocation by the Director General, at the request of the

Executive Committee or at the request of one-fourth of the countries members of the Assembly.

(8) The Assembly shall adopt its own rules of procedure.

Article 14

[Executive Committee]

(1) The Assembly shall have an Executive Committee.

(2)

(a) The Executive Committee shall consist of countries elected by the Assembly from among countries members of the Assembly. Furthermore, the country on whose territory the Organization has its headquarters shall, subject to the provisions of Article 16(7)(b), have an ex officio seat on the Committee.

(b) The Government of each country member of the Executive Committee shall be represented by one delegate, who may be assisted by alternate delegates, advisors, and experts.

(c) The expenses of each delegation shall be borne by the Government which has appointed it.

(3) The number of countries members of the Executive Committee shall correspond to one-fourth of the number of countries members of the Assembly. In establishing the number of seats to be filled, remainders after division by four shall be disregarded.

(4) In electing the members of the Executive Committee, the Assembly shall have due regard to an equitable geographical distribution and to the need for countries party to the Special Agreements established in relation with the Union to be among the countries constituting the Executive Committee.

(5)

(a) Each member of the Executive Committee shall serve from the close of the session of the Assembly which elected it to the close of the next ordinary session of the Assembly.

(b) Members of the Executive Committee may be re-elected, but only up to a maximum of two-thirds of such members.

(c) The Assembly shall establish the details of the rules governing the election and possible re-election of the members of the Executive Committee.

(6)

(a) The Executive Committee shall:

(i) prepare the draft agenda of the Assembly;

    (ii) submit proposals to the Assembly in respect of the draft program and biennial budget of the Union prepared by the Director General;

    (iii) *[deleted]*

    (iv) submit, with appropriate comments, to the Assembly the periodical reports of the Director General and the yearly audit reports on the accounts;

    (v) take all necessary measures to ensure the execution of the program of the Union by the Director General, in accordance with the decisions of the Assembly and having regard to circumstances arising between two ordinary sessions of the Assembly;

    (vi) perform such other functions as are allocated to it under this Convention.

(b) With respect to matters which are of interest also to other Unions administered by the Organization, the Executive Committee shall make its decisions after having heard the advice of the Coordination Committee of the Organization.

(7)

(a) The Executive Committee shall meet once a year in ordinary session upon convocation by the Director General, preferably during the same period and at the same place as the Coordination Committee of the Organization.

(b) The Executive Committee shall meet in extraordinary session upon convocation by the Director General, either on his own initiative, or at the request of its Chairman or one-fourth of its members.

(8)

(a) Each country member of the Executive Committee shall have one vote.

(b) One-half of the members of the Executive Committee shall constitute a quorum.

(c) Decisions shall be made by a simple majority of the votes cast.

(d) Abstentions shall not be considered as votes.

(e) A delegate may represent, and vote in the name of, one country only.

(9) Countries of the Union not members of the Executive Committee shall be admitted to its meetings as observers.

(10) The Executive Committee shall adopt its own rules of procedure.

Article 15

[International Bureau]

(1)

(a) Administrative tasks concerning the Union shall be performed by the International Bureau, which is a continuation of the Bureau of the Union united with the Bureau of the Union established by the International Convention for the Protection of Literary and Artistic Works.

(b) In particular, the International Bureau shall provide the secretariat of the various organs of the Union.

(c) The Director General of the Organization shall be the chief executive of the Union and shall represent the Union.

(2) The International Bureau shall assemble and publish information concerning the protection of industrial property. Each country of the Union shall promptly communicate to the International Bureau all new laws and official texts concerning the protection of industrial property. Furthermore, it shall furnish the International Bureau with all the publications of its industrial property service of direct concern to the protection of industrial property which the International Bureau may find useful in its work.

(3) The International Bureau shall publish a monthly periodical.

(4) The International Bureau shall, on request, furnish any country of the Union with information on matters concerning the protection of industrial property.

(5) The International Bureau shall conduct Studies, and shall provide services, designed to facilitate the protection of industrial property.

(6) The Director General and any staff member designated by him shall participate, without the right to vote, in all meetings of the Assembly, the Executive Committee, and any other committee of experts or working group. The Director General, or a staff member designated by him, shall be ex officio secretary of these bodies.

(7)

(a) The International Bureau shall, in accordance with the directions of the Assembly and in cooperation with the Executive Committee, make the preparations for the conferences of revision of the provisions of the Convention other than Articles 13 to 17.

(b) The International Bureau may consult with intergovernmental and international non governmental organizations concerning preparations for conferences of revision.

(c) The Director General and persons designated by him shall take part, without the right to vote, in the discussions at these conferences.

(8) The International Bureau shall carry out any other tasks assigned to it.

Article 16
[Finances]

(1)

(a) The Union shall have a budget.

(b) The budget of the Union shall include the income and expenses proper to the Union, its contribution to the budget of expenses common to the Unions, and, where applicable, the sum made available to the budget of the Conference of the Organization.

(c) Expenses not attributable exclusively to the Union but also to one or more other Unions administered by the Organization shall be considered as expenses common to the Unions. The share of the Union in such common expenses shall be in proportion to the interest the Union has in them.

(2) The budget of the Union shall be established with due regard to the requirements of coordination with the budgets of the other Unions administered by the Organization.

(3) The budget of the Union shall be financed from the following sources:

(i) contributions of the countries of the Union;

(ii) fees and charges due for services rendered by the International Bureau in relation to the Union;

(iii) sale of, or royalties on, the publications of the International Bureau concerning the Union;

(iv) gifts, bequests, and subventions;

(v) rents, interests, and other miscellaneous income.

(4)

(a) For the purpose of establishing its contribution towards the budget, each country of the Union shall belong to a class, and shall pay its annual contributions on the basis of a number of units fixed as follows:

Class I   25
Class II   20

Class III	15
Class IV	10
Class V	5
Class VI	3
Class VII	1

(b) Unless it has already done so, each country shall indicate, concurrently with depositing its instrument of ratification or accession, the class to which it wishes to belong. Any country may change class. If it chooses a lower class, the country must announce such change to the Assembly at one of its ordinary sessions. Any such change shall take effect at the beginning of the calendar year following the said session.

(c) The annual contribution of each country shall be an amount in the same proportion to the total sum to be contributed to the budget of the Union by all countries as the number of its units is to the total of the units of all contributing countries.

(d) Contributions shall become due on the first of January of each year.

(e) A country which is in arrears in the payment of its contributions may not exercise its right to vote in any of the organs of the Union of which it is a member if the amount of its arrears equals or exceeds the amount of the contributions due from it for the preceding two full years. However, any organ of the Union may allow such a country to continue to exercise its right to vote in that organ if, and as long as, it is satisfied that the delay in payment is due to exceptional and unavoidable circumstances.

(f) If the budget is not adopted before the beginning of a new financial period, it shall be at the same level as the budget of the previous year, as provided in the financial regulations.

(5) The amount of the fees and charges due for services rendered by the International Bureau in relation to the Union shall be established, and shall be reported to the Assembly and the Executive Committee, by the Director General.

(6)

(a) The Union shall have a working capital fund which shall be constituted by a single payment made by each country of the Union. If the fund becomes insufficient, the Assembly shall decide to increase it.

(b) The amount of the initial payment of each country to the said fund or of its participation in the increase thereof shall be a proportion

of the contribution of that country for the year in which the fund is established or the decision to increase it is made.

(c) The proportion and the terms of payment shall be fixed by the Assembly on the proposal of the Director General and after it has heard the advice of the Coordination Committee of the Organization.

(7)

(a) In the headquarters agreement concluded with the country on the territory of which the Organization has its headquarters, it shall be provided that, whenever the working capital fund is insufficient, such country shall grant advances. The amount of these advances and the conditions on which they are granted shall be the subject of separate agreements, in each case, between such country and the Organization. As long as it remains under the obligation to grant advances, such country shall have an ex officio seat on the Executive Committee.

(b) The country referred to in subparagraph *(a)* and the Organization shall each have the right to denounce the obligation to grant advances, by written notification. Denunciation shall take effect three years after the end of the year in which it has been notified.

(8) The auditing of the accounts shall be effected by one or more of the countries of the Union or by external auditors, as provided in the financial regulations. They shall be designated, with their agreement, by the Assembly.

Article 17

[Amendment of Articles 13 to 17]

(1) Proposals for the amendment of Articles 13, 14, 15, 16, and the present Article, may be initiated by any country member of the Assembly, by the Executive Committee, or by the Director General. Such proposals shall be communicated by the Director General to the member countries of the Assembly at least six months in advance of their consideration by the Assembly.

(2) Amendments to the Articles referred to in paragraph (1) shall be adopted by the Assembly. Adoption shall require three-fourths of the votes cast, provided that any amendment to Article 13, and to the present paragraph, shall require four-fifths of the votes cast.

(3) Any amendment to the Articles referred to in paragraph (1) shall enter into force one month after written notifications of acceptance, effected in accordance with their respective constitutional processes, have been received by the Director General from three-fourths of the countries members of the Assembly at the time it adopted the amendment. Any

amendment to the said Articles thus accepted shall bind all the countries which are members of the Assembly at the time the amendment enters into force, or which become members thereof at a subsequent date, provided that any amendment increasing the financial obligations of countries of the Union shall bind only those countries which have notified their acceptance of such amendment.

Article 18

[Revision of Articles 1 to 12 and 18 to 30]

(1)   This Convention shall be submitted to revision with a view to the introduction of amendments designed to improve the system of the Union.

(2)   For that purpose, conferences shall be held successively in one of the countries of the Union among the delegates of the said countries.

(3)   Amendments to Articles 13 to 17 are governed by the provisions of Article 17.

Article 19

[Special Agreements]

It is understood that the countries of the Union reserve the right to make separately between themselves special agreements for the protection of industrial property, in so far as these agreements do not contravene the provisions of this Convention.

Article 20

[Ratification or Accession by Countries
of the Union; Entry Into Force]

(1)

(a)   Any country of the Union which has signed this Act may ratify it, and, if it has not signed it, may accede to it. Instruments of ratification and accession shall be deposited with the Director General.

(b)   Any country of the Union may declare in its instrument of ratification or accession that its ratification or accession shall not apply:

(i)   to Articles 1 to 12, or

(ii)   to Articles 13 to 17.

(c)   Any country of the Union which, in accordance with subparagraph (b), has excluded from the effects of its ratification or accession one of the two groups of Articles referred to in that subparagraph may at any later time declare that it extends the effects of its ratification or accession to that group of Articles. Such declaration shall be deposited with the Director General.

(2)

(a) Articles 1 to 12 shall enter into force, with respect to the first ten countries of the Union which have deposited instruments of ratification or accession without making the declaration permitted under paragraph (1)*(b)*(i), three months after the deposit of the tenth such instrument of ratification or accession.

(b) Articles 13 to 17 shall enter into force, with respect to the first ten countries of the Union which have deposited instruments of ratification or accession without making the declaration permitted under paragraph (1)*(b)*(ii), three months after the deposit of the tenth such instrument of ratification or accession.

(c) Subject to the initial entry into force, pursuant to the provisions of subparagraphs *(a)* and *(b)*, of each of the two groups of Articles referred to in paragraph (1)*(b)*(i) and (ii), and subject to the provisions of paragraph (1)*(b)*, Articles 1 to 17 shall, with respect to any country of the Union, other than those referred to in subparagraphs *(a)* and *(b)*, which deposits an instrument of ratification or accession or any country of the Union which deposits a declaration pursuant to paragraph (1)*(c)*, enter into force three months after the date of notification by the Director General of such deposit, unless a subsequent date has been indicated in the instrument or declaration deposited. In the latter case, this Act shall enter into force with respect to that country on the date thus indicated.

(3) With respect to any country of the Union which deposits an instrument of ratification or accession, Articles 18 to 30 shall enter into force on the earlier of the dates on which any of the groups of Articles referred to in paragraph (1)*(b)* enters into force with respect to that country pursuant to paragraph (2)*(a)*, *(b)*, or *(c)*.

Article 21

[Accession by Countries Outside the Union; Entry Into Force]

(1) Any country outside the Union may accede to this Act and thereby become a member of the Union. Instruments of accession shall be deposited with the Director General.

(2)

(a) With respect to any country outside the Union which deposits its instrument of accession one month or more before the date of entry into force of any provisions of the present Act, this Act shall enter into force, unless a subsequent date has been indicated in the instrument of accession, on the date upon which provisions

first enter into force pursuant to Article 20(2)(a) or (b); provided that:

(i)   if Articles 1 to 12 do not enter into force on that date, such country shall, during the interim period before the entry into force of such provisions, and in substitution therefor, be bound by Articles 1 to 12 of the Lisbon Act,

(ii) if Articles 13 to 17 do not enter into force on that date, such country shall, during the interim period before the entry into force of such provisions, and in substitution therefor, be bound by Articles 13 and 14(3), (4), and (5), of the Lisbon Act.

If a country indicates a subsequent date in its instrument of accession, this Act shall enter into force with respect to that country on the date thus indicated.

(b) With respect to any country outside the Union which deposits its instrument of accession on a date which is subsequent to, or precedes by less than one month, the entry into force of one group of Articles of the present Act, this Act shall, subject to the proviso of subparagraph (a), enter into force three months after the date on which its accession has been notified by the Director General, unless a subsequent date has been indicated in the instrument of accession. In the latter case, this Act shall enter into force with respect to that country on the date thus indicated.

(3) With respect to any country outside the Union which deposits its instrument of accession after the date of entry into force of the present Act in its entirety, or less than one month before such date, this Act shall enter into force three months after the date on which its accession has been notified by the Director General, unless a subsequent date has been indicated in the instrument of accession. In the latter case, this Act shall enter into force with respect to that country on the date thus indicated.

Article 22

[Consequences of Ratification or Accession]

Subject to the possibilities of exceptions provided for in Articles 20(1)(b) and 28(2), ratification or accession shall automatically entail acceptance of all the clauses and admission to all the advantages of this Act.

Article 23

[Accession to Earlier Acts]

After the entry into force of this Act in its entirety, a country may not accede to earlier Acts of this Convention.

Article 24

[Territories]

(1) Any country may declare in its instrument of ratification or accession, or may inform the Director General by written notification any time thereafter, that this Convention shall be applicable to all or part of those territories, designated in the declaration or notification, for the external relations of which it is responsible.

(2) Any country which has made such a declaration or given such a notification may, at any time, notify the Director General that this Convention shall cease to be applicable to all or part of such territories.

(3)

(a) Any declaration made under paragraph (1) shall take effect on the same date as the ratification or accession in the instrument of which it was included, and any notification given under such paragraph shall take effect three months after its notification by the Director General.

(b) Any notification given under paragraph (2) shall take effect twelve months after its receipt by the Director General.

Article 25

[Implementation of the Convention on the Domestic Level]

(1) Any country party to this Convention undertakes to adopt, in accordance with its constitution, the measures necessary to ensure the application of this Convention.

(2) It is understood that, at the time a country deposits its instrument of ratification or accession, it will be in a position under its domestic law to give effect to the provisions of this Convention.

Article 26

[Denunciation]

(1) This Convention shall remain in force without limitation as to time.

(2) Any country may denounce this Act by notification addressed to the Director General. Such denunciation shall constitute also denunciation of all earlier Acts and shall affect only the country making it, the Convention remaining in full force and effect as regards the other countries of the Union.

(3) Denunciation shall take effect one year after the day on which the Director General has received the notification.

(4) The right of denunciation provided by this Article shall not be exercised by any country before the expiration of five years from the date upon which it becomes a member of the Union.

Article 27

[Application of Earlier Acts]

(1) The present Act shall, as regards the relations between the countries to which it applies, and to the extent that it applies, replace the Convention of Paris of March 20, 1883 and the subsequent Acts of revision.

(2)

(a) As regards the countries to which the present Act does not apply, or does not apply in its entirety, but to which the Lisbon Act of October 31, 1958, applies, the latter shall remain in force in its entirety or to the extent that the present Act does not replace it by virtue of paragraph (1).

(b) Similarly, as regards the countries to which neither the present Act, nor portions thereof, nor the Lisbon Act applies, the London Act of June 2, 1934, shall remain in force in its entirety or to the extent that the present Act does not replace it by virtue of paragraph (1).

(c) Similarly, as regards the countries to which neither the present Act, nor portions thereof, nor the Lisbon Act, nor the London Act applies, the Hague Act of November 6, 1925, shall remain in force in its entirety or to the extent that the present Act does not replace it by virtue of paragraph (1).

(3) Countries outside the Union which become party to this Act shall apply it with respect to any country of the Union not party to this Act or which, although party to this Act, has made a declaration pursuant to Article 20(1)(b)(i). Such countries recognize that the said country of the Union may apply, in its relations with them, the provisions of the most recent Act to which it is party.

Article 28

[Disputes]

(1) Any dispute between two or more countries of the Union concerning the interpretation or application of this Convention, not settled by negotiation, may, by any one of the countries concerned, he brought before the International Court of Justice by application in conformity with the Statute of the Court, unless the countries concerned agree on some other method of settlement. The country bringing the dispute before the Court shall inform the International Bureau; the International Bureau shall bring the matter to the attention of the other countries of the Union.

(2) Each country may, at the time it signs this Act or deposits its instrument of ratification or accession, declare that it does not consider itself bound by the provisions of paragraph (1). With regard to any dispute between such country and any other country of the Union, the provisions of paragraph (1) shall not apply.

(3) Any country having made a declaration in accordance with the provisions of paragraph (2) may, at any time, withdraw its declaration by notification addressed to the Director General.

Article 29

[Signature, Languages, Depositary Functions]

(1)

(a) This Act shall be signed in a single copy in the French language and shall be deposited with the Government of Sweden.

(b) Official texts shall be established by the Director General, after consultation with the interested Governments, in the English, German, Italian, Portuguese, Russian and Spanish languages, and such other languages as the Assembly may designate.

(c) In case of differences of opinion on the interpretation of the various texts, the French text shall prevail.

(2) This Act shall remain open for signature at Stockholm until January 13, 1968.

(3) The Director General shall transmit two copies, certified by the Government of Sweden, of the signed text of this Act to the Governments of all countries of the Union and, on request, to the Government of any other country.

(4) The Director General shall register this Act with the Secretariat of the United Nations.

(5) The Director General shall notify the Governments of all countries of the Union of signatures, deposits of instruments of ratification or accession and any declarations included in such instruments or made pursuant to Article 20(1)(c), entry into force of any provisions of this Act, notifications of denunciation, and notifications pursuant to Article 24.

Article 30

[Transitional Provisions]

(1) Until the first Director General assumes office, references in this Act to the International Bureau of the Organization or to the Director General shall be deemed to be references to the Bureau of the Union or its Director, respectively.

(2) Countries of the Union not bound by Articles 13 to 17 may, until five years after the entry into force of the Convention establishing the Organization, exercise, if they so desire, the rights provided under Articles 13 to 17 of this Act as if they were bound by those Articles. Any country desiring to exercise such rights shall give written notification to that effect to the Director General; such notification shall be effective from the date of its receipt. Such countries shall be deemed to be members of the Assembly until the expiration of the said period.

(3) As long as all the countries of the Union have not become Members of the Organization, the International Bureau of the Organization shall also function as the Bureau of the Union, and the Director General as the Director of the said Bureau.

(4) Once all the countries of the Union have become Members of the Organization, the rights, obligations, and property, of the Bureau of the Union shall devolve on the International Bureau of the Organization.

17

PARTIES TO THE PARIS CONVENTION FOR THE PROTECTION OF INDUSTRIAL PROPERTY

Status on October 1, 2020

State	Date on which State became party to the Convention	Latest Act[1] of the Convention to which State is party and date on which State became party to that Act
Afghanistan	May 14, 2017	Stockholm: May 14, 2017
Albania	October 4, 1995	Stockholm: October 4, 1995
Algeria	March 1, 1966	Stockholm: April 20, 1975[2]
Andorra	June 2, 2004	Stockholm: June 2, 2004
Angola	December 27, 2007	Stockholm: December 27, 2007
Antigua and Barbuda	March 17, 2000	Stockholm: March 17, 2000
Argentina	February 10, 1967	Lisbon: February 10, 1967 Stockholm: Articles 13 to 30: October 8, 1980
Armenia	December 25, 1991	Stockholm: December 25, 1991[2]
Australia	October 10, 1925	Stockholm: Articles 1 to 12: September 27, 1975 Stockholm: Articles 13 to 30: August 25, 1972
Austria	January 1, 1909	Stockholm: August 18, 1973

[1]. "Stockholm" means the Paris Convention for the Protection of Industrial Property as revised at Stockholm on July 14, 1967 (Stockholm Act); "Lisbon" means the Paris Convention as revised at Lisbon on October 31, 1958 (Lisbon Act); "London" means the Paris Convention as revised at London on June 2, 1934 (London Act); "The Hague" means the Paris Convention as revised at The Hague on November 6, 1925 (Hague Act).

[2]. With the declaration provided for in Article 28(2) of the Stockholm Act relating to the International Court of Justice.

State	Date on which State became party to the Convention	Latest Act[1] of the Convention to which State is party and date on which State became party to that Act
Azerbaijan	December 25, 1995	Stockholm: December 25, 1995
Bahamas	July 10, 1973	Lisbon: July 10, 1973 Stockholm: Articles 13 to 30: March 10, 1977
Bahrain	October 29, 1997	Stockholm: October 29, 1997
Bangladesh	March 3, 1991	Stockholm: March 3, 1991[2]
Barbados	March 12, 1985	Stockholm: March 12, 1985
Belarus	December 25, 1991	Stockholm: December 25, 1991[2]
Belgium	July 7, 1884	Stockholm: February 12, 1975
Belize	June 17, 2000	Stockholm: June 17, 2000
Benin	January 10, 1967	Stockholm: March 12, 1975
Bhutan	August 4, 2000	Stockholm: August 4, 2000
Bolivia (Plurinational State of)	November 4, 1993	Stockholm: November 4, 1993
Bosnia and Herzegovina	March 1, 1992	Stockholm: March 1, 1992
Botswana	April 15, 1998	Stockholm: April 15, 1998
Brazil	July 7, 1884	Stockholm: Articles 1 to 12: November 24, 1992 Stockholm: Articles 13 to 30: March 24, 1975[2]
Brunei Darussalam	February 17, 2012	Stockholm: February 17, 2012
Bulgaria	June 13, 1921	Stockholm: Articles 1 to 12: May 19 or 27, 1970[3] Stockholm: Articles 13 to 30: May 27, 1970
Burkina Faso	November 19, 1963	Stockholm: September 2, 1975
Burundi	September 3, 1977	Stockholm: September 3, 1977

---

[3]. These are the alternative dates of entry into force which the Director General of WIPO communicated to the States concerned.

State	Date on which State became party to the Convention	Latest Act[1] of the Convention to which State is party and date on which State became party to that Act
Cambodia	September 22, 1998	Stockholm: September 22, 1998
Cameroon	May 10, 1964	Stockholm: April 20, 1975
Canada	September 1, 1923	Stockholm: Articles 1 to 12: May 26, 1996 Stockholm: Articles 13 to 30: July 7, 1970
Central African Republic	November 19, 1963	Stockholm: September 5, 1978
Chad	November 19, 1963	Stockholm: September 26, 1970
Chile	June 14, 1991	Stockholm: June 14, 1991
China[4]	March 19, 1985	Stockholm: March 19, 1985[2]
Colombia	September 3, 1996	Stockholm: September 3, 1996
Comoros	April 3, 2005	Stockholm: April 3, 2005
Congo	September 2, 1963	Stockholm: December 5, 1975
Costa Rica	October 31, 1995	Stockholm: October 31, 1995
Côte d'Ivoire	October 23, 1963	Stockholm: May 4, 1974
Croatia	October 8, 1991	Stockholm: October 8, 1991
Cuba	November 17, 1904	Stockholm: April 8, 1975[2]
Cyprus	January 17, 1966	Stockholm: April 3, 1984
Czech Republic	January 1, 1993	Stockholm: January 1, 1993
Democratic People's Republic of Korea	June 10, 1980	Stockholm: June 10, 1980
Democratic Republic of the Congo	January 31, 1975	Stockholm: January 31, 1975

---

[4]. The Stockholm Act applies also to the Hong Kong Special Administrative Region with effect from July 1, 1997, and to the Macau Special Administrative Region with effect from December 20, 1999.

State	Date on which State became party to the Convention	Latest Act[1] of the Convention to which State is party and date on which State became party to that Act
Denmark[5]	October 1, 1894	Stockholm: Articles 1 to 12: April 26 or May 19, 1970[3]
		Stockholm: Articles 13 to 30: April 26, 1970
Djibouti	May 13, 2002	Stockholm: May 13, 2002
Dominica	August 7, 1999	Stockholm: August 7, 1999
Dominican Republic	July 11, 1890	The Hague: April 6, 1951
Ecuador	June 22, 1999	Stockholm: June 22, 1999[2]
Egypt	July 1, 1951	Stockholm: March 6, 1975[2]
El Salvador	February 19, 1994	Stockholm: February 19, 1994
Equatorial Guinea	June 26, 1997	Stockholm: June 26, 1997
Estonia	August 24, 1994[6]	Stockholm: August 24, 1994
Eswatini	May 12, 1991	Stockholm: May 12, 1991
Finland	September 20, 1921	Stockholm: Articles 1 to 12: October 21, 1975
		Stockholm: Articles 13 to 30: September 15, 1970
France[7]	July 7, 1884	Stockholm: August 12, 1975
Gabon	February 29, 1964	Stockholm: June 10, 1975
Gambia	January 21, 1992	Stockholm: January 21, 1992
Georgia	December 25, 1991	Stockholm: December 25, 1991[2]
Germany	May 1, 1903	Stockholm: September 19, 1970
Ghana	September 28, 1976	Stockholm: September 28, 1976
Greece	October 2, 1924	Stockholm: July 15, 1976
Grenada	September 22, 1998	Stockholm: September 22, 1998

[5]. Denmark extended the application of the Stockholm Act to the Faroe Islands with effect from August 6, 1971.

[6]. Estonia acceded to the Paris Convention (Washington Act, 1911) with effect from February 12, 1924. It lost its independence on August 6, 1940, and regained it on August 20, 1991.

[7]. Including all Overseas Departments and Territories.

State	Date on which State became party to the Convention	Latest Act[1] of the Convention to which State is party and date on which State became party to that Act
Guatemala	August 18, 1998	Stockholm: August 18, 1998[2]
Guinea	February 5, 1982	Stockholm: February 5, 1982
Guinea-Bissau	June 28, 1988	Stockholm: June 28, 1998
Guyana	October 25, 1994	Stockholm: October 25, 1994
Haiti	July 1, 1958	Stockholm: November 3, 1983
Holy See	September 29, 1960	Stockholm: April 24, 1975
Honduras	February 4, 1994	Stockholm: February 4, 1994
Hungary	January 1, 1909	Stockholm: Articles 1 to 12: April 26, 1970[3] Stockholm: Articles 13 to 30: April 26, 1970[2]
Iceland	May 5, 1962	Stockholm: Articles 1 to 12: April 9, 1995 Stockholm: Articles 13 to 30: December 28, 1984
India	December 7, 1998	Stockholm: December 7, 1998[2]
Indonesia	December 24, 1950	Stockholm: Articles 1 to 12: September 5, 1997 Stockholm: Articles 13 to 30: December 20, 1990[2]
Iran (Islamic Republic of)	December 16, 1959	Stockholm: March 12, 1990[2]
Iraq	January 24, 1976	Stockholm: Jan. 24, 1976[2]
Ireland	December 4, 1925	Stockholm: Articles 1 to 12: April 26 or May 19, 1970[3] Stockholm: Articles 13 to 30: April 26, 1970
Israel	March 24, 1950	Stockholm: Articles 1 to 12: April 26, 1970[3] Stockholm: Articles 13 to 30: April 26, 1970
Italy	July 7, 1884	Stockholm: April 24, 1977
Jamaica	December 24, 1999	Stockholm: December 24, 1999

State	Date on which State became party to the Convention	Latest Act[1] of the Convention to which State is party and date on which State became party to that Act
Japan	July 15, 1899	Stockholm: Articles 1 to 12: October 1, 1975
		Stockholm: Articles 13 to 30: April 24, 1975
Jordan	July 17, 1972	Stockholm: July 17, 1972
Kazakhstan	December 25, 1991	Stockholm: December 25, 1991[2]
Kenya	June 14, 1965	Stockholm: October 26, 1971
Kuwait	December 2, 2014	Stockholm: December 2, 2014
Kyrgyzstan	December 25, 1991	Stockholm: December 25, 1991[2]
Lao People's Democratic Republic	October 8, 1998	Stockholm: October 8, 1998
Latvia	September 7, 1993[8]	Stockholm: September 7, 1993
Lebanon	September 1, 1924	London: September 30, 1947
		Stockholm: Articles 13 to 30: December 30, 1986[2]
Lesotho	September 28, 1989	Stockholm: September 28, 1989[2]
Liberia	August 27, 1994	Stockholm: August 27, 1994
Libya	September 28, 1976	Stockholm: September 28, 1976[2]
Liechtenstein	July 14, 1933	Stockholm: May 25, 1972
Lithuania	May 22, 1994	Stockholm: May 22, 1994
Luxembourg	June 30, 1922	Stockholm: March 24, 1975
Madagascar	December 21, 1963	Stockholm: April 10, 1972
Malawi	July 6, 1964	Stockholm: June 25, 1970
Malaysia	January 1, 1989	Stockholm: January 1, 1989
Mali	March 1, 1983	Stockholm: March 1, 1983
Malta	October 20, 1967	Lisbon: October 20, 1967

---

[8]. Latvia acceded to the Paris Convention (Washington Act, 1911) with effect from August 20, 1925. It lost its independence on July 21, 1940, and regained it on August 21, 1991.

State	Date on which State became party to the Convention	Latest Act[1] of the Convention to which State is party and date on which State became party to that Act
		Stockholm: Articles 13 to 30: December 12, 1977[2]
Mauritania	April 11, 1965	Stockholm: September 21, 1978
Mauritius	September 24, 1976	Stockholm: September 24, 1976
Mexico	September 7, 1903	Stockholm: July 26, 1976
Monaco	April 29, 1956	Stockholm: October 4, 1975
Mongolia	April 21, 1985	Stockholm: April 21, 1985[2]
Montenegro	June 3, 2006	Stockholm: June 3, 2006
Morocco	July 30, 1917	Stockholm: August 6, 1971
Mozambique	July 9, 1998	Stockholm: July 9, 1998
Namibia	January 1, 2004	Stockholm: January 1, 2004
Nepal	June 22, 2001	Stockholm: June 22, 2001
Netherlands[9]	July 7, 1884	Stockholm: January 10, 1975
New Zealand[10]	July 29, 1931	London: July 14, 1946
		Stockholm: Articles 13 to 30: June 20, 1984
Nicaragua	July 3, 1996	Stockholm: July 3, 1996[2]
Niger	July 5, 1964	Stockholm: March 6, 1975
Nigeria	September 2, 1963	Lisbon: September 2, 1963
North Macedonia	September 8, 1991	Stockholm: September 8, 1991
Norway	July 1, 1885	Stockholm: June 13, 1974
Oman	July 14, 1999	Stockholm: July 14, 1999[2]
Pakistan	July 22, 2004	Stockholm: July 22, 2004[2]
Panama	October 19, 1996	Stockholm: October 19, 1996
Papua New Guinea	June 15, 1999	Stockholm: June 15, 1999

---

[9]. Ratification for the Kingdom in Europe, the Netherlands Antilles and Aruba. The Netherlands Antilles ceased to exist on October 10, 2010. As from that date, the Stockholm Act continues to apply to Curaçao and Sint Maarten. The Stockholm Act also continues to apply to the islands of Bonaire, Sint Eustatius, and Saba which, with effect from October 10, 2010, have become part of the territory of the Kingdom of the Netherlands in Europe.

[10]. The accession of New Zealand to the Stockholm Act, with the exception of Articles 1 to 12, extends to the Cook Islands, Niue and Tokelau. New Zealand deposited on December 17, 2018, a declaration extending the effects of its accession to Article 1 to 12, in respect of the territory of New Zealand.

State	Date on which State became party to the Convention	Latest Act[1] of the Convention to which State is party and date on which State became party to that Act
Paraguay	May 28, 1994	Stockholm: May 28, 1994
Peru	April 11, 1995	Stockholm: April 11, 1995
Philippines	September 27, 1965	Lisbon: September 27, 1965
		Stockholm: Articles 13 to 30: July 16, 1980
Poland	November 10, 1919	Stockholm: March 24, 1975
Portugal	July 7, 1884	Stockholm: April 30, 1975
Qatar	July 5, 2000	Stockholm: July 5, 2000
Republic of Korea	May 4, 1980	Stockholm: May 4, 1990
Republic of Moldova	December 25, 1991	Stockholm: December 25, 1991[2]
Romania	October 6, 1920	Stockholm: Articles 1 to 12: April 26 or May 19, 1970[3]
		Stockholm: Articles 13 to 30: April 26, 1970[2]
Russian Federation	July 1, 1965[11]	Stockholm: Articles 1 to 12: April 26 or May 19, 1970[3, 11]
		Stockholm: Articles 13 to 30: April 26, 1970[2, 11]
Rwanda	March 1, 1984	Stockholm: March 1, 1984
Saint Kitts and Nevis	April 9, 1995	Stockholm: April 9, 1995
Saint Lucia	June 9, 1995	Stockholm: June 9, 1995[2]
Saint Vincent and the Grenadines	August 29, 1995	Stockholm: August 29, 1995
Samoa	September 21, 2013	Stockholm: September 21, 2013
San Marino	March 4, 1960	Stockholm: June 26, 1991
Sao Tome and Principe	May 12, 1998	Stockholm: May 12, 1998
Saudi Arabia	March 11, 2004	Stockholm: March 11, 2004

[11.] Date of adherence of the Soviet Union, continued by the Russian Federation as from December 25, 1991.

State	Date on which State became party to the Convention	Latest Act[1] of the Convention to which State is party and date on which State became party to that Act
Senegal	December 21, 1963	Stockholm: Articles 1 to 12: April 26 or May 19, 1970[3]
		Stockholm: Articles 13 to 30: April 26, 1970
Serbia[12]	April 27, 1992	Stockholm: April 27, 1992
Seychelles	November 7, 2002	Stockholm: November 7, 2002
Sierra Leone	June 17, 1997	Stockholm: June 17, 1997
Singapore	February 23, 1995	Stockholm: February 23, 1995
Slovakia	January 1, 1993	Stockholm: January 1, 1993
Slovenia	June 25, 1991	Stockholm: June 25, 1991
South Africa	December 1, 1947	Stockholm: March 24, 1975[2]
Spain	July 7, 1884	Stockholm: April 14, 1972
Sri Lanka	December 29, 1952	London: December 29, 1952
		Stockholm: Articles 13 to 30: September 23, 1978
Sudan	April 16, 1984	Stockholm: April 16, 1984
Suriname	November 25, 1975	Stockholm: November 25, 1975
Sweden	July 1, 1885	Stockholm: Articles 1 to 12: October 9, 1970
		Stockholm: Articles 13 to 30: April 26, 1970
Switzerland	July 7, 1884	Stockholm: Articles 1 to 12: April 26 or May 19, 1970[3]
		Stockholm: Articles 13 to 30: April 26, 1970
Syrian Arab Republic	September 1, 1924	Stockholm: December 13, 2002[2]
Tajikistan	December 25, 1991	Stockholm: December 25, 1991[2]
Thailand	August 2, 2008	Stockholm: August 2, 2008

[12.] Serbia is the continuing State from Serbia and Montenegro as from June 3, 2006.

State	Date on which State became party to the Convention	Latest Act[1] of the Convention to which State is party and date on which State became party to that Act
Togo	September 10, 1967	Stockholm: April 30, 1975
Tonga	June 14, 2001	Stockholm: June 14, 2001
Trinidad and Tobago	August 1, 1964	Stockholm: August 16, 1988
Tunisia	July 7, 1884	Stockholm: April 12, 1976[2]
Turkey	October 10, 1925	Stockholm: Articles 1 to 12: February 1, 1995 Stockholm: Articles 13 to 30: May 16, 1976
Turkmenistan	December 25, 1991	Stockholm: December 25, 1991[2]
Uganda	June 14, 1965	Stockholm: October 20, 1973
Ukraine	December 25, 1991	Stockholm: December 25, 1991
United Arab Emirates	September 19, 1996	Stockholm: October 20, 1973[2]
United Kingdom	July 7, 1884	Stockholm: Articles 1 to 12: April 6 or May 19, 1970[3] Stockholm: Articles 13 to 30: April 26, 1970[13, 14, 15]
United Republic of Tanzania	June 16, 1963	Lisbon: June 16, 1963 Stockholm: Articles 13 to 30: December 30, 1983
United States of America	May 30, 1887	Stockholm: Articles 1 to 12: August 25, 1973 Stockholm: Articles 13 to 30: September 5, 1970[16]
Uruguay	March 18, 1967	Stockholm: December 28, 1979

[13.] The United Kingdom extended the application of the Stockholm Act to the Isle of Man with effect from October 29, 1983.

[14.] The United Kingdom extended the application of the Convention to the territories of the Bailiwick of Guernsey and the Bailiwick of Jersey with effect from November 13, 2020.

[15.] The United Kingdom extended the application of the Convention to the territory of Gibraltar with effect from January 1, 2021.

[16.] The United States of America extended the application of the Stockholm Act to all territories and possessions of the United States of America, including the Commonwealth of Puerto Rico, as from August 25, 1973.

State	Date on which State became party to the Convention	Latest Act[1] of the Convention to which State is party and date on which State became party to that Act
Uzbekistan	December 25, 1991	Stockholm: December 25, 1991[2]
Venezuela (Bolivarian Republic of)	September 12, 1995	Stockholm: September 12, 1995
Viet Nam	March 8, 1949	Stockholm: July 2, 1976[2]
Yemen	February 15, 2007	Stockholm: February 15, 2007
Zambia	April 6, 1965	Lisbon: April 6, 1965 Stockholm: Articles 13 to 30: May 14, 1977
Zimbabwe	April 18, 1980	Stockholm: December 30, 1981

Total: 177 States

18

PATENT COOPERATION TREATY

Done at Washington on June 19, 1970, amended on September 28, 1979, modified on February 3, 1984, and on October 3, 2001

The Contracting States,

Desiring to make a contribution to the progress of science and technology,

Desiring to perfect the legal protection of inventions,

Desiring to simplify and render more economical the obtaining of protection for inventions where protection is sought in several countries,

Desiring to facilitate and accelerate access by the public to the technical information contained in documents describing new inventions,

Desiring to foster and accelerate the economic development of developing countries through the adoption of measures designed to increase the efficiency of their legal systems, whether national or regional, instituted for the protection of inventions by providing easily accessible information on the availability of technological solutions applicable to their special needs and by facilitating access to the ever expanding volume of modern technology,

Convinced that cooperation among nations will greatly facilitate the attainment of these aims,

Have concluded the present Treaty.

INTRODUCTORY PROVISIONS

Article 1

Establishment of a Union

(1) The States party to this Treaty (hereinafter called "the Contracting States") constitute a Union for cooperation in the filing, searching, and examination, of applications for the protection of inventions, and for rendering special technical services. The Union shall be known as the International Patent Cooperation Union.

(2) No provision of this Treaty shall be interpreted as diminishing the rights under the Paris Convention for the Protection of Industrial Property of any national or resident of any country party to that Convention.

Article 2

Definitions

For the purposes of this Treaty and the Regulations and unless expressly stated otherwise:

(i)   "application" means an application for the protection of an invention; references to an "application" shall be construed as references to applications for patents for inventions, inventors' certificates, utility certificates, utility models, patents or certificates of addition, inventors' certificates of addition, and utility certificates of addition;

(ii)   references to a "patent" shall be construed as references to patents for inventions, inventors' certificates, utility certificates, utility models, patents or certificates of addition, inventors' certificates of addition, and utility certificates of addition;

(iii)   "national patent" means a patent granted by a national authority;

(iv)   "regional patent" means a patent granted by a national or an intergovernmental authority having the power to grant patents effective in more than one State;

(v)   "regional application" means an application for a regional patent;

(vi)   references to a "national application" shall be construed as references to applications for national patents and regional patents, other than applications filed under this Treaty;

(vii)   "international application" means an application filed under this Treaty;

(viii) references to an "application" shall be construed as references to international applications and national applications;

(ix)   references to a "patent" shall be construed as references to national patents and regional patents;

(x)   references to "national law" shall be construed as references to the national law of a Contracting State or, where a regional application or a regional patent is involved, to the treaty providing for the filing of regional applications or the granting of regional patents;

(xi)   "priority date," for the purposes of computing time limits, means:

(a) where the international application contains a priority claim under Article 8, the filing date of the application whose priority is so claimed;

(b) where the international application contains several priority claims under Article 8, the filing date of the earliest application whose priority is so claimed;

(c) where the international application does not contain any priority claim under Article 8, the international filing date of such application;

(xii) "national Office" means the government authority of a Contracting State entrusted with the granting of patents; references to a "national Office" shall be construed as referring also to any intergovernmental authority which several States have entrusted with the task of granting regional patents, provided that at least one of those States is a Contracting State, and provided that the said States have authorized that authority to assume the obligations and exercise the powers which this Treaty and the Regulations provide for in respect of national Offices;

(xiii) "designated Office" means the national Office of or acting for the State designated by the applicant under Chapter I of this Treaty;

(xiv) "elected Office" means the national Office of or acting for the State elected by the applicant under Chapter II of this Treaty;

(xv) "receiving Office" means the national Office or the intergovernmental organization with which the international application has been filed;

(xvi) "Union" means the International Patent Cooperation Union;

(xvii) "Assembly" means the Assembly of the Union;

(xviii) "Organization" means the World Intellectual Property Organization;

(xix) "International Bureau" means the International Bureau of the Organization and, as long as it subsists, the United International Bureaux for the Protection of Intellectual Property (BIRPI);

(xx) "Director General" means the Director General of the Organization and, as long as BIRPI subsists, the Director of BIRPI.

CHAPTER I

INTERNATIONAL APPLICATION
AND INTERNATIONAL SEARCH

Article 3

The International Application

(1) Applications for the protection of inventions in any of the Contracting States may be filed as international applications under this Treaty.

(2) An international application shall contain, as specified in this Treaty and the Regulations, a request, a description, one or more claims, one or more drawings (where required), and an abstract.

(3) The abstract merely serves the purpose of technical information and cannot be taken into account for any other purpose, particularly not for the purpose of interpreting the scope of the protection sought.

(4) The international application shall:

(i)   be in a prescribed language;

(ii)   comply with the prescribed physical requirements;

(iii) comply with the prescribed requirement of unity of invention;

(iv)   be subject to the payment of the prescribed fees.

Article 4

The Request

(1) The request shall contain:

(i)   a petition to the effect that the international application be processed according to this Treaty;

(ii)   the designation of the Contracting State or States in which protection for the invention is desired on the basis of the international application ("designated States"); if for any designated State a regional patent is available and the applicant wishes to obtain a regional patent rather than a national patent, the request shall so indicate; if, under a treaty concerning a regional patent, the applicant cannot limit his application to certain of the States party to that treaty, designation of one of those States and the indication of the wish to obtain the regional patent shall be treated as designation of all the States party to that treaty; if, under the national law of the designated State, the designation of that State has the effect of an application for a regional patent, the designation of the said State shall be treated as an indication of the wish to obtain the regional patent;

(iii) the name of and other prescribed data concerning the applicant and the agent (if any);

(iv) the title of the invention;

(v) the name of and other prescribed data concerning the inventor where the national law of at least one of the designated States requires that these indications be furnished at the time of filing a national application. Otherwise, the said indications may be furnished either in the request or in separate notices addressed to each designated Office whose national law requires the furnishing of the said indications but allows that they be furnished at a time later than that of the filing of a national application.

(2) Every designation shall be subject to the payment of the prescribed fee within the prescribed time limit.

(3) Unless the applicant asks for any of the other kinds of protection referred to in Article 43, designation shall mean that the desired protection consists of the grant of a patent by or for the designated State. For the purposes of this paragraph, Article 2(ii) shall not apply.

(4) Failure to indicate in the request the name and other prescribed data concerning the inventor shall have no consequence in any designated State whose national law requires the furnishing of the said indications but allows that they be furnished at a time later than that of the filing of a national application. Failure to furnish the said indications in a separate notice shall have no consequence in any designated State whose national law does not require the furnishing of the said indications.

Article 5

The Description

The description shall disclose the invention in a manner sufficiently clear and complete for the invention to be carried out by a person skilled in the art.

Article 6

The Claims

The claim or claims shall define the matter for which protection is sought. Claims shall be clear and concise. They shall be fully supported by the description.

Article 7

The Drawings

(1) Subject to the provisions of paragraph (2)(ii), drawings shall be required when they are necessary for the understanding of the invention.

(2) Where, without being necessary for the understanding of the invention, the nature of the invention admits of illustration by drawings:

(i) the applicant may include such drawings in the international application when filed,

(ii) any designated Office may require that the applicant file such drawings with it within the prescribed time limit.

Article 8

Claiming Priority

(1) The international application may contain a declaration, as prescribed in the Regulations, claiming the priority of one or more earlier applications filed in or for any country party to the Paris Convention for the Protection of Industrial Property.

(2)(a) Subject to the provisions of subparagraph (b), the conditions for, and the effect of, any priority claim declared under paragraph (1) shall be as provided in Article 4 of the Stockholm Act of the Paris Convention for the Protection of Industrial Property.

(b) The international application for which the priority of one or more earlier applications filed in or for a Contracting State is claimed may contain the designation of that State. Where, in the international application, the priority of one or more national applications filed in or for a designated State is claimed, or where the priority of an international application having designated only one State is claimed, the conditions for, and the effect of, the priority claim in that State shall be governed by the national law of that State.

Article 9

The Applicant

(1) Any resident or national of a Contracting State may file an international application.

(2) The Assembly may decide to allow the residents and the nationals of any country party to the Paris Convention for the Protection of Industrial Property which is not party to this Treaty to file international applications.

(3) The concepts of residence and nationality, and the application of those concepts in cases where there are several applicants or where the applicants are not the same for all the designated States, are defined in the Regulations.

Article 10

The Receiving Office

The international application shall be filed with the prescribed receiving Office, which will check and process it as provided in this Treaty and the Regulations.

Article 11

Filing Date and Effects of the International Application

(1) The receiving Office shall accord as the international filing date the date of receipt of the international application, provided that that Office has found that, at the time of receipt:

(i)   the applicant does not obviously lack, for reasons of residence or nationality, the right to file an international application with the receiving Office,

(ii) the international application is in the prescribed language,

(iii) the international application contains at least the following elements:

   (a)   an indication that it is intended as an international application,

   (b)   the designation of at least one Contracting State,

   (c)   the name of the applicant, as prescribed,

   (d)   a part which on the face of it appears to be a description,

   (e)   a part which on the face of it appears to be a claim or claims.

(2)(a)   If the receiving Office finds that the international application did not, at the time of receipt, fulfill the requirements listed in paragraph (1), it shall, as provided in the Regulations, invite the applicant to file the required correction.

   (b)   If the applicant complies with the invitation, as provided in the Regulations, the receiving Office shall accord as the international filing date the date of receipt of the required correction.

(3) Subject to Article 64(4), any international application fulfilling the requirements listed in items (i) to (iii) of paragraph (1) and accorded an international filing date shall have the effect of a regular national application in each designated State as of the international filing date, which date shall be considered to be the actual filing date in each designated State.

(4) Any international application fulfilling the requirements listed in items (i) to (iii) of paragraph (1) shall be equivalent to a regular national

filing within the meaning of the Paris Convention for the Protection of Industrial Property.

Article 12

Transmittal of the International Application to the International Bureau and the International Searching Authority

(1)   One copy of the international application shall be kept by the receiving Office ("home copy"), one copy ("record copy") shall be transmitted to the International Bureau, and another copy ("search copy") shall be transmitted to the competent International Searching Authority referred to in Article 16, as provided in the Regulations.

(2)   The record copy shall be considered the true copy of the international application.

(3)   The international application shall be considered withdrawn if the record copy has not been received by the International Bureau within the prescribed time limit.

Article 13

Availability of Copy of the International Application to Designated Offices

(1)   Any designated Office may ask the International Bureau to transmit to it a copy of the international application prior to the communication provided for in Article 20, and the International Bureau shall transmit such copy to the designated Office as soon as possible after the expiration of one year from the priority date.

(2)(a)   The applicant may, at any time, transmit a copy of his international application to any designated Office.

(b)   The applicant may, at any time, ask the International Bureau to transmit a copy of his international application to any designated Office, and the International Bureau shall transmit such copy to the designated Office as soon as possible.

(c)   Any national Office may notify the International Bureau that it does not wish to receive copies as provided for in subparagraph (b), in which case that subparagraph shall not be applicable in respect of that Office.

Article 14

Certain Defects in the International Application

(1)(a)   The receiving Office shall check whether the international application contains any of the following defects, that is to say:

(i)   it is not signed as provided in the Regulations;

   (ii) it does not contain the prescribed indications concerning the applicant;

   (iii) it does not contain a title;

   (iv) it does not contain an abstract;

   (v)   it does not comply to the extent provided in the Regulations with the prescribed physical requirements.

(b) If the receiving Office finds any of the said defects, it shall invite the applicant to correct the international application within the prescribed time limit, failing which that application shall be considered withdrawn and the receiving Office shall so declare.

(2) If the international application refers to drawings which, in fact, are not included in that application, the receiving Office shall notify the applicant accordingly and he may furnish them within the prescribed time limit and, if he does, the international filing date shall be the date on which the drawings are received by the receiving Office. Otherwise, any reference to the said drawings shall be considered non-existent.

(3)(a)   If the receiving Office finds that, within the prescribed time limits, the fees prescribed under Article 3(4)(iv) have not been paid, or no fee prescribed under Article 4(2) has been paid in respect of any of the designated States, the international application shall be considered withdrawn and the receiving Office shall so declare.

(b) If the receiving Office finds that the fee prescribed under Article 4(2) has been paid in respect of one or more (but less than all) designated States within the prescribed time limit, the designation of those States in respect of which it has not been paid within the prescribed time limit shall be considered withdrawn and the receiving Office shall so declare.

(4) If, after having accorded an international filing date to the international application, the receiving Office finds, within the prescribed time limit, that any of the requirements listed in items (i) to (iii) of Article 11(1) was not complied with at that date, the said application shall be considered withdrawn and the receiving Office shall so declare.

Article 15

The International Search

(1) Each international application shall be the subject of international search.

(2) The objective of the international search is to discover relevant prior art.

(3)　International search shall be made on the basis of the claims, with due regard to the description and the drawings (if any).

(4)　The International Searching Authority referred to in Article 16 shall endeavor to discover as much of the relevant prior art as its facilities permit, and shall, in any case, consult the documentation specified in the Regulations.

(5)(a)　If the national law of the Contracting State so permits, the applicant who files a national application with the national Office of or acting for such State may, subject to the conditions provided for in such law, request that a search similar to an international search ("international-type search") be carried out on such application.

(b)　If the national law of the Contracting State so permits, the national Office of or acting for such State may subject any national application filed with it to an international-type search.

(c)　The international-type search shall be carried out by the International Searching Authority referred to in Article 16 which would be competent for an international search if the national application were an international application and were filed with the Office referred to in subparagraphs (a) and (b). If the national application is in a language which the International Searching Authority considers it is not equipped to handle, the international-type search shall be carried out on a translation prepared by the applicant in a language prescribed for international applications and which the International Searching Authority has undertaken to accept for international applications. The national application and the translation, when required, shall be presented in the form prescribed for international applications.

Article 16

The International Searching Authority

(1)　International search shall be carried out by an International Searching Authority, which may be either a national Office or an intergovernmental organization, such as the International Patent Institute, whose tasks include the establishing of documentary search reports on prior art with respect to inventions which are the subject of applications.

(2)　If, pending the establishment of a single International Searching Authority, there are several International Searching Authorities, each receiving Office shall, in accordance with the provisions of the applicable agreement referred to in paragraph (3)(b), specify the International Searching Authority or Authorities competent for the searching of international applications filed with such Office.

(3)(a)   International Searching Authorities shall be appointed by the Assembly. Any national Office and any intergovernmental organization satisfying the requirements referred to in subparagraph (c) may be appointed as International Searching Authority.

(b)   Appointment shall be conditional on the consent of the national Office or intergovernmental organization to be appointed and the conclusion of an agreement, subject to approval by the Assembly, between such Office or organization and the International Bureau. The agreement shall specify the rights and obligations of the parties, in particular, the formal undertaking by the said Office or organization to apply and observe all the common rules of international search.

(c)   The Regulations prescribe the minimum requirements, particularly as to manpower and documentation, which any Office or organization must satisfy before it can be appointed and must continue to satisfy while it remains appointed.

(d)   Appointment shall be for a fixed period of time and may be extended for further periods.

(e)   Before the Assembly makes a decision on the appointment of any national Office or intergovernmental organization, or on the extension of its appointment, or before it allows any such appointment to lapse, the Assembly shall hear the interested Office or organization and seek the advice of the Committee for Technical Cooperation referred to in Article 56 once that Committee has been established.

Article 17

Procedure before the International Searching Authority

(1)   Procedure before the International Searching Authority shall be governed by the provisions of this Treaty, the Regulations, and the agreement which the International Bureau shall conclude, subject to this Treaty and the Regulations, with the said Authority.

(2)(a)   If the International Searching Authority considers

    (i)   that the international application relates to a subject matter which the International Searching Authority is not required, under the Regulations, to search, and in the particular case decides not to search, or

    (ii)   that the description, the claims, or the drawings, fail to comply with the prescribed requirements to such an extent that a meaningful search could not be carried out, the said Authority shall so declare and shall notify the applicant and the International Bureau that no international search report will be established.

(b) If any of the situations referred to in subparagraph (a) is found to exist in connection with certain claims only, the international search report shall so indicate in respect of such claims, whereas, for the other claims, the said report shall be established as provided in Article 18.

(3)(a)   If the International Searching Authority considers that the international application does not comply with the requirement of unity of invention as set forth in the Regulations, it shall invite the applicant to pay additional fees. The International Searching Authority shall establish the international search report on those parts of the international application which relate to the invention first mentioned in the claims ("main invention") and, provided the required additional fees have been paid within the prescribed time limit, on those parts of the international application which relate to inventions in respect of which the said fees were paid.

(b) The national law of any designated State may provide that, where the national Office of that State finds the invitation, referred to in subparagraph (a), of the International Searching Authority justified and where the applicant has not paid all additional fees, those parts of the international application which consequently have not been searched shall, as far as effects in that State are concerned, be considered withdrawn unless a special fee is paid by the applicant to the national Office of that State.

Article 18

The International Search Report

(1) The international search report shall be established within the prescribed time limit and in the prescribed form.

(2) The international search report shall, as soon as it has been established, be transmitted by the International Searching Authority to the applicant and the International Bureau.

(3) The international search report or the declaration referred to in Article 17(2)(a) shall be translated as provided in the Regulations. The translations shall be prepared by or under the responsibility of the International Bureau.

Article 19

Amendment of the Claims before the International Bureau

(1) The applicant shall, after having received the international search report, be entitled to one opportunity to amend the claims of the international application by filing amendments with the International

Bureau within the prescribed time limit. He may, at the same time, file a brief statement, as provided in the Regulations, explaining the amendments and indicating any impact that such amendments might have on the description and the drawings.

(2) The amendments shall not go beyond the disclosure in the international application as filed.

(3) If the national law of any designated State permits amendments to go beyond the said disclosure, failure to comply with paragraph (2) shall have no consequence in that State.

Article 20

Communication to Designated Offices

(1)(a)   The international application, together with the international search report (including any indication referred to in Article 17(2)(b)) or the declaration referred to in Article 17(2)(a), shall be communicated to each designated Office, as provided in the Regulations, unless the designated Office waives such requirement in its entirety or in part.

(b)   The communication shall include the translation (as prescribed) of the said report or declaration.

(2) If the claims have been amended by virtue of Article 19(1), the communication shall either contain the full text of the claims both as filed and as amended or shall contain the full text of the claims as filed and specify the amendments, and shall include the statement, if any, referred to in Article 19(1).

(3) At the request of the designated Office or the applicant, the International Searching Authority shall send to the said Office or the applicant, respectively, copies of the documents cited in the international search report, as provided in the Regulations.

Article 21

International Publication

(1) The International Bureau shall publish international applications.

(2)(a)   Subject to the exceptions provided for in subparagraph (b) and in Article 64(3), the international publication of the international application shall be effected promptly after the expiration of 18 months from the priority date of that application.

(b)   The applicant may ask the International Bureau to publish his international application any time before the expiration of the time limit referred to in subparagraph (a). The International Bureau shall proceed accordingly, as provided in the Regulations.

(3)   The international search report or the declaration referred to in Article 17(2)(a) shall be published as prescribed in the Regulations.

(4)   The language and form of the international publication and other details are governed by the Regulations.

(5)   There shall be no international publication if the international application is withdrawn or is considered withdrawn before the technical preparations for publication have been completed.

(6)   If the international application contains expressions or drawings which, in the opinion of the International Bureau, are contrary to morality or public order, or if, in its opinion, the international application contains disparaging statements as defined in the Regulations, it may omit such expressions, drawings, and statements, from its publications, indicating the place and number of words or drawings omitted, and furnishing, upon request, individual copies of the passages omitted.

Article 22

Copy, Translation, and Fee, to Designated Offices

(1)   The applicant shall furnish a copy of the international application (unless the communication provided for in Article 20 has already taken place) and a translation thereof (as prescribed), and pay the national fee (if any), to each designated Office not later than at the expiration of 30[1] months from the priority date. Where the national law of the designated State requires the indication of the name of and other prescribed data concerning the inventor but allows that these indications be furnished at a time later than that of the filing of a national application, the applicant shall, unless they were contained in the request, furnish the said indications to the national Office of or acting for the State not later than at the expiration of 30[1] months from the priority date.

(2)   Where the International Searching Authority makes a declaration, under Article 17(2)(a), that no international search report will be established, the time limit for performing the acts referred to in paragraph (1) of this Article shall be the same as that provided for in paragraph (1).

[1.]   *Editor's Note:* The 30-month time limit, as in force from April 1, 2002, does not apply in respect of any designated Office which has notified the International Bureau of incompatibility with the national law applied by that Office. The 20-month time limit, as in force until March 31, 2002, continues to apply after that date in respect of any such designated Office for as long as Article 22(1), as modified, continues not to be compatible with the applicable national law. Information received by the International Bureau concerning any such incompatibility is published in the Gazette and on the WIPO website at: www.wipo.int/pct/en/texts/reservations/res_incomp.html. [The specific time limits are listed at: https://www.wipo.int/pct/en/texts/time_limits.html.]

(3) Any national law may, for performing the acts referred to in paragraphs (1) or (2), fix time limits which expire later than the time limit provided for in those paragraphs.

Article 23

Delaying of National Procedure

(1) No designated Office shall process or examine the international application prior to the expiration of the applicable time limit under Article 22.

(2) Notwithstanding the provisions of paragraph (1), any designated Office may, on the express request of the applicant, process or examine the international application at any time.

Article 24

Possible Loss of Effect in Designated States

(1) Subject, in case (ii) below, to the provisions of Article 25, the effect of the international application provided for in Article 11(3) shall cease in any designated State with the same consequences as the withdrawal of any national application in that State:

(i) if the applicant withdraws his international application or the designation of that State;

(ii) if the international application is considered withdrawn by virtue of Articles 12(3), 14(1)(b), 14(3)(a), or 14(4), or if the designation of that State is considered withdrawn by virtue of Article 14(3)(b);

(iii) if the applicant fails to perform the acts referred to in Article 22 within the applicable time limit.

(2) Notwithstanding the provisions of paragraph (1), any designated Office may maintain the effect provided for in Article 11(3) even where such effect is not required to be maintained by virtue of Article 25(2).

Article 25

Review by Designated Offices

(1)(a) Where the receiving Office has refused to accord an international filing date or has declared that the international application is considered withdrawn, or where the International Bureau has made a finding under Article 12(3), the International Bureau shall promptly send, at the request of the applicant, copies of any document in the file to any of the designated Offices named by the applicant.

(b) Where the receiving Office has declared that the designation of any given State is considered withdrawn, the International

Bureau shall promptly send, at the request of the applicant, copies of any document in the file to the national Office of such State.

(c) The request under subparagraphs (a) or (b) shall be presented within the prescribed time limit.

(2)(a) Subject to the provisions of subparagraph (b), each designated Office shall, provided that the national fee (if any) has been paid and the appropriate translation (as prescribed) has been furnished within the prescribed time limit, decide whether the refusal, declaration, or finding, referred to in paragraph (1) was justified under the provisions of this Treaty and the Regulations, and, if it finds that the refusal or declaration was the result of an error or omission on the part of the receiving Office or that the finding was the result of an error or omission on the part of the International Bureau, it shall, as far as effects in the State of the designated Office are concerned, treat the international application as if such error or omission had not occurred.

(b) Where the record copy has reached the International Bureau after the expiration of the time limit prescribed under Article 12(3) on account of any error or omission on the part of the applicant, the provisions of subparagraph (a) shall apply only under the circumstances referred to in Article 48(2).

Article 26

Opportunity to Correct before Designated Offices

No designated Office shall reject an international application on the grounds of non-compliance with the requirements of this Treaty and the Regulations without first giving the applicant the opportunity to correct the said application to the extent and according to the procedure provided by the national law for the same or comparable situations in respect of national applications.

Article 27

National Requirements

(1) No national law shall require compliance with requirements relating to the form or contents of the international application different from or additional to those which are provided for in this Treaty and the Regulations.

(2) The provisions of paragraph (1) neither affect the application of the provisions of Article 7(2) nor preclude any national law from requiring, once the processing of the international application has started in the designated Office, the furnishing:

(i) when the applicant is a legal entity, of the name of an officer entitled to represent such legal entity,

(ii) of documents not part of the international application but which constitute proof of allegations or statements made in that application, including the confirmation of the international application by the signature of the applicant when that application, as filed, was signed by his representative or agent.

(3) Where the applicant, for the purposes of any designated State, is not qualified according to the national law of that State to file a national application because he is not the inventor, the international application may be rejected by the designated Office.

(4) Where the national law provides, in respect of the form or contents of national applications, for requirements which, from the viewpoint of applicants, are more favorable than the requirements provided for by this Treaty and the Regulations in respect of international applications, the national Office, the courts and any other competent organs of or acting for the designated State may apply the former requirements, instead of the latter requirements, to international applications, except where the applicant insists that the requirements provided for by this Treaty and the Regulations be applied to his international application.

(5) Nothing in this Treaty and the Regulations is intended to be construed as prescribing anything that would limit the freedom of each Contracting State to prescribe such substantive conditions of patentability as it desires. In particular, any provision in this Treaty and the Regulations concerning the definition of prior art is exclusively for the purposes of the international procedure and, consequently, any Contracting State is free to apply, when determining the patentability of an invention claimed in an international application, the criteria of its national law in respect of prior art and other conditions of patentability not constituting requirements as to the form and contents of applications.

(6) The national law may require that the applicant furnish evidence in respect of any substantive condition of patentability prescribed by such law.

(7) Any receiving Office or, once the processing of the international application has started in the designated Office, that Office may apply the national law as far as it relates to any requirement that the applicant be represented by an agent having the right to represent applicants before the said Office and/or that the applicant have an address in the designated State for the purpose of receiving notifications.

(8) Nothing in this Treaty and the Regulations is intended to be construed as limiting the freedom of any Contracting State to apply measures deemed necessary for the preservation of its national security or to limit, for the protection of the general economic interests of that State, the right of its own residents or nationals to file international applications.

Article 28

Amendment of the Claims, the Description, and the Drawings, before Designated Offices

(1)   The applicant shall be given the opportunity to amend the claims, the description, and the drawings, before each designated Office within the prescribed time limit. No designated Office shall grant a patent, or refuse the grant of a patent, before such time limit has expired except with the express consent of the applicant.

(2)   The amendments shall not go beyond the disclosure in the international application as filed unless the national law of the designated State permits them to go beyond the said disclosure.

(3)   The amendments shall be in accordance with the national law of the designated State in all respects not provided for in this Treaty and the Regulations.

(4)   Where the designated Office requires a translation of the international application, the amendments shall be in the language of the translation.

Article 29

Effects of the International Publication

(1)   As far as the protection of any rights of the applicant in a designated State is concerned, the effects, in that State, of the international publication of an international application shall, subject to the provisions of paragraphs (2) to (4), be the same as those which the national law of the designated State provides for the compulsory national publication of unexamined national applications as such.

(2)   If the language in which the international publication has been effected is different from the language in which publications under the national law are effected in the designated State, the said national law may provide that the effects provided for in paragraph (1) shall be applicable only from such time as:

(i)   a translation into the latter language has been published as provided by the national law, or

(ii)   a translation into the latter language has been made available to the public, by laying open for public inspection as provided by the national law, or

(iii) a translation into the latter language has been transmitted by the applicant to the actual or prospective unauthorized user of the invention claimed in the international application, or

(iv)   both the acts described in (i) and (iii), or both the acts described in (ii) and (iii), have taken place.

(3) The national law of any designated State may provide that, where the international publication has been effected, on the request of the applicant, before the expiration of 18 months from the priority date, the effects provided for in paragraph (1) shall be applicable only from the expiration of 18 months from the priority date.

(4) The national law of any designated State may provide that the effects provided for in paragraph (1) shall be applicable only from the date on which a copy of the international application as published under Article 21 has been received in the national Office of or acting for such State. The said Office shall publish the date of receipt in its gazette as soon as possible.

Article 30

Confidential Nature of the International Application

(1)(a) Subject to the provisions of subparagraph (b), the International Bureau and the International Searching Authorities shall not allow access by any person or authority to the international application before the international publication of that application, unless requested or authorized by the applicant.

(b) The provisions of subparagraph (a) shall not apply to any transmittal to the competent International Searching Authority, to transmittals provided for under Article 13, and to communications provided for under Article 20.

(2)(a) No national Office shall allow access to the international application by third parties, unless requested or authorized by the applicant, before the earliest of the following dates:

(i) date of the international publication of the international application,

(ii) date of the receipt of the communication of the international application under Article 20,

(iii) date of the receipt of a copy of the international application under Article 22.

(b) The provisions of subparagraph (a) shall not prevent any national Office from informing third parties that it has been designated, or from publishing that fact. Such information or publication may, however, contain only the following data: identification of the receiving Office, name of the applicant, international filing date, international application number, and title of the invention.

(c) The provisions of subparagraph (a) shall not prevent any designated Office from allowing access to the international application for the purposes of the judicial authorities.

(3) The provisions of paragraph (2)(a) shall apply to any receiving Office except as far as transmittals provided for under Article 12(1) are concerned.

(4) For the purposes of this Article, the term "access" covers any means by which third parties may acquire cognizance, including individual communication and general publication, provided, however, that no national Office shall generally publish an international application or its translation before the international publication or, if international publication has not taken place by the expiration of 20 months from the priority date, before the expiration of 20 months from the said priority date.

CHAPTER II

INTERNATIONAL PRELIMINARY EXAMINATION

Article 31

Demand for International Preliminary Examination

(1) On the demand of the applicant, his international application shall be the subject of an international preliminary examination as provided in the following provisions and the Regulations.

(2)(a)   Any applicant who is a resident or national, as defined in the Regulations, of a Contracting State bound by Chapter II, and whose international application has been filed with the receiving Office of or acting for such State, may make a demand for international preliminary examination.

(b)   The Assembly may decide to allow persons entitled to file international applications to make a demand for international preliminary examination even if they are residents or nationals of a State not party to this Treaty or not bound by Chapter II.

(3) The demand for international preliminary examination shall be made separately from the international application. The demand shall contain the prescribed particulars and shall be in the prescribed language and form.

(4)(a)   The demand shall indicate the Contracting State or States in which the applicant intends to use the results of the international preliminary examination ("elected States"). Additional Contracting States may be elected later. Election may relate only to Contracting States already designated under Article 4.

(b)   Applicants referred to in paragraph (2)(a) may elect any Contracting State bound by Chapter II. Applicants referred to in paragraph (2)(b) may elect only such Contracting States bound by Chapter II as have declared that they are prepared to be elected by such applicants.

(5) The demand shall be subject to the payment of the prescribed fees within the prescribed time limit.

(6)(a) The demand shall be submitted to the competent International Preliminary Examining Authority referred to in Article 32.

(b) Any later election shall be submitted to the International Bureau.

(7) Each elected Office shall be notified of its election.

Article 32

The International Preliminary Examining Authority

(1) International preliminary examination shall be carried out by the International Preliminary Examining Authority.

(2) In the case of demands referred to in Article 31(2)(a), the receiving Office, and, in the case of demands referred to in Article 31(2)(b), the Assembly, shall, in accordance with the applicable agreement between the interested International Preliminary Examining Authority or Authorities and the International Bureau, specify the International Preliminary Examining Authority or Authorities competent for the preliminary examination.

(3) The provisions of Article 16(3) shall apply, *mutatis mutandis*, in respect of International Preliminary Examining Authorities.

Article 33

The International Preliminary Examination

(1) The objective of the international preliminary examination is to formulate a preliminary and non-binding opinion on the questions whether the claimed invention appears to be novel, to involve an inventive step (to be non-obvious), and to be industrially applicable.

(2) For the purposes of the international preliminary examination, a claimed invention shall be considered novel if it is not anticipated by the prior art as defined in the Regulations.

(3) For the purposes of the international preliminary examination, a claimed invention shall be considered to involve an inventive step if, having regard to the prior art as defined in the Regulations, it is not, at the prescribed relevant date, obvious to a person skilled in the art.

(4) For the purposes of the international preliminary examination, a claimed invention shall be considered industrially applicable if, according to its nature, it can be made or used (in the technological sense) in any kind of industry. "Industry" shall be understood in its broadest sense, as in the Paris Convention for the Protection of Industrial Property.

(5) The criteria described above merely serve the purposes of international preliminary examination. Any Contracting State may apply additional or different criteria for the purpose of deciding whether, in that State, the claimed invention is patentable or not.

(6) The international preliminary examination shall take into consideration all the documents cited in the international search report. It may take into consideration any additional documents considered to be relevant in the particular case.

Article 34

Procedure before the International Preliminary Examining Authority

(1) Procedure before the International Preliminary Examining Authority shall be governed by the provisions of this Treaty, the Regulations, and the agreement which the International Bureau shall conclude, subject to this Treaty and the Regulations, with the said Authority.

(2)(a) The applicant shall have a right to communicate orally and in writing with the International Preliminary Examining Authority.

(b) The applicant shall have a right to amend the claims, the description, and the drawings, in the prescribed manner and within the prescribed time limit, before the international preliminary examination report is established. The amendment shall not go beyond the disclosure in the international application as filed.

(c) The applicant shall receive at least one written opinion from the International Preliminary Examining Authority unless such Authority considers that all of the following conditions are fulfilled:

(i) the invention satisfies the criteria set forth in Article 33(1),

(ii) the international application complies with the requirements of this Treaty and the Regulations in so far as checked by that Authority,

(iii) no observations are intended to be made under Article 35(2), last sentence.

(d) The applicant may respond to the written opinion.

(3)(a) If the International Preliminary Examining Authority considers that the international application does not comply with the requirement of unity of invention as set forth in the Regulations, it may invite the applicant, at his option, to restrict the claims so as to comply with the requirement or to pay additional fees.

(b) The national law of any elected State may provide that, where the applicant chooses to restrict the claims under subparagraph (a), those parts of the international application which, as a consequence of the restriction, are not to be the subject of international preliminary examination shall, as far as effects in that State are concerned, be considered withdrawn unless a special fee is paid by the applicant to the national Office of that State.

(c) If the applicant does not comply with the invitation referred to in subparagraph (a) within the prescribed time limit, the International Preliminary Examining Authority shall establish an international preliminary examination report on those parts of the international application which relate to what appears to be the main invention and shall indicate the relevant facts in the said report. The national law of any elected State may provide that, where its national Office finds the invitation of the International Preliminary Examining Authority justified, those parts of the international application which do not relate to the main invention shall, as far as effects in that State are concerned, be considered withdrawn unless a special fee is paid by the applicant to that Office.

(4)(a) If the International Preliminary Examining Authority considers

(i) that the international application relates to a subject matter on which the International Preliminary Examining Authority is not required, under the Regulations, to carry out an international preliminary examination, and in the particular case decides not to carry out such examination, or

(ii) that the description, the claims, or the drawings, are so unclear, or the claims are so inadequately supported by the description, that no meaningful opinion can be formed on the novelty, inventive step (non-obviousness), or industrial applicability, of the claimed invention, the said Authority shall not go into the questions referred to in Article 33(1) and shall inform the applicant of this opinion and the reasons therefor.

(b) If any of the situations referred to in subparagraph (a) is found to exist in, or in connection with, certain claims only, the provisions of that subparagraph shall apply only to the said claims.

Article 35

The International Preliminary Examination Report

(1) The international preliminary examination report shall be established within the prescribed time limit and in the prescribed form.

(2) The international preliminary examination report shall not contain any statement on the question whether the claimed invention is or seems to be patentable or unpatentable according to any national law. It shall state, subject to the provisions of paragraph (3), in relation to each claim, whether the claim appears to satisfy the criteria of novelty, inventive step (non-obviousness), and industrial applicability, as defined for the purposes of the international preliminary examination in Article 33(1) to (4). The statement shall be accompanied by the citation of the documents believed to support the stated conclusion with such explanations as the circumstances of the case may require. The statement shall also be accompanied by such other observations as the Regulations provide for.

(3)(a)   If, at the time of establishing the international preliminary examination report, the International Preliminary Examining Authority considers that any of the situations referred to in Article 34(4)(a) exists, that report shall state this opinion and the reasons therefor. It shall not contain any statement as provided in paragraph (2).

(b)   If a situation under Article 34(4)(b) is found to exist, the international preliminary examination report shall, in relation to the claims in question, contain the statement as provided in subparagraph (a), whereas, in relation to the other claims, it shall contain the statement as provided in paragraph (2).

Article 36

Transmittal, Translation, and Communication, of the International Preliminary Examination Report

(1) The international preliminary examination report, together with the prescribed annexes, shall be transmitted to the applicant and to the International Bureau.

(2)(a)   The international preliminary examination report and its annexes shall be translated into the prescribed languages.

(b)   Any translation of the said report shall be prepared by or under the responsibility of the International Bureau, whereas any translation of the said annexes shall be prepared by the applicant.

(3)(a)   The international preliminary examination report, together with its translation (as prescribed) and its annexes (in the original language), shall be communicated by the International Bureau to each elected Office.

(b) The prescribed translation of the annexes shall be transmitted within the prescribed time limit by the applicant to the elected Offices.

(4) The provisions of Article 20(3) shall apply, *mutatis mutandis*, to copies of any document which is cited in the international preliminary examination report and which was not cited in the international search report.

Article 37

Withdrawal of Demand or Election

(1) The applicant may withdraw any or all elections.

(2) If the election of all elected States is withdrawn, the demand shall be considered withdrawn.

(3)(a) Any withdrawal shall be notified to the International Bureau.

(b) The elected Offices concerned and the International Preliminary Examining Authority concerned shall be notified accordingly by the International Bureau.

(4)(a) Subject to the provisions of subparagraph (b), withdrawal of the demand or of the election of a Contracting State shall, unless the national law of that State provides otherwise, be considered to be withdrawal of the international application as far as that State is concerned.

(b) Withdrawal of the demand or of the election shall not be considered to be withdrawal of the international application if such withdrawal is effected prior to the expiration of the applicable time limit under Article 22; however, any Contracting State may provide in its national law that the aforesaid shall apply only if its national Office has received, within the said time limit, a copy of the international application, together with a translation (as prescribed), and the national fee.

Article 38

Confidential Nature of the International Preliminary Examination

(1) Neither the International Bureau nor the International Preliminary Examining Authority shall, unless requested or authorized by the applicant, allow access within the meaning, and with the proviso, of Article 30(4) to the file of the international preliminary examination by any person or authority at any time, except by the elected Offices once the international preliminary examination report has been established.

(2) Subject to the provisions of paragraph (1) and Articles 36(1) and (3) and 37(3)(b), neither the International Bureau nor the International

Preliminary Examining Authority shall, unless requested or authorized by the applicant, give information on the issuance or nonissuance of an international preliminary examination report and on the withdrawal or nonwithdrawal of the demand or of any election.

Article 39

Copy, Translation, and Fee, to Elected Offices

(1)(a)   If the election of any Contracting State has been effected prior to the expiration of the 19th month from the priority date, the provisions of Article 22 shall not apply to such State and the applicant shall furnish a copy of the international application (unless the communication under Article 20 has already taken place) and a translation thereof (as prescribed), and pay the national fee (if any), to each elected Office not later than at the expiration of 30 months from the priority date.

(b) Any national law may, for performing the acts referred to in subparagraph (a), fix time limits which expire later than the time limit provided for in that subparagraph.

(2) The effect provided for in Article 11(3) shall cease in the elected State with the same consequences as the withdrawal of any national application in that State if the applicant fails to perform the acts referred to in paragraph (1)(a) within the time limit applicable under paragraph (1)(a) or (b).

(3) Any elected Office may maintain the effect provided for in Article 11(3) even where the applicant does not comply with the requirements provided for in paragraph (1)(a) or (b).

Article 40

Delaying of National Examination and Other Processing

(1) If the election of any Contracting State has been effected prior to the expiration of the 19th month from the priority date, the provisions of Article 23 shall not apply to such State and the national Office of or acting for that State shall not proceed, subject to the provisions of paragraph (2), to the examination and other processing of the international application prior to the expiration of the applicable time limit under Article 39.

(2) Notwithstanding the provisions of paragraph (1), any elected Office may, on the express request of the applicant, proceed to the examination and other processing of the international application at any time.

Article 41

Amendment of the Claims, the Description, and the Drawings, before Elected Offices

(1) The applicant shall be given the opportunity to amend the claims, the description, and the drawings, before each elected Office within the prescribed time limit. No elected Office shall grant a patent, or refuse the grant of a patent, before such time limit has expired, except with the express consent of the applicant.

(2) The amendments shall not go beyond the disclosure in the international application as filed, unless the national law of the elected State permits them to go beyond the said disclosure.

(3) The amendments shall be in accordance with the national law of the elected State in all respects not provided for in this Treaty and the Regulations.

(4) Where an elected Office requires a translation of the international application, the amendments shall be in the language of the translation.

Article 42

Results of National Examination in Elected Offices

No elected Office receiving the international preliminary examination report may require that the applicant furnish copies, or information on the contents, of any papers connected with the examination relating to the same international application in any other elected Office.

CHAPTER III

COMMON PROVISIONS

Article 43

Seeking Certain Kinds of Protection

In respect of any designated or elected State whose law provides for the grant of inventors' certificates, utility certificates, utility models, patents or certificates of addition, inventors' certificates of addition, or utility certificates of addition, the applicant may indicate, as prescribed in the Regulations, that his international application is for the grant, as far as that State is concerned, of an inventor's certificate, a utility certificate, or a utility model, rather than a patent, or that it is for the grant of a patent or certificate of addition, an inventor's certificate of addition, or a utility certificate of addition, and the ensuing effect shall be governed by the applicant's choice. For the purposes of this Article and any Rule thereunder, Article 2(ii) shall not apply.

Article 44

Seeking Two Kinds of Protection

In respect of any designated or elected State whose law permits an application, while being for the grant of a patent or one of the other kinds of protection referred to in Article 43, to be also for the grant of another of the said kinds of protection, the applicant may indicate, as prescribed in the Regulations, the two kinds of protection he is seeking, and the ensuing effect shall be governed by the applicant's indications. For the purposes of this Article, Article 2(ii) shall not apply.

Article 45

Regional Patent Treaties

(1)   Any treaty providing for the grant of regional patents ("regional patent treaty"), and giving to all persons who, according to Article 9, are entitled to file international applications the right to file applications for such patents, may provide that international applications designating or electing a State party to both the regional patent treaty and the present Treaty may be filed as applications for such patents.

(2)   The national law of the said designated or elected State may provide that any designation or election of such State in the international application shall have the effect of an indication of the wish to obtain a regional patent under the regional patent treaty.

Article 46

Incorrect Translation of the International Application

If, because of an incorrect translation of the international application, the scope of any patent granted on that application exceeds the scope of the international application in its original language, the competent authorities of the Contracting State concerned may accordingly and retroactively limit the scope of the patent, and declare it null and void to the extent that its scope has exceeded the scope of the international application in its original language.

Article 47

Time Limits

(1)   The details for computing time limits referred to in this Treaty are governed by the Regulations.

(2)(a)   All time limits fixed in Chapters I and II of this Treaty may, outside any revision under Article 60, be modified by a decision of the Contracting States.

(b)   Such decisions shall be made in the Assembly or through voting by correspondence and must be unanimous.

(c)   The details of the procedure are governed by the Regulations.

Article 48

Delay in Meeting Certain Time Limits

(1)   Where any time limit fixed in this Treaty or the Regulations is not met because of interruption in the mail service or unavoidable loss or delay in the mail, the time limit shall be deemed to be met in the cases and subject to the proof and other conditions prescribed in the Regulations.

(2)(a)   Any Contracting State shall, as far as that State is concerned, excuse, for reasons admitted under its national law, any delay in meeting any time limit.

(b)   Any Contracting State may, as far as that State is concerned, excuse, for reasons other than those referred to in subparagraph (a), any delay in meeting any time limit.

Article 49

Right to Practice before International Authorities

Any attorney, patent agent, or other person, having the right to practice before the national Office with which the international application was filed, shall be entitled to practice before the International Bureau and the competent International Searching Authority and competent International Preliminary Examining Authority in respect of that application.

CHAPTER IV

TECHNICAL SERVICES

Article 50

Patent Information Services

(1)   The International Bureau may furnish services by providing technical and any other pertinent information available to it on the basis of published documents, primarily patents and published applications (referred to in this Article as "the information services").

(2)   The International Bureau may provide these information services either directly or through one or more International Searching Authorities or other national or international specialized institutions, with which the International Bureau may reach agreement.

(3)   The information services shall be operated in a way particularly facilitating the acquisition by Contracting States which are developing countries of technical knowledge and technology, including available published know-how.

(4) The information services shall be available to Governments of Contracting States and their nationals and residents. The Assembly may decide to make these services available also to others.

(5)(a)   Any service to Governments of Contracting States shall be furnished at cost, provided that, when the Government is that of a Contracting State which is a developing country, the service shall be furnished below cost if the difference can be covered from profit made on services furnished to others than Governments of Contracting States or from the sources referred to in Article 51(4).

(b)   The cost referred to in subparagraph (a) is to be understood as cost over and above costs normally incident to the performance of the services of a national Office or the obligations of an International Searching Authority.

(6) The details concerning the implementation of the provisions of this Article shall be governed by decisions of the Assembly and, within the limits to be fixed by the Assembly, such working groups as the Assembly may set up for that purpose.

(7) The Assembly shall, when it considers it necessary, recommend methods of providing financing supplementary to those referred to in paragraph (5).

Article 51

Technical Assistance

(1) The Assembly shall establish a Committee for Technical Assistance (referred to in this Article as "the Committee").

(2)(a)   The members of the Committee shall be elected among the Contracting States, with due regard to the representation of developing countries.

(b)   The Director General shall, on his own initiative or at the request of the Committee, invite representatives of intergovernmental organizations concerned with technical assistance to developing countries to participate in the work of the Committee.

(3)(a)   The task of the Committee shall be to organize and supervise technical assistance for Contracting States which are developing countries in developing their patent systems individually or on a regional basis.

(b)   The technical assistance shall comprise, among other things, the training of specialists, the loaning of experts, and the supply of equipment both for demonstration and for operational purposes.

(4) The International Bureau shall seek to enter into agreements, on the one hand, with international financing organizations and

intergovernmental organizations, particularly the United Nations, the agencies of the United Nations, and the Specialized Agencies connected with the United Nations concerned with technical assistance, and, on the other hand, with the Governments of the States receiving the technical assistance, for the financing of projects pursuant to this Article.

(5) The details concerning the implementation of the provisions of this Article shall be governed by decisions of the Assembly and, within the limits to be fixed by the Assembly, such working groups as the Assembly may set up for that purpose.

Article 52

Relations with Other Provisions of the Treaty

Nothing in this Chapter shall affect the financial provisions contained in any other Chapter of this Treaty. Such provisions are not applicable to the present Chapter or to its implementation.

CHAPTER V

ADMINISTRATIVE PROVISIONS

Article 53

Assembly

(1)(a)   The Assembly shall, subject to Article 57(8), consist of the Contracting States.

(b)   The Government of each Contracting State shall be represented by one delegate, who may be assisted by alternate delegates, advisors, and experts.

(2)(a)   The Assembly shall:

(i)   deal with all matters concerning the maintenance and development of the Union and the implementation of this Treaty;

(ii)   perform such tasks as are specifically assigned to it under other provisions of this Treaty;

(iii)   give directions to the International Bureau concerning the preparation for revision conferences;

(iv)   review and approve the reports and activities of the Director General concerning the Union, and give him all necessary instructions concerning matters within the competence of the Union;

(v)   review and approve the reports and activities of the Executive Committee established under paragraph (9), and give instructions to such Committee;

    (vi)   determine the program and adopt the triennial[2] budget of the Union, and approve its final accounts;

    (vii)   adopt the financial regulations of the Union;

    (viii)   establish such committees and working groups as it deems appropriate to achieve the objectives of the Union;

    (ix)   determine which States other than Contracting States and, subject to the provisions of paragraph (8), which intergovernmental and international non-governmental organizations shall be admitted to its meetings as observers;

    (x)   take any other appropriate action designed to further the objectives of the Union and perform such other functions as are appropriate under this Treaty.

(b)   With respect to matters which are of interest also to other Unions administered by the Organization, the Assembly shall make its decisions after having heard the advice of the Coordination Committee of the Organization.

(3)   A delegate may represent, and vote in the name of, one State only.

(4)   Each Contracting State shall have one vote.

(5)(a) One-half of the Contracting States shall constitute a quorum.

(b)   In the absence of the quorum, the Assembly may make decisions but, with the exception of decisions concerning its own procedure, all such decisions shall take effect only if the quorum and the required majority are attained through voting by correspondence as provided in the Regulations.

(6)(a)   Subject to the provisions of Articles 47(2)(b), 58(2)(b), 58(3) and 61(2)(b), the decisions of the Assembly shall require two-thirds of the votes cast.

(b)   Abstentions shall not be considered as votes.

(7)   In connection with matters of exclusive interest to States bound by Chapter II, any reference to Contracting States in paragraphs (4), (5), and (6), shall be considered as applying only to States bound by Chapter II.

(8)   Any intergovernmental organization appointed as International Searching or Preliminary Examining Authority shall be admitted as observer to the Assembly.

(9)   When the number of Contracting States exceeds forty, the Assembly shall establish an Executive Committee. Any reference to the

---

2. *Editor's Note:* Since 1980, the program and budget of the Union have been biennial.

Executive Committee in this Treaty and the Regulations shall be construed as references to such Committee once it has been established.

(10) Until the Executive Committee has been established, the Assembly shall approve, within the limits of the program and triennial[3] budget, the annual programs and budgets prepared by the Director General.

(11)(a) The Assembly shall meet in every second calendar year in ordinary session upon convocation by the Director General and, in the absence of exceptional circumstances, during the same period and at the same place as the General Assembly of the Organization.

(b) The Assembly shall meet in extraordinary session upon convocation by the Director General, at the request of the Executive Committee, or at the request of one-fourth of the Contracting States.

(12) The Assembly shall adopt its own rules of procedure.

Article 54

Executive Committee

(1) When the Assembly has established an Executive Committee, that Committee shall be subject to the provisions set forth hereinafter.

(2)(a) The Executive Committee shall, subject to Article 57(8), consist of States elected by the Assembly from among States members of the Assembly.

(b) The Government of each State member of the Executive Committee shall be represented by one delegate, who may be assisted by alternate delegates, advisors, and experts.

(3) The number of States members of the Executive Committee shall correspond to one-fourth of the number of States members of the Assembly. In establishing the number of seats to be filled, remainders after division by four shall be disregarded.

(4) In electing the members of the Executive Committee, the Assembly shall have due regard to an equitable geographical distribution.

(5)(a) Each member of the Executive Committee shall serve from the close of the session of the Assembly which elected it to the close of the next ordinary session of the Assembly.

(b) Members of the Executive Committee may be re-elected but only up to a maximum of two-thirds of such members.

[3.] *Editor's Note:* Since 1980, the program and budget of the Union have been biennial.

(c) The Assembly shall establish the details of the rules governing the election and possible re-election of the members of the Executive Committee.

(6)(a)   The Executive Committee shall:

(i) prepare the draft agenda of the Assembly;

(ii) submit proposals to the Assembly in respect of the draft program and biennial budget of the Union prepared by the Director General;

(iii) *[deleted]*

(iv) submit, with appropriate comments, to the Assembly the periodical reports of the Director General and the yearly audit reports on the accounts;

(v) take all necessary measures to ensure the execution of the program of the Union by the Director General, in accordance with the decisions of the Assembly and having regard to circumstances arising between two ordinary sessions of the Assembly;

(vi) perform such other functions as are allocated to it under this Treaty.

(b) With respect to matters which are of interest also to other Unions administered by the Organization, the Executive Committee shall make its decisions after having heard the advice of the Coordination Committee of the Organization.

(7)(a)   The Executive Committee shall meet once a year in ordinary session upon convocation by the Director General, preferably during the same period and at the same place as the Coordination Committee of the Organization.

(b) The Executive Committee shall meet in extraordinary session upon convocation by the Director General, either on his own initiative or at the request of its Chairman or one-fourth of its members.

(8)(a)   Each State member of the Executive Committee shall have one vote.

(b) One-half of the members of the Executive Committee shall constitute a quorum.

(c) Decisions shall be made by a simple majority of the votes cast.

(d) Abstentions shall not be considered as votes.

(e) A delegate may represent, and vote in the name of, one State only.

(9) Contracting States not members of the Executive Committee shall be admitted to its meetings as observers, as well as any intergovernmental organization appointed as International Searching or Preliminary Examining Authority.

(10) The Executive Committee shall adopt its own rules of procedure.

Article 55

International Bureau

(1) Administrative tasks concerning the Union shall be performed by the International Bureau.

(2) The International Bureau shall provide the secretariat of the various organs of the Union.

(3) The Director General shall be the chief executive of the Union and shall represent the Union.

(4) The International Bureau shall publish a Gazette and other publications provided for by the Regulations or required by the Assembly.

(5) The Regulations shall specify the services that national Offices shall perform in order to assist the International Bureau and the International Searching and Preliminary Examining Authorities in carrying out their tasks under this Treaty.

(6) The Director General and any staff member designated by him shall participate, without the right to vote, in all meetings of the Assembly, the Executive Committee and any other committee or working group established under this Treaty or the Regulations. The Director General, or a staff member designated by him, shall be *ex officio* secretary of these bodies.

(7)(a)   The International Bureau shall, in accordance with the directions of the Assembly and in cooperation with the Executive Committee, make the preparations for the revision conferences.

(b)   The International Bureau may consult with intergovernmental and international non-governmental organizations concerning preparations for revision conferences.

(c)   The Director General and persons designated by him shall take part, without the right to vote, in the discussions at revision conferences.

(8) The International Bureau shall carry out any other tasks assigned to it.

Article 56

Committee for Technical Cooperation

(1) The Assembly shall establish a Committee for Technical Cooperation (referred to in this Article as "the Committee").

(2)(a)   The Assembly shall determine the composition of the Committee and appoint its members, with due regard to an equitable representation of developing countries.

(b)   The International Searching and Preliminary Examining Authorities shall be *ex officio* members of the Committee. In the case where such an Authority is the national Office of a Contracting State, that State shall not be additionally represented on the Committee.

(c)   If the number of Contracting States so allows, the total number of members of the Committee shall be more than double the number of *ex officio* members.

(d)   The Director General shall, on his own initiative or at the request of the Committee, invite representatives of interested organizations to participate in discussions of interest to them.

(3)   The aim of the Committee shall be to contribute, by advice and recommendations:

(i)   to the constant improvement of the services provided for under this Treaty,

(ii)   to the securing, so long as there are several International Searching Authorities and several International Preliminary Examining Authorities, of the maximum degree of uniformity in their documentation and working methods and the maximum degree of uniformly high quality in their reports, and

(iii)   on the initiative of the Assembly or the Executive Committee, to the solution of the technical problems specifically involved in the establishment of a single International Searching Authority.

(4)   Any Contracting State and any interested international organization may approach the Committee in writing on questions which fall within the competence of the Committee.

(5)   The Committee may address its advice and recommendations to the Director General or, through him, to the Assembly, the Executive Committee, all or some of the International Searching and Preliminary Examining Authorities, and all or some of the receiving Offices.

(6)(a) In any case, the Director General shall transmit to the Executive Committee the texts of all the advice and recommendations of the Committee. He may comment on such texts.

(b) The Executive Committee may express its views on any advice, recommendation, or other activity of the Committee, and may invite the Committee to study and report on questions falling within its competence. The Executive Committee may submit to the Assembly, with appropriate comments, the advice, recommendations and report of the Committee.

(7) Until the Executive Committee has been established, references in paragraph (6) to the Executive Committee shall be construed as references to the Assembly.

(8) The details of the procedure of the Committee shall be governed by the decisions of the Assembly.

Article 57

Finances

(1)(a) The Union shall have a budget.

(b) The budget of the Union shall include the income and expenses proper to the Union and its contribution to the budget of expenses common to the Unions administered by the Organization.

(c) Expenses not attributable exclusively to the Union but also to one or more other Unions administered by the Organization shall be considered as expenses common to the Unions. The share of the Union in such common expenses shall be in proportion to the interest the Union has in them.

(2) The budget of the Union shall be established with due regard to the requirements of coordination with the budgets of the other Unions administered by the Organization.

(3) Subject to the provisions of paragraph (5), the budget of the Union shall be financed from the following sources:

(i) fees and charges due for services rendered by the International Bureau in relation to the Union;

(ii) sale of, or royalties on, the publications of the International Bureau concerning the Union;

(iii) gifts, bequests, and subventions;

(iv) rents, interests, and other miscellaneous income.

(4) The amounts of fees and charges due to the International Bureau and the prices of its publications shall be so fixed that they should, under

normal circumstances, be sufficient to cover all the expenses of the International Bureau connected with the administration of this Treaty.

(5)(a)   Should any financial year close with a deficit, the Contracting States shall, subject to the provisions of subparagraphs (b) and (c), pay contributions to cover such deficit.

(b)   The amount of the contribution of each Contracting State shall be decided by the Assembly with due regard to the number of international applications which has emanated from each of them in the relevant year.

(c)   If other means of provisionally covering any deficit or any part thereof are secured, the Assembly may decide that such deficit be carried forward and that the Contracting States should not be asked to pay contributions.

(d)   If the financial situation of the Union so permits, the Assembly may decide that any contributions paid under subparagraph (a) be reimbursed to the Contracting States which have paid them.

(e)   A Contracting State which has not paid, within two years of the due date as established by the Assembly, its contribution under subparagraph (b) may not exercise its right to vote in any of the organs of the Union. However, any organ of the Union may allow such a State to continue to exercise its right to vote in that organ so long as it is satisfied that the delay in payment is due to exceptional and unavoidable circumstances.

(6)   If the budget is not adopted before the beginning of a new financial period, it shall be at the same level as the budget of the previous year, as provided in the financial regulations.

(7)(a)   The Union shall have a working capital fund which shall be constituted by a single payment made by each Contracting State. If the fund becomes insufficient, the Assembly shall arrange to increase it. If part of the fund is no longer needed, it shall be reimbursed.

(b)   The amount of the initial payment of each Contracting State to the said fund or of its participation in the increase thereof shall be decided by the Assembly on the basis of principles similar to those provided for under paragraph (5)(b).

(c)   The terms of payment shall be fixed by the Assembly on the proposal of the Director General and after it has heard the advice of the Coordination Committee of the Organization.

(d)   Any reimbursement shall be proportionate to the amounts paid by each Contracting State, taking into account the dates at which they were paid.

(8)(a) In the headquarters agreement concluded with the State on the territory of which the Organization has its headquarters, it shall be provided that, whenever the working capital fund is insufficient, such State shall grant advances. The amount of these advances and the conditions on which they are granted shall be the subject of separate agreements, in each case, between such State and the Organization. As long as it remains under the obligation to grant advances, such State shall have an *ex officio* seat in the Assembly and on the Executive Committee.

(b) The State referred to in subparagraph (a) and the Organization shall each have the right to denounce the obligation to grant advances, by written notification. Denunciation shall take effect three years after the end of the year in which it has been notified.

(9) The auditing of the accounts shall be effected by one or more of the Contracting States or by external auditors, as provided in the financial regulations. They shall be designated, with their agreement, by the Assembly.

Article 58

Regulations

(1) The Regulations annexed to this Treaty provide Rules:

(i) concerning matters in respect of which this Treaty expressly refers to the Regulations or expressly provides that they are or shall be prescribed,

(ii) concerning any administrative requirements, matters, or procedures,

(iii) concerning any details useful in the implementation of the provisions of this Treaty.

(2)(a) The Assembly may amend the Regulations.

(b) Subject to the provisions of paragraph (3), amendments shall require three-fourths of the votes cast.

(3)(a) The Regulations specify the Rules which may be amended

(i) only by unanimous consent, or

(ii) only if none of the Contracting States whose national Office acts as an International Searching or Preliminary Examining Authority dissents, and, where such Authority is an intergovernmental organization, if the Contracting State member of that organization authorized for that purpose by the other member States within the competent body of such organization does not dissent.

(b) Exclusion, for the future, of any such Rules from the applicable requirement shall require the fulfillment of the conditions referred to in subparagraph (a)(i) or (a)(ii), respectively.

(c) Inclusion, for the future, of any Rule in one or the other of the requirements referred to in subparagraph (a) shall require unanimous consent.

(4) The Regulations provide for the establishment, under the control of the Assembly, of Administrative Instructions by the Director General.

(5) In the case of conflict between the provisions of the Treaty and those of the Regulations, the provisions of the Treaty shall prevail.

CHAPTER VI

DISPUTES

Article 59

Disputes

Subject to Article 64(5), any dispute between two or more Contracting States concerning the interpretation or application of this Treaty or the Regulations, not settled by negotiation, may, by any one of the States concerned, be brought before the International Court of Justice by application in conformity with the Statute of the Court, unless the States concerned agree on some other method of settlement. The Contracting State bringing the dispute before the Court shall inform the International Bureau; the International Bureau shall bring the matter to the attention of the other Contracting States.

CHAPTER VII

REVISION AND AMENDMENT

Article 60

Revision of the Treaty

(1) This Treaty may be revised from time to time by a special conference of the Contracting States.

(2) The convocation of any revision conference shall be decided by the Assembly.

(3) Any intergovernmental organization appointed as International Searching or Preliminary Examining Authority shall be admitted as observer to any revision conference.

(4) Articles 53(5), (9) and (11), 54, 55(4) to (8), 56, and 57, may be amended either by a revision conference or according to the provisions of Article 61.

Article 61

Amendment of Certain Provisions of the Treaty

(1)(a)   Proposals for the amendment of Articles 53(5), (9) and (11), 54. 55(4) to (8), 56, and 57, may be initiated by any State member of the Assembly, by the Executive Committee, or by the Director General.

(b)   Such proposals shall be communicated by the Director General to the Contracting States at least six months in advance of their consideration by the Assembly.

(2)(a)   Amendments to the Articles referred to in paragraph (1) shall be adopted by the Assembly.

(b)   Adoption shall require three-fourths of the votes cast.

(3)(a)   Any amendment to the Articles referred to in paragraph (1) shall enter into force one month after written notifications of acceptance, effected in accordance with their respective constitutional processes, have been received by the Director General from three-fourths of the States members of the Assembly at the time it adopted the amendment.

(b)   Any amendment to the said Articles thus accepted shall bind all the States which are members of the Assembly at the time the amendment enters into force, provided that any amendment increasing the financial obligations of the Contracting States shall bind only those States which have notified their acceptance of such amendment.

(c)   Any amendment accepted in accordance with the provisions of subparagraph (a) shall bind all States which become members of the Assembly after the date on which the amendment entered into force in accordance with the provisions of subparagraph (a).

CHAPTER VIII

FINAL PROVISIONS

Article 62

Becoming Party to the Treaty

(1)   Any State member of the International Union for the Protection of Industrial Property may become party to this Treaty by:

     (i)   signature followed by the deposit of an instrument of ratification, or

     (ii)   deposit of an instrument of accession.

(2)   Instruments of ratification or accession shall be deposited with the Director General.

(3) The provisions of Article 24 of the Stockholm Act of the Paris Convention for the Protection of Industrial Property shall apply to this Treaty.

(4) Paragraph (3) shall in no way be understood as implying the recognition or tacit acceptance by a Contracting State of the factual situation concerning a territory to which this Treaty is made applicable by another Contracting State by virtue of the said paragraph.

Article 63

Entry into Force of the Treaty

(1)(a) Subject to the provisions of paragraph (3), this Treaty shall enter into force three months after eight States have deposited their instruments of ratification or accession, provided that at least four of those States each fulfill any of the following conditions:

(i) the number of applications filed in the State has exceeded 40,000 according to the most recent annual statistics published by the International Bureau,

(ii) the nationals or residents of the State have filed at least 1,000 applications in one foreign country according to the most recent annual statistics published by the International Bureau,

(iii) the national Office of the State has received at least 10,000 applications from nationals or residents of foreign countries according to the most recent annual statistics published by the International Bureau.

(b) For the purposes of this paragraph, the term "applications" does not include applications for utility models.

(2) Subject to the provisions of paragraph (3), any State which does not become party to this Treaty upon entry into force under paragraph (1) shall become bound by this Treaty three months after the date on which such State has deposited its instrument of ratification or accession.

(3) The provisions of Chapter II and the corresponding provisions of the Regulations annexed to this Treaty shall become applicable, however, only on the date on which three States each of which fulfill at least one of the three requirements specified in paragraph (1) have become party to this Treaty without declaring, as provided in Article 64(1), that they do not intend to be bound by the provisions of Chapter II. That date shall not, however, be prior to that of the initial entry into force under paragraph (1).

Article 64

Reservations

(1)(a)   Any State may declare that it shall not be bound by the provisions of Chapter II.

(b)   States making a declaration under subparagraph (a) shall not be bound by the provisions of Chapter II and the corresponding provisions of the Regulations.

(2)(a)   Any State not having made a declaration under paragraph (1)(a) may declare that:

(i)   it shall not be bound by the provisions of Article 39(1) with respect to the furnishing of a copy of the international application and a translation thereof (as prescribed),

(ii)   the obligation to delay national processing, as provided for under Article 40, shall not prevent publication, by or through its national Office, of the international application or a translation thereof, it being understood, however, that it is not exempted from the limitations provided for in Articles 30 and 38.

(b)   States making such a declaration shall be bound accordingly.

(3)(a)   Any State may declare that, as far as it is concerned, international publication of international applications is not required.

(b)   Where, at the expiration of 18 months from the priority date, the international application contains the designation only of such States as have made declarations under subparagraph (a), the international application shall not be published by virtue of Article 21(2).

(c)   Where the provisions of subparagraph (b) apply, the international application shall nevertheless be published by the International Bureau:

(i)   at the request of the applicant, as provided in the Regulations,

(ii)   when a national application or a patent based on the international application is published by or on behalf of the national Office of any designated State having made a declaration under subparagraph (a), promptly after such publication but not before the expiration of 18 months from the priority date.

(4)(a)   Any State whose national law provides for prior art effect of its patents as from a date before publication, but does not equate for prior art purposes the priority date claimed under the Paris Convention for the Protection of Industrial Property to the actual filing date in that State, may declare that the filing outside that State of an international application designating that State is not equated to an actual filing in that State for prior art purposes.

(b) Any State making a declaration under subparagraph (a) shall to that extent not be bound by the provisions of Article 11(3).

(c) Any State making a declaration under subparagraph (a) shall, at the same time, state in writing the date from which, and the conditions under which, the prior art effect of any international application designating that State becomes effective in that State. This statement may be modified at any time by notification addressed to the Director General.

(5) Each State may declare that it does not consider itself bound by Article 59. With regard to any dispute between any Contracting State having made such a declaration and any other Contracting State, the provisions of Article 59 shall not apply.

(6)(a)   Any declaration made under this Article shall be made in writing. It may be made at the time of signing this Treaty, at the time of depositing the instrument of ratification or accession, or, except in the case referred to in paragraph (5), at any later time by notification addressed to the Director General. In the case of the said notification, the declaration shall take effect six months after the day on which the Director General has received the notification, and shall not affect international applications filed prior to the expiration of the said six-month period.

(b) Any declaration made under this Article may be withdrawn at any time by notification addressed to the Director General. Such withdrawal shall take effect three months after the day on which the Director General has received the notification and, in the case of the withdrawal of a declaration made under paragraph (3), shall not affect international applications filed prior to the expiration of the said three-month period.

(7) No reservations to this Treaty other than the reservations under paragraphs (1) to (5) are permitted.

Article 65

Gradual Application

(1) If the agreement with any International Searching or Preliminary Examining Authority provides, transitionally, for limits on the number or kind of international applications that such Authority undertakes to process, the Assembly shall adopt the measures necessary for the gradual

application of this Treaty and the Regulations in respect of given categories of international applications. This provision shall also apply to requests for an international-type search under Article 15(5).

(2) The Assembly shall fix the dates from which, subject to the provision of paragraph (1), international applications may be filed and demands for international preliminary examination may be submitted. Such dates shall not be later than six months after this Treaty has entered into force according to the provisions of Article 63(1), or after Chapter II has become applicable under Article 63(3), respectively.

Article 66

Denunciation

(1) Any Contracting State may denounce this Treaty by notification addressed to the Director General.

(2) Denunciation shall take effect six months after receipt of the said notification by the Director General. It shall not affect the effects of the international application in the denouncing State if the international application was filed, and, where the denouncing State has been elected, the election was made, prior to the expiration of the said six-month period.

Article 67

Signature and Languages

(1)(a) This Treaty shall be signed in a single original in the English and French languages, both texts being equally authentic.

(b) Official texts shall be established by the Director General, after consultation with the interested Governments, in the German, Japanese, Portuguese, Russian and Spanish languages, and such other languages as the Assembly may designate.

(2) This Treaty shall remain open for signature at Washington until December 31, 1970.

Article 68

Depositary Functions

(1) The original of this Treaty, when no longer open for signature, shall be deposited with the Director General.

(2) The Director General shall transmit two copies, certified by him, of this Treaty and the Regulations annexed hereto to the Governments of all States party to the Paris Convention for the Protection of Industrial Property and, on request, to the Government of any other State.

(3) The Director General shall register this Treaty with the Secretariat of the United Nations.

(4)   The Director General shall transmit two copies, certified by him, of any amendment to this Treaty and the Regulations to the Governments of all Contracting States and, on request, to the Government of any other State.

Article 69

Notifications

The Director General shall notify the Governments of all States party to the Paris Convention for the Protection of Industrial Property of:

(i)   signatures under Article 62,

(ii)   deposits of instruments of ratification or accession under Article 62,

(iii) the date of entry into force of this Treaty and the date from which Chapter II is applicable in accordance with Article 63(3),

(iv)   any declarations made under Article 64(1) to (5),

(v)   withdrawals of any declarations made under Article 64(6)(b),

(vi)   denunciations received under Article 66, and

(vii) any declarations made under Article 31(4).

19

PARTIES TO THE PATENT COOPERATION TREATY

Status as of December 23, 2020

Contracting Party	Entry into Force
Albania	October 4, 1995
Algeria[1]	March 8, 2000
Angola	December 27, 2007
Antigua and Barbuda	March 17, 2000
Armenia[1]	December 25, 1991
Australia	March 31, 1980
Austria	April 23, 1979
Azerbaijan	December 25, 1995
Bahrain[1]	March 18, 2007
Barbados	March 12, 1985
Belarus[1]	December 25, 1991
Belgium	December 14, 1981
Belize	June 17, 2000
Benin	February 26, 1987
Bosnia and Herzegovina	September 7, 1996
Botswana	October 30, 2003
Brazil	April 9, 1978
Brunei Darussalam	July 24, 2012
Bulgaria	May 21, 1984
Burkina Faso	March 21, 1989
Cambodia[1]	December 8, 2016
Cameroon	January 24, 1978
Canada	January 2, 1990
Central African Republic	January 24, 1978
Chad	January 24, 1978
Chile[1]	June 2, 2009

---

[1] With the declaration provided for in Article 64(5).

Contracting Party	Entry into Force
China[2, 3]	January 1, 1994
Colombia	February 28, 2001
Comoros	April 3, 2005
Congo	January 24, 1978
Costa Rica	August 3, 1999
Côte d'Ivoire	April 30, 1991
Croatia	July 1, 1998
Cuba[1]	July 16, 1996
Cyprus	April 1, 1998
Czech Republic	January 1, 1993
Democratic People's Republic of Korea	July 8, 1980
Denmark	December 1, 1978
Djibouti	September 23, 2016
Dominica	August 7, 1999
Dominican Republic	May 28, 2007
Ecuador	May 7, 2001
Egypt	September 6, 2003
El Salvador	August 17, 2006
Equatorial Guinea	July 17, 2001
Estonia	August 24, 1994
Eswatini	September 20, 1994
Finland[4]	October 1, 1980
France[1, 5]	February 25, 1978
Gabon	January 24, 1978
Gambia	December 9, 1997
Georgia[1]	December 25, 1991
Germany	January 24, 1978
Ghana	February 26, 1997
Greece	October 9, 1990
Grenada	September 22, 1998
Guatemala	October 14, 2006
Guinea	May 27, 1991
Guinea-Bissau	December 12, 1997

[2.] Applies also to Hong Kong, China with effect from July 1, 1997.

[3.] Not applicable to Macao, China.

[4.] With the declaration provided for in Article 64(2)(a)(ii).

[5.] Including all Overseas Departments and Territories.

Contracting Party	Entry into Force
Honduras	June 20, 2006
Hungary[1]	June 27, 1980
Iceland	March 23, 1995
India[1]	December 7, 1998
Indonesia[1]	September 5, 1997
Iran[1] (Islamic Republic of)	October 4, 2013
Ireland	August 1, 1992
Israel	June 1, 1996
Italy	March 28, 1985
Japan	October 1, 1978
Jordan	June 9, 2017
Kazakhstan[1]	December 25, 1991
Kenya	June 8, 1994
Kuwait	September 9, 2016
Kyrgyzstan[1]	December 25, 1991
Lao People's Democratic Republic[1]	June 14, 2006
Latvia	September 7, 1993
Lesotho	October 21, 1995
Liberia	August 27, 1994
Libya	September 15, 2005
Liechtenstein	March 19, 1980
Lithuania	July 5, 1994
Luxembourg	April 30, 1978
Madagascar	January 24, 1978
Malawi	January 24, 1978
Malaysia[1]	August 16, 2006
Mali	October 19, 1984
Malta[1]	March 1, 2007
Mauritania	April 13, 1983
Mexico	January 1, 1995
Monaco	June 22, 1979
Mongolia	May 27, 1991
Montenegro	June 3, 2006
Morocco	October 8, 1999
Mozambique[1]	May 18, 2000
Namibia	January 1, 2004

Contracting Party	Entry into Force
Netherlands[6]	July 10, 1979
New Zealand	December 1, 1992
Nicaragua	March 6, 2003
Niger	March 21, 1993
Nigeria	May 8, 2005
North Macedonia	August 10, 1995
Norway[4]	January 1, 1980
Oman[1]	October 26, 2001
Panama	September 7, 2012
Papua New Guinea	June 14, 2003
Peru	June 6, 2009
Philippines	August 17, 2001
Poland[4]	December 25, 1990
Portugal	November 24, 1992
Qatar[1]	August 3, 2011
Republic of Korea	August 10, 1984
Republic of Moldova[1]	December 25, 1991
Romania[1]	July 23, 1979
Russian Federation[1]	March 29, 1978[7]
Rwanda	August 31, 2011
Saint Kitts and Nevis	October 27, 2005
Saint Lucia[1]	August 30, 1996
Saint Vincent and the Grenadines[1]	August 6, 2002
Samoa	January 2, 2020[1]
San Marino	December 14, 2004
Sao Tome and Principe	July 3, 2008
Saudi Arabia	August 3, 2013
Senegal	January 24, 1978
Serbia[8]	February 1, 1997
Seychelles	November 7, 2002
Sierra Leone	June 17, 1997
Singapore	February 23, 1995

[6.] Ratification for the Kingdom in Europe, the Netherlands Antilles and Aruba. The Netherlands Antilles ceased to exist on October 10, 2010. As from that date, the PCT continues to apply to Curaçao and Sint Maarten. The PCT also continues to apply to the islands of Bonaire, Sint Eustatius and Saba which, with effect from October 10, 2010, have become part of the territory of the Kingdom of the Netherlands in Europe.

[7.] Date of ratification of the Soviet Union, continued by the Russian Federation as from December 25, 1991.

[8.] Serbia is the continuing State from Serbia and Montenegro as from June 3, 2006.

Contracting Party	Entry into Force
Slovakia	January 1, 1993
Slovenia	March 1, 1994
South Africa[1]	March 16, 1999
Spain	November 16, 1989
Sri Lanka	February 26, 1982
Sudan	April 16, 1984
Sweden[4]	May 17, 1978
Switzerland	January 24, 1978
Syrian Arab Republic	June 26, 2003
Tajikistan[1]	December 25, 1991
Thailand[1]	December 24, 2009
Togo	January 24, 1978
Trinidad and Tobago	March 10, 1994
Tunisia	December 10, 2001
Turkey	January 1, 1996
Turkmenistan[1]	December 25, 1991
Uganda	February 9, 1995
Ukraine[1]	December 25, 1991
United Arab Emirates	March 10, 1999
United Kingdom[9, 10, 11]	January 24, 1978
United Republic of Tanzania	September 14, 1999
United States of America[12, 13]	January 24, 1978
Uzbekistan[1]	December 25, 1991
Viet Nam	March 10, 1993
Zambia	November 15, 2001
Zimbabwe	June 11, 1997

Total: 153 States

[9.] The United Kingdom extended the application of the PCT to the Isle of Man with effect from October 29, 1983.

[10.] The United Kingdom extended the application of the PCT to the territory of Gibraltar with effect from January 1, 2021.

[11.] The United Kingdom extended the application of the PCT to the territory of the Bailiwick of Guernsey with effect from March 23, 2021.

[12.] With the declarations provided for in Articles 64(3)(a) and 64(4)(a).

[13.] Extends to all areas for which the United States of America has international responsibility.

20

EUROPEAN PATENT CONVENTION

CONVENTION

ON THE GRANT OF EUROPEAN PATENTS of 5 October 1973

Text as amended by the act revising Article 63 EPC of 17 December 1991 and the Act revising the EPC of 29 November 2000.

PREAMBLE

The Contracting States,

DESIRING to strengthen co-operation between the States of Europe in respect of the protection of inventions,

DESIRING that such protection may be obtained in those States by a single procedure for the grant of patents and by the establishment of certain standard rules governing patents so granted,

DESIRING, for this purpose, to conclude a Convention which establishes a European Patent Organisation and which constitutes a special agreement within the meaning of Article 19 of the Convention for the Protection of Industrial Property, signed in Paris on 20 March 1883 and last revised on 14 July 1967, and a regional patent treaty within the meaning of Article 45, paragraph 1, of the Patent Cooperation Treaty of 1, June 1970,

HAVE AGREED on the following provisions:

PART I—GENERAL AND INSTITUTIONAL PROVISIONS

CHAPTER I—General provisions

Article 1

European law for the grant of patents

A system of law, common to the Contracting States, for the grant of patents for invention is hereby established.

Article 2

European patent

(1) Patents granted by virtue of this Convention shall be called European patents.

(2) The European patent shall, in each of the Contracting States for which it is granted, have the effect of and be subject to the same conditions

as a national patent granted by that State, unless otherwise provided in this Convention.

Article 3

Territorial effect

The grant of a European patent may be requested for one or more of the Contracting States.

Article 4

European Patent Organisation

(1) A European Patent Organisation, hereinafter referred to as the Organisation, is established by this Convention. It shall have administrative and financial autonomy.

(2) The organs of the Organisation shall be:

(a) a European Patent Office;

(b) an Administrative Council.

(3) The task of the Organisation shall be to grant European patents. This shall be carried out by the European Patent Office supervised by the Administrative Council.

Article 4a

Conference of ministers of the Contracting States

A conference of ministers of the Contracting States responsible for patent matters shall meet at least every five years to discuss issues pertaining to the Organisation and to the European patent system.

Chapter II—The European Patent Organisation

Article 5

Legal status

(1) The Organisation shall have legal personality.

(2) In each of the Contracting States, the Organisation shall enjoy the most extensive legal capacity accorded to legal persons under the national law of that State; it may in particular acquire or dispose of movable and immovable property and may be a party to legal proceedings.

(3) The President of the European Patent Office shall represent the Organisation.

Article 6

Headquarters

(1) The Organisation shall have its headquarters at Munich.

(2) The European Patent Office shall be located in Munich. It shall have a branch at The Hague.

Article 7

Sub-offices of the European Patent Office

By decision of the Administrative Council, sub-offices of the European Patent Office may be created if need be, for the purpose of information and liaison, in the Contracting States and with inter-governmental organisations in the field of industrial property, subject to the approval of the Contracting State or organisation concerned.

Article 8

Privileges and immunities

The Protocol on Privileges and Immunities annexed to this Convention shall define the conditions under which the Organisation, the members of the Administrative Council, the employees of the European Patent Office and such other persons specified in that Protocol as take part in the work of the Organisation, shall enjoy, in the territory of each Contracting State, the privileges and immunities necessary for the performance of their duties.

Article 9

Liability

(1) The contractual liability of the Organisation shall be governed by the law applicable to the relevant contract.

(2) The non-contractual liability of the Organisation in respect of any damage caused by it or by the employees of the European Patent Office in the performance of their duties shall be governed by the provisions of the law of the Federal Republic of Germany. Where the damage is caused by the branch at The Hague or a sub-office or employees attached thereto, the provisions of the law of the Contracting State in which such branch or sub-office is located shall apply.

(3) The personal liability of the employees of the European Patent Office towards the Organisation shall be laid down in their Service Regulations or conditions of employment.

(4) The courts with jurisdiction to settle disputes under paragraphs 1 and 2 shall be:

(a) for disputes under paragraph 1, the courts of competent jurisdiction in the Federal Republic of Germany, unless the contract concluded between the parties designates the courts of another State;

(b) for disputes under paragraph 2, either the courts of competent jurisdiction in the Federal Republic of Germany, or the courts of competent jurisdiction in the State in which the branch or sub-office is located.

Chapter III—The European Patent Office

Article 10

Management

(1) The European Patent Office shall be managed by the President who shall be responsible for its activities to the Administrative Council.

(2) To this end, the President shall have in particular the following functions and powers:

(a) he shall take all necessary steps to ensure the functioning of the European Patent Office, including the adoption of internal administrative instructions and information to the public;

(b) unless this Convention provides otherwise, he shall prescribe which acts are to be performed at the European Patent Office in Munich and its branch at The Hague respectively;

(c) he may submit to the Administrative Council any proposal for amending this Convention, for general regulations, or for decisions which come within the competence of the Administrative Council;

(d) he shall prepare and implement the budget and any amending or supplementary budget;

(e) he shall submit a management report to the Administrative Council each year;

(f) he shall exercise supervisory authority over the staff;

(g) subject to Article 11, he shall appoint the employees and decide on their promotion;

(h) he shall exercise disciplinary authority over the employees other than those referred to in Article 11, and may propose disciplinary action to the Administrative Council with regard to employees referred to in Article 11, paragraphs 2 and 3;

(i) he may delegate his functions and powers.

(3) The President shall be assisted by a number of Vice-Presidents. If the President is absent or indisposed, one of the Vice-Presidents shall take his place in accordance with the procedure laid down by the Administrative Council.

Article 11

Appointment of senior employees

(1) The President of the European Patent Office shall be appointed by the Administrative Council.

(2) The Vice-Presidents shall be appointed by the Administrative Council after the President of the European Patent Office has been consulted.

(3) The members, including the Chairmen, of the Boards of Appeal and of the Enlarged Board of Appeal shall be appointed by the Administrative Council on a proposal from the President of the European Patent Office. They may be re-appointed by the Administrative Council after the President of the European Patent Office has been consulted.

(4) The Administrative Council shall exercise disciplinary authority over the employees referred to in paragraphs 1 to 3.

(5) The Administrative Council, after consulting the President of the European Patent Office, may also appoint as members of the Enlarged Board of Appeal legally qualified members of the national courts or quasi-judicial authorities of the Contracting States, who may continue their judicial activities at the national level. They shall be appointed for a term of three years and may be re-appointed.

Article 12

Duties of office

The employees of the European Patent Office shall be bound, even after the termination of their employment, neither to disclose nor to make use of information which by its nature is a professional secret.

Article 13

Disputes between the Organisation and the employees of the European Patent Office

(1) Employees and former employees of the European Patent Office or their successors in title may apply to the Administrative Tribunal of the International Labour Organisation in the case of disputes with the European Patent Organisation in accordance with the Statute of the Tribunal and within the limits and subject to the conditions laid down in the Service Regulations for permanent employees or the Pension Scheme Regulations or arising from the conditions of employment of other employees.

(2) An appeal shall only be admissible if the person concerned has exhausted such other means of appeal as are available to him under the Service Regulations, the Pension Scheme Regulations or the conditions of employment, as the case may be.

Article 14

Languages of the European Patent Office, European patent applications and other documents

(1) The official languages of the European Patent Office shall be English, French and German.

(2) A European patent application shall be filed in one of the official languages or, if filed in any other language, translated into one of the official languages in accordance with the Implementing Regulations. Throughout the proceedings before the European Patent Office, such translation may be brought into conformity with the application as filed. If a required translation is not filed in due time, the application shall be deemed to be withdrawn.

(3) The official language of the European Patent Office in which the European patent application is filed or into which it is translated shall be used as the language of the proceedings in all proceedings before the European Patent Office, unless the Implementing Regulations provide otherwise.

(4) Natural or legal persons having their residence or principal place of business within a Contracting State having a language other than English, French or German as an official language, and nationals of that State who are resident abroad, may file documents which have to be filed within a time limit in an official language of that State. They shall, however, file a translation in an official language of the European Patent Office in accordance with the Implementing Regulations. If any document, other than those documents making up the European patent application, is not filed in the prescribed language, or if any required translation is not filed in due time, the document shall be deemed not to have been filed.

(5) European patent applications shall be published in the language of the proceedings.

(6) Specifications of European patents shall be published in the language of the proceedings and shall include a translation of the claims in the other two official languages of the European Patent Office.

(7) The following shall be published in the three official languages of the European Patent Office:

(a) the European Patent Bulletin;

(b) the Official Journal of the European Patent Office.

(8) Entries in the European Patent Register shall be made in the three official languages of the European Patent Office. In cases of doubt, the entry in the language of the proceedings shall be authentic.

Article 15

Departments entrusted with the procedure

For implementing the procedures laid down in this Convention, there shall be set up within the European Patent Office:

(a) a Receiving Section;

(b) Search Divisions;

(c) Examining Divisions;

(d) Opposition Divisions;

(e) a Legal Division;

(f) Boards of Appeal;

(g) an Enlarged Board of Appeal.

Article 16

Receiving Section

The Receiving Section shall be responsible for the examination on filing and the examination as to formal requirements of European patent applications.

Article 17

Search Divisions

The Search Divisions shall be responsible for drawing up European search reports.

Article 18

Examining Divisions

(1) The Examining Divisions shall be responsible for the examination of European patent applications.

(2) An Examining Division shall consist of three technically qualified examiners. However, before a decision is taken on a European patent application, its examination shall, as a general rule, be entrusted to one member of the Examining Division. Oral proceedings shall be before the Examining Division itself. If the Examining Division considers that the nature of the decision so requires, it shall be enlarged by the addition of a legally qualified examiner. In the event of parity of votes, the vote of the Chairman of the Examining Division shall be decisive.

Article 19

Opposition Divisions

(1) An Opposition Division shall be responsible for the examination of oppositions against any European patent.

(2)   An Opposition Division shall consist of three technical examiners, at least two of whom shall not have taken part in the proceedings for grant of the patent to which the opposition relates. An examiner who has taken part in the proceedings for the grant of the European patent shall not be the Chairman. Prior to the taking of a final decision on the opposition, the Opposition Division may entrust the examination of the opposition to one of its members. Oral proceedings shall be before the Opposition Division itself. If the Opposition Division considers that the nature of the decision so requires, it shall be enlarged by the addition of a legally qualified examiner who shall not have taken part in the proceedings for grant of the patent. In the event of parity of votes, the vote of the Chairman of the Division shall be decisive.

Article 20

Legal Division

(1)   The Legal Division shall be responsible for decisions in respect of entries in the Register of European Patents and in respect of registration on, and deletion from, the list of professional representatives.

(2)   Decisions of the Legal Division shall be taken by one legally qualified member.

Article 21

Boards of Appeal

(1)   The Boards of Appeal shall be responsible for the examination of appeals from decisions of the Receiving Section, the Examining Divisions and Opposition Divisions, and the Legal Division.

(2)   For appeals from decisions of the Receiving Section or the Legal Division, a Board of Appeal shall consist of three legally qualified members.

(3)   For appeals from a decision of an Examining Division, a Board of Appeal shall consist of:

(a)   two technically qualified members and one legally qualified member, when the decision concerns the refusal of a European patent application or the grant, limitation or revocation of a European patent, and was taken by an Examining Division consisting of less than four members;

(b)   three technically and two legally qualified members, when the decision was taken by an Examining Division consisting of four members, or when the Board of Appeal considers that the nature of the appeal so requires;

(c)   three legally qualified members in all other cases.

(4) For appeals from a decision of an Opposition Division, a Board of Appeal shall consist of:

(a) two technically qualified members and one legally qualified member, when the decision was taken by an Opposition Division consisting of three members;

(b) three technically and two legally qualified members, when the decision was taken by an Opposition Division consisting of four members, or when the Board of Appeal considers that the nature of the appeal so requires.

Article 22

Enlarged Board of Appeal

(1) The Enlarged Board of Appeal shall be responsible for:

(a) deciding on points of law referred to it by Boards of Appeal under Article 112;

(b) giving opinions on points of law referred to it by the President of the European Patent Office under Article 112;

(c) deciding on petitions for review of decisions of the Boards of Appeal under Article 112a.

(2) In proceedings under paragraph 1(a) and (b), the Enlarged Board of Appeal shall consist of five legally and two technically qualified members. In proceedings under paragraph 1(c), the Enlarged Board of Appeal shall consist of three or five members as laid down in the Implementing Regulations. In all proceedings, a legally qualified member shall be the Chairman.

Article 23

Independence of the members of the Boards

(1) The members of the Enlarged Board of Appeal and of the Boards of Appeal shall be appointed for a term of five years and may not be removed from office during this term, except if there are serious grounds for such removal and if the Administrative Council, on a proposal from the Enlarged Board of Appeal, takes a decision to this effect. Notwithstanding sentence 1, the term of office of members of the Boards shall end if they resign or are retired in accordance with the Service Regulations for permanent employees of the European Patent Office.

(2) The members of the Boards may not be members of the Receiving Section, Examining Divisions, Opposition Divisions or Legal Division.

(3) In their decisions the members of the Boards shall not be bound by any instructions and shall comply only with the provisions of this Convention.

(4) The Rules of Procedure of the Boards of Appeal and the Enlarged Board of Appeal shall be adopted in accordance with the Implementing Regulations. They shall be subject to the approval of the Administrative Council.

Article 24

Exclusion and objection

(1) Members of the Boards of Appeal or of the Enlarged Board of Appeal may not take part in any appeal if they have any personal interest therein, if they have previously been involved as representatives of one of the parties, or if they participated in the decision under appeal.

(2) If, for one of the reasons mentioned in paragraph 1, or for any other reason, a member of a Board of Appeal or of the Enlarged Board of Appeal considers that he should not take part in any appeal, he shall inform the Board accordingly.

(3) Members of a Board of Appeal or of the Enlarged Board of Appeal may be objected to by any party for one of the reasons mentioned in paragraph 1, or if suspected of partiality. An objection shall not be admissible if, while being aware of a reason for objection, the party has taken a procedural step. No objection may be based upon the nationality of members.

(4) The Boards of Appeal and the Enlarged Board of Appeal shall decide as to the action to be taken in the cases specified in paragraphs 2 and 3 without the participation of the member concerned. For the purposes of taking this decision the member objected to shall be replaced by his alternate.

Article 25

Technical opinion

At the request of the competent national court trying an infringement or revocation action, the European Patent Office shall be obliged, against payment of an appropriate fee, to give a technical opinion concerning the European patent which is the subject of the action. The Examining Divisions shall be responsible for the issue of such options.

Chapter IV—The Administrative Council

Article 26

Membership

(1) The Administrative Council shall be composed of the Representatives and the alternate Representatives of the Contracting States. Each Contracting State shall be entitled to appoint one Representative and one alternate Representative to the Administrative Council.

(2) The members of the Administrative Council may, subject to the provisions of its Rules of Procedure, be assisted by advisers or experts.

Article 27

Chairmanship

(1) The Administrative Council shall elect a Chairman and a Deputy Chairman from among the Representatives and alternate Representatives of the Contracting States. The Deputy Chairman shall ex officio replace the Chairman in the event of his being prevented from attending to his duties.

(2) The duration of the terms of office of the Chairman and the Deputy Chairman shall be three years. The terms of office shall be renewable.

Article 28

Board

(1) When there are at least eight Contracting States, the Administrative Council may set up a Board composed of five of its members.

(2) The Chairman and the Deputy Chairman of the Administrative Council shall be members of the Board ex officio; the other three members shall be elected by the Administrative Council.

(3) The term of office of the members elected by the Administrative Council shall be three years. This term of office shall not be renewable.

(4) The Board shall perform the duties given to it by the Administrative Council in accordance with the Rules of Procedure.

Article 29

Meetings

(1) Meetings of the Administrative Council shall be convened by its Chairman.

(2) The President of the European Patent Office shall take part in the deliberations of the Administrative Council.

(3) The Administrative Council shall hold an ordinary meeting once each year. In addition, it shall meet on the initiative of its Chairman or at the request of one-third of the Contracting States.

(4) The deliberations of the Administrative Council shall be based on an agenda, and shall be held in accordance with its Rules of Procedure.

(5) The provisional agenda shall contain any question whose inclusion is requested by any Contracting State in accordance with the Rules of Procedure.

Article 30

Attendance of observers

(1) The World Intellectual Property Organization shall be represented at the meetings of the Administrative Council, in accordance with the provisions of an agreement to be concluded between the European Patent Organization and the World Intellectual Property Organisation.

(2) Any other inter-governmental organisation charged with the implementation of international procedures in the field of patents with which the Organisation has concluded an agreement shall be represented at the meetings of the Administrative Council, in accordance with any provisions contained in such agreement.

(3) Any other inter-governmental and international non-governmental organisations exercising an activity of interest to the Organisation may be invited by the Administrative Council to arrange to be represented at its meetings during any discussion of matters of mutual interest.

Article 31

Languages of the Administrative Council

(1) The languages in use in the deliberations of the Administrative Council shall be English, French and German.

(2) Documents submitted to the Administrative Council, and the minutes of its deliberations, shall be drawn up in the three languages mentioned in paragraph 1.

Article 32

Staff, premises and equipment

The European Patent Office shall place at the disposal of the Administrative Council and any body established by it such staff, premises and equipment as may be necessary for the performance of their duties.

Article 33

Competence of the Administrative Council in certain cases

(1) The Administrative Council shall be competent to amend:

(a) the time limits laid down in this Convention;

(b) Parts II to VIII and Part X of this Convention, to bring them into line with an international treaty relating to patents or European Community legislation relating to patents;

(c) the Implementing Regulations.

(2) The Administrative Council shall be competent, in conformity with this Convention, to adopt or amend:

(a) the Financial Regulations;

(b) the Service Regulations for permanent employees and the conditions of employment of other employees of the European Patent Office, the salary scales of the said permanent and other employees, and also the nature of any supplementary benefits and the rules for granting them;

(c) the Pension Scheme Regulations and any appropriate increases in existing pensions to correspond to increases in salaries;

(d) the Rules relating to Fees;

(e) its Rules of Procedure.

(3) Notwithstanding Article 18, paragraph 2, the Administrative Council shall be competent to decide, in the light of experience, that in certain categories of cases Examining Divisions shall consist of one technically qualified examiner only. Such decision may be rescinded.

(4) The Administrative Council shall be competent to authorise the President of the European Patent Office to negotiate and, subject to its approval, to conclude agreements on behalf of the European Patent Organisation with States, with intergovernmental organisations and with documentation centres set up on the basis of agreements with such organisations.

(5) The Administrative Council may not take a decision under paragraph 1(b):

— concerning an international treaty, before its entry into force;

— concerning European Community legislation, before its entry into force or, where that legislation lays down a period for its implementation, before the expiry of that period.

Article 34

Voting rights

(1) The right to vote in the Administrative Council shall be restricted to the Contracting States.

(2) Each Contracting State shall have one vote, subject to the application of the provisions of Article 36.

Article 35

Voting rules

(1) The Administrative Council shall take its decisions, other than those referred to in paragraphs 2 and 3, by a simple majority of the Contracting States represented and voting.

(2)   A majority of three-quarters of the votes of the Contracting States represented and voting shall be required for the decisions which the Administrative Council is empowered to take under Article 7, Article 11, paragraph 1, Article 33, paragraphs 1(a) and (c), and 2 to 4, Article 39, paragraph 1, Article 40, paragraphs 2 and 4, Article 46, Article 134a, Article 149a, paragraph 2, Article 152, Article 153, paragraph 7, Article 166 and Article 172.

(3)   Unanimity of the Contracting States voting shall be required for the decisions which the Administrative Council is empowered to take under Article 33, paragraph 1(b). The Administrative Council shall take such decisions only if all the Contracting States are represented. A decision taken on the basis of Article 33, paragraph 1(b), shall not take effect if a Contracting State declares, within twelve months of the date of the decision, that it does not wish to be bound by that decision.

(4)   Abstentions shall not be considered as votes.

Article 36

Weighting of votes

(1)   In respect of the adoption or amendment of the Rules relating to Fees and, if the financial contribution to be made by the Contracting States would thereby be increased, the adoption of the budget of the Organisation and of any amending or supplementary budget, any Contracting State may require, following a first ballot in which each Contracting State shall have one vote, and whatever the result of this ballot, that a second ballot be taken immediately, in which votes shall be given to the States in accordance with paragraph 2. The decision shall be determined by the result of this second ballot.

(2)   The number of votes that each Contracting State shall have in the second ballot shall be calculated as follows:

(a)   the percentage obtained for each Contracting State in respect of the scale for the special financial contributions, pursuant to Article 40, paragraphs 3 and 4, shall be multiplied by the number of Contracting States and divided by five;

(b)   the number of votes thus given shall be rounded upwards to the next higher whole number;

(c)   five additional votes shall be added to this number;

(d)   nevertheless no Contracting State shall have more than 30 votes.

Chapter V—Financial Provisions

Article 37

Budgetary funding

The budget of the Organisation shall be financed:

(a) by the Organisation's own resources;

(b) by payments made by the Contracting States in respect of renewal fees for European patents levied in these States;

(c) where necessary, by special financial contributions made by the Contracting States;

(d) where appropriate, by the revenue provided for in Article 146;

(e) where appropriate, and for tangible assets only, by third-party borrowings secured on land or buildings;

(f) where appropriate, by third-party funding for specific projects.

Article 38

The Organisation's own resources

The Organisation's own resources shall comprise:

(a) all income from fees and other sources and also the reserves of the Organisation;

(b) the resources of the Pension Reserve Fund, which shall be treated as a special class of asset of the Organisation, designed to support the Organisation's pension scheme by providing the appropriate reserves.

Article 39

Payments by the Contracting States in respect of renewal fees for European patents

(1) Each Contracting State shall pay to the Organisation in respect of each renewal fee received for a European patent in that State an amount equal to a proportion of that fee, to be fixed by the Administrative Council; the proportion shall not exceed 75 per cent and shall be the same for all Contracting States. However, if the said proportion corresponds to an amount which is less than a uniform minimum amount fixed by the Administrative Council, the Contracting State shall pay that minimum to the Organisation.

(2) Each Contracting State shall communicate to the Organisation such information as the Administrative Council considers to be necessary to determine the amount of its payments.

(3) The due dates for these payments shall be determined by the Administrative Council.

(4) If a payment is not remitted fully by the due date, the Contracting State shall pay interest from the due date on the amount remaining unpaid.

Article 40

Level of fees and payments—Special financial contributions

(1) The amounts of the fees referred to under Article 38 and the proportion referred to under Article 39 shall be fixed at such a level as to ensure that the revenue in respect thereof is sufficient for the budget of the Organisation to be balanced.

(2) However, if the Organisation is unable to balance its budget under the conditions laid down in paragraph 1, the Contracting States shall remit to the Organisation special financial contributions, the amount of which shall be determined by the Administrative Council for the accounting period in question.

(3) These special financial contributions shall be determined in respect of any Contracting State on the basis of the number of patent applications filed in the last year but one prior to that of entry into force of this Convention, and calculated in the following manner:

(a) one half in proportion to the number of patent applications filed in that Contracting State;

(b) one half in proportion to the second highest number of patent applications filed in the other Contracting States by natural or legal persons having their residence or principal place of business in that Contracting State.

However, the amounts to be contributed by States in which the number of patent applications filed exceeds 25,000 shall then be taken as a whole and a new scale drawn up determined in proportion to the total number of patent applications filed in these States.

(4) Where, in respect of any Contracting State, its scale position cannot be established in accordance with paragraph 3, the Administrative Council shall, with the consent of that State, decide its scale position.

(5) Article 39, paragraphs 3 and 4, shall apply mutatis mutandis to the special financial contributions.

(6) The special financial contributions shall be repaid together with interest at a rate which shall be the same for all Contracting States. Repayments shall be made in so far as it is possible to provide for this purpose in the budget; the amount thus provided shall be distributed

among the Contracting States in accordance with the scale mentioned in paragraphs 3 and 4 above.

(7) The special financial contributions remitted in any accounting period shall be wholly repaid before any such contributions or parts thereof remitted in any subsequent accounting period are repaid.

Article 41

Advances

(1) At the request of the President of the European Patent Office, the Contracting States shall make advances to the Organisation, on account of their payments and contributions, within the limit of the amount fixed by the Administrative Council. Such advances shall be apportioned in proportion to the amounts due by the Contracting States for the accounting period in question.

(2) Article 39, paragraphs 3 and 4, shall apply mutatis mutandis to the advances.

Article 42

Budget

(1) The budget of the Organisation shall be balanced. It shall be drawn up in accordance with the generally accepted accounting principles laid down in the Financial Regulations. If necessary, there may be amending or supplementary budgets.

(2) The budget shall be drawn up in the unit of account fixed in the Financial Regulations.

Article 43

Authorisation for expenditure

(1) The expenditure entered in the budget shall be authorised for the duration of one accounting period, unless any provisions to the contrary are contained in the Financial Regulations.

(2) Subject to the conditions to be laid down in the Financial Regulations, any appropriations, other than those relating to staff costs, which are unexpended at the end of the accounting period may be carried forward, but not beyond the end of the following accounting period.

(3) Appropriations shall be set out under different headings according to type and purpose of the expenditure and subdivided, as far as necessary, in accordance with the Financial Regulations.

Article 44

Appropriations for unforeseeable expenditure

(1) The budget of the Organisation may contain appropriations for unforeseeable expenditure.

(2) The employment of these appropriations by the Organisation shall be subject to the prior approval of the Administrative Council.

Article 45

Accounting period

The accounting period shall commence on 1 January and end on 31 December.

Article 46

Preparation and adoption of the budget

(1) The President of the European Patent Office shall lay the draft budget before the Administrative Council not later than the date prescribed in the Financial Regulations.

(2) The budget and any amending or supplementary budget shall be adopted by the Administrative Council.

Article 47

Provisional budget

(1) If, at the beginning of the accounting period, the budget has not been adopted by the Administrative Council, expenditures may be effected on a monthly basis per heading or other division of the budget, according to the provisions of the Financial Regulations, up to one-12th of the budget appropriations for the preceding accounting period, provided that the appropriations thus made available to the President of the European Patent Office shall not exceed one-12th of those provided for in the draft budget.

(2) The Administrative Council may, subject to the observance of the other provisions laid down in paragraph 1, authorise expenditure in excess of one-12th of the appropriations.

(3) The payments referred to in Article 37, sub-paragraph (b), shall continue to be made, on a provisional basis, under the conditions determined under Article 39 for the year preceding that to which the draft budget relates.

(4) The Contracting States shall pay each month, on a provisional basis and in accordance with the scale referred to in Article 40, paragraphs 3 and 4, any special financial contributions necessary to ensure implementation of paragraphs 1 and 2 above. Article 39, paragraph 4, shall apply mutatis mutandis to these contributions.

Article 48

Budget implementation

(1) The President of the European Patent Office shall implement the budget and any amending or supplementary budget on his own responsibility and within the limits of the allocated appropriations.

(2) Within the budget, the President of the European Patent Office may, subject to the limits and conditions laid down in the Financial Regulations, transfer funds as between the various headings or subheadings.

Article 49

Auditing of accounts

(1) The income and expenditure account and a balance sheet of the Organisation shall be examined by auditors whose independence is beyond doubt, appointed by the Administrative Council for a period of five years, which shall be renewable or extensible.

(2) The audit, which shall be based on vouchers and shall take place, if necessary, in situ, shall ascertain, that all income has been received and all expenditure effected in a lawful and proper manner and that the financial management is sound. The auditors shall draw up a report after the end of each accounting period.

(3) The President of the European Patent Office shall annually submit to the Administrative Council the accounts of the preceding accounting period in respect of the budget and the balance sheet showing the assets and liabilities of the Organisation together with the report of the auditors.

(4) The Administrative Council shall approve the annual accounts together with the report of the auditors and shall give the President of the European Patent Office a discharge in respect of the implementation of the budget.

Article 50

Financial regulations

The Financial Regulations shall lay down in particular:

(a) the arrangements relating to the establishment and implementation of the budget and for the rendering and auditing of accounts;

(b) the method and procedure whereby the payments and contributions provided for in Article 37 and the advances provided for in Article 41 are to be made available to the Organisation by the Contracting States;

(c) the rules concerning the responsibilities of authorising and accounting officers and the arrangements for their supervision;

(d) the rates of interest provided for in Articles 39, 40 and 47;

(e) the method of calculating the contributions payable by virtue of Article 146;

(f) the composition of and duties to be assigned to a Budget and Finance Committee which should be set up by the Administrative Council;

(g) the generally accepted accounting principles on which the budget and the annual financial statements shall be based.

Article 51

Fees

(1) The European Patent Office may levy fees for any official task or procedure carried out under this Convention.

(2) Time limits for the payment of fees other than those fixed by this Convention shall be laid down in the Implementing Regulations.

(3) Where the Implementing Regulations provide that a fee shall be paid, they shall also lay down the legal consequences of failure to pay such fee in due time.

(4) The Rules relating to Fees shall determine in particular the amounts of the fees and the ways in which they are to be paid.

PART II—SUBSTANTIVE PATENT LAW

Chapter I—Patentability

Article 52

Patentable inventions

(1) European patents shall be granted for any inventions, in all fields of technology, provided that they are new, involve an inventive step and are susceptible of industrial application.

(2) The following in particular shall not be regarded as inventions within the meaning of paragraph 1:

(a) discoveries, scientific theories and mathematical methods;

(b) aesthetic creations;

(c) schemes, rules and methods for performing mental acts, playing games or doing business, and programs for computers;

(d) presentations of information.

(3) Paragraph 2 shall exclude the patentability of the subject-matter or activities referred to therein only to the extent to which a European

patent application or European patent relates to such subject-matter or activities as such.

Article 53

Exceptions to patentability

European patents shall not be granted in respect of:

(a) inventions the commercial exploitation of which would be contrary to "ordre public" or morality; such exploitation shall not be deemed to be so contrary merely because it is prohibited by law or regulation in some or all of the Contracting States;

(b) plant or animal varieties or essentially biological processes for the production of plants or animals; this provision shall not apply to microbiological processes or the products thereof;

(c) methods for treatment of the human or animal body by surgery or therapy and diagnostic methods practised on the human or animal body; this provision shall not apply to products, in particular substances or compositions, for use in any of these methods.

Article 54

Novelty

(1) An invention shall be considered to be new if it does not form part of the state of the art.

(2) The state of the art shall be held to comprise everything made available to the public by means of a written or oral description, by use, or in any other way, before the date of filing of the European patent application.

(3) Additionally, the content of European patent applications as filed, the dates of filing of which are prior to the date referred to in paragraph 2 and which were published on or after that date, shall be considered as comprised in the state of the art.

(4) Paragraphs 2 and 3 shall not exclude the patentability of any substance or composition, comprised in the state of the art, for use in a method referred to in Article 53(c), provided that its use for any such method is not comprised in the state of the art.

(5) Paragraphs 2 and 3 shall also not exclude the patentability of any substance or composition referred to in paragraph 4 for any specific use in a method referred to in Article 53(c), provided that such use is not comprised in the state of the art.

Article 55

Non-prejudicial disclosures

(1) For the application of Article 54 a disclosure of the invention shall not be taken into consideration if it occurred no earlier than six months preceding the filing of the European patent application and if it was due to, or in consequence of:

(a) an evident abuse in relation to the applicant or his legal predecessor, or

(b) the fact that the applicant or his legal predecessor has displayed the invention at an official, or officially recognised, international exhibition falling within the terms of the Convention on international exhibitions signed at Paris on 22 November 1928 and last revised on 30 November 1972.

(2) In the case of paragraph 1(b), paragraph 1 shall apply only if the applicant states, when filing the European patent application, that the invention has been so displayed and files a supporting certificate within the period and under the conditions laid down in the Implementing Regulations.

Article 56

Inventive step

An invention shall be considered as involving an inventive step if, having regard to the state of the art, it is not obvious to a person skilled in the art. If the state of the art also includes documents within the meaning of Article 54, paragraph 3, these documents are not to be considered in deciding whether there has been an inventive step.

Article 57

Industrial application

An invention shall be considered as susceptible of industrial application if it can be made or used in any kind of industry, including agriculture.

Chapter II—Persons entitled to apply for and obtain a European patents—Mention of the inventor

Article 58

Entitlement to file a European patent application

A European patent application may be filed by any natural or legal person, or any body equivalent to a legal person by virtue of the law governing it.

Article 59

Multiple applicants

A European patent application may also be filed either by joint applicants or by two or more applicants designating different Contracting States.

Article 60

Right to a European patent

(1) The right to a European patent shall belong to the inventor or his successor in title. If the inventor is an employee, the right to a European patent shall be determined in accordance with the law of the State in which the employee is mainly employed; if the State in which the employee is mainly employed cannot be determined, the law to be applied shall be that of the State in which the employer has the place of business to which the employee is attached.

(2) If two or more persons have made an invention independently of each other, the right to a European patent therefor shall belong to the person whose European patent application has the earliest date of filing, provided that this first application has been published.

(3) In proceedings before the European Patent Office, the applicant shall be deemed to be entitled to exercise the right to a European patent.

Article 61

European patent applications filed by non-entitled persons

(1) If by a final decision it is adjudged that a person other than the applicant is entitled to the grant of the European patent, that person may, in accordance with the Implementing Regulations:

(a) prosecute the European patent application as his own application in place of the applicant;

(b) file a new European patent application in respect of the same invention; or

(c) request that the European patent application be refused.

(2) Article 76, paragraph 1, shall apply mutatis mutandis to a new European patent application filed under paragraph 1(b).

Article 62

Right of the inventor to be mentioned

The inventor shall have the right, vis-a-vis the applicant for or proprietor of a European patent, to be mentioned as such before the European Patent Office.

Chapter III—Effects of the European patent and application

Article 63

Term of the European patent

(1) The term of the European patent shall be 20 years from the date of filing of the application.

(2) Nothing in the preceding paragraph shall limit the right of a Contracting State to extend the term of a European patent, or to grant corresponding protection which follows immediately on expiry of the term of the patent, under the same conditions as those applying to national patents:

  (a) in order to take account of a state of war or similar emergency conditions affecting that State;

  (b) if the subject-matter of the European patent is a product or a process for manufacturing a product or a use of a product which has to undergo an administrative authorisation procedure required by law before it can be put on the market in that State.

(3) Paragraph 2 shall apply mutatis mutandis to European patents granted jointly for a group of Contracting States in accordance with Article 142.

(4) A Contracting State which makes provision for extension of the term or corresponding protection under paragraph 2(b) may, in accordance with an agreement concluded with the Organisation, entrust to the European Patent Office tasks associated with implementation of the relevant provisions.

Article 64

Rights conferred by a European patent

(1) A European patent shall, subject to the provisions of paragraph 2, confer on its proprietor from the date of publication of the mention of its grant, in each Contracting State in respect of which it is granted, the same rights as would be conferred by a national patent granted in that State.

(2) If the subject-matter of the European patent is a process, the protection conferred by the patent shall extend to the products directly obtained by such process.

(3) Any infringement of a European patent shall be dealt with by national law.

Article 65

Translation of the European patent

(1) Any Contracting State may, if the European patent as granted, amended or limited by the European Patent Office is not drawn up in one of its official languages, prescribe that the proprietor of the patent shall supply to its central industrial property office a translation of the patent as granted, amended or limited in one of its official languages at his option or, where that State has prescribed the use of one specific official language, in that language. The period for supplying the translation shall end three months after the date on which the mention of the grant, maintenance in amended form or limitation of the European patent is published in the European Patent Bulletin, unless the State concerned prescribes a longer period.

(2) Any Contracting State which has adopted provisions pursuant to paragraph 1 may prescribe that the proprietor of the patent must pay all or part of the costs of publication of such translation within a period laid down by that State.

(3) Any Contracting State may prescribe that in the event of failure to observe the provisions adopted in accordance with paragraphs 1 and 2, the European patent shall be deemed to be void ab initio in that State.

Article 66

Equivalence of European filing with national filing

A European patent application which has been accorded a date of filing shall, in the designated Contracting States, be equivalent to a regular national filing, where appropriate with the priority claimed for the European patent application.

Article 67

Rights conferred by a European patent application after publication

(1) A European patent application shall, from the date of its publication, provisionally confer upon the applicant the protection provided for by Article 64, in the Contracting States designated in the application.

(2) Any Contracting State may prescribe that a European patent application shall not confer such protection as is conferred by Article 64. However, the protection attached to the publication of the European patent application may not be less than that which the laws of the State concerned attach to the compulsory publication of unexamined national patent applications. In any event, each State shall ensure at least that, from the date of publication of a European patent application, the applicant can claim compensation reasonable in the circumstances from any person who

has used the invention in that State in circumstances where that person would be liable under national law for infringement of a national patent.

(3) Any Contracting State which does not have as an official language the language of the proceedings may prescribe that provisional protection in accordance with paragraphs 1 and 2 above shall not be effective until such time as a translation of the claims in one of its official languages at the option of the applicant or, where that State has prescribed the use of one specific official language, in that language:

(a) has been made available to the public in the manner prescribed by national law, or

(b) has been communicated to the person using the invention in the said State.

(4) The European patent application shall be deemed never to have had the effects set out in paragraphs 1 and 2 when it has been withdrawn, deemed to be withdrawn or finally refused. The same shall apply in respect of the effects of the European patent application in a Contracting State the designation of which is withdrawn or deemed to be withdrawn.

Article 68

Effect of revocation or limitation of the European patent

The European patent application and the resulting European patent shall be deemed not to have had, from the outset, the effects specified in Articles 64 and 67, to the extent that the patent has been revoked or limited in opposition, limitation or revocation proceedings.

Article 69

Extent of protection

(1) The extent of the protection conferred by a European patent or a European patent application shall be determined by the claims. Nevertheless, the description and drawings shall be used to interpret the claims.

(2) For the period up to grant of the European patent, the extent of the protection conferred by the European patent application shall be determined by the claims contained in the application as published. However, the European patent as granted or as amended in opposition, limitation or revocation proceedings shall determine retroactively the protection conferred by the application, in so far as such protection is not thereby extended.

Article 70

Authentic text of a European patent application or European patent

(1) The text of a European patent application or a European patent in the language of the proceedings shall be the authentic text in any proceedings before the European Patent Office and in any Contracting State.

(2) If, however, the European patent application has been filed in a language which is not an official language of the European Patent Office, that text shall be the application as filed within the meaning of this Convention.

(3) Any Contracting State may provide that a translation into one of its official languages, as prescribed by it according to this Convention, shall in that State be regarded as authentic, except for revocation proceedings, in the event of the European patent application or European patent in the language of the translation conferring protection which is narrower than that conferred by it in the language of the proceedings.

(4) Any Contracting State which adopts a provision under paragraph 3:

(a) shall allow the applicant for or proprietor of the patent to file a corrected translation of the European patent application or European patent. Such corrected translation shall not have any legal effect until any conditions established by the Contracting State under Article 65, paragraph 2, or Article 67, paragraph 3, have been complied with;

(b) may prescribe that any person who, in that State, in good faith has used or has made effective and serious preparations for using an invention the use of which would not constitute infringement of the application or patent in the original translation, may, after the corrected translation takes effect, continue such use in the course of his business or for the needs thereof without payment.

Chapter IV—The European patent application as an object of property

Article 71

Transfer and constitution of rights

A European patent application may be transferred or give rise to rights for one or more of the designated Contracting States.

Article 72

Assignment

An assignment of a European patent application shall be made in writing and shall require the signature of the parties to the contract.

Article 73

Contractual licensing

A European patent application may be licensed in whole or in part for the whole or part of the territories of the designated Contracting States.

Article 74

Law applicable

Unless otherwise specified in this Convention, the European patent application as an object of property shall, in each designated Contracting State and with effect for such State, be subject to the law applicable in that State to national patent applications.

PART III—THE EUROPEAN PATENT APPLICATION

Chapter I—Filing and requirements of the European patent application

Article 75

Filing of a European patent application

(1) A European patent application may be filed:

(a) with the European Patent Office, or

(b) if the law of a Contracting State so permits, and subject to Article 76, paragraph 1, with the central industrial property office or other competent authority of that State. Any application filed in this way shall have the same effect as if it had been filed on the same date with the European Patent Office.

(2) Paragraph 1 shall not preclude the application of legislative or regulatory provisions which, in any Contracting State:

(a) govern inventions which, owing to the nature of their subject-matter, may not be communicated abroad without the prior authorisation of the competent authorities of that State, or

(b) prescribe that any application is to be filed initially with a national authority, or make direct filing with another authority subject to prior authorisation.

Article 76

European divisional applications

(1) A European divisional application shall be filed directly with the European Patent Office in accordance with the Implementing Regulations. It may be filed only in respect of subject-matter which does not extend beyond the content of the earlier application as filed; in so far as this requirement is complied with, the divisional application shall be deemed to have been filed on the date of filing of the earlier application and shall enjoy any right of priority.

(2) All the Contracting States designated in the earlier application at the time of filing of a European divisional application shall be deemed to be designated in the divisional application.

Article 77

Forwarding of European patent applications

(1) The central industrial property office of a Contracting State shall forward to the European Patent Office any European patent application filed with it or any other competent authority in that State, in accordance with the Implementing Regulations.

(2) A European patent application the subject of which has been made secret shall not be forwarded to the European Patent Office.

(3) A European patent application not forwarded to the European Patent Office in due time shall be deemed to be withdrawn.

Article 78

Requirements of a European patent application

(1) A European patent application shall contain:

(a) a request for the grant of a European patent;

(b) a description of the invention;

(c) one or more claims;

(d) any drawings referred to in the description or the claims;

(e) an abstract,

and satisfy the requirements laid down in the Implementing Regulations.

(2) A European patent application shall be subject to the payment of the filing fee and the search fee. If the filing fee or the search fee is not paid in due time, the application shall be deemed to be withdrawn.

Article 79

Designation of Contracting States

(1) All the Contracting States party to this Convention at the time of filing of the European patent application shall be deemed to be designated in the request for grant of a European patent.

(2) The designation of a Contracting State may be subject to the payment of a designation fee.

(3) The designation of a Contracting State may be withdrawn at any time up to the grant of the European patent.

Article 80

Date of filing

The date of filing of a European patent application shall be the date on which the requirements laid down in the Implementing Regulations are fulfilled.

Article 81

Designation of the inventor

The European patent application shall designate the inventor. If the applicant is not the inventor or is not the sole inventor, the designation shall contain a statement indicating the origin of the right to the European patent.

Article 82

Unity of invention

The European patent application shall relate to one invention only or to a group of inventions so linked as to form a single general inventive concept.

Article 83

Disclosure of the invention

The European patent application must disclose the invention in a manner sufficiently clear and complete for it to be carried out by a person skilled in the art.

Article 84

Claims

The claims shall define the matter for which protection is sought. They shall be clear and concise and be supported by the description.

Article 85

Abstract

The abstract shall merely serve for use as technical information; it may not be taken into account for any other purpose, in particular not for the purpose of interpreting the scope of the protection sought nor for the purpose of applying Article 54, paragraph 3.

Article 86

Renewal fees for the European patent application

(1) Renewal fees for the European patent application shall be paid to the European Patent Office in accordance with the Implementing Regulations. These fees shall be due in respect of the third year and each subsequent year, calculated from the date of filing of the application. If a renewal fee is not paid in due time, the application shall be deemed to be withdrawn.

(2) The obligation to pay renewal fees shall terminate with the payment of the renewal fee due in respect of the year in which the mention of the grant of the European patent is published in the European Patent Bulletin.

Chapter II—Priority

Article 87

Priority right

(1) Any person who has duly filed, in or for

(a) any State party to the Paris Convention for the Protection of Industrial Property or

(b) any Member of the World Trade Organization,

an application for a patent, a utility model or a utility certificate, or his successor in title, shall enjoy, for the purpose of filing a European patent application in respect of the same invention, a right of priority during a period of twelve months from the date of filing of the first application.

(2) Every filing that is equivalent to a regular national filing under the national law of the State where it was made or under bilateral or multilateral agreements, including this Convention, shall be recognised as giving rise to a right of priority.

(3) A regular national filing shall mean any filing that is sufficient to establish the date on which the application was filed, whatever the outcome of the application may be.

(4) A subsequent application in respect of the same subject-matter as a previous first application and filed in or for the same State shall be

considered as the first application for the purposes of determining priority, provided that, at the date of filing the subsequent application, the previous application has been withdrawn, abandoned or refused, without being open to public inspection and without leaving any rights outstanding, and has not served as a basis for claiming a right of priority. The previous application may not thereafter serve as a basis for claiming a right of priority.

(5) If the first filing has been made with an industrial property authority which is not subject to the Paris Convention for the Protection of Industrial Property or the Agreement Establishing the World Trade Organization, paragraphs 1 to 4 shall apply if that authority, according to a communication issued by the President of the European Patent Office, recognises that a first filing made with the European Patent Office gives rise to a right of priority under conditions and with effects equivalent to those laid down in the Paris Convention.

Article 88

Claiming priority

(1) An applicant desiring to take advantage of the priority of a previous application shall file a declaration of priority and any other document required, in accordance with the Implementing Regulations.

(2) Multiple priorities may be claimed in respect of a European patent application, notwithstanding the fact that they originated in different countries. Where appropriate, multiple priorities may be claimed for any one claim. Where multiple priorities are claimed, time limits which run from the date of priority shall run from the earliest date of priority.

(3) If one or more priorities are claimed in respect of a European patent application, the right of priority shall cover only those elements of the European patent application which are included in the application or applications whose priority is claimed.

(4) If certain elements of the invention for which priority is claimed do not appear among the claims formulated in the previous application, priority may nonetheless be granted, provided that the documents of the previous application as a whole specifically disclose such elements.

Article 89

Effect of priority right

The right of priority shall have the effect that the date of priority shall count as the date of filing of the European patent application for the purposes of Article 54, paragraphs 2 and 3, and Article 60, paragraph 2.

PART IV—PROCEDURE UP TO GRANT

Article 90

Examination on filing and examination as to formal requirements

(1) The European Patent Office shall examine, in accordance with the Implementing Regulations, whether the application satisfies the requirements for the accordance of a date of filing.

(2) If a date of filing cannot be accorded following the examination under paragraph 1, the application shall not be dealt with as a European patent application.

(3) If the European patent application has been accorded a date of filing, the European Patent Office shall examine, in accordance with the Implementing Regulations, whether the requirements in Articles 14, 78 and 81, and, where applicable, Article 88, paragraph 1, and Article 133, paragraph 2, as well as any other requirement laid down in the Implementing Regulations, have been satisfied.

(4) Where the European Patent Office in carrying out the examination under paragraphs 1 or 3 notes that there are deficiencies which may be corrected, it shall give the applicant an opportunity to correct them.

(5) If any deficiency noted in the examination under paragraph 3 is not corrected, the European patent application shall be refused unless a different legal consequence is provided for by this Convention. Where the deficiency concerns the right of priority, this right shall be lost for the application.

Article 91

(Deleted by the Act revising the European Patent Convention of 29.11.2000.)

Article 92

Drawing up of the European search report

The European Patent Office shall, in accordance with the Implementing Regulations, draw up and publish a European search report in respect of the European patent application on the basis of the claims, with due regard to the description and any drawings.

Article 93

Publication of the European patent application

(1) The European Patent Office shall publish the European patent application as soon as possible

(a) after the expiry of a period of eighteen months from the date of filing or, if priority has been claimed, from the date of priority, or

(b)   at the request of the applicant, before the expiry of that period.

(2)   The European patent application shall be published at the same time as the specification of the European patent when the decision to grant the patent becomes effective before the expiry of the period referred to in paragraph 1(a).

Article 94

Examination of the European patent application

(1)   The European Patent Office shall, in accordance with the Implementing Regulations, examine on request whether the European patent application and the invention to which it relates meet the requirements of this Convention. The request shall not be deemed to be filed until the examination fee has been paid.

(2)   If no request for examination has been made in due time, the application shall be deemed to be withdrawn.

(3)   If the examination reveals that the application or the invention to which it relates does not meet the requirements of this Convention, the Examining Division shall invite the applicant, as often as necessary, to file his observations and, subject to Article 123, paragraph 1, to amend the application.

(4)   If the applicant fails to reply in due time to any communication from the Examining Division, the application shall be deemed to be withdrawn.

Article 95

(Deleted by the Act revising the European Patent Convention of 29.11.2000.)

Article 96

(Deleted by the Act revising the European Patent Convention of 29.11.2000.)

Article 97

Grant or refusal

(1)   If the Examining Division is of the opinion that the European patent application and the invention to which it relates meet the requirements of this Convention, it shall decide to grant a European patent, provided that the conditions laid down in the Implementing Regulations are fulfilled.

(2)   If the Examining Division is of the opinion that the European patent application or the invention to which it relates does not meet the requirements of this Convention, it shall refuse the application unless this Convention provides for a different legal consequence.

(3) The decision to grant a European patent shall take effect on the date on which the mention of the grant is published in the European Patent Bulletin.

Article 98

Publication of the specification of the European patent

The European Patent Office shall publish the specification of the European patent as soon as possible after the mention of the grant of the European patent has been published in the European Patent Bulletin.

PART V—OPPOSITION AND LIMITATION PROCEDURE

Article 99

Opposition

(1) Within nine months of the publication of the mention of the grant of the European patent in the European Patent Bulletin, any person may give notice to the European Patent Office of opposition to that patent, in accordance with the Implementing Regulations. Notice of opposition shall not be deemed to have been filed until the opposition fee has been paid.

(2) The opposition shall apply to the European patent in all the Contracting States in which that patent has effect.

(3) Opponents shall be parties to the opposition proceedings as well as the proprietor of the patent.

(4) Where a person provides evidence that in a Contracting State, following a final decision, he has been entered in the patent register of such State instead of the previous proprietor, such person shall, at his request, replace the previous proprietor in respect of such State. Notwithstanding Article 118, the previous proprietor and the person making the request shall not be regarded as joint proprietors unless both so request.

Article 100

Grounds for opposition

Opposition may only be filed on the grounds that:

(a) the subject-matter of the European patent is not patentable under Articles 52 to 57;

(b) the European patent does not disclose the invention in a manner sufficiently clear and complete for it to be carried out by a person skilled in the art;

(c) the subject-matter of the European patent extends beyond the content of the application as filed, or, if the patent was granted on a divisional application or on a new application filed under Article 61, beyond the content of the earlier application as filed.

Article 101

Examination of the opposition—Revocation or maintenance of the European patent

(1) If the opposition is admissible, the Opposition Division shall examine, in accordance with the Implementing Regulations, whether at least one ground for opposition under Article 100 prejudices the maintenance of the European patent. During this examination, the Opposition Division shall invite the parties, as often as necessary, to file observations on communications from another party or issued by itself.

(2) If the Opposition Division is of the opinion that at least one ground for opposition prejudices the maintenance of the European patent, it shall revoke the patent. Otherwise, it shall reject the opposition.

(3) If the Opposition Division is of the opinion that, taking into consideration the amendments made by the proprietor of the European patent during the opposition proceedings, the patent and the invention to which it relates

(a) meet the requirements of this Convention, it shall decide to maintain the patent as amended, provided that the conditions laid down in the Implementing Regulations are fulfilled;

(b) do not meet the requirements of this Convention, it shall revoke the patent.

Article 102

(Deleted by the Act revising the European Patent Convention of 29.11.2000.)

Article 103

Publication of a new specification of the European Patent

If the European patent is maintained as amended under Article 101, paragraph 3(a), the European Patent Office shall publish a new specification of the European patent as soon as possible after the mention of the opposition decision has been published in the European Patent Bulletin.

Article 104

Costs

(1) Each party to the opposition proceedings shall bear the costs it has incurred, unless the Opposition Division, for reasons of equity, orders, in accordance with the Implementing Regulations, a different apportionment of costs.

(2) The procedure for fixing costs shall be laid down in the Implementing Regulations.

(3) Any final decision of the European Patent Office fixing the amount of costs shall be dealt with, for the purpose of enforcement in the Contracting States, in the same way as a final decision given by a civil court of the State in which enforcement is to take place. Verification of such decision shall be limited to its authenticity.

Article 105

Intervention of the assumed infringer

(1) Any third party may, in accordance with the Implementing Regulations, intervene in opposition proceedings after the opposition period has expired, if the third party proves that

 (a) proceedings for infringement of the same patent have been instituted against him, or

 (b) following a request of the proprietor of the patent to cease alleged infringement, the third party has instituted proceedings for a ruling that he is not infringing the patent.

(2) An admissible intervention shall be treated as an opposition.

Article 105a

Request for limitation or revocation

(1) At the request of the proprietor, the European patent may be revoked or be limited by an amendment of the claims. The request shall be filed with the European Patent Office in accordance with the Implementing Regulations. It shall not be deemed to have been filed until the limitation or revocation fee has been paid.

(2) The request may not be filed while opposition proceedings in respect of the European patent are pending.

Article 105b

Limitation or revocation of the European patent

(1) The European Patent Office shall examine whether the requirements laid down in the Implementing Regulations for limiting or revoking the European patent have been met.

(2) If the European Patent Office considers that the request for limitation or revocation of the European patent meets these requirements, it shall decide to limit or revoke the European patent in accordance with the Implementing Regulations. Otherwise, it shall reject the request.

(3) The decision to limit or revoke the European patent shall apply to the European patent in all the Contracting States in respect of which it has been granted. It shall take effect on the date on which the mention of the decision is published in the European Patent Bulletin.

Article 105c

Publication of the amended specification of the European patent

If the European patent is limited under Article 105b, paragraph 2, the European Patent Office shall publish the amended specification of the European patent as soon as possible after the mention of the limitation has been published in the European Patent Bulletin.

PART VI—APPEALS PROCEDURE

Article 106

Decisions subject to appeal

(1) An appeal shall lie from decisions of the Receiving Section, Examining Divisions, Opposition Divisions and the Legal Division. It shall have suspensive effect.

(2) A decision which does not terminate proceedings as regards one of the parties can only be appealed together with the final decision, unless the decision allows a separate appeal.

(3) The right to file an appeal against decisions relating to the apportionment or fixing of costs in opposition proceedings may be restricted in the Implementing Regulations.

Article 107

Persons entitled to appeal and to be parties to appeal proceedings

Any party to proceedings adversely affected by a decision may appeal. Any other parties to the proceedings shall be parties to the appeal proceedings as of right.

Article 108

Time limit and form

Notice of appeal shall be filed, in accordance with the Implementing Regulations, at the European Patent Office within two months of notification of the decision. Notice of appeal shall not be deemed to have been filed until the fee for appeal has been paid. Within four months of notification of the decision, a statement setting out the grounds of appeal shall be filed in accordance with the Implementing Regulations.

Article 109

Interlocutory revision

(1) If the department whose decision is contested considers the appeal to be admissible and well founded, it shall rectify its decision. This shall not apply where the appellant is opposed by another party to the proceedings.

(2)   If the appeal is not allowed within one month after receipt of the statement of grounds, it shall be remitted to the Board of Appeal without delay, and without comment as to its merit.

Article 110

Examination of appeals

If the appeal is admissible, the Board of Appeal shall examine whether the appeal is allowable. The examination of the appeal shall be conducted in accordance with the Implementing Regulations.

Article 111

Decision in respect of appeals

(1)   Following the examination as to the allowability of the appeal, the Board of Appeal shall decide on the Appeal. The Board of Appeal may either exercise any power within the competence of the department which was responsible for the decision appealed or remit the case to that department for further prosecution.

(2)   If the Board of Appeal remits the case for further prosecution to the department whose decision was appealed, that department shall be bound by the ratio decidendi of the Board of Appeal, in so far as the facts are the same. If the decision which was appealed emanated from the Receiving Section, the Examining Division shall similarly be bound by the ratio decidendi of the Board of Appeal.

Article 112

Decision or opinion of the Enlarged Board of Appeal

(1)   In order to ensure uniform application of the law, or if an important point of law arises:

(a)   the Board of Appeal shall, during proceedings on a case and either of its own motion or following a request from a party to the appeal, refer any question to the Enlarged Board of Appeal if it considers that a decision is required for the above purposes. If the Board of Appeal rejects the request, it shall give the reasons in its final decision;

(b)   the President of the European Patent Office may refer a point of law to the Enlarged Board of Appeal where two Boards of Appeal have given different decisions on that question.

(2)   In the cases covered by paragraph 1(a) the parties to the appeal proceedings shall be parties to the proceedings before the Enlarged Board of Appeal.

(3) The decision of the Enlarged Board of Appeal referred to in paragraph 1(a) shall be binding on the Board of Appeal in respect of the appeal in question.

Article 112a

Petition for review by the Enlarged Board of Appeal

(1) Any party to appeal proceedings adversely affected by the decision of the Board of Appeal may file a petition for review of the decision by the Enlarged Board of Appeal.

(2) The petition may only be filed on the grounds that:

(a) a member of the Board of Appeal took part in the decision in breach of Article 24, paragraph 1, or despite being excluded pursuant to a decision under Article 24, paragraph 4;

(b) the Board of Appeal included a person not appointed as a member of the Boards of Appeal;

(c) a fundamental violation of Article 113 occurred;

(d) any other fundamental procedural defect defined in the Implementing Regulations occurred in the appeal proceedings; or

(e) a criminal act established under the conditions laid down in the Implementing Regulations may have had an impact on the decision.

(3) The petition for review shall not have suspensive effect.

(4) The petition for review shall be filed in a reasoned statement, in accordance with the Implementing Regulations. If based on paragraph 2(a) to (d), the petition shall be filed within two months of notification of the decision of the Board of Appeal. If based on paragraph 2(e), the petition shall be filed within two months of the date on which the criminal act has been established and in any event no later than five years from notification of the decision of the Board of Appeal. The petition shall not be deemed to have been filed until after the prescribed fee has been paid.

(5) The Enlarged Board of Appeal shall examine the petition for review in accordance with the Implementing Regulations. If the petition is allowable, the Enlarged Board of Appeal shall set aside the decision and shall re-open proceedings before the Boards of Appeal in accordance with the Implementing Regulations.

(6) Any person who, in a designated Contracting State, has in good faith used or made effective and serious preparations for using an invention which is the subject of a published European patent application or a European patent in the period between the decision of the Board of Appeal and publication in the European Patent Bulletin of the mention of the decision of the Enlarged Board of Appeal on the petition, may without

payment continue such use in the course of his business or for the needs thereof.

PART VII—COMMON PROVISIONS

Chapter I—Common provisions governing procedure

Article 113

Right to be heard and basis of decisions

(1) The decisions of the European Patent Office may only be based on grounds or evidence on which the parties concerned have had an opportunity to present their comments.

(2) The European Patent Office shall consider and decide upon the European patent application or the European patent only in the text submitted to it, or agreed, by the applicant for or proprietor of the patent.

Article 114

Examination by the European Patent Office of its own motion

(1) In proceedings before it, the European Patent Office shall examine the facts of its own motion; it shall not be restricted in this examination to the facts, evidence and arguments provided by the parties and the relief sought.

(2) The European Patent Office may disregard facts or evidence which are not submitted in due time by the parties concerned.

Article 115

Observations by third parties

In proceedings before the European Patent Office, following the publication of the European patent application, any third party may, in accordance with the Implementing Regulations, present observations concerning the patentability of the invention to which the application or patent relates. That person shall not be a party to the proceedings.

Article 116

Oral proceedings

(1) Oral proceedings shall take place either at the instance of the European Patent Office if it considers this to be expedient or at the request of any party to the proceedings. However, the European Patent Office may reject a request for further oral proceedings before the same department where the parties and the subject of the proceedings are the same.

(2) Nevertheless, oral proceedings shall take place before the Receiving Section at the request of the applicant only where the Receiving

Section considers this to be expedient or where it envisages refusing the European patent application.

(3) Oral proceedings before the Receiving Section, the Examining Divisions and the Legal Division shall not be public.

(4) Oral proceedings, including delivery of the decision, shall be public, as regards the Boards of Appeal and the Enlarged Board of Appeal, after publication of the European patent application, and also before the Opposition Divisions, in so far as the department before which the proceedings are taking place does not decide otherwise in cases where admission of the public could have serious and unjustified disadvantages, in particular for a party to the proceedings.

Article 117

Means and taking of evidence

(1) In proceedings before the European Patent Office the means of giving or obtaining evidence shall include the following:

(a) hearing the parties;

(b) requests for information;

(c) production of documents;

(d) hearing witnesses;

(e) opinions by experts;

(f) inspection;

(g) sworn statements in writing.

(2) The procedure for taking such evidence shall be laid down in the Implementing Regulations.

Article 118

Unity of the European patent application or European patent

Where the applicants for or proprietors of a European patent are not the same in respect of different designated Contracting States, they shall be regarded as joint applicants or proprietors for the purposes of proceedings before the European Patent Office. The unity of the application or patent in these proceedings shall not be affected; in particular the text of the application or patent shall be uniform for all designated Contracting States unless otherwise provided for in this Convention.

Article 119

Notification

Decisions, summonses, notices and communications shall be notified by the European Patent Office of its own motion in accordance with the Implementing Regulations. Notification may, where exceptional circumstances so require, be effected through the intermediary of the central industrial property offices of the Contracting States.

Article 120

Time limits

The Implementing Regulations shall specify:

(a) the time limits which are to be observed in proceedings before the European Patent Office and are not fixed by this Convention;

(b) the manner of computation of time limits and the conditions under which time limits may be extended;

(c) the minima and maxima for time limits to be determined by the European Patent Office.

Article 121

Further processing of the European patent application

(1) If an applicant fails to observe a time limit vis-à-vis the European Patent Office, he may request further processing of the European patent application.

(2) The European Patent Office shall grant the request, provided that the requirements laid down in the Implementing Regulations are met. Otherwise, it shall reject the request.

(3) If the request is granted, the legal consequences of the failure to observe the time limit shall be deemed not to have ensued.

(4) Further processing shall be ruled out in respect of the time limits in Article 87, paragraph 1, Article 108 and Article 112a, paragraph 4, as well as the time limits for requesting further processing or re-establishment of rights. The Implementing Regulations may rule out further processing for other time limits.

Article 122

Re-establishment of rights

(1) An applicant for or proprietor of a European patent who, in spite of all due care required by the circumstances having been taken, was unable to observe a time limit vis-à-vis the European Patent Office shall have his rights re-established upon request if the non-observance of this time limit has the direct consequence of causing the refusal of the

European patent application or of a request, or the deeming of the application to have been withdrawn, or the revocation of the European patent, or the loss of any other right or means of redress.

(2) The European Patent Office shall grant the request, provided that the conditions of paragraph 1 and any other requirements laid down in the Implementing Regulations are met. Otherwise, it shall reject the request.

(3) If the request is granted, the legal consequences of the failure to observe the time limit shall be deemed not to have ensued.

(4) Re-establishment of rights shall be ruled out in respect of the time limit for requesting re-establishment of rights. The Implementing Regulations may rule out re-establishment for other time limits.

(5) Any person who, in a designated Contracting State, has in good faith used or made effective and serious preparations for using an invention which is the subject of a published European patent application or a European patent in the period between the loss of rights referred to in paragraph 1 and publication in the European Patent Bulletin of the mention of re-establishment of those rights, may without payment continue such use in the course of his business or for the needs thereof.

(6) Nothing in this Article shall limit the right of a Contracting State to grant re-establishment of rights in respect of time limits provided for in this Convention and to be observed vis-à-vis the authorities of such State.

Article 123

Amendments

(1) The European patent application or European patent may be amended in proceedings before the European Patent Office, in accordance with the Implementing Regulations. In any event, the applicant shall be given at least one opportunity to amend the application of his own volition.

(2) The European patent application or European patent may not be amended in such a way that it contains subject-matter which extends beyond the content of the application as filed.

(3) The European patent may not be amended in such a way as to extend the protection it confers.

Article 124

Information on prior art

(1) The European Patent Office may, in accordance with the Implementing Regulations, invite the applicant to provide information on prior art taken into consideration in national or regional patent proceedings and concerning an invention to which the European patent application relates.

(2) If the applicant fails to reply in due time to an invitation under paragraph 1, the European patent application shall be deemed to be withdrawn.

Article 125

Reference to general principles

In the absence of procedural provisions in this Convention, the European Patent Office shall take into account the principles of procedural law generally recognised in the Contracting States.

Article 126

(Deleted by the Act revising the European Patent Convention of 29.11.2000.)

Chapter II—Information to the public or official authorities

Article 127

European Patent Register

The European Patent Office shall keep a European Patent Register, in which the particulars specified in the Implementing Regulations shall be recorded. No entry shall be made in the European Patent Register before the publication of the European patent application. The European Patent Register shall be open to public inspection.

Article 128

Inspection of files

(1) Files relating to European patent applications which have not yet been published shall not be made available for inspection without the consent of the applicant.

(2) Any person who can prove that the applicant has invoked the rights under the European patent application against him may obtain inspection of the files before the publication of that application and without the consent of the applicant.

(3) Where a European divisional application or a new European patent application filed under Article 61, paragraph 1, is published, any person may obtain inspection of the files of the earlier application before the publication of that application and without the consent of the applicant.

(4) After the publication of the European patent application, the files relating to the application and the resulting European patent may be inspected on request, subject to the restrictions laid down in the Implementing Regulations.

(5) Even before the publication of the European patent application, the European Patent Office may communicate to third parties or publish the particulars specified in the Implementing Regulations.

Article 129

Periodical publications

The European Patent Office shall periodically publish:

(a) a European Patent Bulletin containing the particulars the publication of which is prescribed by this Convention, the Implementing Regulations or the President of the European Patent Office;

(b) an Official Journal containing notices and information of a general character issued by the President of the European Patent Office, as well as any other information relevant to this Convention or its implementation.

Article 130

Exchange of information

(1) Unless this Convention or national laws provide otherwise, the European Patent Office and the central industrial property office of any Contracting State shall, on request, communicate to each other any useful information regarding European or national patent applications and patents and any proceedings concerning them.

(2) Paragraph 1 shall apply to the communication of information by virtue of working agreements between the European Patent Office and

(a) the central industrial property offices of other States;

(b) any intergovernmental organisation entrusted with the task of granting patents;

(c) any other organisation.

(3) Communications under paragraphs 1 and 2(a) and (b) shall not be subject to the restrictions laid down in Article 128. The Administrative Council may decide that communications under paragraph 2(c) shall not be subject to such restrictions, provided that the organisation concerned treats the information communicated as confidential until the European patent application has been published.

Article 131

Administrative and legal co-operation

(1) Unless otherwise provided in this Convention or in national laws, the European Patent Office and the courts or authorities of Contracting States shall on request give assistance to each other by communicating information or opening files for inspection. Where the European Patent Office lays files open to inspection by courts, Public Prosecutors' Offices or central industrial property offices, the inspection shall not be subject to the restrictions laid down in Article 128.

(2) Upon receipt of letters rogatory from the European Patent Office, the courts or other competent authorities of Contracting States shall undertake, on behalf of that Office and within the limits of their jurisdiction, any necessary enquiries or other legal measures.

Article 132

Exchange of publications

(1) The European Patent Office and the central industrial property offices of the Contracting States shall despatch to each other on request and for their own use one or more copies of their respective publications free of charge.

(2) The European Patent Office may conclude agreements relating to the exchange or supply of publications.

Chapter III—Representation

Article 133

General principles of representation

(1) Subject to paragraph 2, no person shall be compelled to be represented by a professional representative in proceedings established by this Convention.

(2) Natural or legal persons not having their residence or principal place of business in a Contracting State shall be represented by a professional representative and act through him in all proceedings established by this Convention, other than in filing a European patent application; the Implementing Regulations may permit other exceptions.

(3) Natural or legal persons having their residence or principal place of business in a Contracting State may be represented in proceedings established by this Convention by an employee, who need not be a professional representative but who shall be authorised in accordance with the Implementing Regulations. The Implementing Regulations may provide whether and under what conditions an employee of a legal person may also represent other legal persons which have their principal place of business in a Contracting State and which have economic connections with the first legal person.

(4) The Implementing Regulations may lay down special provisions concerning the common representation of parties acting in common.

Article 134

Representation before the European Patent Office

(1) Representation of natural or legal persons in proceedings established by this Convention may only be undertaken by professional

representatives whose names appear on a list maintained for this purpose by the European Patent Office.

(2)   Any natural person who

(a)   is a national of a Contracting State,

(b)   has his place of business or employment in a Contracting State and

(c)   has passed the European qualifying examination

may be entered on the list of professional representatives.

(3)   During a period of one year from the date on which the accession of a State to this Convention takes effect, entry on that list may also be requested by any natural person who

(a)   is a national of a Contracting State,

(b)   has his place of business or employment in the State having acceded to the Convention and

(c)   is entitled to represent natural or legal persons in patent matters before the central industrial property office of that State. Where such entitlement is not conditional upon the requirement of special professional qualifications, the person shall have regularly so acted in that State for at least five years.

(4)   Entry shall be effected upon request, accompanied by certificates indicating that the conditions laid down in paragraph 2 or 3 are fulfilled.

(5)   Persons whose names appear on the list of professional representatives shall be entitled to act in all proceedings established by this Convention.

(6)   For the purpose of acting as a professional representative, any person whose name appears on the list of professional representatives shall be entitled to establish a place of business in any Contracting State in which proceedings established by this Convention may be conducted, having regard to the Protocol on Centralisation annexed to this Convention. The authorities of such State may remove that entitlement in individual cases only in application of legal provisions adopted for the purpose of protecting public security and law and order. Before such action is taken, the President of the European Patent Office shall be consulted.

(7)   The President of the European Patent Office may grant exemption from:

(a)   the requirement of paragraphs 2(a) or 3(a) in special circumstances;

(b) the requirement of paragraph 3(c), second sentence, if the applicant furnishes proof that he has acquired the requisite qualification in another way.

(8) Representation in proceedings established by this Convention may also be undertaken, in the same way as by a professional representative, by any legal practitioner qualified in a Contracting State and having his place of business in that State, to the extent that he is entitled in that State to act as a professional representative in patent matters. Paragraph 6 shall apply mutatis mutandis. of parties acting in common.

Article 134a

Institute of Professional Representatives before the European Patent Office

(1) The Administrative Council shall be competent to adopt and amend provisions governing:

(a) the Institute of Professional Representatives before the European Patent Office, hereinafter referred to as the Institute;

(b) the qualifications and training required of a person for admission to the European qualifying examination and the conduct of such examination;

(c) the disciplinary power exercised by the Institute or the European Patent Office in respect of professional representatives;

(d) the obligation of confidentiality on the professional representative and the privilege from disclosure in proceedings before the European Patent Office in respect of communications between a professional representative and his client or any other person.

(2) Any person entered on the list of professional representatives referred to in Article 134, paragraph 1, shall be a member of the Institute.

PART VIII—IMPACT ON NATIONAL LAW

Chapter I—Conversion into a national patent application

Article 135

Request for conversion

(1) The central industrial property office of a designated Contracting State shall, at the request of the applicant for or proprietor of a European patent, apply the procedure for the grant of a national patent in the following circumstances:

(a) where the European patent application is deemed to be withdrawn under Article 77, paragraph 3;

(b) in such other cases as are provided for by the national law, in which the European patent application is refused or withdrawn or deemed to be withdrawn, or the European patent is revoked under this Convention.

(2) In the case referred to in paragraph 1(a), the request for conversion shall be filed with the central industrial property office with which the European patent application has been filed. That office shall, subject to the provisions governing national security, transmit the request directly to the central industrial property offices of the Contracting States specified therein.

(3) In the cases referred to in paragraph 1(b), the request for conversion shall be submitted to the European Patent Office in accordance with the Implementing Regulations. It shall not be deemed to be filed until the conversion fee has been paid. The European Patent Office shall transmit the request to the central industrial property offices of the Contracting States specified therein.

(4) The effect of the European patent application referred to in Article 66 shall lapse if the request for conversion is not submitted in due time.

Article 136

(Deleted by the Act revising the European Patent Convention of 29.11.2000.)

Article 137

Formal requirements for conversion

(1) A European patent application transmitted in accordance with Article 135, paragraph 2 or 3, shall not be subjected to formal requirements of national law which are different from or additional to those provided for in this Convention.

(2) Any central industrial property office to which the European patent application is transmitted may require that the applicant shall, within a period of not less than two months:

(a) pay the national application fee; and

(b) file a translation of the original text of the European patent application in an official language of the State in question and, where appropriate, of the text as amended during proceedings before the European Patent Office which the applicant wishes to use as the basis for the national procedure.

Chapter II—Revocation and prior rights

Article 138

Revocation of European patents

(1) Subject to Article 139, a European patent may be revoked with effect for a Contracting State only on the grounds that:

    (a) the subject-matter of the European patent is not patentable under Articles 52 to 57;

    (b) the European patent does not disclose the invention in a manner sufficiently clear and complete for it to be carried out by a person skilled in the art;

    (c) the subject-matter of the European patent extends beyond the content of the application as filed or, if the patent was granted on a divisional application or on a new application filed under Article 61, beyond the content of the earlier application as filed;

    (d) the protection conferred by the European patent has been extended; or

    (e) the proprietor of the European patent is not entitled under Article 60, paragraph 1.

(2) If the grounds for revocation affect the European patent only in part, the patent shall be limited by a corresponding amendment of the claims and revoked in part.

(3) In proceedings before the competent court or authority relating to the validity of the European patent, the proprietor of the patent shall have the right to limit the patent by amending the claims. The patent as thus limited shall form the basis for the proceedings.

Article 139

Prior rights and rights arising on the same date

(1) In any designated Contracting State a European patent application and a European patent shall have with regard to a national patent application and a national patent the same prior right effect as a national patent application and a national patent.

(2) A national patent application and a national patent in a Contracting State shall have with regard to a European patent in which that Contracting State is designated the same prior right effect as they have with regard to a national patent.

(3) Any Contracting State may prescribe whether and on what terms an invention disclosed in both a European patent application or patent and a national application or patent having the same date of filing or, where

priority is claimed, the same date of priority, may be protected simultaneously by both applications or patents.

Chapter III—Miscellaneous effects

Article 140

National utility models and utility certificates

Articles 66, 124, 135, 137 and 139 shall apply to utility models and utility certificates and to applications for utility models and utility certificates registered or deposited in the Contracting States whose laws make provision for such models or certificates.

Article 141

Renewal fees for European patents

(1) Renewal fees for a European patent may only be imposed for the years which follow that referred to in Article 86, paragraph 2.

(2) Any renewal fees falling due within two months of the publication in the European Patent Bulletin of the mention of the grant of the European patent shall be deemed to have been validly paid if they are paid within that period. Any additional fee provided for under national law shall not be charged.

PART IX—SPECIAL AGREEMENTS

Article 142

Unitary patents

(1) Any group of Contracting States, which has provided by a special agreement that a European patent granted for those States has a unitary character throughout their territories, may provide that a European patent may only be granted jointly in respect of all those States.

(2) Where any group of Contracting States has availed itself of the authorisation given in paragraph 1, the provisions of this Part shall apply.

Article 143

Special departments of the European Patent Office

(1) The group of Contracting States may give additional tasks to the European Patent Office.

(2) Special departments common to the Contracting States in the group may be set up within the European Patent Office in order to carry out the additional tasks. The President of the European Patent Office shall direct such special departments; Article 10, paragraphs 2 and 3, shall apply mutatis mutandis.

Article 144

Representation before special departments

The group of Contracting States may lay down special provisions to govern representation of parties before the departments referred to in Article 143, paragraph 2.

Article 145

Select committee of the Administrative Council

(1)   The group of Contracting States may set up a select committee of the Administrative Council for the purpose of supervising the activities of the special departments set up under Article 143, paragraph 2; the European Patent Office shall place at its disposal such staff, premises and equipment as may be necessary for the performance of its duties. The President of the European Patent Office shall be responsible for the activities of the special departments to the select committee of the Administrative Council.

(2)   The composition, powers and functions of the select committee shall be determined by the group of Contracting States.

Article 146

Cover for expenditure for carrying out special tasks

Where additional tasks have been given to the European Patent Office under Article 143, the group of Contracting States shall bear the expenses incurred by the Organisation in carrying out these tasks. Where special departments have been set up in the European Patent Office to carry out these additional tasks, the group shall bear the expenditure on staff, premises and equipment chargeable in respect of these departments. Article 39, paragraphs 3 and 4, Article 41 and Article 47 shall apply mutatis mutandis.

Article 147

Payments in respect of renewal fees for unitary patents

If the group of Contracting States has fixed a common scale of renewal fees in respect of European patents the proportion referred to in Article 39, paragraph 1, shall be calculated on the basis of the common scale; the minimum amount referred to in Article 39, paragraph 1, shall apply to the unitary patent. Article 39, paragraphs 3 and 4, shall apply mutatis mutandis.

Article 148

The European patent application as an object of property

(1)   Article 74 shall apply unless the group of Contracting States has specified otherwise.

(2)   The group of Contracting States may provide that a European patent application for which these Contracting States are designated may only be transferred, mortgaged or subjected to any legal means of execution in respect of all the Contracting States of the group and in accordance with the provisions of the special agreement.

Article 149

Joint designation

(1)   The group of Contracting States may provide that these States may only be designated jointly, and that the designation of one or some only of such States shall be deemed to constitute the designation of all the States of the group.

(2)   Where the European Patent Office acts as a designated Office under Article 153, paragraph 1, paragraph 1 shall apply if the applicant has indicated in the international application that he wishes to obtain a European patent for one or more of the designated States of the group. The same shall apply if the applicant designates in the international application one of the Contracting States in the group, whose national law provides that the designation of that State shall have the effect of the application being for a European patent.

Article 149a

Other agreements between the Contracting States

(1)   Nothing in this Convention shall be construed as limiting the right of some or all of the Contracting States to conclude special agreements on any matters concerning European patent applications or European patents which under this Convention are subject to and governed by national law, such as, in particular

(a)   an agreement establishing a European patent court common to the Contracting States party to it;

(b)   an agreement establishing an entity common to the Contracting States party to it to deliver, at the request of national courts or quasi-judicial authorities, opinions on issues of European or harmonised national patent law;

(c)   an agreement under which the Contracting States party to it dispense fully or in part with translations of European patents under Article 65;

(d) an agreement under which the Contracting States party to it provide that translations of European patents as required under Article 65 may be filed with, and published by, the European Patent Office.

(2) The Administrative Council shall be competent to decide that:

(a) the members of the Boards of Appeal or the Enlarged Board of Appeal may serve on a European patent court or a common entity and take part in proceedings before that court or entity in accordance with any such agreement;

(b) the European Patent Office shall provide a common entity with such support staff, premises and equipment as may be necessary for the performance of its duties, and the expenses incurred by that entity shall be borne fully or in part by the Organisation.

PART X—INTERNATIONAL APPLICATION UNDER THE PATENT COOPERATION TREATY— EURO-PCT APPLICATIONS

Article 150

Application of the Patent Cooperation Treaty

(1) The Patent Cooperation Treaty of 19 June 1970, hereinafter referred to as the PCT, shall be applied in accordance with the provisions of this Part.

(2) International applications filed under the PCT may be the subject of proceedings before the European Patent Office. In such proceedings, the provisions of the PCT and its Regulations shall be applied, supplemented by the provisions of this Convention. In case of conflict, the provisions of the PCT or its Regulations shall prevail.

Article 151

The European Patent Office as a receiving Office

The European Patent Office shall act as a receiving Office within the meaning of the PCT, in accordance with the Implementing Regulations. Article 75, paragraph 2, shall apply.

Article 152

The European Patent Office as an International Searching Authority or International Preliminary Examining Authority

The European Patent Office shall act as an International Searching Authority and International Preliminary Examining Authority within the meaning of the PCT, in accordance with an agreement between the Organisation and the International Bureau of the World Intellectual Property Organization, for applicants who are residents or nationals of a

State party to this Convention. This agreement may provide that the European Patent Office shall also act for other applicants.

Article 153

The European Patent Office as a designated Office or elected Office

(1) The European Patent Office shall be

(a) a designated Office for any State party to this Convention in respect of which the PCT is in force, which is designated in the international application and for which the applicant wishes to obtain a European patent, and

(b) an elected Office, if the applicant has elected a State designated pursuant to letter (a).

(2) An international application for which the European Patent Office is a designated or elected Office, and which has been accorded an international date of filing, shall be equivalent to a regular European application (Euro-PCT application).

(3) The international publication of a Euro-PCT application in an official language of the European Patent Office shall take the place of the publication of the European patent application and shall be mentioned in the European Patent Bulletin.

(4) If the Euro-PCT application is published in another language, a translation into one of the official languages shall be filed with the European Patent Office, which shall publish it. Subject to Article 67, paragraph 3, the provisional protection under Article 67, paragraphs 1 and 2, shall be effective from the date of that publication.

(5) The Euro-PCT application shall be treated as a European patent application and shall be considered as comprised in the state of the art under Article 54, paragraph 3, if the conditions laid down in paragraph 3 or 4 and in the Implementing Regulations are fulfilled.

(6) The international search report drawn up in respect of a Euro-PCT application or the declaration replacing it, and their international publication, shall take the place of the European search report and the mention of its publication in the European Patent Bulletin.

(7) A supplementary European search report shall be drawn up in respect of any Euro-PCT application under paragraph 5. The Administrative Council may decide that the supplementary search report is to be dispensed with or that the search fee is to be reduced.

Article 154

(Deleted by the Act revising the European Patent Convention of 29.11.2000.)

Article 155

(Deleted by the Act revising the European Patent Convention of 29.11.2000.)

Article 156

(Deleted by the Act revising the European Patent Convention of 29.11.2000.)

Article 157

(Deleted by the Act revising the European Patent Convention of 29.11.2000.)

Article 158

(Deleted by the Act revising the European Patent Convention of 29.11.2000.)

PART XI—TRANSITIONAL PROVISIONS

(Articles 159, 160, 161, 162 and 163 were deleted by the Act revising the European Patent Convention of 29.11.2000.)

PART XII—FINAL PROVISIONS

Article 164

Implementing Regulations and Protocols

(1) The Implementing Regulations, the Protocol on Recognition, the Protocol on Privileges and Immunities, the Protocol on Centralisation, the Protocol on the Interpretation of Article 69 and the Protocol on Staff Complement shall be integral parts of this Convention.

(2) In case of conflict between the provisions of this Convention and those of the Implementing Regulations, the provisions of this Convention shall prevail. A supplementary European search report shall be drawn up in respect of any Euro-PCT application under paragraph 5. The Administrative Council may decide that the supplementary search report is to be dispensed with or that the search fee is to be reduced.

Article 165

Signature-Ratification

(1) This Convention shall be open for signature until 5 April 1974 by the States which took part in the Inter-Governmental Conference for the setting up of a European System for the Grant of Patents or were informed of the holding of that conference and offered the option of taking part therein.

(2) This Convention shall be subject to ratification; instruments of ratification shall be deposited with the Government of the Federal Republic of Germany.

Article 166

Accession

(1) This Convention shall be open to accession by:

(a) the States referred to in Article 165, paragraph 1;

(b) any other European State at the invitation of the Administrative Council.

(2) Any State which has been a party to the Convention and has ceased so to be as a result of the application of Article 172, paragraph 4, may again become a party to the Convention by acceding to it.

(3) Instruments of accession shall be deposited with the Government of the Federal Republic of Germany.

Article 167

(Deleted by the Act revising the European Patent Convention of 29.11.2000.)

Article 168

Territorial field of application

(1) Any Contracting State may declare in its instrument of ratification or accession, or may inform the Government of the Federal Republic of Germany by written notification any time thereafter, that this Convention shall be applicable to one or more of the territories for the external relations of which it is responsible. European patents granted for that Contracting State shall also have effect in the territories for which such a declaration has taken effect.

(2) If the declaration referred to in paragraph 1 is contained in the instrument of ratification or accession, it shall take effect on the same date as the ratification or accession; if the declaration is made in a notification after the deposit of the instrument of ratification or accession, such notification shall take effect six months after the date of its receipt by the Government of the Federal Republic of Germany.

(3) Any Contracting State may at any time declare that the Convention shall cease to apply to some or to all of the territories in respect of which it has given a notification pursuant to paragraph 1. Such declaration shall take effect one year after the date on which the Government of the Federal Republic of Germany received notification thereof.

Article 169

Entry into force

(1) This Convention shall enter into force three months after the deposit of the last instrument of ratification or accession by six States on

whose territory the total number of patent applications filed in 1970 amounted to at least 180,000 for all the said States.

(2) Any ratification or accession after the entry into force of this Convention shall take effect on the first day of the third month after the deposit of the instrument of ratification or accession.

Article 170

Initial contribution

(1) Any State which ratifies or accedes to this Convention after its entry into force shall pay to the Organisation an initial contribution, which shall not be refunded.

(2) The initial contribution shall be five per cent of an amount calculated by applying the percentage obtained for the State in question, on the date on which ratification or accession takes effect, in accordance with the scale provided for in Article 40, paragraphs 3 and 4, to the sum of the special financial contributions due from the other Contracting States in respect of the accounting periods preceding the date referred to above.

(3) In the event that special financial contributions were not required in respect of the accounting period immediately preceding the date referred to in paragraph 2, the scale of contributions referred to in that paragraph shall be the scale that would have been applicable to the State concerned in respect of the last year for which financial contributions were required.

Article 171

Duration of the Convention

The present Convention shall be of unlimited duration.

Article 172

Revision

(1) This Convention may be revised by a Conference of the Contracting States.

(2) The Conference shall be prepared and convened by the Administrative Council. The Conference shall not be deemed to be validly constituted unless at least three-quarters of the Contracting States are represented at it. In order to adopt the revised text there must be a majority of three-quarters of the Contracting States represented and voting at the Conference. Abstentions shall not be considered as votes.

(3) The revised text shall enter into force when it has been ratified or acceded to by the number of Contracting States specified by the Conference, and at the time specified by that Conference.

(4) Such States as have not ratified or acceded to the revised text of the Convention at the time of its entry into force shall cease to be parties to this Convention as from that time.

Article 173

Disputes between Contracting States

(1) Any dispute between Contracting States concerning the interpretation or application of the present Convention which is not settled by negotiation shall be submitted, at the request of one of the States concerned, to the Administrative Council, which shall endeavour to bring about agreement between the States concerned.

(2) If such agreement is not reached within six months from the date when the Administrative Council was seized of the dispute, any one of the States concerned may submit the dispute to the International Court of Justice for a binding decision.

Article 174

Denunciation

Any Contracting State may at any time denounce this Convention. Notification of denunciation shall be given to the Government of the Federal Republic of Germany. Denunciation shall take effect one year after the date of receipt of such notification.

Article 175

Preservation of acquired rights

(1) In the event of a State ceasing to be party to this Convention in accordance with Article 172, paragraph 4, or Article 174, rights already acquired pursuant to this Convention shall not be impaired.

(2) A European patent application which is pending when a designated State ceases to be party to the Convention shall be processed by the European Patent Office, in so far as that State is concerned, as if the Convention in force thereafter were applicable to that State.

(3) The provisions of paragraph 2 shall apply to European patents in respect of which, on the date mentioned in that paragraph, an opposition is pending or the opposition period has not expired.

(4) Nothing in this article shall affect the right of any State that has ceased to be a party to this Convention to treat any European patent in accordance with the text to which it was a party.

Article 176

Financial rights and obligations
of former Contracting States

(1) Any State which has ceased to be a party to this Convention in accordance with Article 172, paragraph 4, or Article 174, shall have the special financial contributions which it has paid pursuant to Article 40, paragraph 2, refunded to it by the Organisation only at the time and under the conditions whereby the Organisation refunds special financial contributions paid by other States during the same accounting period.

(2) The State referred to in paragraph 1 shall, even after ceasing to be a party to this Convention, continue to pay the proportion pursuant to Article 39 of renewal fees in respect of European patents remaining in force in that State, at the rate current on the date on which it ceased to be a party.

Article 177

Languages of the Convention

(1) This Convention, drawn up in a single original, in the English, French and German languages, shall be deposited in the archives of the Government of the Federal Republic of Germany, the three texts being equally authentic.

(2) The texts of this Convention drawn up in official languages of Contracting States other than those referred to in paragraph 1 shall, if they have been approved by the Administrative Council, be considered as official texts. In the event of conflict on the interpretation of the various texts, the texts referred to in paragraph 1 shall be authentic.

Article 178

Transmission and notifications

(1) The Government of the Federal Republic of Germany shall draw up certified true copies of this Convention and shall transmit them to the Governments of all signatory or acceding States.

(2) The Government of the Federal Republic of Germany shall notify to the Governments of the States referred to in paragraph 1:

(a) any signature;

(b) the deposit of any instrument of ratification or accession;

(c) any reservation or withdrawal of reservation pursuant to the provisions of Article 167;

(d) any declaration or notification received pursuant to the provisions of Article 168;

(e) the date of entry into force of this Convention;

(f)   any denunciation received pursuant to the provisions of Article 174 and the date on which such denunciation comes into force.

(3) The Government of the Federal Republic of Germany shall register this Convention with the Secretariat of the United Nations.

IN WITNESS WHEREOF, the Plenipotentiaries authorised thereto, having presented their Full Powers, found to be in good and due form, have signed this Convention.

DONE at Munich this fifth day of October, one thousand nine hundred and seventy-three.

21

PARTIES TO THE EUROPEAN PATENT CONVENTION

Contracting Party	Date of Entry into Force
Albania	1 May 1, 2010
Austria	1 May 1, 1979
Belgium	7 October 7, 1977
Bulgaria	1 July 1, 2002
Switzerland	7 October 7, 1977
Cyprus	1 April 1, 1998
Czech Republic	1 July 1, 2002
Germany	7 October 7, 1977
Denmark	1 January 1, 1990
Estonia	1 July 1, 2002
Spain	1 October 1, 1986
Finland	1 March 1, 1996
France	7 October 7, 1977
Greece	1 October 1, 1986
Croatia	1 January 1, 2008
Hungary	1 January 1, 2003
Ireland	1 August 1, 1992
Iceland	November 1, 2004
Italy	1 December 1, 1978
Liechtenstein	1 April 1, 1980
Lithuania	1 December 1, 2004
Luxembourg	7 October 7, 1977
Latvia	1 July 1, 2005
Monaco	1 December 1, 1991
Malta	1 March 1, 2007
Netherlands	7 October 7, 1977
Norway	1 January 1, 2008
North Macedonia	1 January 1, 2009
Poland	1 March 1, 2004
Portugal	1 January 1, 1992

Contracting Party	Date of Entry into Force
Romania	1 March 1, 2003
Serbia	1 October 1, 2010
Sweden	1 May 1, 1978
Slovenia	1 December 1, 2002
Slovakia	1 July 1, 2002
San Marino	1 July 1, 2009
Turkey	1 November 1, 2000
United Kingdom	7 October 7, 1977

Total: 38 Parties

22

DOHA WTO MINISTERIAL 2001
WT/MIN(01)/DEC/2

20 November 2001

MINISTERIAL CONFERENCE

Fourth Session

Doha, 9–14 November 2001

DECLARATION ON THE TRIPS
AGREEMENT AND PUBLIC HEALTH

Adopted on 14 November 2001

(1) We recognize the gravity of the public health problems afflicting many developing and least-developed countries, especially those resulting from HIV/AIDS, tuberculosis, malaria and other epidemics.

(2) We stress the need for the WTO Agreement on Trade-Related Aspects of Intellectual Property Rights (TRIPS Agreement) to be part of the wider national and international action to address these problems.

(3) We recognize that intellectual property protection is important for the development of new medicines. We also recognize the concerns about its effects on prices.

(4) We agree that the TRIPS Agreement does not and should not prevent Members from taking measures to protect public health. Accordingly, while reiterating our commitment to the TRIPS Agreement, we affirm that the Agreement can and should be interpreted and implemented in a manner supportive of WTO Members' right to protect public health and, in particular, to promote access to medicines for all. In this connection, we reaffirm the right of WTO Members to use, to the full, the provisions in the TRIPS Agreement, which provide flexibility for this purpose.

(5) Accordingly and in the light of paragraph 4 above, while maintaining our commitments in the TRIPS Agreement, we recognize that these flexibilities include:

(a) In applying the customary rules of interpretation of public international law, each provision of the TRIPS Agreement shall be read in the light of the object and purpose of the Agreement as expressed, in particular, in its objectives and principles.

(b) Each Member has the right to grant compulsory licences and the freedom to determine the grounds upon which such licences are granted.

(c) Each Member has the right to determine what constitutes a national emergency or other circumstances of extreme urgency, it being understood that public health crises, including those relating to HIV/AIDS, tuberculosis, malaria and other epidemics, can represent a national emergency or other circumstances of extreme urgency.

(d) The effect of the provisions in the TRIPS Agreement that are relevant to the exhaustion of intellectual property rights is to leave each Member free to establish its own regime for such exhaustion without challenge, subject to the MFN and national treatment provisions of Articles 3 and 4.

(6) We recognize that WTO Members with insufficient or no manufacturing capacities in the pharmaceutical sector could face difficulties in making effective use of compulsory licensing under the TRIPS Agreement. We instruct the Council for TRIPS to find an expeditious solution to this problem and to report to the General Council before the end of 2002.

(7) We reaffirm the commitment of developed-country Members to provide incentives to their enterprises and institutions to promote and encourage technology transfer to least-developed country Members pursuant to Article 66.2. We also agree that the least-developed country Members will not be obliged, with respect to pharmaceutical products, to implement or apply Sections 5 and 7 of Part II of the TRIPS Agreement or to enforce rights provided for under these Sections until 1 January 2016, without prejudice to the right of least-developed country Members to seek other extensions of the transition periods as provided for in Article 66.1 of the TRIPS Agreement. We instruct the Council for TRIPS to take the necessary action to give effect to this pursuant to Article 66.1 of the TRIPS Agreement.

23

IMPLEMENTATION OF PARAGRAPH 6 OF THE DOHA DECLARATION ON THE TRIPS AGREEMENT AND PUBLIC HEALTH

WT/L/540

2 September 2003

Decision of 30 August 2003*

The General Council,

Having regard to paragraphs 1, 3 and 4 of Article IX of the Marrakesh Agreement Establishing the World Trade Organization ("the WTO Agreement");

Conducting the functions of the Ministerial Conference in the interval between meetings pursuant to paragraph 2 of Article IV of the WTO Agreement;

Noting the Declaration on the TRIPS Agreement and Public Health (WT/MIN(01)/DEC/2) (the "Declaration") and, in particular, the instruction of the Ministerial Conference to the Council for TRIPS contained in paragraph 6 of the Declaration to find an expeditious solution to the problem of the difficulties that WTO Members with insufficient or no manufacturing capacities in the pharmaceutical sector could face in making effective use of compulsory licensing under the TRIPS Agreement and to report to the General Council before the end of 2002;

Recognizing, where eligible importing Members seek to obtain supplies under the system set out in this Decision, the importance of a rapid response to those needs consistent with the provisions of this Decision;

Noting that, in the light of the foregoing, exceptional circumstances exist justifying waivers from the obligations set out in paragraphs (f) and (h) of Article 31 of the TRIPS Agreement with respect to pharmaceutical products;

---

*   This Decision was adopted by the General Council in the light of a statement read out by the Chairman, which can be found in JOB(03)/177. This statement will be reproduced in the minutes of the General Council to be issued as WT/GC/M/82.

Decides as follows:

(1) For the purposes of this Decision:

(a) "pharmaceutical product" means any patented product, or product manufactured through a patented process, of the pharmaceutical sector needed to address the public health problems as recognized in paragraph 1 of the Declaration. It is understood that active ingredients necessary for its manufacture and diagnostic kits needed for its use would be included[1];

(b) "eligible importing Member" means any least-developed country Member, and any other Member that has made a notification[2] to the Council for TRIPS of its intention to use the system as an importer, it being understood that a Member may notify at any time that it will use the system in whole or in a limited way, for example only in the case of a national emergency or other circumstances of extreme urgency or in cases of public noncommercial use. It is noted that some Members will not use the system set out in this Decision as importing Members[3] and that some other Members have stated that, if they use the system, it would be in no more than situations of national emergency or other circumstances of extreme urgency;

(c) "exporting Member" means a Member using the system set out in this Decision to produce pharmaceutical products for, and export them to, an eligible importing Member.

(2) The obligations of an exporting Member under Article 31(f) of the TRIPS Agreement shall be waived with respect to the grant by it of a compulsory licence to the extent necessary for the purposes of production of a pharmaceutical product(s) and its export to an eligible importing Member(s) in accordance with the terms set out below in this paragraph:

(a) the eligible importing Member(s)[4] has made a notification[2] to the Council for TRIPS, that:

    (i) specifies the names and expected quantities of the product(s) needed[5];

---

[1]. This subparagraph is without prejudice to subparagraph 1(b).

[2]. It is understood that this notification does not need to be approved by a WTO body in order to use the system set out in this Decision.

[3]. Australia, Austria, Belgium, Canada, Denmark, Finland, France, Germany, Greece, Iceland, Ireland, Italy, Japan, Luxembourg, the Netherlands, New Zealand, Norway, Portugal, Spain, Sweden, Switzerland, the United Kingdom and the United States.

[4]. Joint notifications providing the information required under this subparagraph may be made by the regional organizations referred to in paragraph 6 of this Decision on behalf of eligible importing Members using the system that are parties to them, with the agreement of those parties.

[5]. The notification will be made available publicly by the WTO Secretariat through a page on the WTO website dedicated to this Decision.

(ii) confirms that the eligible importing Member in question, other than a least-developed country Member, has established that it has insufficient or no manufacturing capacities in the pharmaceutical sector for the product(s) in question in one of the ways set out in the Annex to this Decision; and

(iii) confirms that, where a pharmaceutical product is patented in its territory, it has granted or intends to grant a compulsory licence in accordance with Article 31 of the TRIPS Agreement and the provisions of this Decision[6];

(b) the compulsory licence issued by the exporting Member under this Decision shall contain the following conditions:

(i) only the amount necessary to meet the needs of the eligible importing Member(s) may be manufactured under the licence and the entirety of this production shall be exported to the Member(s) which has notified its needs to the Council for TRIPS;

(ii) products produced under the licence shall be clearly identified as being produced under the system set out in this Decision through specific labelling or marking. Suppliers should distinguish such products through special packaging and/or special colouring/shaping of the products themselves, provided that such distinction is feasible and does not have a significant impact on price; and

(iii) before shipment begins, the licensee shall post on a website[7] the following information:

the quantities being supplied to each destination as referred to in indent (i) above; and

the distinguishing features of the product(s) referred to in indent (ii) above;

(c) the exporting Member shall notify[8] the Council for TRIPS of the grant of the licence, including the conditions attached to it.[9] The information provided shall include the name and address of the licensee, the product(s) for which the licence has been granted, the quantity(ies) for which it has been granted, the country(ies) to

---

6. This subparagraph is without prejudice to Article 66.1 of the TRIPS Agreement.

7. The licensee may use for this purpose its own website or, with the assistance of the WTO Secretariat, the page on the WTO website dedicated to this Decision.

8. It is understood that this notification does not need to be approved by a WTO body in order to use the system set out in this Decision.

9. The notification will be made available publicly by the WTO Secretariat through a page on the WTO website dedicated to this Decision.

which the product(s) is (are) to be supplied and the duration of the licence. The notification shall also indicate the address of the website referred to in subparagraph (b)(iii) above.

(3) Where a compulsory licence is granted by an exporting Member under the system set out in this Decision, adequate remuneration pursuant to Article 31(h) of the TRIPS Agreement shall be paid in that Member taking into account the economic value to the importing Member of the use that has been authorized in the exporting Member. Where a compulsory licence is granted for the same products in the eligible importing Member, the obligation of that Member under Article 31(h) shall be waived in respect of those products for which remuneration in accordance with the first sentence of this paragraph is paid in the exporting Member.

(4) In order to ensure that the products imported under the system set out in this Decision are used for the public health purposes underlying their importation, eligible importing Members shall take reasonable measures within their means, proportionate to their administrative capacities and to the risk of trade diversion to prevent re-exportation of the products that have actually been imported into their territories under the system. In the event that an eligible importing Member that is a developing country Member or a least-developed country Member experiences difficulty in implementing this provision, developed country Members shall provide, on request and on mutually agreed terms and conditions, technical and financial cooperation in order to facilitate its implementation.

(5) Members shall ensure the availability of effective legal means to prevent the importation into, and sale in, their territories of products produced under the system set out in this Decision and diverted to their markets inconsistently with its provisions, using the means already required to be available under the TRIPS Agreement. If any Member considers that such measures are proving insufficient for this purpose, the matter may be reviewed in the Council for TRIPS at the request of that Member.

(6) With a view to harnessing economies of scale for the purposes of enhancing purchasing power for, and facilitating the local production of, pharmaceutical products:

(i)   where a developing or least-developed country WTO Member is a party to a regional trade agreement within the meaning of Article XXIV of the GATT 1994 and the Decision of 28 November 1979 on Differential and More Favourable Treatment Reciprocity and Fuller Participation of Developing Countries (L/4903), at least half of the current membership of which is made up of countries presently on the United Nations list of least-developed countries, the obligation of that Member under Article 31(f) of the TRIPS Agreement shall be waived to the extent necessary to enable a pharmaceutical product produced or imported under a compulsory licence in that Member to be exported to the markets of those other developing or least-developed country parties to the regional trade agreement that share the health problem in question. It is understood that this will not prejudice the territorial nature of the patent rights in question;

(ii) it is recognized that the development of systems providing for the grant of regional patents to be applicable in the above Members should be promoted. To this end, developed country Members undertake to provide technical cooperation in accordance with Article 67 of the TRIPS Agreement, including in conjunction with other relevant intergovernmental organizations.

(7) Members recognize the desirability of promoting the transfer of technology and capacity building in the pharmaceutical sector in order to overcome the problem identified in paragraph 6 of the Declaration. To this end, eligible importing Members and exporting Members are encouraged to use the system set out in this Decision in a way which would promote this objective. Members undertake to cooperate in paying special attention to the transfer of technology and capacity building in the pharmaceutical sector in the work to be undertaken pursuant to Article 66.2 of the TRIPS Agreement, paragraph 7 of the Declaration and any other relevant work of the Council for TRIPS.

(8) The Council for TRIPS shall review annually the functioning of the system set out in this Decision with a view to ensuring its effective operation and shall annually report on its operation to the General Council. This review shall be deemed to fulfil the review requirements of Article IX:4 of the WTO Agreement.

(9) This Decision is without prejudice to the rights, obligations and flexibilities that Members have under the provisions of the TRIPS Agreement other than paragraphs (f) and (h) of Article 31, including those reaffirmed by the Declaration, and to their interpretation. It is also without prejudice to the extent to which pharmaceutical products produced under a compulsory licence can be exported under the present provisions of Article 31(f) of the TRIPS Agreement.

(10) Members shall not challenge any measures taken in conformity with the provisions of the waivers contained in this Decision under subparagraphs 1(b) and 1(c) of Article XXIII of GATT 1994.

(11) This Decision, including the waivers granted in it, shall terminate for each Member on the date on which an amendment to the TRIPS Agreement replacing its provisions takes effect for that Member. The TRIPS Council shall initiate by the end of 2003 work on the preparation of such an amendment with a view to its adoption within six months, on the understanding that the amendment will be based, where appropriate, on

this Decision and on the further understanding that it will not be part of the negotiations referred to in paragraph 45 of the Doha Ministerial Declaration (WT/MIN(01)/DEC/1).

ANNEX

Assessment of Manufacturing Capacities in the Pharmaceutical Sector

Least-developed country Members are deemed to have insufficient or no manufacturing capacities in the pharmaceutical sector.

For other eligible importing Members insufficient or no manufacturing capacities for the product(s) in question may be established in either of the following ways:

(i) the Member in question has established that it has no manufacturing capacity in the pharmaceutical sector;

OR

(ii) where the Member has some manufacturing capacity in this sector, it has examined this capacity and found that, excluding any capacity owned or controlled by the patent owner, it is currently insufficient for the purposes of meeting its needs. When it is established that such capacity has become sufficient to meet the Member's needs, the system shall no longer apply.

PART 3

TRADEMARKS AND GEOGRAPHICAL INDICATIONS

24

PROTOCOL RELATING TO THE MADRID AGREEMENT CONCERNING THE INTERNATIONAL REGISTRATION OF MARKS (MADRID PROTOCOL)

Adopted at Madrid on June 27, 1989, as amended on October 3, 2006 and on November 12, 2007

Article 1

Membership in the Madrid Union

The States party to this Protocol (hereinafter referred to as "the Contracting States"), even where they are not party to the Madrid Agreement Concerning the International Registration of Marks as revised at Stockholm in 1967 and as amended in 1979 (hereinafter referred to as "the Madrid (Stockholm) Agreement"), and the organizations referred to in Article 14(1)(b) which are party to this Protocol (hereinafter referred to as "the Contracting Organizations") shall be members of the same Union of which countries party to the Madrid (Stockholm) Agreement are members. Any reference in this Protocol to "Contracting Parties" shall be construed as a reference to both Contracting States and Contracting Organizations.

Article 2

Securing Protection through International Registration

(1) Where an application for the registration of a mark has been filed with the Office of a Contracting Party, or where a mark has been registered in the register of the Office of a Contracting Party, the person in whose name that application (hereinafter referred to as "the basic application") or that registration (hereinafter referred to as "the basic registration") stands may, subject to the provisions of this Protocol, secure protection for his mark in the territory of the Contracting Parties, by obtaining the registration of that mark in the register of the International Bureau of the World Intellectual Property Organization (hereinafter referred to as "the international registration," "the International Register," "the International Bureau" and "the Organization," respectively), provided that,

    (i) where the basic application has been filed with the Office of a Contracting State or where the basic registration has been made by such an Office, the person in whose name that application or registration stands is a national of that Contracting State, or is domiciled, or has a real and effective industrial or commercial establishment, in the said Contracting State,

(ii) where the basic application has been filed with the Office of a Contracting Organization or where the basic registration has been made by such an Office, the person in whose name that application or registration stands is a national of a State member of that Contracting Organization, or is domiciled, or has a real and effective industrial or commercial establishment, in the territory of the said Contracting Organization.

(2) The application for international registration (hereinafter referred to as "the international application") shall be filed with the International Bureau through the intermediary of the Office with which the basic application was filed or by which the basic registration was made (hereinafter referred to as "the Office of origin"), as the case may be.

(3) Any reference in this Protocol to an "Office" or an "Office of a Contracting Party" shall be construed as a reference to the office that is in charge, on behalf of a Contracting Party, of the registration of marks, and any reference in this Protocol to "marks" shall be construed as a reference to trademarks and service marks.

(4) For the purposes of this Protocol, "territory of a Contracting Party" means, where the Contracting Party is a State, the territory of that State and, where the Contracting Party is an intergovernmental organization, the territory in which the constituting treaty of that intergovernmental organization applies.

Article 3

International Application

(1) Every international application under this Protocol shall be presented on the form prescribed by the Regulations. The Office of origin shall certify that the particulars appearing in the international application correspond to the particulars appearing, at the time of the certification, in the basic application or basic registration, as the case may be. Furthermore, the said Office shall indicate,

(i) in the case of a basic application, the date and number of that application,

(ii) in the case of a basic registration, the date and number of that registration as well as the date and number of the application from which the basic registration resulted.

The Office of origin shall also indicate the date of the international application.

(2) The applicant must indicate the goods and services in respect of which protection of the mark is claimed and also, if possible, the corresponding class or classes according to the classification established by the Nice Agreement Concerning the International Classification of Goods and Services for the Purposes of the Registration of Marks. If the applicant does not give such indication, the International Bureau shall classify the goods and services in the appropriate classes of the said classification. The indication of classes given by the applicant shall be subject to control by the International Bureau, which shall exercise the said control in association with the Office of origin. In the event of disagreement between the said Office and the International Bureau, the opinion of the latter shall prevail.

(3) If the applicant claims color as a distinctive feature of his mark, he shall be required

(i) to state the fact, and to file with his international application a notice specifying the color or the combination of colors claimed;

(ii) to append to his international application copies in color of the said mark, which shall be attached to the notifications given by the International Bureau; the number of such copies shall be fixed by the Regulations.

(4) The International Bureau shall register immediately the marks filed in accordance with Article 2. The international registration shall bear the date on which the international application was received in the Office of origin, provided that the international application has been received by the International Bureau within a period of two months from that date. If the international application has not been received within that period, the international registration shall bear the date on which the said international application was received by the International Bureau. The International Bureau shall notify the international registration without delay to the Offices concerned. Marks registered in the International Register shall be published in a periodical gazette issued by the International Bureau, on the basis of the particulars contained in the international application.

(5) With a view to the publicity to be given to marks registered in the International Register, each Office shall receive from the International Bureau a number of copies of the said gazette free of charge and a number of copies at a reduced price, under the conditions fixed by the Assembly referred to in Article 10 (hereinafter referred to as "the Assembly"). Such publicity shall be deemed to be sufficient for the purposes of all the Contracting Parties, and no other publicity may be required of the holder of the international registration.

Article 3*bis*

Territorial Effect

The protection resulting from the international registration shall extend to any Contracting Party only at the request of the person who files the international application or who is the holder of the international registration. However, no such request can be made with respect to the Contracting Party whose Office is the Office of origin.

Article 3*ter*

Request for "Territorial Extension"

(1) Any request for extension of the protection resulting from the international registration to any Contracting Party shall be specially mentioned in the international application.

(2) A request for territorial extension may also be made subsequently to the international registration. Any such request shall be presented on the form prescribed by the Regulations. It shall be immediately recorded by the International Bureau, which shall notify such recordal without delay to the Office or Offices concerned. Such recordal shall be published in the periodical gazette of the International Bureau. Such territorial extension shall be effective from the date on which it has been recorded in the International Register; it shall cease to be valid on the expiry of the international registration to which it relates.

Article 4

Effects of International Registration

(1)(a)   From the date of the registration or recordal effected in accordance with the provisions of Articles 3 and 3*ter*, the protection of the mark in each of the Contracting Parties concerned shall be the same as if the mark had been deposited direct with the Office of that Contracting Party. If no refusal has been notified to the International Bureau in accordance with Article 5(1) and (2) or if a refusal notified in accordance with the said Article has been withdrawn subsequently, the protection of the mark in the Contracting Party concerned shall, as from the said date, be the same as if the mark had been registered by the Office of that Contracting Party.

(b)   The indication of classes of goods and services provided for in Article 3 shall not bind the Contracting Parties with regard to the determination of the scope of the protection of the mark.

(2) Every international registration shall enjoy the right of priority provided for by Article 4 of the Paris Convention for the Protection of Industrial Property, without it being necessary to comply with the formalities prescribed in Section D of that Article.

Article 4*bis*

Replacement of a National or Regional Registration by an International Registration

(1) Where a mark that is the subject of a national or regional registration in the Office of a Contracting Party is also the subject of an international registration and both registrations stand in the name of the same person, the international registration is deemed to replace the national or regional registration, without prejudice to any rights acquired by virtue of the latter, provided that

(i)   the protection resulting from the international registration extends to the said Contracting Party under Article 3*ter*(1) or (2),

(ii) all the goods and services listed in the national or regional registration are also listed in the international registration in respect of the said Contracting Party,

(iii) such extension takes effect after the date of the national or regional registration.

(2) The Office referred to in paragraph (1) shall, upon request, be required to take note in its register of the international registration.

Article 5

Refusal and Invalidation of Effects of International Registration in Respect of Certain Contracting Parties

(1) Where the applicable legislation so authorizes, any Office of a Contracting Party which has been notified by the International Bureau of an extension to that Contracting Party, under Article 3*ter*(1) or (2), of the protection resulting from the international registration shall have the right to declare in a notification of refusal that protection cannot be granted in the said Contracting Party to the mark which is the subject of such extension. Any such refusal can be based only on the grounds which would apply, under the Paris Convention for the Protection of Industrial Property, in the case of a mark deposited direct with the Office which notifies the refusal. However, protection may not be refused, even partially, by reason only that the applicable legislation would permit registration only in a limited number of classes or for a limited number of goods or services.

(2)(a)   Any Office wishing to exercise such right shall notify its refusal to the International Bureau, together with a statement of all grounds, within the period prescribed by the law applicable to that Office and at the latest, subject to subparagraphs (b) and (c), before the expiry of one year from the date on which the notification of the extension referred to in paragraph (1) has been sent to that Office by the International Bureau.

(b)   Notwithstanding subparagraph (a), any Contracting Party may declare that, for international registrations made under this Protocol, the time limit of one year referred to in subparagraph (a) is replaced by 18 months.

(c)   Such declaration may also specify that, when a refusal of protection may result from an opposition to the granting of protection, such refusal may be notified by the Office of the said Contracting Party to the International Bureau after the expiry of the 18-month time limit. Such an Office may, with respect to any given international registration, notify a refusal of protection after the expiry of the 18-month time limit, but only if

    (i)   it has, before the expiry of the 18-month time limit, informed the International Bureau of the possibility that oppositions may be filed after the expiry of the 18-month time limit, and

    (ii)   the notification of the refusal based on an opposition is made within a time limit of one month from the expiry of the opposition period and, in any case, not later than seven months from the date on which the opposition period begins; if the opposition period expires before this time limit of seven months, the notification must be made within a time limit of one month from the expiry of the opposition period.

(d)   Any declaration under subparagraphs (b) or (c) may be made in the instruments referred to in Article 14(2), and the effective date of the declaration shall be the same as the date of entry into force of this Protocol with respect to the State or intergovernmental organization having made the declaration. Any such declaration may also be made later, in which case the declaration shall have effect three months after its receipt by the Director General of the Organization (hereinafter referred to as "the Director General"), or at any later date indicated in the declaration, in respect of any international registration whose date is the same as or is later than the effective date of the declaration.

(e)   Upon the expiry of a period of ten years from the entry into force of this Protocol, the Assembly shall examine the operation of the system established by subparagraphs (a) to (d). Thereafter, the provisions of the said subparagraphs may be modified by a unanimous decision of the Assembly.

(3)   The International Bureau shall, without delay, transmit one of the copies of the notification of refusal to the holder of the international registration. The said holder shall have the same remedies as if the mark had been deposited by him direct with the Office which has notified its refusal. Where the International Bureau has received information under

paragraph (2)(c)(i), it shall, without delay, transmit the said information to the holder of the international registration.

(4) The grounds for refusing a mark shall be communicated by the International Bureau to any interested party who may so request.

(5) Any Office which has not notified, with respect to a given international registration, any provisional or final refusal to the International Bureau in accordance with paragraphs (1) and (2) shall, with respect to that international registration, lose the benefit of the right provided for in paragraph (1).

(6) Invalidation, by the competent authorities of a Contracting Party, of the effects, in the territory of that Contracting Party, of an international registration may not be pronounced without the holder of such international registration having, in good time, been afforded the opportunity of defending his rights. Invalidation shall be notified to the International Bureau.

Article 5*bis*

Documentary Evidence of Legitimacy of Use of Certain Elements of the Mark

Documentary evidence of the legitimacy of the use of certain elements incorporated in a mark, such as armorial bearings, escutcheons, portraits, honorary distinctions, titles, trade names, names of persons other than the name of the applicant, or other like inscriptions, which might be required by the Offices of the Contracting Parties shall be exempt from any legalization as well as from any certification other than that of the Office of origin.

Article 5*ter*

Copies of Entries in International Register; Searches for Anticipations; Extracts from International Register

(1) The International Bureau shall issue to any person applying therefor, upon the payment of a fee fixed by the Regulations, a copy of the entries in the International Register concerning a specific mark.

(2) The International Bureau may also, upon payment, undertake searches for anticipations among marks that are the subject of international registrations.

(3) Extracts from the International Register requested with a view to their production in one of the Contracting Parties shall be exempt from any legalization.

Article 6

Period of Validity of International Registration; Dependence and Independence of International Registration

(1) Registration of a mark at the International Bureau is effected for ten years, with the possibility of renewal under the conditions specified in Article 7.

(2) Upon expiry of a period of five years from the date of the international registration, such registration shall become independent of the basic application or the registration resulting therefrom, or of the basic registration, as the case may be, subject to the following provisions.

(3) The protection resulting from the international registration, whether or not it has been the subject of a transfer, may no longer be invoked if, before the expiry of five years from the date of the international registration, the basic application or the registration resulting therefrom, or the basic registration, as the case may be, has been withdrawn, has lapsed, has been renounced or has been the subject of a final decision of rejection, revocation, cancellation or invalidation, in respect of all or some of the goods and services listed in the international registration. The same applies if

(i) an appeal against a decision refusing the effects of the basic application,

(ii) an action requesting the withdrawal of the basic application or the revocation, cancellation or invalidation of the registration resulting from the basic application or of the basic registration, or

(iii) an opposition to the basic application results, after the expiry of the five-year period, in a final decision of rejection, revocation, cancellation or invalidation, or ordering the withdrawal, of the basic application, or the registration resulting therefrom, or the basic registration, as the case may be, provided that such appeal, action or opposition had begun before the expiry of the said period. The same also applies if the basic application is withdrawn, or the registration resulting from the basic application or the basic registration is renounced, after the expiry of the five-year period, provided that, at the time of the withdrawal or renunciation, the said application or registration was the subject of a proceeding referred to in item (i), (ii) or (iii) and that such proceeding had begun before the expiry of the said period.

(4) The Office of origin shall, as prescribed in the Regulations, notify the International Bureau of the facts and decisions relevant under paragraph (3), and the International Bureau shall, as prescribed in the Regulations, notify the interested parties and effect any publication accordingly. The Office of origin shall, where applicable, request the

International Bureau to cancel, to the extent applicable, the international registration, and the International Bureau shall proceed accordingly.

Article 7

Renewal of International Registration

(1) Any international registration may be renewed for a period of ten years from the expiry of the preceding period, by the mere payment of the basic fee and, subject to Article 8(7), of the supplementary and complementary fees provided for in Article 8(2).

(2) Renewal may not bring about any change in the international registration in its latest form.

(3) Six months before the expiry of the term of protection, the International Bureau shall, by sending an unofficial notice, remind the holder of the international registration and his representative, if any, of the exact date of expiry.

(4) Subject to the payment of a surcharge fixed by the Regulations, a period of grace of six months shall be allowed for renewal of the international registration.

Article 8

Fees for International Application and Registration

(1) The Office of origin may fix, at its own discretion, and collect, for its own benefit, a fee which it may require from the applicant for international registration or from the holder of the international registration in connection with the filing of the international application or the renewal of the international registration.

(2) Registration of a mark at the International Bureau shall be subject to the advance payment of an international fee which shall, subject to the provisions of paragraph (7)(a), include,

(i) a basic fee;

(ii) a supplementary fee for each class of the International Classification, beyond three, into which the goods or services to which the mark is applied will fall;

(iii) a complementary fee for any request for extension of protection under Article 3*ter*.

(3) However, the supplementary fee specified in paragraph (2)(ii) may, without prejudice to the date of the international registration, be paid within the period fixed by the Regulations if the number of classes of goods or services has been fixed or disputed by the International Bureau. If, upon expiry of the said period, the supplementary fee has not been paid or the list of goods or services has not been reduced to the required extent by the

applicant, the international application shall be deemed to have been abandoned.

(4) The annual product of the various receipts from international registration, with the exception of the receipts derived from the fees mentioned in paragraph (2)(ii) and (iii), shall be divided equally among the Contracting Parties by the International Bureau, after deduction of the expenses and charges necessitated by the implementation of this Protocol.

(5) The amounts derived from the supplementary fees provided for in paragraph (2)(ii) shall be divided, at the expiry of each year, among the interested Contracting Parties in proportion to the number of marks for which protection has been applied for in each of them during that year, this number being multiplied, in the case of Contracting Parties which make an examination, by a coefficient which shall be determined by the Regulations.

(6) The amounts derived from the complementary fees provided for in paragraph (2)(iii) shall be divided according to the same rules as those provided for in paragraph (5).

(7)(a)   Any Contracting Party may declare that, in connection with each international registration in which it is mentioned under Article 3*ter*, and in connection with the renewal of any such international registration, it wants to receive, instead of a share in the revenue produced by the supplementary and complementary fees, a fee (hereinafter referred to as "the individual fee") whose amount shall be indicated in the declaration, and can be changed in further declarations, but may not be higher than the equivalent of the amount which the said Contracting Party's Office would be entitled to receive from an applicant for a ten-year registration, or from the holder of a registration for a ten-year renewal of that registration, of the mark in the register of the said Office, the said amount being diminished by the savings resulting from the international procedure. Where such an individual fee is payable,

(i)   no supplementary fees referred to in paragraph (2)(ii) shall be payable if only Contracting Parties which have made a declaration under this subparagraph are mentioned under Article 3*ter*, and

(ii) no complementary fee referred to in paragraph (2)(iii) shall be payable in respect of any Contracting Party which has made a declaration under this subparagraph.

(b) Any declaration under subparagraph (a) may be made in the instruments referred to in Article 14(2), and the effective date of the declaration shall be the same as the date of entry into force of this Protocol with respect to the State or intergovernmental organization having made the declaration. Any such declaration may also be made later, in which case the declaration shall have effect three months after its receipt by the Director General, or at any later date indicated in the declaration, in respect of any international registration whose date is the same as or is later than the effective date of the declaration.

Article 9

Recordal of Change in the Ownership of an International Registration

At the request of the person in whose name the international registration stands, or at the request of an interested Office made ex officio or at the request of an interested person, the International Bureau shall record in the International Register any change in the ownership of that registration, in respect of all or some of the Contracting Parties in whose territories the said registration has effect and in respect of all or some of the goods and services listed in the registration, provided that the new holder is a person who, under Article 2(1), is entitled to file international applications.

Article 9*bis*

Recordal of Certain Matters Concerning an International Registration

The International Bureau shall record in the International Register

(i)   any change in the name or address of the holder of the international registration,

(ii) the appointment of a representative of the holder of the international registration and any other relevant fact concerning such representative,

(iii) any limitation, in respect of all or some of the Contracting Parties, of the goods and services listed in the international registration,

(iv) any renunciation, cancellation or invalidation of the international registration in respect of all or some of the Contracting Parties,

(v)   any other relevant fact, identified in the Regulations, concerning the rights in a mark that is the subject of an international registration.

Article 9*ter*

Fees for Certain Recordals

Any recordal under Article 9 or under Article 9*bis* may be subject to the payment of a fee.

Article 9*quater*

Common Office of Several Contracting States

(1)   If several Contracting States agree to effect the unification of their domestic legislations on marks, they may notify the Director General

(i)   that a common Office shall be substituted for the national Office of each of them, and

(ii) that the whole of their respective territories shall be deemed to be a single State for the purposes of the application of all or part of the provisions preceding this Article as well as the provisions of Articles 9*quinquies* and 9*sexies*.

(2)   Such notification shall not take effect until three months after the date of the communication thereof by the Director General to the other Contracting Parties.

Article 9*quinquies*

Transformation of an International Registration into National or Regional Applications

Where, in the event that the international registration is cancelled at the request of the Office of origin under Article 6(4), in respect of all or some of the goods and services listed in the said registration, the person who was the holder of the international registration files an application for the registration of the same mark with the Office of any of the Contracting Parties in the territory of which the international registration had effect, that application shall be treated as if it had been filed on the date of the international registration according to Article 3(4) or on the date of recordal of the territorial extension according to Article 3*ter*(2) and, if the international registration enjoyed priority, shall enjoy the same priority, provided that

(i)   such application is filed within three months from the date on which the international registration was cancelled,

(ii) the goods and services listed in the application are in fact covered by the list of goods and services contained in the international registration in respect of the Contracting Party concerned, and

(iii) such application complies with all the requirements of the applicable law, including the requirements concerning fees.

Article 9*sexies*

Relations Between States Party to both this Protocol and the Madrid (Stockholm) Agreement

(1)(a)   This Protocol alone shall be applicable as regards the mutual relations of States party to both this Protocol and the Madrid (Stockholm) Agreement.

(b)   Notwithstanding subparagraph (a), a declaration made under Article 5(2)(b), Article 5(2)(c) or Article 8(7) of this Protocol, by a State party to both this Protocol and the Madrid (Stockholm) Agreement, shall have no effect in the relations with another State party to both this Protocol and the Madrid (Stockholm) Agreement.

(2)   The Assembly shall, after the expiry of a period of three years from September 1, 2008, review the application of paragraph (1)(b) and may, at any time thereafter, either repeal it or restrict its scope, by a three-fourths majority. In the vote of the Assembly, only those States which are party to both the Madrid (Stockholm) Agreement and this Protocol shall have the right to participate.

Article 10

Assembly

(1)(a)   The Contracting Parties shall be members of the same Assembly as the countries party to the Madrid (Stockholm) Agreement.

(b)   Each Contracting Party shall be represented in that Assembly by one delegate, who may be assisted by alternate delegates, advisors, and experts.

(c)   The expenses of each delegation shall be borne by the Contracting Party which has appointed it, except for the travel expenses and the subsistence allowance of one delegate for each Contracting Party, which shall be paid from the funds of the Union.

(2)   The Assembly shall, in addition to the functions which it has under the Madrid (Stockholm) Agreement, also

(i)   deal with all matters concerning the implementation of this Protocol;

(ii)   give directions to the International Bureau concerning the preparation for conferences of revision of this Protocol, due account being taken of any comments made by those countries of the Union which are not party to this Protocol;

(iii) adopt and modify the provisions of the Regulations concerning the implementation of this Protocol;

(iv) perform such other functions as are appropriate under this Protocol.

(3)(a) Each Contracting Party shall have one vote in the Assembly. On matters concerning only countries that are party to the Madrid (Stockholm) Agreement, Contracting Parties that are not party to the said Agreement shall not have the right to vote, whereas, on matters concerning only Contracting Parties, only the latter shall have the right to vote.

(b) One-half of the members of the Assembly which have the right to vote on a given matter shall constitute the quorum for the purposes of the vote on that matter.

(c) Notwithstanding the provisions of subparagraph (b), if, in any session, the number of the members of the Assembly having the right to vote on a given matter which are represented is less than one-half but equal to or more than one-third of the members of the Assembly having the right to vote on that matter, the Assembly may make decisions but, with the exception of decisions concerning its own procedure, all such decisions shall take effect only if the conditions set forth hereinafter are fulfilled. The International Bureau shall communicate the said decisions to the members of the Assembly having the right to vote on the said matter which were not represented and shall invite them to express in writing their vote or abstention within a period of three months from the date of the communication. If, at the expiry of this period, the number of such members having thus expressed their vote or abstention attains the number of the members which was lacking for attaining the quorum in the session itself, such decisions shall take effect provided that at the same time the required majority still obtains.

(d) Subject to the provisions of Articles 5(2)(e), 9sexies(2), 12 and 13(2), the decisions of the Assembly shall require two-thirds of the votes cast.

(e) Abstentions shall not be considered as votes.

(f) A delegate may represent, and vote in the name of, one member of the Assembly only.

(4) In addition to meeting in ordinary sessions and extraordinary sessions as provided for by the Madrid (Stockholm) Agreement, the Assembly shall meet in extraordinary session upon convocation by the Director General, at the request of one-fourth of the members of the Assembly having the right to vote on the matters proposed to be included in the agenda of the session. The agenda of such an extraordinary session shall be prepared by the Director General.

Article 11

International Bureau

(1) International registration and related duties, as well as all other administrative tasks, under or concerning this Protocol, shall be performed by the International Bureau.

(2)(a) The International Bureau shall, in accordance with the directions of the Assembly, make the preparations for the conferences of revision of this Protocol.

(b) The International Bureau may consult with intergovernmental and international non-governmental organizations concerning preparations for such conferences of revision.

(c) The Director General and persons designated by him shall take part, without the right to vote, in the discussions at such conferences of revision.

(3) The International Bureau shall carry out any other tasks assigned to it in relation to this Protocol.

Article 12

Finances

As far as Contracting Parties are concerned, the finances of the Union shall be governed by the same provisions as those contained in Article 12 of the Madrid (Stockholm) Agreement, provided that any reference to Article 8 of the said Agreement shall be deemed to be a reference to Article 8 of this Protocol. Furthermore, for the purposes of Article 12(6)(b) of the said Agreement, Contracting Organizations shall, subject to a unanimous decision to the contrary by the Assembly, be considered to belong to contribution class I (one) under the Paris Convention for the Protection of Industrial Property.

Article 13

Amendment of Certain Articles of the Protocol

(1) Proposals for the amendment of Articles 10, 11, 12, and the present Article, may be initiated by any Contracting Party, or by the Director General. Such proposals shall be communicated by the Director General to the Contracting Parties at least six months in advance of their consideration by the Assembly.

(2) Amendments to the Articles referred to in paragraph (1) shall be adopted by the Assembly. Adoption shall require three-fourths of the votes cast, provided that any amendment to Article 10, and to the present paragraph, shall require four-fifths of the votes cast.

(3) Any amendment to the Articles referred to in paragraph (1) shall enter into force one month after written notifications of acceptance, effected in accordance with their respective constitutional processes, have been received by the Director General from three-fourths of those States and intergovernmental organizations which, at the time the amendment was adopted, were members of the Assembly and had the right to vote on the amendment. Any amendment to the said Articles thus accepted shall bind all the States and intergovernmental organizations which are Contracting Parties at the time the amendment enters into force, or which become Contracting Parties at a subsequent date.

Article 14

Becoming Party to the Protocol; Entry into Force

(1)(a) Any State that is a party to the Paris Convention for the Protection of Industrial Property may become party to this Protocol.

(b) Furthermore, any intergovernmental organization may also become party to this Protocol where the following conditions are fulfilled:

(i) at least one of the member States of that organization is a party to the Paris Convention for the Protection of Industrial Property;

(ii) that organization has a regional Office for the purposes of registering marks with effect in the territory of the organization, provided that such Office is not the subject of a notification under Article 9*quater*.

(2) Any State or organization referred to in paragraph (1) may sign this Protocol. Any such State or organization may, if it has signed this Protocol, deposit an instrument of ratification, acceptance or approval of this Protocol or, if it has not signed this Protocol, deposit an instrument of accession to this Protocol.

(3) The instruments referred to in paragraph (2) shall be deposited with the Director General.

(4)(a) This Protocol shall enter into force three months after four instruments of ratification, acceptance, approval or accession have been deposited, provided that at least one of those instruments has been deposited by a country party to the Madrid (Stockholm) Agreement and at least one other of those instruments has been deposited by a State not party to the Madrid (Stockholm) Agreement or by any of the organizations referred to in paragraph (1)(b).

(b) With respect to any other State or organization referred to in paragraph (1), this Protocol shall enter into force three months after the date on which its ratification, acceptance, approval or accession has been notified by the Director General.

(5) Any State or organization referred to in paragraph (1) may, when depositing its instrument of ratification, acceptance or approval of, or accession to, this Protocol, declare that the protection resulting from any international registration effected under this Protocol before the date of entry into force of this Protocol with respect to it cannot be extended to it.

Article 15

Denunciation

(1) This Protocol shall remain in force without limitation as to time.

(2) Any Contracting Party may denounce this Protocol by notification addressed to the Director General.

(3) Denunciation shall take effect one year after the day on which the Director General has received the notification.

(4) The right of denunciation provided for by this Article shall not be exercised by any Contracting Party before the expiry of five years from the date upon which this Protocol entered into force with respect to that Contracting Party.

(5)(a)   Where a mark is the subject of an international registration having effect in the denouncing State or intergovernmental organization at the date on which the denunciation becomes effective, the holder of such registration may file an application for the registration of the same mark with the Office of the denouncing State or intergovernmental organization, which shall be treated as if it had been filed on the date of the international registration according to Article 3(4) or on the date of recordal of the territorial extension according to Article 3ter(2) and, if the international registration enjoyed priority, enjoy the same priority, provided that

(i)   such application is filed within two years from the date on which the denunciation became effective,

(ii)   the goods and services listed in the application are in fact covered by the list of goods and services contained in the international registration in respect of the denouncing State or intergovernmental organization, and

(iii)   such application complies with all the requirements of the applicable law, including the requirements concerning fees.

(b) The provisions of subparagraph (a) shall also apply in respect of any mark that is the subject of an international registration having effect in Contracting Parties other than the denouncing State or intergovernmental organization at the date on which denunciation becomes effective and whose holder, because of the denunciation, is no longer entitled to file international applications under Article 2(1).

Article 16

Signature; Languages; Depositary Functions

(1)(a) This Protocol shall be signed in a single copy in the English, French and Spanish languages, and shall be deposited with the Director General when it ceases to be open for signature at Madrid. The texts in the three languages shall be equally authentic.

(b) Official texts of this Protocol shall be established by the Director General, after consultation with the interested governments and organizations, in the Arabic, Chinese, German, Italian, Japanese, Portuguese and Russian languages, and in such other languages as the Assembly may designate.

(2) This Protocol shall remain open for signature at Madrid until December 31, 1989.

(3) The Director General shall transmit two copies, certified by the Government of Spain, of the signed texts of this Protocol to all States and intergovernmental organizations that may become party to this Protocol.

(4) The Director General shall register this Protocol with the Secretariat of the United Nations.

(5) The Director General shall notify all States and international organizations that may become or are party to this Protocol of signatures, deposits of instruments of ratification, acceptance, approval or accession, the entry into force of this Protocol and any amendment thereto, any notification of denunciation and any declaration provided for in this Protocol.

25

PARTIES TO THE MADRID PROTOCOL

Status as of February 24, 2021

State/IGO	Date on which State/IGO became party to the Madrid Protocol
Afghanistan	June 26, 2018
African Intellectual Property Organization	March 5, 2015[3, 4]
Albania	July 30, 2003
Algeria	October 31, 2015[3]
Antigua and Barbuda	March 17, 2000[3, 4]
Armenia	October 19, 2000[3, 8]
Australia	July 11, 2001[3, 4]
Austria	April 13, 1999
Azerbaijan	April 15, 2007
Bahrain	December 15, 2005[8]
Belarus	January 18, 2002[4, 8]
Belgium	April 1, 1998[1, 4]
Bhutan	August 4, 2000
Bosnia and Herzegovina	January 27, 2009
Botswana	December 5, 2006
Brazil	October 2, 2019[3, 4, 6]
Brunei Darussalam	January 6, 2017[3, 4]
Bulgaria	October 2, 2001[4]
Cambodia	June 5, 2015
Canada	June 17, 2019[3, 4]
China	December 1, 1995[2, 3]

[1.] The territories of Belgium, Luxembourg and the Kingdom of the Netherlands in Europe are to be deemed a single country, for the application of the Madrid Agreement as from January 1, 1971, and for the application of the Protocol as from April 1, 1998.

[2.] Not applicable to either Hong Kong, China or Macao, China

[3.] In accordance with Article 5(2)(b) and (c) of the Protocol, this Contracting Party has declared that the time limit to notify a refusal of protection shall be 18 months and that, where a refusal of protection results from an opposition to the granting of protection, such refusal may be notified after the expiry of the 18-month time limit.

State/IGO	Date on which State/IGO became party to the Madrid Protocol
Colombia	August 29, 2012[3, 4]
Croatia	January 23, 2004
Cuba	December 26, 1995
Cyprus	November 4, 2003[3]
Czech Republic	September 25, 1996
Democratic People's Republic of Korea	October 3, 1996
Denmark	February 13, 1996[3, 4, 5]
Egypt	September 3, 2009
Estonia	November 18, 1998[3, 4, 6]
Eswatini	December 14, 1998
European Union	October 1, 2004[4, 8]
Finland	April 1, 1996[3, 4]
France	November 7, 1997[7]
Gambia	December 18, 2015[3, 4]
Georgia	August 20, 1998[4, 8]
Germany	March 20, 1996
Ghana	September 16, 2008[3, 4]
Greece	August 10, 2000[3, 4]
Hungary	October 3, 1997
Iceland	April 15, 1997[4, 8]
India	July 8, 2013[3, 4, 6]
Indonesia	January 2, 2018[4, 8]
Iran (Islamic Republic of)	December 25, 2003[3]
Ireland	October 19, 2001[3, 4]
Israel	September 1, 2010[3, 4]
Italy	April 17, 2000[3, 4]
Japan	March 14, 2000[4, 8]
Kazakhstan	December 8, 2010
Kenya	June 26, 1998[3, 4]

[4.] In accordance with Article 8(7)(a) of the Protocol, this Contracting Party has declared that, in connection with each request for territorial extension to it of the protection of an international registration and the renewal of any such international registration, it wants to receive an individual fee, instead of a share in the revenue produced by the supplementary and complementary fees.

[5.] Applicable to Greenland as of January 11, 2011 and the Faroe Islands as of April 13, 2016.

[6.] In accordance with Article 14(5) of the Protocol, this Contracting Party has declared that the protection resulting from any international registration effected under this Protocol before the date of entry into force of this Protocol with respect to it cannot be extended to it.

[7.] Including all Overseas Departments and Territories.

State/IGO	Date on which State/IGO became party to the Madrid Protocol
Kyrgyzstan	June 17, 2004[4]
Lao People's Democratic Republic	March 7, 2016[4, 8]
Latvia	January 5, 2000
Lesotho	February 12, 1999
Liberia	December 11, 2009
Liechtenstein	March 17, 1998
Lithuania	November 15, 1997[3]
Luxembourg	April 1, 1998[1, 4]
Madagascar	April 28, 2008[8]
Malawi	December 25, 2018[3]
Malaysia	December 27, 2019[3, 4]
Mexico	February 19, 2013[4, 8]
Monaco	September 27, 1996
Mongolia	June 16, 2001
Montenegro	June 3, 2006
Morocco	October 8, 1999[4]
Mozambique	October 7, 1998
Namibia	June 30, 2004[6]
Netherlands	April 1, 1998[1, 4, 9]
New Zealand	December 10, 2012[3, 4, 10]
North Macedonia	August 30, 2020
Norway	March 29, 1996[3, 4]
Oman	October 16, 2007[8]
Pakistan	May 23, 2021[3, 4]
Philippines	April 25, 2012[3, 4, 6]
Poland	March 4, 1997[8]
Portugal	March 20, 1997
Republic of Korea	April 10, 2003[3, 4]

[8]. In accordance with Article 5(2)(b) of the Protocol, this Contracting Party has declared that the time limit to notify a refusal of protection shall be 18 months.

[9]. The instrument of ratification of the Stockholm Act and the instrument of acceptance of the Protocol were deposited for the Kingdom in Europe. The Netherlands extended the application of the Madrid Protocol to the Netherlands Antilles with effect from April 28, 2003. The Netherlands Antilles ceased to exist on October 10, 2010. As from that date, the Protocol continues to apply to Curaçao and Sint Maarten. The Protocol also continues to apply to the islands of Bonaire, Sint Eustatius and Saba which, with effect from October 10, 2010, have become part of the territory of the Kingdom of the Netherlands in Europe.

[10]. With a declaration that this accession shall not extend to Tokelau unless and until a declaration to this effect is lodged by the Government of New Zealand with the depositary on the basis of appropriate consultation with that territory.

State/IGO	Date on which State/IGO became party to the Madrid Protocol
Republic of Moldova	December 1, 1997[4]
Romania	July 28, 1998
Russian Federation	June 10, 1997
Rwanda	August 17, 2013
Samoa	March 4, 2019[3, 4]
San Marino	September 12, 2007[4, 8]
Sao Tome and Principe	December 8, 2008
Serbia[11]	February 17, 1998
Sierra Leone	December 28, 1999
Singapore	October 31, 2000[3, 4]
Slovakia	September 13, 1997[8]
Slovenia	March 12, 1998
Spain	December 1, 1995
Sudan	February 16, 2010
Sweden	December 1, 1995[3, 4]
Switzerland	May 1, 1997[4, 8]
Syrian Arab Republic	August 5, 2004[3]
Tajikistan	June 30, 2011[4, 8]
Thailand	November 7, 2017[3, 4]
Trinidad and Tobago	January 12, 2021[3, 4]
Tunisia	October 16, 2013[3, 4]
Turkey	January 1, 1999[3, 4]
Turkmenistan	September 28, 1999[4, 8]
Ukraine	December 29, 2000[3, 4]
United Kingdom	December 1, 1995[3, 4, 12, 13]
United States of America	November 2, 2003[3, 4]
Uzbekistan	December 27, 2006[4, 8]
Viet Nam	July 11, 2006[4]
Zambia	November 15, 2001[4]
Zimbabwe	March 11, 2015[3, 4]
Total: 108	

[11.] Serbia is the continuing State from Serbia and Montenegro as from June 3, 2006.

[12.] Ratification in respect of the United Kingdom and the Isle of Man.

[13.] The United Kingdom extended the application of the Madrid Protocol to the territories of Gibraltar and the Bailiwick of Guernsey with effect from January 1, 2021.

26

MADRID AGREEMENT CONCERNING THE INTERNATIONAL REGISTRATION OF MARKS

of April 14, 1891, as revised at Brussels on December 14, 1900, at Washington on June 2, 1911, at The Hague on November 6, 1925, at London on June 2, 1934, at Nice on June 15, 1957, and at Stockholm on July 14, 1967, and as amended on September 28, 1979

Article 1

(1) The countries to which this Agreement applies constitute a Special Union for the International registration of marks.

(2) Nationals of any of the contracting countries may, in all the other countries party to this Agreement, secure protection for their marks applicable to goods or services, registered in the country of origin, by filing the said marks at the International Bureau of Intellectual Property (hereinafter designated as "the International Bureau") referred to in the Convention establishing the World Intellectual Property Organization (hereinafter designated as "the Organization"), through the intermediary of the Office of the said country of origin.

(3) Shall be considered the country of origin the country of the Special Union where the applicant has a real and effective industrial or commercial establishment; if he has no such establishment in a country of the Special Union, the country of the Special Union where he has his domicile; if he has no domicile within the Special Union but is a national of a country of the Special Union, the country of which he is a national.

Article 2

Nationals of countries not having acceded to this Agreement who, within the territory of the Special Union constituted by the said Agreement, satisfy the conditions specified in Article 3 of the Paris Convention for the Protection of Industrial Property shall be treated in the same manner as nationals of the contracting countries.

Article 3

(1) Every application for international registration must be presented on the form prescribed by the Regulations; the Office of the country of origin of the mark shall certify that the particulars appearing in such

application correspond to the particulars in the national register, and shall mention the dates and numbers of the filing and registration of the mark in the country of origin and also the date of the application for international registration.

(2) The applicant must indicate the goods or services in respect of which protection of the mark is claimed and also, if possible, the corresponding class or classes according to the classification established by the Nice Agreement concerning the International Classification of Goods and Services for the Purposes of the Registration of Marks. If the applicant does not give such indication, the International Bureau shall classify the goods or services in the appropriate classes of the said classification. The indication of classes given by the applicant shall be subject to control by the International Bureau, which shall exercise the said control in association with the national Office. In the event of disagreement between the national Office and the International Bureau, the opinion of the latter shall prevail.

(3) If the applicant claims color as a distinctive feature of his mark, he shall be required:

1. to state the fact, and to file with his application a notice specifying the color or the combination of colors claimed;

2. to append to his application copies in color of the said mark, which shall be attached to the notification given by the International Bureau. The number of such copies shall be fixed by the Regulations.

(4) The International Bureau shall register immediately the marks filed in accordance with Article 1. The registration shall bear the date of the application for international registration in the country of origin, provided that the application has been received by the International Bureau within a period of two months from that date. If the application has not been received within that period, the International Bureau shall record it as at the date on which it received the said application. The International Bureau shall notify such registration without delay to the Offices concerned. Registered marks shall be published in a periodical journal issued by the International Bureau, on the basis of the particulars contained in the application for registration. In the case of marks comprising a figurative element or a special form of writing, the Regulations shall determine whether a printing block must be supplied by the applicant.

(5) With a view to the publicity to be given in the contracting countries to registered marks, each Office shall receive from the International Bureau a number of copies of the said publication free of charge and a number of copies at a reduced price, in proportion to the number of units mentioned in Article 16(4)(a) of the Paris Convention for

the Protection of Industrial Property, under the conditions fixed by the Regulations. Such publicity shall be deemed in all the contracting countries to be sufficient, and no other publicity may be required of the applicant.

Article 3*bis*

(1) Any contracting country may, at any time, notify the Director General of the Organization (hereinafter designated as "the Director General") in writing that the protection resulting from the international registration shall extend to that country only at the express request of the proprietor of the mark.

(2) Such notification shall not take effect until six months after the date of the communication thereof by the Director General to the other contracting countries.

Article 3*ter*

(1) Any request for extension of the protection resulting from the international registration to a country which has availed itself of the right provided for in Article 3*bis* must be specially mentioned in the application referred to in Article 3(1).

(2) Any request for territorial extension made subsequently to the international registration must be presented through the intermediary of the Office of the country of origin on a form prescribed by the Regulations. It shall be immediately registered by the International Bureau, which shall notify it without delay to the Office or Offices concerned. It shall be published in the periodical journal issued by the International Bureau. Such territorial extension shall be effective from the date on which it has been recorded in the International Register; it shall cease to be valid on the expiration of the international registration of the mark to which it relates.

Article 4

(1) From the date of the registration so effected at the International Bureau in accordance with the provisions of Articles 3 and 3*ter*, the protection of the mark in each of the contracting countries concerned shall be the same as if the mark had been filed therein direct. The indication of classes of goods or services provided for in Article 3 shall not bind the contracting countries with regard to the determination of the scope of the protection of the mark.

(2) Every mark which has been the subject of an international registration shall enjoy the right of priority provided for by Article 4 of the Paris Convention for the Protection of Industrial Property, without requiring compliance with the formalities prescribed in Section D of that Article.

Article 4*bis*

(1) When a mark already filed in one or more of the contracting countries is later registered by the International Bureau in the name of the same proprietor or his successor in title, the international registration shall be deemed to have replaced the earlier national registrations, without prejudice to any rights acquired by reason of such earlier registrations.

(2) The national Office shall, upon request, be required to take note in its registers of the international registration.

Article 5

(1) In countries where the legislation so authorizes, Offices notified by the International Bureau of the registration of a mark or of a request for extension of protection made in accordance with Article 3*ter* shall have the right to declare that protection cannot be granted to such mark in their territory. Any such refusal can be based only on the grounds which would apply, under the Paris Convention for the Protection of Industrial Property, in the case of a mark filed for national registration. However, protection may not be refused, even partially, by reason only that national legislation would not permit registration except in a limited number of classes or for a limited number of goods or services.

(2) Offices wishing to exercise such right must give notice of their refusal to the International Bureau, together with a statement of all grounds, within the period prescribed by their domestic law and, at the latest, before the expiration of one year from the date of the international registration of the mark or of the request for extension of protection made in accordance with Article 3*ter*.

(3) The International Bureau shall, without delay, transmit to the Office of the country of origin and to the proprietor of the mark, or to his agent if an agent has been mentioned to the Bureau by the said Office, one of the copies of the declaration of refusal so notified. The interested party shall have the same remedies as if the mark had been filed by him direct in the country where protection is refused.

(4) The grounds for refusing a mark shall be communicated by the International Bureau to any interested party who may so request.

(5) Offices which, within the aforesaid maximum period of one year, have not communicated to the International Bureau any provisional or final decision of refusal with regard to the registration of a mark or a request for extension of protection shall lose the benefit of the right provided for in paragraph (1) of this Article with respect to the mark in question.

(6) Invalidation of an international mark may not be pronounced by the competent authorities without the proprietor of the mark having, in

good time, been afforded the opportunity of defending his rights. Invalidation shall be notified to the International Bureau.

Article 5*bis*

Documentary evidence of the legitimacy of the use of certain elements incorporated in a mark, such as armorial bearings, escutcheons, portraits, honorary distinctions, titles, trade names, names of persons other than the name of the applicant, or other like inscriptions, which might be required by the Offices of the contracting countries shall be exempt from any legalization or certification other than that of the Office of the country of origin.

Article 5*ter*

(1) The International Bureau shall issue to any person applying therefor, subject to a fee fixed by the Regulations, a copy of the entries in the Register relating to a specific mark.

(2) The International Bureau may also, upon payment, undertake searches for anticipation among international marks.

(3) Extracts from the International Register requested with a view to their production in one of the contracting countries shall be exempt from all legalization.

Article 6

(1) Registration of a mark at the International Bureau is effected for twenty years, with the possibility of renewal under the conditions specified in Article 7.

(2) Upon expiration of a period of five years from the date of the international registration, such registration shall become independent of the national mark registered earlier in the country of origin, subject to the following provisions.

(3) The protection resulting from the international registration, whether or not it has been the subject of a transfer, may no longer be invoked, in whole or in part, if, within five years from the date of the international registration, the national mark, registered earlier in the country of origin in accordance with Article 1, no longer enjoys, in whole or in part, legal protection in that country. This provision shall also apply when legal protection has later ceased as the result of an action begun before the expiration of the period of five years.

(4) In the case of voluntary or ex officio cancellation, the Office of the country of origin shall request the cancellation of the mark at the International Bureau, and the latter shall effect the cancellation. In the case of judicial action, the said Office shall send to the International Bureau, ex officio or at the request of the plaintiff, a copy of the complaint or any other documentary evidence that an action has begun, and also of

the final decision of the court; the Bureau shall enter notice thereof in the International Register.

Article 7

(1) Any registration may be renewed for a period of twenty years from the expiration of the preceding period, by payment only of the basic fee and, where necessary, of the supplementary and complementary fees provided for in Article 8(2).

(2) Renewal may not include any change in relation to the previous registration in its latest form.

(3) The first renewal effected under the provisions of the Nice Act of June 15, 1957, or of this Act, shall include an indication of the classes of the International Classification to which the registration relates.

(4) Six months before the expiration of the term of protection, the International Bureau shall, by sending an unofficial notice, remind the proprietor of the mark and his agent of the exact date of expiration.

(5) Subject to the payment of a surcharge fixed by the Regulations, a period of grace of six months shall be granted for renewal of the international registration.

Article 8

(1) The Office of the country of origin may fix, at its own discretion, and collect, for its own benefit, a national fee which it may require from the proprietor of the mark in respect of which international registration or renewal is applied for.

(2) Registration of a mark at the International Bureau shall be subject to the advance payment of an international fee which shall include:

(a) a basic fee;

(b) a supplementary fee for each class of the International Classification, beyond three, into which the goods or services to which the mark is applied will fall;

(c) a complementary fee for any request for extension of protection under Article 3*ter*.

(3) However, the supplementary fee specified in paragraph (2)(b) may, without prejudice to the date of registration, be paid within a period fixed by the Regulations if the number of classes of goods or services has been fixed or disputed by the International Bureau. If, upon expiration of the said period, the supplementary fee has not been paid or the list of goods or services has not been reduced to the required extent by the applicant, the application for international registration shall be deemed to have been abandoned.

(4)   The annual returns from the various receipts from international registration, with the exception of those provided for under (b) and (c) of paragraph (2), shall he divided equally among the countries party to this Act by the International Bureau, after deduction of the expenses and charges necessitated by the implementation of the said Act. If, at the time this Act enters into force, a country has not yet ratified or acceded to the said Act, it shall be entitled, until the date on which its ratification or accession becomes effective, to a share of the excess receipts calculated on the basis of that earlier Act which is applicable to it.

(5)   The amounts derived from the supplementary fees provided for in paragraph (2)(b) shall be divided at the expiration of each year among the countries party to this Act or to the Nice Act of June 15, 1957, in proportion to the number of marks for which protection has been applied for in each of them during that year, this number being multiplied, in the case of countries which make a preliminary examination, by a coefficient which shall be determined by the Regulations. If, at the time this Act enters into force, a country has not yet ratified or acceded to the said Act, it shall be entitled, until the date on which its ratification or accession becomes effective, to a share of the amounts calculated on the basis of the Nice Act.

(6)   The amounts derived from the complementary fees provided for in paragraph (2)(c) shall be divided according to the requirements of paragraph (5) among the countries availing themselves of the right provided for in Article 3*bis*. If, at the time this Act enters into force, a country has not yet ratified or acceded to the said Act, it shall be entitled, until the date on which its ratification or accession becomes effective, to a share of the amounts calculated on the basis of the Nice Act.

Article 8*bis*

The person in whose name the international registration stands may at any time renounce protection in one or more of the contracting countries by means of a declaration filed with the Office of his own country, for communication to the International Bureau, which shall notify accordingly the countries in respect of which renunciation has been made. Renunciation shall not be subject to any fee.

Article 9

(1)   The Office of the country of the person in whose name the international registration stands shall likewise notify the International Bureau of all annulments, cancellations, renunciations, transfers, and other changes made in the entry of the mark in the national register, if such changes also affect the international registration.

(2)   The Bureau shall record those changes in the International Register, shall notify them in turn to the Offices of the contracting countries, and shall publish them in its journal.

(3) A similar procedure shall be followed when the person in whose name the international registration stands requests a reduction of the list of goods or services to which the registration applies.

(4) Such transactions may be subject to a fee, which shall be fixed by the Regulations.

(5) The subsequent addition of new goods or services to the said list can be obtained only by filing a new application as prescribed in Article 3.

(6) The substitution of one of the goods or services for another shall be treated as an addition.

Article 9*bis*

(1) When a mark registered in the International Register is transferred to a person established in a contracting country other than the country of the person in whose name the international registration stands, the transfer shall be notified to the International Bureau by the Office of the latter country. The International Bureau shall record the transfer, shall notify the other Offices thereof, and shall publish it in its journal. If the transfer has been effected before the expiration of a period of five years from the international registration, the International Bureau shall seek the consent of the Office of the country of the new proprietor, and shall publish, if possible, the date and registration number of the mark in the country of the new proprietor.

(2) No transfer of a mark registered in the International Register for the benefit of a person who is not entitled to file an international mark shall be recorded.

(3) When it has not been possible to record a transfer in the International Register, either because the country of the new proprietor has refused its consent or because the said transfer has been made for the benefit of a person who is not entitled to apply for international registration, the Office of the country of the former proprietor shall have the right to demand that the International Bureau cancel the mark in its Register.

Article 9*ter*

(1) If the assignment of an international mark for part only of the registered goods or services is notified to the International Bureau, the Bureau shall record it in its Register. Each of the contracting countries shall have the right to refuse to recognize the validity of such assignment if the goods or services included in the part so assigned are similar to those in respect of which the mark remains registered for the benefit of the assignor.

(2)   The International Bureau shall likewise record the assignment of an international mark in respect of one or several of the contracting countries only.

(3)   If, in the above cases, a change occurs in the country of the proprietor, the Office of the country to which the new proprietor belongs shall, if the international mark has been transferred before the expiration of a period of five years from the international registration, give its consent as required by Article 9*bis*.

(4)   The provisions of the foregoing paragraphs shall apply subject to Article 6*quater* of the Paris Convention for the Protection of Industrial Property.

Article 9*quater*

(1)   If several countries of the Special Union agree to effect the unification of their domestic legislations on marks, they may notify the Director General:

(a)   that a common Office shall be substituted for the national Office of each of them, and

(b)   that the whole of their respective territories shall be deemed to be a single country for the purposes of the application of all or part of the provisions preceding this Article.

(2)   Such notification shall not take effect until six months after the date of the communication thereof by the Director General to the other contracting countries.

Article 10

(1)(a)   The Special Union shall have an Assembly consisting of those countries which have ratified or acceded to this Act.

(b)   The Government of each country shall be represented by one delegate, who may be assisted by alternate delegates, advisors, and experts.

(c)   The expenses of each delegation shall be borne by the Government which has appointed it, except for the travel expenses and the subsistence allowance of one delegate for each member country, which shall be paid from the funds of the Special Union.

(2)(a)   The Assembly shall:

(i)   deal with all matters concerning the maintenance and development of the Special Union and the implementation of this Agreement;

(ii)   give directions to the International Bureau concerning the preparation for conferences of revision, due account being taken of any comments made by those countries of the Special Union which have not ratified or acceded to this Act;

(iii) modify the Regulations, including the fixation of the amounts of the fees referred to in Article 8(2) and other fees relating to international registration;

(iv) review and approve the reports and activities of the Director General concerning the Special Union, and give him all necessary instructions concerning matters within the competence of the Special Union;

(v) determine the program and adopt the biennal budget of the Special Union, and approve its final accounts;

(vi) adopt the financial regulations of the Special Union;

(vii) establish such committees of experts and working groups as it may deem necessary to achieve the objectives of the Special Union;

(viii) determine which countries not members of the Special Union and which intergovernmental and international non-governmental organizations shall be admitted to its meetings as observers;

(ix) adopt amendments to Articles 10 to 13;

(x) take any other appropriate action designed to further the objectives of the Special Union;

(xi) perform such other functions as are appropriate under this Agreement.

(b) With respect to matters which are of interest also to other Unions administered by the Organization, the Assembly shall make its decisions after having heard the advice of the Coordination Committee of the Organization.

(3)(a) Each country member of the Assembly shall have one vote.

(b) One-half of the countries members of the Assembly shall constitute a quorum.

(c) Notwithstanding the provisions of subparagraph (b), if, in any session, the number of countries represented is less than one-half but equal to or more than one-third of the countries members of the Assembly, the Assembly may make decisions but, with the exception of decisions concerning its own procedure, all such decisions shall take effect only if the conditions set forth hereinafter are fulfilled. The International Bureau shall communicate the said decisions to the countries members of the Assembly which were not represented and shall invite them to express in writing their vote or abstention within a period of three months from the date of the communication. If, at the expiration of this period, the number of countries having thus expressed their vote or abstention attains the number of countries which was lacking for attaining the quorum in the session itself, such decisions shall take effect provided that at the same time the required majority still obtains.

(d) Subject to the provisions of Article 13(2), the decisions of the Assembly shall require two-thirds of the votes cast.

(e) Abstentions shall not be considered as votes.

(f) A delegate may represent, and vote in the name of, one country only.

(g) Countries of the Special Union not members of the Assembly shall be admitted to the meetings of the latter as observers.

(4)(a)   The Assembly shall meet once in every second calendar year in ordinary session upon convocation by the Director General and, in the absence of exceptional circumstances, during the same period and at the same place as the General Assembly of the Organization.

(b) The Assembly shall meet in extraordinary session upon convocation by the Director General, at the request of one-fourth of the countries members of the Assembly.

(c) The agenda of each session shall be prepared by the Director General.

(5) The Assembly shall adopt its own rules of procedure.

Article 11

(1)(a)   International registration and related duties, as well as all other administrative tasks concerning the Special Union, shall be performed by the International Bureau.

(b) In particular, the International Bureau shall prepare the meetings and provide the secretariat of the Assembly and of such committees of experts and working groups as may have been established by the Assembly.

(c) The Director General shall be the chief executive of the Special Union and shall represent the Special Union.

(2) The Director General and any staff member designated by him shall participate, without the right to vote, in all meetings of the Assembly and of such committees of experts or working groups as may have been established by the Assembly. The Director General, or a staff member designated by him, shall be ex officio secretary of those bodies.

(3)(a)   The International Bureau shall, in accordance with the directions of the Assembly, make the preparations for the conferences of revision of the provisions of the Agreement other than Articles 10 to 13.

(b)   The International Bureau may consult with intergovernmental and international non-governmental organizations concerning preparations for conferences of revision.

(c)   The Director General and persons designated by him shall take part, without the right to vote, in the discussions at those conferences.

(4)   The International Bureau shall carry out any other tasks assigned to it.

Article 12

(1)(a)   The Special Union shall have a budget.

(b)   The budget of the Special Union shall include the income and expenses proper to the Special Union, its contribution to the budget of expenses common to the Unions, and, where applicable, the sum made available to the budget of the Conference of the Organization.

(c)   Expenses not attributable exclusively to the Special Union but also to one or more other Unions administered by the Organization shall be considered as expenses common to the Unions. The share of the Special Union in such common expenses shall be in proportion to the interest the Special Union has in them.

(2)   The budget of the Special Union shall be established with due regard to the requirements of coordination with the budgets of the other Unions administered by the Organization.

(3)   The budget of the Special Union shall be financed from the following sources:

(i)   international registration fees and other fees and charges due for other services rendered by the International Bureau in relation to the Special Union;

(ii)   sale of, or royalties on, the publications of the International Bureau concerning the Special Union;

(iii)   gifts, bequests, and subventions;

(iv)   rents, interests, and other miscellaneous income.

(4)(a)   The amounts of the fees referred to in Article 8(2) and other fees relating to international registration shall be fixed by the Assembly on the proposal of the Director General.

(b)   The amounts of such fees shall be so fixed that the revenues of the Special Union from fees, other than the supplementary and complementary fees referred to in Article 8(2)(b) and (c), and other sources shall be at least sufficient to cover the expenses of the International Bureau concerning the Special Union.

(c)   If the budget is not adopted before the beginning of a new financial period, it shall be at the same level as the budget of the previous year, as provided in the financial regulations.

(5)   Subject to the provisions of paragraph (4)(a), the amount of fees and charges due for other services rendered by the International Bureau in relation to the Special Union shall be established, and shall be reported to the Assembly, by the Director General.

(6)(a)   The Special Union shall have a working capital fund which shall be constituted by a single payment made by each country of the Special Union. If the fund becomes insufficient, the Assembly shall decide to increase it.

(b)   The amount of the initial payment of each country to the said fund or of its participation in the increase thereof shall be a proportion of the contribution of that country as a member of the Paris Union for the Protection of Industrial Property to the budget of the said Union for the year in which the fund is established or the decision to increase it is made.

(c)   The proportion and the terms of payment shall be fixed by the Assembly on the proposal of the Director General and after it has beard the advice of the Coordination Committee of the Organization.

(d)   As long as the Assembly authorizes the use of the reserve fund of the Special Union as a working capital fund, the Assembly may suspend the application of the provisions of subparagraphs (a), (b), and (c).

(7)(a)   In the headquarters agreement concluded with the country on the territory of which the Organization has its headquarters, it shall be provided that, whenever the working capital fund is insufficient, such country shall grant advances. The amount of those advances and the conditions on which they are granted shall be the subject of separate agreements, in each case, between such country and the Organization.

(b) The country referred to in subparagraph (a) and the Organization shall each have the right to denounce the obligation to grant advances, by written notification. Denunciation shall take effect three years after the end of the year in which it has been notified.

(8) The auditing of the accounts shall be effected by one or more of the countries of the Special Union or by external auditors, as provided in the financial regulations. They shall be designated, with their agreement, by the Assembly.

Article 13

(1) Proposals for the amendment of Articles 10, 11, 12, and the present Article, may be initiated by any country member of the Assembly, or by the Director General. Such proposals shall be communicated by the Director General to the member countries of the Assembly at least six months in advance of their consideration by the Assembly.

(2) Amendments to the Articles referred to in paragraph (1) shall be adopted by the Assembly. Adoption shall require three-fourths of the votes cast, provided that any amendment to Article 10, and to the present paragraph, shall require four-fifths of the votes cast.

(3) Any amendment to the Articles referred to in paragraph (1) shall enter into force one month after written notifications of acceptance, effected in accordance with their respective constitutional processes, have been received by the Director General from three-fourths of the countries members of the Assembly at the time it adopted the amendment. Any amendment to the said Articles thus accepted shall bind all the countries which are members of the Assembly at the time the amendment enters into force, or which become members thereof at a subsequent date.

Article 14

(1) Any country of the Special Union which has signed this Act may ratify it, and, if it has not signed it, may accede to it.

(2)(a)   Any country outside the Special Union which is party to the Paris Convention for the Protection of Industrial Property may accede to this Act and thereby become a member of the Special Union.

(b) As soon as the International Bureau is informed that such a country has acceded to this Act, it shall address to the Office of that country, in accordance with Article 3, a collective notification of the marks which, at that time, enjoy international protection.

(c) Such notification shall, of itself, ensure to the said marks the benefits of the foregoing provisions in the territory of the said country, and shall mark the commencement of the period of one year during which the Office concerned may make the declaration provided for in Article 5.

(d) However, any such country may, in acceding to this Act, declare that, except in the case of international marks which have already been the subject in that country of an earlier identical national registration still in force, and which shall be immediately recognized upon the request of the interested parties, application of this Act shall be limited to marks registered from the date on which its accession enters into force.

(e) Such declaration shall dispense the International Bureau from making the collective notification referred to above. The International Bureau shall notify only those marks in respect of which it receives, within a period of one year from the accession of the new country, a request, with the necessary particulars, to take advantage of the exception provided for in subparagraph (d).

(f) The International Bureau shall not make the collective notification to such countries as declare, in acceding to this Act, that they are availing themselves of the right provided for in Article 3*bis*. The said countries may also declare at the same time that the application of this Act shall be limited to marks registered from the day on which their accessions enter into force; however, such limitation shall not affect international marks which have already been the subject of an earlier identical national registration in those countries, and which could give rise to requests for extension of protection made and notified in accordance with Articles 3*ter* and 8(2)(c).

(g) Registrations of marks which have been the subject of one of the notifications provided for in this paragraph shall be regarded as replacing registrations effected direct in the new contracting country before the date of entry into force of its accession.

(3) Instruments of ratification and accession shall be deposited with the Director General.

(4)(a) With respect to the first five countries which have deposited their instruments of ratification or accession, this Act shall enter into force three months after the deposit of the fifth such instrument.

(b) With respect to any other country, this Act shall enter into force three months after the date on which its ratification or accession has been notified by the Director General, unless a subsequent date has been indicated in the instrument of ratification or accession. In the latter case, this Act shall enter into force with respect to that country on the date thus indicated.

(5) Ratification or accession shall automatically entail acceptance of all the clauses and admission to all the advantages of this Act.

(6) After the entry into force of this Act, a country may accede to the Nice Act of June 15, 1957, only in conjunction with ratification of, or accession to, this Act. Accession to Acts earlier than the Nice Act shall not be permitted, not even in conjunction with ratification of, or accession to, this Act.

(7) The provisions of Article 24 of the Paris Convention for the Protection of Industrial Property shall apply to this Agreement.

Article 15

(1) This Agreement shall remain in force without limitation as to time.

(2) Any country may denounce this Act by notification addressed to the Director General. Such denunciation shall constitute also denunciation of all earlier Acts and shall affect only the country making it, the Agreement remaining in full force and effect as regards the other countries of the Special Union.

(3) Denunciation shall take effect one year after the day on which the Director General has received the notification.

(4) The right of denunciation provided for by this Article shall not be exercised by any country before the expiration of five years from the date upon which it becomes a member of the Special Union.

(5) International marks registered up to the date on which denunciation becomes effective, and not refused within the period of one year provided for in Article 5, shall continue, throughout the period of international protection, to enjoy the same protection as if they had been filed direct in the denouncing country.

Article 16

(1)(a) This Act shall, as regards the relations between the countries of the Special Union by which it has been ratified or acceded to, replace, as from the day on which it enters into force with respect to them, the Madrid Agreement of 1891, in its texts earlier than this Act.

(b) However, any country of the Special Union which has ratified or acceded to this Act shall remain bound by the earlier texts which it has not previously denounced by virtue of Article 12(4) of the Nice Act of June 15, 1957, as regards its relations with countries which have not ratified or acceded to this Act.

(2) Countries outside the Special Union which become party to this Act shall apply it to international registrations effected at the

International Bureau through the intermediary of the national Office of any country of the Special Union not party to this Act, provided that such registrations satisfy, with respect to the said countries, the requirements of this Act. With regard to international registrations effected at the International Bureau through the intermediary of the national Offices of the said countries outside the Special Union which become party to this Act, such countries recognize that the aforesaid country of the Special Union may demand compliance with the requirements of the most recent Act to which it is party.

Article 17

(1)(a)   This Act shall be signed in a single copy in the French language and shall be deposited with the Government of Sweden.

(b)   Official texts shall be established by the Director General, after consultation with the interested Governments, in such other languages as the Assembly may designate.

(2)   This Act shall remain open for signature at Stockholm until January 13, 1968.

(3)   The Director General shall transmit two copies, certified by the Government of Sweden, of the signed text of this Act to the Governments of all countries of the Special Union and, on request, to the Government of any other country.

(4)   The Director General shall register this Act with the Secretariat of the United Nations.

(5)   The Director General shall notify the Governments of all countries of the Special Union of signatures, deposits of instruments of ratification or accession and any declarations included in such instruments, entry into force of any provisions of this Act, notifications of denunciation, and notifications pursuant to Articles 3*bis*, 9*quater*, 13, 14(7), and 15(2).

Article 18

(1)   Until the first Director General assumes office, references in this Act to the International Bureau of the Organization or to the Director General shall be construed as references to the Bureau of the Union established by the Paris Convention for the Protection of Industrial Property or its Director, respectively.

(2)   Countries of the Special Union not having ratified or acceded to this Act may, until five years after the entry into force of the Convention establishing the Organization, exercise, if they so desire, the rights provided for under Articles 10 to 13 of this Act as if they were bound by those Articles. Any country desiring to exercise such rights shall give written notification to that effect to the Director General; such notification shall be effective from the date of its receipt. Such countries shall be

deemed to be members of the Assembly until the expiration of the said period.

27

PARTIES TO THE MADRID AGREEMENT CONCERNING THE INTERNATIONAL REGISTRATION OF MARKS

Status on February 24, 2021

State	Date on which State became party to the Madrid Agreement[1]
Albania	October 4, 1995
Algeria	July 5, 1972
Armenia	December 25, 1991
Austria	January 1, 1909
Azerbaijan	December 25, 1995
Belarus	December 25, 1991
Belgium	July 15, 1892[2]
Bhutan	August 4, 2000
Bosnia and Herzegovina	March 1, 1992
Bulgaria	August 1, 1985
China	October 4, 1989[3]
Croatia	October 8, 1991
Cuba	December 6, 1989
Cyprus	November 4, 2003
Czech Republic	January 1, 1993
Democratic People's Republic of Korea	June 10, 1980
Egypt	July 1, 1952
Eswatini	December 14, 1998
France	July 15, 1892[4]

[1.] All the States party to the Madrid Agreement have declared, under Article 3bis of the Nice or Stockholm Act, that the protection arising from international registration shall not extend to them unless the proprietor of the mark so requests.

[2.] The territories of Belgium, Luxembourg and the Kingdom of the Netherlands in Europe are to be deemed a single country, for the application of the Madrid Agreement as from January 1, 1971, and for the application of the Protocol as from April 1, 1998.

[3.] Not applicable to either Hong Kong, China or Macao, China.

[4.] Including all Overseas Departments and Territories.

State	Date on which State became party to the Madrid Agreement[1]
Germany	December 1, 1922
Hungary	January 1, 1909
Iran (Islamic Republic of)	December 25, 2003
Italy	October 15, 1894
Kazakhstan	December 25, 1991
Kenya	June 26, 1998
Kyrgyzstan	December 25, 1991
Latvia	January 1, 1995
Lesotho	February 12, 1999
Liberia	December 25, 1995
Liechtenstein	July 14, 1933
Luxembourg	September 1, 1924[2]
Monaco	April 29, 1956
Mongolia	April 21, 1985
Montenegro	June 3, 2006
Morocco	July 30, 1917
Mozambique	October 7, 1998
Namibia	June 30, 2004
Netherlands	March 1, 1893[2, 5]
North Macedonia	September 8, 1991
Poland	March 18, 1991
Portugal	October 31, 1893
Republic of Moldova	December 25, 1991
Romania	October 6, 1920
Russian Federation	July 1, 1976[6]
San Marino	September 25, 1960
Serbia[7]	April 27, 1992
Sierra Leone	June 17, 1997
Slovakia	January 1, 1993
Slovenia	June 25, 1991

[5] The instrument of ratification of the Stockholm Act and the instrument of acceptance of the Protocol were deposited for the Kingdom in Europe. The Netherlands extended the application of the Madrid Protocol to the Netherlands Antilles with effect from April 28, 2003. The Netherlands Antilles ceased to exist on October 10, 2010. As from that date, the Protocol continues to apply to Curaçao and Sint Maarten. The Protocol also continues to apply to the islands of Bonaire, Sint Eustatius and Saba which, with effect from October 10, 2010, have become part of the territory of the Kingdom of the Netherlands in Europe.

[6] Date of accession by the Soviet Union, continued by the Russian Federation as from December 25, 1991.

[7] Serbia is the continuing State from Serbia and Montenegro as from June 3, 2006.

State	Date on which State became party to the Madrid Agreement[1]
Spain	July 15, 1892
Sudan	May 16, 1984
Switzerland	July 15, 1892
Tajikistan	December 25, 1991
Ukraine	December 25, 1991
Viet Nam	March 8, 1949

Total: 55

28

EU Trade Mark Directive

DIRECTIVE (EU) 2015/2436 OF THE EUROPEAN PARLIAMENT AND OF THE COUNCIL

of 16 December 2015

to approximate the laws of the member states relating to trade marks

(Recast)

(Text with EEA relevance)

THE EUROPEAN PARLIAMENT AND THE COUNCIL OF THE EUROPEAN UNION,

Having regard to the Treaty on the Functioning of the European Union, and in particular Article 114(1) thereof,

Having regard to the proposal from the European Commission,

After transmission of the draft legislative act to the national parliaments,

Having regard to the opinion of the European Economic and Social Committee[1],

Acting in accordance with the ordinary legislative procedure[2],

Whereas:

(1)   A number of amendments should be made to Directive 2008/95/EC of the European Parliament and of the Council[3]. In the interests of clarity, that Directive should be recast.

(2)   Directive 2008/95/EC has harmonised central provisions of substantive trade mark law which at the time of adoption were considered as most directly affecting the functioning of the internal market by impeding the free movement of goods and the freedom to provide services in the Union.

---

[1]   OJ C 327, 12.11.2013, p. 42.

[2]   Position of the European Parliament of 25 February 2014 (not yet published in the Official Journal) and position of the Council at first reading of 10 November 2015 (not yet published in the Official Journal). Position of the European Parliament of 15 December 2015.

[3]   Directive 2008/95/EC of the European Parliament and of the Council of 22 October 2008 to approximate the laws of the Member States relating to trade marks (OJ L 299, 8.11.2008, p. 25).

(3) Trade mark protection in the Member States coexists with protection available at Union level through European Union trade marks ('EU trade marks') which are unitary in character and valid throughout the Union as laid down in Council Regulation (EC) No 207/2009[4]. The coexistence and balance of trade mark systems at national and Union level in fact constitutes a cornerstone of the Union's approach to intellectual property protection.

(4) Further to the Commission's communication of 16 July 2008 on an industrial property rights strategy for Europe, the Commission carried out a comprehensive evaluation of the overall functioning of the trade mark system in Europe as a whole, covering Union and national levels and the interrelation between the two.

(5) In its conclusions of 25 May 2010 on the future revision of the trade mark system in the European Union, the Council called on the Commission to present proposals for the revision of Regulation (EC) No 207/2009 and Directive 2008/95/EC. The revision of that Directive should include measures to make it more consistent with Regulation (EC) No 207/2009, which would thus reduce the areas of divergence within the trade mark system in Europe as a whole, while maintaining national trade mark protection as an attractive option for applicants. In this context, the complementary relationship between the EU trade mark system and national trade mark systems should be ensured.

(6) The Commission concluded in its communication of 24 May 2011 entitled 'A single market for intellectual property rights' that in order to meet increased demands from stakeholders for faster, higher quality, more streamlined trade mark registration systems, which are also more consistent, user friendly, publicly accessible and technologically up to date, there is a necessity to modernise the trade mark system in the Union as a whole and adapt it to the internet era.

(7) Consultation and evaluation for the purpose of this Directive has revealed that, in spite of the previous partial harmonisation of national laws, there remain areas where further harmonisation could have a positive impact on competitiveness and growth.

(8) In order to serve the objective of fostering and creating a well-functioning internal market and to facilitate acquiring and protecting trade marks in the Union, to the benefit of the growth and the competitiveness of European businesses, in particular small and medium-sized enterprises, it is necessary to go beyond the limited scope of approximation achieved by Directive 2008/95/EC and extend approximation to other aspects of substantive trade mark law governing

---

[4] Council Regulation (EC) No 207/2009 of 26 February 2009 on the Community trade mark (OJ L 78, 24.3.2009, p. 1).

trade marks protected through registration pursuant to Regulation (EC) No 207/2009.

(9) For the purpose of making trade mark registrations throughout the Union easier to obtain and administer, it is essential to approximate not only provisions of substantive law but also procedural rules. Therefore, the principal procedural rules in the area of trade mark registration in the Member States and in the EU trade mark system should be aligned. As regards procedures under national law, it is sufficient to lay down general principles, leaving the Member States free to establish more specific rules.

(10) It is essential to ensure that registered trade marks enjoy the same protection under the legal systems of all the Member States. In line with the extensive protection granted to EU trade marks which have a reputation in the Union, extensive protection should also be granted at national level to all registered trade marks which have a reputation in the Member State concerned.

(11) This Directive should not deprive the Member States of the right to continue to protect trade marks acquired through use but should take them into account only with regard to their relationship with trade marks acquired by registration.

(12) Attainment of the objectives of this approximation of laws requires that the conditions for obtaining and continuing to hold a registered trade mark be, in general, identical in all Member States.

(13) To this end, it is necessary to list examples of signs which are capable of constituting a trade mark, provided that such signs are capable of distinguishing the goods or services of one undertaking from those of other undertakings. In order to fulfil the objectives of the registration system for trade marks, namely to ensure legal certainty and sound administration, it is also essential to require that the sign is capable of being represented in a manner which is clear, precise, self-contained, easily accessible, intelligible, durable and objective. A sign should therefore be permitted to be represented in any appropriate form using generally available technology, and thus not necessarily by graphic means, as long as the representation offers satisfactory guarantees to that effect.

(14) Furthermore, the grounds for refusal or invalidity concerning the trade mark itself, including the absence of any distinctive character, or concerning conflicts between the trade mark and earlier rights, should be listed in an exhaustive manner, even if some of those grounds are listed as an option for the Member States which should therefore be able to maintain or introduce them in their legislation.

(15) In order to ensure that the levels of protection afforded to geographical indications by Union legislation and national law are applied in a uniform and exhaustive manner in the examination of absolute and

relative grounds for refusal throughout the Union, this Directive should include the same provisions in relation to geographical indications as contained in Regulation (EC) No 207/2009. Furthermore, it is appropriate to ensure that the scope of absolute grounds is extended to also cover protected traditional terms for wine and traditional specialties guaranteed.

(16) The protection afforded by the registered trade mark, the function of which is in particular to guarantee the trade mark as an indication of origin, should be absolute in the event of there being identity between the mark and the corresponding sign and the goods or services. The protection should apply also in the case of similarity between the mark and the sign and the goods or services. It is indispensable to give an interpretation of the concept of similarity in relation to the likelihood of confusion. The likelihood of confusion, the appreciation of which depends on numerous elements and, in particular, on the recognition of the trade mark on the market, the association which can be made with the used or registered sign, the degree of similarity between the trade mark and the sign and between the goods or services identified, should constitute the specific condition for such protection. The ways in which a likelihood of confusion can be established, and in particular the onus of proof in that regard, should be a matter for national procedural rules which should not be prejudiced by this Directive.

(17) In order to ensure legal certainty and full consistency with the principle of priority, under which a registered earlier trade mark takes precedence over later registered trade marks, it is necessary to provide that the enforcement of rights which are conferred by a trade mark should be without prejudice to the rights of proprietors acquired prior to the filing or priority date of the trade mark. Such an approach is in conformity with Article 16(1) of the Agreement on trade-related aspects of intellectual property rights of 15 April 1994 ('TRIPS Agreement').

(18) It is appropriate to provide that an infringement of a trade mark can only be established if there is a finding that the infringing mark or sign is used in the course of trade for the purposes of distinguishing goods or services. Use of the sign for purposes other than for distinguishing goods or services should be subject to the provisions of national law.

(19) The concept of infringement of a trade mark should also comprise the use of the sign as a trade name or similar designation, as long as such use is made for the purposes of distinguishing goods or services.

(20) In order to ensure legal certainty and full consistency with specific Union legislation, it is appropriate to provide that the proprietor of a trade mark should be entitled to prohibit a third party from using a sign in

comparative advertising where such comparative advertising is contrary to Directive 2006/114/EC of the European Parliament and of the Council[5].

(21) In order to strengthen trade mark protection and combat counterfeiting more effectively, and in line with international obligations of the Member States under the World Trade Organisation (WTO) framework, in particular Article V of the General Agreement on Tariffs and Trade on freedom of transit and, as regards generic medicines, the 'Declaration on the TRIPS Agreement and public health' adopted by the Doha WTO Ministerial Conference on 14 November 2001, the proprietor of a trade mark should be entitled to prevent third parties from bringing goods, in the course of trade, into the Member State where the trade mark is registered without being released for free circulation there, where such goods come from third countries and bear without authorisation a trade mark which is identical or essentially identical with the trade mark registered in respect of such goods.

(22) To this effect, it should be permissible for trade mark proprietors to prevent the entry of infringing goods and their placement in all customs situations, including, in particular transit, transhipment, warehousing, free zones, temporary storage, inward processing or temporary admission, also when such goods are not intended to be placed on the market of the Member State concerned. In performing customs controls, the customs authorities should make use of the powers and procedures laid down in Regulation (EU) No 608/2013 of the European Parliament and of the Council[6], also at the request of the right holders. In particular, the customs authorities should carry out the relevant controls on the basis of risk analysis criteria.

(23) In order to reconcile the need to ensure the effective enforcement of trade mark rights with the necessity to avoid hampering the free flow of trade in legitimate goods, the entitlement of the proprietor of the trade mark should lapse where, during the subsequent proceedings initiated before the judicial or other authority competent to take a substantive decision on whether the registered trade mark has been infringed, the declarant or the holder of the goods is able to prove that the proprietor of the registered trade mark is not entitled to prohibit the placing of the goods on the market in the country of final destination.

(24) Article 28 of Regulation (EU) No 608/2013 provides that a right holder is to be liable for damages towards the holder of the goods where,

[5]. Directive 2006/114/EC of the European Parliament and of the Council of 12 December 2006 concerning misleading and comparative advertising (OJ L 376, 27.12.2006, p. 21).

[6]. Regulation (EU) No 608/2013 of the European Parliament and of the Council of 12 June 2013 concerning customs enforcement of intellectual property rights and repealing Council Regulation (EC) No 1383/2003 (OJ L 181, 29.6.2013, p. 15).

inter alia, the goods in question are subsequently found not to infringe an intellectual property right.

(25) Appropriate measures should be taken with a view to ensuring the smooth transit of generic medicines. With respect to international non-proprietary names (INN) as globally recognised generic names for active substances in pharmaceutical preparations, it is vital to take due account of the existing limitations on the effect of trade mark rights. Consequently, the proprietor of a trade mark should not have the right to prevent a third party from bringing goods into a Member State where the trade mark is registered without being released for free circulation there based upon similarities between the INN for the active ingredient in the medicines and the trade mark.

(26) In order to enable proprietors of registered trade marks to combat counterfeiting more effectively, they should be entitled to prohibit the affixing of an infringing trade mark to goods, and certain preparatory acts carried out prior to such affixing.

(27) The exclusive rights conferred by a trade mark should not entitle the proprietor to prohibit the use of signs or indications by third parties which are used fairly and thus in accordance with honest practices in industrial and commercial matters. In order to create equal conditions for trade names and trade marks against the background that trade names are regularly granted unrestricted protection against later trade marks, such use should only be considered to include the use of the personal name of the third party. Such use should further permit the use of descriptive or non-distinctive signs or indications in general. Furthermore, the proprietor should not be entitled to prevent the fair and honest use of the mark for the purpose of identifying or referring to the goods or services as those of the proprietor. Use of a trade mark by third parties to draw the consumer's attention to the resale of genuine goods that were originally sold by, or with the consent of, the proprietor of the trade mark in the Union should be considered as being fair as long as it is at the same time in accordance with honest practices in industrial and commercial matters. Use of a trade mark by third parties for the purpose of artistic expression should be considered as being fair as long as it is at the same time in accordance with honest practices in industrial and commercial matters. Furthermore, this Directive should be applied in a way that ensures full respect for fundamental rights and freedoms, and in particular the freedom of expression.

(28) It follows from the principle of free movement of goods that the proprietor of a trade mark should not be entitled to prohibit its use by a third party in relation to goods which have been put into circulation in the Union, under the trade mark, by him or with his consent, unless the

proprietor has legitimate reasons to oppose further commercialisation of the goods.

(29) It is important, for reasons of legal certainty to provide that, without prejudice to his interests as a proprietor of an earlier trade mark, the latter may no longer request a declaration of invalidity or oppose the use of a trade mark subsequent to his own trade mark, of which he has knowingly tolerated the use for a substantial length of time, unless the application for the subsequent trade mark was made in bad faith.

(30) In order to ensure legal certainty and safeguard legitimately acquired trade mark rights, it is appropriate and necessary to provide that, without prejudice to the principle that the later trade mark cannot be enforced against the earlier trade mark, proprietors of earlier trade marks should not be entitled to obtain refusal or invalidation or to oppose the use of a later trade mark if the later trade mark was acquired at a time when the earlier trade mark was liable to be declared invalid or revoked, for example because it had not yet acquired distinctiveness through use, or if the earlier trade mark could not be enforced against the later trade mark because the necessary conditions were not applicable, for example when the earlier mark had not yet obtained a reputation.

(31) Trade marks fulfil their purpose of distinguishing goods or services and allowing consumers to make informed choices only when they are actually used on the market. A requirement of use is also necessary in order to reduce the total number of trade marks registered and protected in the Union and, consequently, the number of conflicts which arise between them. It is therefore essential to require that registered trade marks actually be used in connection with the goods or services for which they are registered, or, if not used in that connection within five years of the date of the completion of the registration procedure, be liable to be revoked.

(32) Consequently, a registered trade mark should only be protected in so far as it is actually used and a registered earlier trade mark should not enable its proprietor to oppose or invalidate a later trade mark if that proprietor has not put his trade mark to genuine use. Furthermore, Member States should provide that a trade mark may not be successfully invoked in infringement proceedings if it is established, as a result of a plea, that the trade mark could be revoked or, when the action is brought against a later right, could have been revoked at the time when the later right was acquired.

(33) It is appropriate to provide that, where the seniority of a national mark or a trade mark registered under international arrangements having effect in the Member State has been claimed for an EU trade mark and the mark providing the basis for the seniority claim has thereafter been surrendered or allowed to lapse, the validity of that mark can still be

challenged. Such a challenge should be limited to situations where the mark could have been declared invalid or revoked at the time it was removed from the register.

(34) For reasons of coherence and in order to facilitate the commercial exploitation of trade marks in the Union, the rules applicable to trade marks as objects of property should be aligned to the extent appropriate with those already in place for EU trade marks, and should include rules on assignment and transfer, licensing, rights *in rem* and levy of execution.

(35) Collective trade marks have proven a useful instrument for promoting goods or services with specific common properties. It is therefore appropriate to subject national collective trade marks to rules similar to the rules applicable to European Union collective marks.

(36) In order to improve and facilitate access to trade mark protection and to increase legal certainty and predictability, the procedure for the registration of trade marks in the Member States should be efficient and transparent and should follow rules similar to those applicable to EU trade marks.

(37) In order to ensure legal certainty with regard to the scope of trade mark rights and to facilitate access to trade mark protection, the designation and classification of goods and services covered by a trade mark application should follow the same rules in all Member States and should be aligned to those applicable to EU trade marks. In order to enable the competent authorities and economic operators to determine the extent of the trade mark protection sought on the basis of the application alone, the designation of goods and services should be sufficiently clear and precise. The use of general terms should be interpreted as including only goods and services clearly covered by the literal meaning of a term. In the interest of clarity and legal certainty, the Member States' central industrial property offices and the Benelux Office for Intellectual Property should, in cooperation with each other, endeavour to compile a list reflecting their respective administrative practices with regard to the classification of goods and services.

(38) For the purpose of ensuring effective trade mark protection, Member States should make available an efficient administrative opposition procedure, allowing at least the proprietor of earlier trade mark rights and any person authorised under the relevant law to exercise the rights arising from a protected designation of origin or a geographical indication to oppose the registration of a trade mark application. Furthermore, in order to offer efficient means of revoking trademarks or declaring them invalid, Member States should provide for an administrative procedure for revocation or declaration of invalidity within the longer transposition period of seven years, after the entry into force of this Directive.

(39) It is desirable that Member States' central industrial property offices and the Benelux Office for Intellectual Property cooperate with each other and with the European Union Intellectual Property Office in all fields of trade mark registration and administration in order to promote convergence of practices and tools, such as the creation and updating of common or connected databases and portals for consultation and search purposes. The Member States should further ensure that their offices cooperate with each other and with the European Union Intellectual Property Office in all other areas of their activities which are relevant for the protection of trade marks in the Union.

(40) This Directive should not exclude the application to trade marks of provisions of law of the Member States other than trade mark law, such as provisions relating to unfair competition, civil liability or consumer protection.

(41) Member States are bound by the Paris Convention for the Protection of Industrial Property ('the Paris Convention') and the TRIPS Agreement. It is necessary that this Directive be entirely consistent with that Convention and that Agreement. The obligations of the Member States resulting from that Convention and that Agreement should not be affected by this Directive. Where appropriate, the second paragraph of Article 351 of the Treaty on the Functioning of the European Union should apply.

(42) Since the objectives of this Directive, namely to foster and create a well-functioning internal market and to facilitate the registration, administration and protection of trade marks in the Union to the benefit of growth and competitiveness, cannot be sufficiently achieved by the Member States but can rather, by reason of its scale and effects, be better achieved at Union level, the Union may adopt measures, in accordance with the principle of subsidiarity as set out in Article 5 of the Treaty on European Union. In accordance with the principle of proportionality as set out in that Article, this Directive does not go beyond what is necessary in order to achieve those objectives.

(43) Directive 95/46/EC of the European Parliament and of the Council[7] governs the processing of personal data carried out in the Member States in the context of this Directive.

(44) The European Data Protection Supervisor was consulted in accordance with Article 28(2) of Regulation (EC) No 45/2001 of the

---

7. Directive 95/46/EC of the European Parliament and of the Council of 24 October 1995 on the protection of individuals with regard to the processing of personal data and on the free movement of such data (OJ L 281, 23.11.1995, p. 31).

European Parliament and of the Council[8] and delivered an opinion on 11 July 2013.

(45) The obligation to transpose this Directive into national law should be confined to those provisions which represent a substantive amendment as compared with the earlier Directive. The obligation to transpose the provisions which are unchanged arises under the earlier Directive.

(46) This Directive should be without prejudice to the obligations of the Member States under Directive 2008/95/EC relating to the time limit for transposition of Council Directive 89/104/EEC[9] into national law as set out in Part B of Annex I to Directive 2008/95/EC,

HAVE ADOPTED THIS DIRECTIVE:

CHAPTER 1

GENERAL PROVISIONS

Article 1

Scope

This Directive applies to every trade mark in respect of goods or services which is the subject of registration or of an application for registration in a Member State as an individual trade mark, a guarantee or certification mark or a collective mark, or which is the subject of a registration or an application for registration in the Benelux Office for Intellectual Property or of an international registration having effect in a Member State.

Article 2

Definitions

For the purpose of this Directive, the following definitions apply:

(a) 'office' means the central industrial property office of the Member State or the Benelux Office for Intellectual Property, entrusted with the registration of trade marks;

(b) 'register' means the register of trade marks kept by an office.

---

[8]. Regulation (EC) No 45/2001 of the European Parliament and of the Council of 18 December 2000 on the protection of individuals with regard to the processing of personal data by the Community institutions and bodies and on the free movement of such data (OJ L 8, 12.1.2001, p. 1).

[9]. First Council Directive 89/104/EEC of 21 December 1988 to approximate the laws of the Member States relating to trade marks (OJ L 40, 11.2.1989, p. 1).

CHAPTER 2

SUBSTANTIVE LAW ON TRADE MARKS

SECTION 1

Signs of which a trade mark may consist

Article 3

Signs of which a trade mark may consist

A trade mark may consist of any signs, in particular words, including personal names, or designs, letters, numerals, colours, the shape of goods or of the packaging of goods, or sounds, provided that such signs are capable of:

(a) distinguishing the goods or services of one undertaking from those of other undertakings; and

(b) being represented on the register in a manner which enables the competent authorities and the public to determine the clear and precise subject matter of the protection afforded to its proprietor.

SECTION 2

Grounds for refusal or invalidity

Article 4

Absolute grounds for refusal or invalidity

1.   The following shall not be registered or, if registered, shall be liable to be declared invalid:

(a) signs which cannot constitute a trade mark;

(b) trade marks which are devoid of any distinctive character;

(c) trade marks which consist exclusively of signs or indications which may serve, in trade, to designate the kind, quality, quantity, intended purpose, value, geographical origin, or the time of production of the goods or of rendering of the service, or other characteristics of the goods or services;

(d) trade marks which consist exclusively of signs or indications which have become customary in the current language or in the bona fide and established practices of the trade;

(e) signs which consist exclusively of:

(i) the shape, or another characteristic, which results from the nature of the goods themselves;

(ii) the shape, or another characteristic, of goods which is necessary to obtain a technical result;

(iii) the shape, or another characteristic, which gives substantial value to the goods;

(f) trade marks which are contrary to public policy or to accepted principles of morality;

(g) trade marks which are of such a nature as to deceive the public, for instance, as to the nature, quality or geographical origin of the goods or service;

(h) trade marks which have not been authorised by the competent authorities and are to be refused or invalidated pursuant to Article 6ter of the Paris Convention;

(i) trade marks which are excluded from registration pursuant to Union legislation or the national law of the Member State concerned, or to international agreements to which the Union or the Member State concerned is party, providing for protection of designations of origin and geographical indications;

(j) trade marks which are excluded from registration pursuant to Union legislation or international agreements to which the Union is party, providing for protection of traditional terms for wine;

(k) trade marks which are excluded from registration pursuant to Union legislation or international agreements to which the Union is party, providing for protection of traditional specialities guaranteed;

(*l*) trade marks which consist of, or reproduce in their essential elements, an earlier plant variety denomination registered in accordance with Union legislation or the national law of the Member State concerned, or international agreements to which the Union or the Member State concerned is party, providing protection for plant variety rights, and which are in respect of plant varieties of the same or closely related species.

2.   A trade mark shall be liable to be declared invalid where the application for registration of the trade mark was made in bad faith by the applicant. Any Member State may also provide that such a trade mark is not to be registered.

3.   Any Member State may provide that a trade mark is not to be registered or, if registered, is liable to be declared invalid where and to the extent that:

(a) the use of that trade mark may be prohibited pursuant to provisions of law other than trade mark law of the Member State concerned or of the Union;

(b) the trade mark includes a sign of high symbolic value, in particular a religious symbol;

(c) the trade mark includes badges, emblems and escutcheons other than those covered by Article 6ter of the Paris Convention and which are of public interest, unless the consent of the competent authority to their registration has been given in conformity with the law of the Member State.

4. A trade mark shall not be refused registration in accordance with paragraph 1(b), (c) or (d) if, before the date of application for registration, following the use which has been made of it, it has acquired a distinctive character. A trade mark shall not be declared invalid for the same reasons if, before the date of application for a declaration of invalidity, following the use which has been made of it, it has acquired a distinctive character.

5. Any Member State may provide that paragraph 4 is also to apply where the distinctive character was acquired after the date of application for registration but before the date of registration.

Article 5

Relative grounds for refusal or invalidity

1. A trade mark shall not be registered or, if registered, shall be liable to be declared invalid where:

(a) it is identical with an earlier trade mark, and the goods or services for which the trade mark is applied for or is registered are identical with the goods or services for which the earlier trade mark is protected;

(b) because of its identity with, or similarity to, the earlier trade mark and the identity or similarity of the goods or services covered by the trade marks, there exists a likelihood of confusion on the part of the public; the likelihood of confusion includes the likelihood of association with the earlier trade mark.

2. 'Earlier trade marks' within the meaning of paragraph 1 means:

(a) trade marks of the following kinds with a date of application for registration which is earlier than the date of application for registration of the trade mark, taking account, where appropriate, of the priorities claimed in respect of those trade marks:

(i)   EU trade marks;

(ii) trade marks registered in the Member State concerned or, in the case of Belgium, Luxembourg or the Netherlands, at the Benelux Office for Intellectual Property;

(iii) trade marks registered under international arrangements which have effect in the Member State concerned;

(b) EU trade marks which validly claim seniority, in accordance with Regulation (EC) No 207/2009, of a trade mark referred to in points (a)(ii) and (iii), even when the latter trade mark has been surrendered or allowed to lapse;

(c) applications for the trade marks referred to in points (a) and (b), subject to their registration;

(d) trade marks which, on the date of application for registration of the trade mark, or, where appropriate, of the priority claimed in respect of the application for registration of the trade mark, are well known in the Member State concerned, in the sense in which the words 'well-known' are used in Article 6bis of the Paris Convention.

3. Furthermore, a trade mark shall not be registered or, if registered, shall be liable to be declared invalid where:

(a) it is identical with, or similar to, an earlier trade mark irrespective of whether the goods or services for which it is applied or registered are identical with, similar to or not similar to those for which the earlier trade mark is registered, where the earlier trade mark has a reputation in the Member State in respect of which registration is applied for or in which the trade mark is registered or, in the case of an EU trade mark, has a reputation in the Union and the use of the later trade mark without due cause would take unfair advantage of, or be detrimental to, the distinctive character or the repute of the earlier trade mark;

(b) an agent or representative of the proprietor of the trade mark applies for registration thereof in his own name without the proprietor's authorisation, unless the agent or representative justifies his action;

(c) and to the extent that, pursuant to Union legislation or the law of the Member State concerned providing for protection of designations of origin and geographical indications:

(i) an application for a designation of origin or a geographical indication had already been submitted in accordance with Union legislation or the law of the Member State concerned prior to the date of application for registration of the trade mark or the date of the priority claimed for the application, subject to its subsequent registration;

(ii) that designation of origin or geographical indication confers on the person authorised under the relevant law to exercise the rights arising therefrom the right to prohibit the use of a subsequent trade mark.

4.   Any Member State may provide that a trade mark is not to be registered or, if registered, is liable to be declared invalid where, and to the extent that:

(a)   rights to a non-registered trade mark or to another sign used in the course of trade were acquired prior to the date of application for registration of the subsequent trade mark, or the date of the priority claimed for the application for registration of the subsequent trade mark, and that non-registered trade mark or other sign confers on its proprietor the right to prohibit the use of a subsequent trade mark;

(b)   the use of the trade mark may be prohibited by virtue of an earlier right, other than the rights referred to in paragraph 2 and point (a) of this paragraph, and in particular:

(i)   a right to a name;

(ii)   a right of personal portrayal;

(iii) a copyright;

(iv)   an industrial property right;

(c)   the trade mark is liable to be confused with an earlier trade mark protected abroad, provided that, at the date of the application, the applicant was acting in bad faith.

5.   The Member States shall ensure that in appropriate circumstances there is no obligation to refuse registration or to declare a trade mark invalid where the proprietor of the earlier trade mark or other earlier right consents to the registration of the later trade mark.

6.   Any Member State may provide that, by way of derogation from paragraphs 1 to 5, the grounds for refusal of registration or invalidity in force in that Member State prior to the date of the entry into force of the provisions necessary to comply with Directive 89/104/EEC are to apply to trade marks for which an application has been made prior to that date.

Article 6

Establishment a posteriori of invalidity or revocation of a trade mark

Where the seniority of a national trade mark or of a trade mark registered under international arrangements having effect in the Member State, which has been surrendered or allowed to lapse, is claimed for an EU trade mark, the invalidity or revocation of the trade mark providing the basis for the seniority claim may be established *a posteriori*, provided that the invalidity or revocation could have been declared at the time the mark was surrendered or allowed to lapse. In such a case, the seniority shall cease to produce its effects.

Article 7

Grounds for refusal or invalidity relating to only some of the goods or services

Where grounds for refusal of registration or for invalidity of a trade mark exist in respect of only some of the goods or services for which that trade mark has been applied or registered, refusal of registration or invalidity shall cover those goods or services only.

Article 8

Lack of distinctive character or of reputation of an earlier trade mark precluding a declaration of invalidity of a registered trade mark

An application for a declaration of invalidity on the basis of an earlier trade mark shall not succeed at the date of application for invalidation if it would not have been successful at the filing date or the priority date of the later trade mark for any of the following reasons:

(a) the earlier trade mark, liable to be declared invalid pursuant to Article 4(1)(b), (c) or (d), had not yet acquired a distinctive character as referred to in Article 4(4);

(b) the application for a declaration of invalidity is based on Article 5(1)(b) and the earlier trade mark had not yet become sufficiently distinctive to support a finding of likelihood of confusion within the meaning of Article 5(1)(b);

(c) the application for a declaration of invalidity is based on Article 5(3)(a) and the earlier trade mark had not yet acquired a reputation within the meaning of Article 5(3)(a).

Article 9

Preclusion of a declaration of invalidity due to acquiescence

1.   Where, in a Member State, the proprietor of an earlier trade mark as referred to in Article 5(2) or Article 5(3)(a) has acquiesced, for a period of five successive years, in the use of a later trade mark registered in that Member State while being aware of such use, that proprietor shall no longer be entitled on the basis of the earlier trade mark to apply for a declaration that the later trade mark is invalid in respect of the goods or services for which the later trade mark has been used, unless registration of the later trade mark was applied for in bad faith.

2.   Member States may provide that paragraph 1 of this Article is to apply to the proprietor of any other earlier right referred to in Article 5(4)(a) or (b).

3.   In the cases referred to in paragraphs 1 and 2, the proprietor of a later registered trade mark shall not be entitled to oppose the use of the

earlier right, even though that right may no longer be invoked against the later trade mark.

SECTION 3

Rights conferred and limitations

Article 10

Rights conferred by a trade mark

1.   The registration of a trade mark shall confer on the proprietor exclusive rights therein.

2.   Without prejudice to the rights of proprietors acquired before the filing date or the priority date of the registered trade mark, the proprietor of that registered trade mark shall be entitled to prevent all third parties not having his consent from using in the course of trade, in relation to goods or services, any sign where:

(a)   the sign is identical with the trade mark and is used in relation to goods or services which are identical with those for which the trade mark is registered;

(b)   the sign is identical with, or similar to, the trade mark and is used in relation to goods or services which are identical with, or similar to, the goods or services for which the trade mark is registered, if there exists a likelihood of confusion on the part of the public; the likelihood of confusion includes the likelihood of association between the sign and the trade mark;

(c)   the sign is identical with, or similar to, the trade mark irrespective of whether it is used in relation to goods or services which are identical with, similar to, or not similar to, those for which the trade mark is registered, where the latter has a reputation in the Member State and where use of that sign without due cause takes unfair advantage of, or is detrimental to, the distinctive character or the repute of the trade mark.

3.   The following, in particular, may be prohibited under paragraph 2:

(a)   affixing the sign to the goods or to the packaging thereof;

(b)   offering the goods or putting them on the market, or stocking them for those purposes, under the sign, or offering or supplying services thereunder;

(c)   importing or exporting the goods under the sign;

(d)   using the sign as a trade or company name or part of a trade or company name;

(e)   using the sign on business papers and in advertising;

(f) using the sign in comparative advertising in a manner that is contrary to Directive 2006/114/EC.

4. Without prejudice to the rights of proprietors acquired before the filing date or the priority date of the registered trade mark, the proprietor of that registered trade mark shall also be entitled to prevent all third parties from bringing goods, in the course of trade, into the Member State where the trade mark is registered, without being released for free circulation there, where such goods, including the packaging thereof, come from third countries and bear without authorisation a trade mark which is identical with the trade mark registered in respect of such goods, or which cannot be distinguished in its essential aspects from that trade mark.

The entitlement of the trade mark proprietor pursuant to the first subparagraph shall lapse if, during the proceedings to determine whether the registered trade mark has been infringed, initiated in accordance with Regulation (EU) No 608/2013, evidence is provided by the declarant or the holder of the goods that the proprietor of the registered trade mark is not entitled to prohibit the placing of the goods on the market in the country of final destination.

5. Where, under the law of a Member State, the use of a sign under the conditions referred to in paragraph 2 (b) or (c) could not be prohibited before the date of entry into force of the provisions necessary to comply with Directive 89/104/EEC in the Member State concerned, the rights conferred by the trade mark may not be relied on to prevent the continued use of the sign.

6. Paragraphs 1, 2, 3 and 5 shall not affect provisions in any Member State relating to the protection against the use of a sign other than use for the purposes of distinguishing goods or services, where use of that sign without due cause takes unfair advantage of, or is detrimental to, the distinctive character or the repute of the trade mark.

Article 11

The right to prohibit preparatory acts in relation to the use of packaging or other means

Where the risk exists that the packaging, labels, tags, security or authenticity features or devices, or any other means to which the trade mark is affixed, could be used in relation to goods or services and that use would constitute an infringement of the rights of the proprietor of a trade mark under Article 10(2) and (3), the proprietor of that trade mark shall have the right to prohibit the following acts if carried out in the course of trade:

(a) affixing a sign identical with, or similar to, the trade mark on packaging, labels, tags, security or authenticity features or devices, or any other means to which the mark may be affixed;

(b) offering or placing on the market, or stocking for those purposes, or importing or exporting, packaging, labels, tags, security or authenticity features or devices, or any other means to which the mark is affixed.

Article 12

Reproduction of trade marks in dictionaries

If the reproduction of a trade mark in a dictionary, encyclopaedia or similar reference work, in print or electronic form, gives the impression that it constitutes the generic name of the goods or services for which the trade mark is registered, the publisher of the work shall, at the request of the proprietor of the trade mark, ensure that the reproduction of the trade mark is, without delay, and in the case of works in printed form at the latest in the next edition of the publication, accompanied by an indication that it is a registered trade mark.

Article 13

Prohibition of the use of a trade mark registered in the name of an agent or representative

1.   Where a trade mark is registered in the name of the agent or representative of a person who is the proprietor of that trade mark, without the proprietor's consent, the latter shall be entitled to do either or both of the following:

(a) oppose the use of the trade mark by his agent or representative;

(b) demand the assignment of the trade mark in his favour.

2.   Paragraph 1 shall not apply where the agent or representative justifies his action.

Article 14

Limitation of the effects of a trade mark

1.   A trade mark shall not entitle the proprietor to prohibit a third party from using, in the course of trade:

(a) the name or address of the third party, where that third party is a natural person;

(b) signs or indications which are not distinctive or which concern the kind, quality, quantity, intended purpose, value, geographical origin, the time of production of goods or of rendering of the service, or other characteristics of goods or services;

(c) the trade mark for the purpose of identifying or referring to goods or services as those of the proprietor of that trade mark, in particular, where the use of the trade mark is necessary to indicate the intended purpose of a product or service, in particular as accessories or spare parts.

2.   Paragraph 1 shall only apply where the use made by the third party is in accordance with honest practices in industrial or commercial matters.

3.   A trade mark shall not entitle the proprietor to prohibit a third party from using, in the course of trade, an earlier right which only applies in a particular locality, if that right is recognised by the law of the Member State in question and the use of that right is within the limits of the territory in which it is recognised.

Article 15

Exhaustion of the rights conferred by a trade mark

1.   A trade mark shall not entitle the proprietor to prohibit its use in relation to goods which have been put on the market in the Union under that trade mark by the proprietor or with the proprietor's consent.

2.   Paragraph 1 shall not apply where there exist legitimate reasons for the proprietor to oppose further commercialisation of the goods, especially where the condition of the goods is changed or impaired after they have been put on the market.

Article 16

Use of trade marks

1.   If, within a period of five years following the date of the completion of the registration procedure, the proprietor has not put the trade mark to genuine use in the Member State in connection with the goods or services in respect of which it is registered, or if such use has been suspended during a continuous five-year period, the trade mark shall be subject to the limits and sanctions provided for in Article 17, Article 19(1), Article 44(1) and (2), and Article 46(3) and (4), unless there are proper reasons for non-use.

2.   Where a Member State provides for opposition proceedings following registration, the five-year period referred to in paragraph 1 shall be calculated from the date when the mark can no longer be opposed or, in the event that an opposition has been lodged, from the date when a decision terminating the opposition proceedings became final or the opposition was withdrawn.

3.   With regard to trade marks registered under international arrangements and having effect in the Member State, the five-year period referred to in paragraph 1 shall be calculated from the date when the mark can no longer be rejected or opposed. Where an opposition has been lodged or when an objection on absolute or relative grounds has been notified, the period shall be calculated from the date when a decision terminating the

opposition proceedings or a ruling on absolute or relative grounds for refusal became final or the opposition was withdrawn.

4.   The date of commencement of the five-year period, as referred to in paragraphs 1 and 2, shall be entered in the register.

5.   The following shall also constitute use within the meaning of paragraph 1:

(a)   use of the trade mark in a form differing in elements which do not alter the distinctive character of the mark in the form in which it was registered, regardless of whether or not the trade mark in the form as used is also registered in the name of the proprietor;

(b)   affixing of the trade mark to goods or to the packaging thereof in the Member State concerned solely for export purposes.

6.   Use of the trade mark with the consent of the proprietor shall be deemed to constitute use by the proprietor.

Article 17

Non-use as defence in infringement proceedings

The proprietor of a trade mark shall be entitled to prohibit the use of a sign only to the extent that the proprietor's rights are not liable to be revoked pursuant to Article 19 at the time the infringement action is brought. If the defendant so requests, the proprietor of the trade mark shall furnish proof that, during the five-year period preceding the date of bringing the action, the trade mark has been put to genuine use as provided in Article 16 in connection with the goods or services in respect of which it is registered and which are cited as justification for the action, or that there are proper reasons for non-use, provided that the registration procedure of the trade mark has at the date of bringing the action been completed for not less than five years.

Article 18

Intervening right of the proprietor of a later registered trade mark as defence in infringement proceedings

1.   In infringement proceedings, the proprietor of a trade mark shall not be entitled to prohibit the use of a later registered mark where that later trade mark would not be declared invalid pursuant to Article 8, Article 9(1) or (2) or Article 46(3).

2.   In infringement proceedings, the proprietor of a trade mark shall not be entitled to prohibit the use of a later registered EU trade mark where that later trade mark would not be declared invalid pursuant to Article 53(1), (3) or (4), 54(1) or (2) or 57(2) of Regulation (EC) No 207/2009.

3.   Where the proprietor of a trade mark is not entitled to prohibit the use of a later registered trade mark pursuant to paragraph 1 or 2, the

proprietor of that later registered trade mark shall not be entitled to prohibit the use of the earlier trade mark in infringement proceedings, even though that earlier right may no longer be invoked against the later trade mark.

SECTION 4

Revocation of trade mark rights

Article 19

Absence of genuine use as ground for revocation

1.   A trade mark shall be liable to revocation if, within a continuous five-year period, it has not been put to genuine use in the Member State in connection with the goods or services in respect of which it is registered, and there are no proper reasons for non-use.

2.   No person may claim that the proprietor's rights in a trade mark should be revoked where, during the interval between expiry of the five-year period and filing of the application for revocation, genuine use of the trade mark has been started or resumed.

3.   The commencement or resumption of use within the three-month period preceding the filing of the application for revocation which began at the earliest on expiry of the continuous five-year period of non-use shall be disregarded where preparations for the commencement or resumption occur only after the proprietor becomes aware that the application for revocation may be filed.

Article 20

Trade mark having become generic or misleading indication as grounds for revocation

A trade mark shall be liable to revocation if, after the date on which it was registered:

(a)   as a result of acts or inactivity of the proprietor, it has become the common name in the trade for a product or service in respect of which it is registered;

(b)   as a result of the use made of it by the proprietor of the trade mark or with the proprietor's consent in respect of the goods or services for which it is registered, it is liable to mislead the public, particularly as to the nature, quality or geographical origin of those goods or services.

Article 21

Revocation relating to only some of the goods or services

Where grounds for revocation of a trade mark exist in respect of only some of the goods or services for which that trade mark has been registered, revocation shall cover those goods or services only.

SECTION 5

Trade marks as objects of property

Article 22

Transfer of registered trade marks

1. A trade mark may be transferred, separately from any transfer of the undertaking, in respect of some or all of the goods or services for which it is registered.

2. A transfer of the whole of the undertaking shall include the transfer of the trade mark except where there is agreement to the contrary or circumstances clearly dictate otherwise. This provision shall apply to the contractual obligation to transfer the undertaking.

3. Member States shall have procedures in place to allow for the recordal of transfers in their registers.

Article 23

Rights in rem

1. A trade mark may, independently of the undertaking, be given as security or be the subject of rights *in rem*.

2. Member States shall have procedures in place to allow for the recordal of rights *in rem* in their registers.

Article 24

Levy of execution

1. A trade mark may be levied in execution.

2. Member States shall have procedures in place to allow for the recordal of levy of execution in their registers.

Article 25

Licensing

1. A trade mark may be licensed for some or all of the goods or services for which it is registered and for the whole or part of the Member State concerned. A licence may be exclusive or non-exclusive.

2. The proprietor of a trade mark may invoke the rights conferred by that trade mark against a licensee who contravenes any provision in his licensing contract with regard to:

(a) its duration;

(b) the form covered by the registration in which the trade mark may
     be used;

(c) the scope of the goods or services for which the licence is granted;

(d) the territory in which the trade mark may be affixed; or

(e) the quality of the goods manufactured or of the services provided
     by the licensee.

3.   Without prejudice to the provisions of the licensing contract, the
licensee may bring proceedings for infringement of a trade mark only if its
proprietor consents thereto. However, the holder of an exclusive licence
may bring such proceedings if the proprietor of the trade mark, after formal
notice, does not himself bring infringement proceedings within an
appropriate period.

4.   A licensee shall, for the purpose of obtaining compensation for
damage suffered by him, be entitled to intervene in infringement
proceedings brought by the proprietor of the trade mark.

5.   Member States shall have procedures in place to allow for the
recordal of licences in their registers.

Article 26

Applications for a trade mark as an object of property

Articles 22 to 25 shall apply to applications for trade marks.

SECTION 6

Guarantee or certification marks and collective marks

Article 27

Definitions

For the purposes of this Directive, the following definitions apply:

(a) 'guarantee or certification mark' means a trade mark which is
     described as such when the mark is applied for and is capable of
     distinguishing goods or services which are certified by the
     proprietor of the mark in respect of material, mode of manufacture
     of goods or performance of services, quality, accuracy or other
     characteristics, from goods and services which are not so certified;

(b) 'collective mark' means a trade mark which is described as such
     when the mark is applied for and is capable of distinguishing the
     goods or services of the members of an association which is the
     proprietor of the mark from the goods or services of other
     undertakings.

Article 28

Guarantee or certification marks

1.   Member States may provide for the registration of guarantee or certification marks.

2.   Any natural or legal person, including institutions, authorities and bodies governed by public law, may apply for guarantee or certification marks provided that such person does not carry on a business involving the supply of goods or services of the kind certified.

Member States may provide that a guarantee or certification mark is not to be registered unless the applicant is competent to certify the goods or services for which the mark is to be registered.

3.   Member States may provide that guarantee or certification marks are not to be registered, or are to be revoked or declared invalid, on grounds other than those specified in Articles 4, 19 and 20, where the function of those marks so requires.

4.   By way of derogation from Article 4(1)(c), Member States may provide that signs or indications which may serve, in trade, to designate the geographical origin of the goods or services may constitute guarantee or certification marks. Such a guarantee or certification mark shall not entitle the proprietor to prohibit a third party from using in the course of trade such signs or indications, provided that third party uses them in accordance with honest practices in industrial or commercial matters. In particular, such a mark may not be invoked against a third party who is entitled to use a geographical name.

5.   The requirements laid down in Article 16 shall be satisfied where genuine use of a guarantee or certification mark in accordance with Article 16 is made by any person who has the authority to use it.

Article 29

Collective marks

1.   Member States shall provide for the registration of collective marks.

2.   Associations of manufacturers, producers, suppliers of services or traders, which, under the terms of the law governing them, have the capacity in their own name to have rights and obligations, to make contracts or accomplish other legal acts, and to sue and be sued, as well as legal persons governed by public law, may apply for collective marks.

3.   By way of derogation from Article 4(1)(c), Member States may provide that signs or indications which may serve, in trade, to designate the geographical origin of the goods or services may constitute collective marks. Such a collective mark shall not entitle the proprietor to prohibit a

third party from using, in the course of trade, such signs or indications, provided that third party uses them in accordance with honest practices in industrial or commercial matters. In particular, such a mark may not be invoked against a third party who is entitled to use a geographical name.

Article 30

Regulations governing use of a collective mark

1.   An applicant for a collective mark shall submit the regulations governing its use to the office.

2.   The regulations governing use shall specify at least the persons authorised to use the mark, the conditions of membership of the association and the conditions of use of the mark, including sanctions. The regulations governing use of a mark referred to in Article 29(3) shall authorise any person whose goods or services originate in the geographical area concerned to become a member of the association which is the proprietor of the mark, provided that the person fulfils all the other conditions of the regulations.

Article 31

Refusal of an application

1.   In addition to the grounds for refusal of a trade mark application provided for in Article 4, where appropriate with the exception of Article 4(1)(c) concerning signs or indications which may serve, in trade, to designate the geographical origin of the goods or services, and Article 5, and without prejudice to the right of an office not to undertake examination *ex officio* of relative grounds, an application for a collective mark shall be refused where the provisions of point (b) of Article 27, Article 29 or Article 30 are not satisfied, or where the regulations governing use of that collective mark are contrary to public policy or to accepted principles of morality.

2.   An application for a collective mark shall also be refused if the public is liable to be misled as regards the character or the significance of the mark, in particular if it is likely to be taken to be something other than a collective mark.

3.   An application shall not be refused if the applicant, as a result of amendment of the regulations governing use of the collective mark, meets the requirements referred to in paragraphs 1 and 2.

Article 32

Use of collective marks

The requirements of Article 16 shall be satisfied where genuine use of a collective mark in accordance with that Article is made by any person who has authority to use it.

Article 33

Amendments to the regulations governing use of a collective mark

1.   The proprietor of a collective mark shall submit to the office any amended regulations governing use.

2.   Amendments to the regulations governing use shall be mentioned in the register unless the amended regulations do not satisfy the requirements of Article 30 or involve one of the grounds for refusal referred to in Article 31.

3.   For the purposes of this Directive, amendments to the regulations governing use shall take effect only from the date of entry of the mention of those amendments in the register.

Article 34

Persons entitled to bring an action for infringement

1.   Article 25(3) and (4) shall apply to every person who has the authority to use a collective mark.

2.   The proprietor of a collective mark shall be entitled to claim compensation on behalf of persons who have authority to use the mark where those persons have sustained damage as a result of unauthorised use of the mark.

Article 35

Additional grounds for revocation

In addition to the grounds for revocation provided for in Articles 19 and 20, the rights of the proprietor of a collective mark shall be revoked on the following grounds:

(a)   the proprietor does not take reasonable steps to prevent the mark being used in a manner that is incompatible with the conditions of use laid down in the regulations governing use, including any amendments thereto mentioned in the register;

(b)   the manner in which the mark has been used by authorised persons has caused it to become liable to mislead the public in the manner referred to in Article 31(2);

(c)   an amendment to the regulations governing use of the mark has been mentioned in the register in breach of Article 33(2), unless the proprietor of the mark, by further amending the regulations governing use, complies with the requirements of that Article.

Article 36

Additional grounds for invalidity

In addition to the grounds for invalidity provided for in Article 4, where appropriate with the exception of Article 4(1)(c) concerning signs or indications which may serve, in trade, to designate the geographical origin of the goods or services, and Article 5, a collective mark which is registered in breach of Article 31 shall be declared invalid unless the proprietor of the mark, by amending the regulations governing use, complies with the requirements of Article 31.

CHAPTER 3

PROCEDURES

SECTION 1

Application and registration

Article 37

Application requirements

1.   An application for registration of a trade mark shall contain at least all of the following:

(a)   a request for registration;

(b)   information identifying the applicant;

(c)   a list of the goods or services in respect of which the registration is requested;

(d)   a representation of the trade mark, which satisfies the requirements set out in point (b) of Article 3.

2.   The application for a trade mark shall be subject to the payment of a fee determined by the Member State concerned.

Article 38

Date of filing

1.   The date of filing of a trade mark application shall be the date on which the documents containing the information specified in Article 37(1) are filed with the office by the applicant.

2.   Member States may, in addition, provide that the accordance of the date of filing is to be subject to the payment of a fee as referred to in Article 37(2).

Article 39

Designation and classification of goods and services

1.   The goods and services in respect of which trade mark registration is applied for shall be classified in conformity with the system of

classification established by the Nice Agreement Concerning the International Classification of Goods and Services for the Purposes of the Registration of Marks of 15 June 1957 ('the Nice Classification').

2.   The goods and services for which protection is sought shall be identified by the applicant with sufficient clarity and precision to enable the competent authorities and economic operators, on that sole basis, to determine the extent of the protection sought.

3.   For the purposes of paragraph 2, the general indications included in the class headings of the Nice Classification or other general terms may be used, provided that they comply with the requisite standards of clarity and precision set out in this Article.

4.   The office shall reject an application in respect of indications or terms which are unclear or imprecise, where the applicant does not suggest an acceptable wording within a period set by the office to that effect.

5.   The use of general terms, including the general indications of the class headings of the Nice Classification, shall be interpreted as including all the goods or services clearly covered by the literal meaning of the indication or term. The use of such terms or indications shall not be interpreted as comprising a claim to goods or services which cannot be so understood.

6.   Where the applicant requests registration for more than one class, the applicant shall group the goods and services according to the classes of the Nice Classification, each group being preceded by the number of the class to which that group of goods or services belongs, and shall present them in the order of the classes.

7.   Goods and services shall not be regarded as being similar to each other on the ground that they appear in the same class under the Nice Classification. Goods and services shall not be regarded as being dissimilar from each other on the ground that they appear in different classes under the Nice Classification.

Article 40

Observations by third parties

1.   Member States may provide that prior to registration of a trade mark, any natural or legal person and any group or body representing manufacturers, producers, suppliers of services, traders or consumers may submit to the office written observations, explaining on which grounds the trade mark should not be registered *ex officio*.

Persons and groups or bodies, as referred to in the first subparagraph, shall not be parties to the proceedings before the office.

2.   In addition to the grounds referred to in paragraph 1 of this Article, any natural or legal person and any group or body representing

manufacturers, producers, suppliers of services, traders or consumers may submit to the office written observations based on the particular grounds on which the application for a collective mark should be refused under Article 31(1) and (2). This provision may be extended to cover certification and guarantee marks where regulated in Member States.

Article 41

Division of applications and registrations

The applicant or proprietor may divide a national trade mark application or registration into two or more separate applications or registrations by sending a declaration to the office and indicating for each divisional application or registration the goods or services covered by the original application or registration which are to be covered by the divisional applications or registrations.

Article 42

Class fees

Member States may provide that the application and renewal of a trade mark is to be subject to an additional fee for each class of goods and services beyond the first class.

SECTION 2

Procedures for opposition, revocation and invalidity

Article 43

Opposition procedure

1.   Member States shall provide for an efficient and expeditious administrative procedure before their offices for opposing the registration of a trade mark application on the grounds provided for in Article 5.

2.   The administrative procedure referred to in paragraph 1 of this Article shall at least provide that the proprietor of an earlier trade mark as referred to in Article 5(2) and Article 5(3)(a), and the person authorised under the relevant law to exercise the rights arising from a protected designation of origin or geographical indication as referred to in Article 5(3)(c) shall be entitled to file a notice of opposition. A notice of opposition may be filed on the basis of one or more earlier rights, provided that they all belong to the same proprietor, and on the basis of part or the totality of the goods or services in respect of which the earlier right is protected or applied for, and may be directed against part or the totality of the goods or services in respect of which the contested mark is applied for.

3.   The parties shall be granted, at their joint request, a minimum of two months in the opposition proceedings in order to allow for the possibility of a friendly settlement between the opposing party and the applicant.

Article 44

Non-use as defence in opposition proceedings

1.   In opposition proceedings pursuant to Article 43, where at the filing date or date of priority of the later trade mark, the five-year period within which the earlier trade mark must have been put to genuine use as provided for in Article 16 had expired, at the request of the applicant, the proprietor of the earlier trade mark who has given notice of opposition shall furnish proof that the earlier trade mark has been put to genuine use as provided for in Article 16 during the five-year period preceding the filing date or date of priority of the later trade mark, or that proper reasons for non-use existed. In the absence of proof to this effect, the opposition shall be rejected.

2.   If the earlier trade mark has been used in relation to only part of the goods or services for which it is registered, it shall, for the purpose of the examination of the opposition as provided for in paragraph 1, be deemed to be registered in respect of that part of the goods or services only.

3.   Paragraphs 1 and 2 of this Article shall also apply where the earlier trade mark is an EU trade mark. In such a case, the genuine use of the EU trade mark shall be determined in accordance with Article 15 of Regulation (EC) No 207/2009.

Article 45

Procedure for revocation or declaration of invalidity

1.   Without prejudice to the right of the parties to appeal to the courts, Member States shall provide for an efficient and expeditious administrative procedure before their offices for the revocation or declaration of invalidity of a trade mark.

2.   The administrative procedure for revocation shall provide that the trade mark is to be revoked on the grounds provided for in Articles 19 and 20.

3.   The administrative procedure for invalidity shall provide that the trade mark is to be declared invalid at least on the following grounds:

(a)   the trade mark should not have been registered because it does not comply with the requirements provided for in Article 4;

(b)   the trade mark should not have been registered because of the existence of an earlier right within the meaning of Article 5(1) to (3).

4.   The administrative procedure shall provide that at least the following are to be entitled to file an application for revocation or for a declaration of invalidity:

(a)   in the case of paragraph 2 and paragraph 3(a), any natural or legal person and any group or body set up for the purpose of representing the interests of manufacturers, producers, suppliers of services, traders or consumers, and which, under the terms of the law governing it, has the capacity to sue in its own name and to be sued;

(b)   in the case of paragraph 3(b) of this Article, the proprietor of an earlier trade mark as referred to in Article 5(2) and Article 5(3)(a), and the person authorised under the relevant law to exercise the rights arising from a protected designation of origin or geographical indication as referred to in Article 5(3)(c).

5.   An application for revocation or for a declaration of invalidity may be directed against a part or the totality of the goods or services in respect of which the contested mark is registered.

6.   An application for a declaration of invalidity may be filed on the basis of one or more earlier rights, provided they all belong to the same proprietor.

Article 46

Non-use as a defence in proceedings seeking a declaration of invalidity

1.   In proceedings for a declaration of invalidity based on a registered trade mark with an earlier filing date or priority date, if the proprietor of the later trade mark so requests, the proprietor of the earlier trade mark shall furnish proof that, during the five-year period preceding the date of the application for a declaration of invalidity, the earlier trade mark has been put to genuine use, as provided for in Article 16, in connection with the goods or services in respect of which it is registered and which are cited as justification for the application, or that there are proper reasons for non-use, provided that the registration process of the earlier trade mark has at the date of the application for a declaration of invalidity been completed for not less than five years.

2.   Where, at the filing date or date of priority of the later trade mark, the five-year period within which the earlier trade mark was to have been put to genuine use, as provided for in Article 16, had expired, the proprietor of the earlier trade mark shall, in addition to the proof required under paragraph 1 of this Article, furnish proof that the trade mark was put to genuine use during the five-year period preceding the filing date or date of priority, or that proper reasons for non-use existed.

3.   In the absence of the proof referred to in paragraphs 1 and 2, an application for a declaration of invalidity on the basis of an earlier trade mark shall be rejected.

4.   If the earlier trade mark has been used in accordance with Article 16 in relation to only part of the goods or services for which it is registered, it shall, for the purpose of the examination of the application for a declaration of invalidity, be deemed to be registered in respect of that part of the goods or services only.

5.   Paragraphs 1 to 4 of this Article shall also apply where the earlier trade mark is an EU trade mark. In such a case, genuine use of the EU trade mark shall be determined in accordance with Article 15 of Regulation (EC) No 207/2009.

Article 47

Consequences of revocation and invalidity

1.   A registered trade mark shall be deemed not to have had, as from the date of the application for revocation, the effects specified in this Directive, to the extent that the rights of the proprietor have been revoked. An earlier date, on which one of the grounds for revocation occurred, may be fixed in the decision on the application for revocation, at the request of one of the parties.

2.   A registered trade mark shall be deemed not to have had, as from the outset, the effects specified in this Directive, to the extent that the trade mark has been declared invalid.

SECTION 3

Duration and renewal of registration

Article 48

Duration of registration

1.   Trade marks shall be registered for a period of 10 years from the date of filing of the application.

2.   Registration may be renewed in accordance with Article 49 for further 10-year periods.

Article 49

Renewal

1.   Registration of a trade mark shall be renewed at the request of the proprietor of the trade mark or any person authorised to do so by law or by contract, provided that the renewal fees have been paid. Member States may provide that receipt of payment of the renewal fees is to be deemed to constitute such a request.

2.   The office shall inform the proprietor of the trade mark of the expiry of the registration at least six months before the said expiry. The office shall not be held liable if it fails to give such information.

3.   The request for renewal shall be submitted and the renewal fees shall be paid within a period of at least six months immediately preceding the expiry of the registration. Failing that, the request may be submitted within a further period of six months immediately following the expiry of the registration or of the subsequent renewal thereof. The renewal fees and an additional fee shall be paid within that further period.

4.   Where the request is submitted or the fees paid in respect of only some of the goods or services for which the trade mark is registered, registration shall be renewed for those goods or services only.

5.   Renewal shall take effect from the day following the date on which the existing registration expires. The renewal shall be recorded in the register.

SECTION 4

Communication with the office

Article 50

Communication with the office

Parties to the proceedings or, where appointed, their representatives, shall designate an official address for all official communication with the office. Member States shall have the right to require that such an official address be situated in the European Economic Area.

CHAPTER 4

ADMINISTRATIVE COOPERATION

Article 51

Cooperation in the area of trade mark registration and administration

The offices shall be free to cooperate effectively with each other and with the European Union Intellectual Property Office in order to promote convergence of practices and tools in relation to the examination and registration of trade marks.

Article 52

Cooperation in other areas

The offices shall be free to cooperate effectively with each other and with the European Union Intellectual Property Office in all areas of their activities other than those referred to in Article 51 which are of relevance for the protection of trade marks in the Union.

CHAPTER 5

FINAL PROVISIONS

Article 53

Data protection

The processing of any personal data carried out in the Member States in the framework of this Directive shall be subject to national law implementing Directive 95/46/EC.

Article 54

Transposition

1.   Member States shall bring into force the laws, regulations and administrative provisions necessary to comply with Articles 3 to 6, Articles 8 to 14, Articles 16, 17 and 18, Articles 22 to 39, Article 41, Articles 43 to 50 by 14 January 2019. Member States shall bring into force the laws, regulations and administrative provisions to comply with Article 45 by 14 January 2023. They shall immediately communicate the text of those measures to the Commission.

When Member States adopt those measures, they shall contain a reference to this Directive or be accompanied by such a reference on the occasion of their official publication. They shall also include a statement that references in existing laws, regulations and administrative provisions to the Directive repealed by this Directive shall be construed as references to this Directive. Member States shall determine how such reference is to be made and how that statement is to be formulated.

2.   Member States shall communicate to the Commission the text of the main provisions of national law which they adopt in the field covered by this Directive.

Article 55

Repeal

Directive 2008/95/EC is repealed with effect from 15 January 2019, without prejudice to the obligations of the Member States relating to the time limit for the transposition into national law of Directive 89/104/EEC set out in Part B of Annex I to Directive 2008/95/EC.

References to the repealed Directive shall be construed as references to this Directive and shall be read in accordance with the correlation table in the Annex.

Article 56

Entry into Force

This Directive shall enter into force on the twentieth day following that of its publication in the *Official Journal of the European Union*.

Articles 1, 7, 15, 19, 20, 21 and 54 to 57 shall apply from 15 January 2019.

Article 57

Addressees

This Directive is addressed to the Member States.

Done at Strasbourg, 16 December 2015.

For the European Parliament

The President

M. SCHULZ

For the Council

The President

N. SCHMIT

ANNEX

Correlation table

Directive 2008/95/EC	This Directive
Article 1	Article 1
—	Article 2
Article 2	Article 3
Article 3(1)(a) to (h)	Article 4(1)(a) to (h)
—	Article 4(1)(i) to (*l*)
Article 3(2)(a) to (c)	Article 4(3)(a) to (c)
Article 3(2)(d)	Article 4(2)
Article 3(3), first sentence	Article 4(4), first sentence
—	Article 4(4), second sentence
Article 3(3), second sentence	Article 4(5)
Article 3(4)	—
Article 4(1) and (2)	Article 5(1) and (2)
Article 4(3) and (4)(a)	Article 5(3)(a)
—	Article 5(3)(b)

Directive 2008/95/EC	This Directive
—	Article 5(3)(c)
Article 4(4)(b) and (c)	Article 5(4)(a) and (b)
Article 4(4)(d) to (f)	—
Article 4(4)(g)	Article 5(4)(c)
Article 4(5) and (6)	Article 5(5) and (6)
—	Article 8
Article 5(1), first sentence	Article 10(1)
Article 5(1), second sentence, introductory part	Article 10(2), introductory part of the sentence
Article 5(1)(a) and (b)	Article 10(2)(a) and (b)
Article 5(2)	Article 10(2)(c)
Article 5(3)(a) to (c)	Article 10(3)(a) to (c)
—	Article 10(3)(d)
Article 5(3)(d)	Article 10(3)(e)
—	Article 10(3)(f)
—	Article 10(4)
Article 5(4) and (5)	Article 10(5) and (6)
—	Article 11
—	Article 12
—	Article 13
Article 6(1)(a) to (c)	Article 14(1)(a) to (c), and (2)
Article 6(2)	Article 14(3)
Article 7	Article 15
Article 8(1) and (2)	Article 25(1) and (2)
—	Article 25(3) to (5)
Article 9	Article 9
Article 10(1), first subparagraph	Article 16(1)
—	Article 16(2) to (4)

Directive 2008/95/EC	This Directive
Article 10(1), second subparagraph	Article 16(5)
Article 10(2)	Article 16(6)
Article 10(3)	—
Article 11(1)	Article 46(1) to (3)
Article 11(2)	Article 44(1)
Article 11(3)	Article 17
Article 11(4)	Articles 17, 44(2) and Article 46(4)
—	Article 18
Article 12(1), first subparagraph	Article 19(1)
Article 12(1), second subparagraph	Article 19(2)
Article 12(1), third subparagraph	Article 19(3)
Article 12(2)	Article 20
Article 13	Article 7 and Article 21
Article 14	Article 6
—	Articles 22 to 24
—	Article 26
—	Article 27
Article 15(1)	Article 28(1) and (3)
Article 15(2)	Article 28(4)
—	Article 28(2) and (5)
—	Articles 29 to 54(1)
Article 16	Article 54(2)
Article 17	Article 55
Article 18	Article 56
Article 19	Article 57

29

EU Regulation on Quality Schemes for Agricultural Products and Foodstuffs

REGULATION (EU) NO 1151/2012 OF THE EUROPEAN PARLIAMENT AND OF THE COUNCIL

of 21 November 2012

on quality schemes for agricultural products and foodstuffs

amended by Regulation (EU) 2017/625

THE EUROPEAN PARLIAMENT AND THE COUNCIL OF THE EUROPEAN UNION,

Having regard to the Treaty on the Functioning of the European Union, and in particular Article 43(2) and the first paragraph of Article 118 thereof,

Having regard to the proposal from the European Commission,

After transmission of the draft legislative act to the national parliaments,

Having regard to the opinion of the European Economic and Social Committee[1],

Having regard to the opinion of the Committee of the Regions[2],

Acting in accordance with the ordinary legislative procedure[3],

Whereas:

(1) The quality and diversity of the Union's agricultural, fisheries and aquaculture production is one of its important strengths, giving a competitive advantage to the Union's producers and making a major contribution to its living cultural and gastronomic heritage. This is due to the skills and determination of Union farmers and producers who have

---

[1] OJ C 218, 23.7.2011, p. 114.

[2] OJ C 192, 1.7.2011, p. 28.

[3] Position of the European Parliament of 13 September 2012 (not yet published in the Official Journal) and decision of the Council of 13 November 2012.

kept traditions alive while taking into account the developments of new production methods and material.

(2)   Citizens and consumers in the Union increasingly demand quality as well as traditional products. They are also concerned to maintain the diversity of the agricultural production in the Union. This generates a demand for agricultural products or foodstuffs with identifiable specific characteristics, in particular those linked to their geographical origin.

(3)   Producers can only continue to produce a diverse range of quality products if they are rewarded fairly for their effort. This requires that they are able to communicate to buyers and consumers the characteristics of their product under conditions of fair competition. It also requires them to be able to correctly identify their products on the marketplace.

(4)   Operating quality schemes for producers which reward them for their efforts to produce a diverse range of quality products can benefit the rural economy. This is particularly the case in less favoured areas, in mountain areas and in the most remote regions, where the farming sector accounts for a significant part of the economy and production costs are high. In this way quality schemes are able to contribute to and complement rural development policy as well as market and income support policies of the common agricultural policy (CAP). In particular, they may contribute to areas in which the farming sector is of greater economic importance and, especially, to disadvantaged areas.

(5)   The Europe 2020 policy priorities as set out in the Commission Communication entitled 'Europe 2020: A strategy for smart, sustainable and inclusive growth', include the aims of achieving a competitive economy based on knowledge and innovation and fostering a high-employment economy delivering social and territorial cohesion. Agricultural product quality policy should therefore provide producers with the right tools to better identify and promote those of their products that have specific characteristics while protecting those producers against unfair practices.

(6)   The set of complementary measures envisaged should respect the principles of subsidiarity and proportionality.

(7) Agricultural product quality policy measures are laid down in Council Regulation (EEC) No 1601/91 of 10 June 1991 laying down general rules on the definition, description and presentation of aromatized wines, aromatized wine-based drinks and aromatized wine-product cocktails[4]; Council Directive 2001/110/EC of 20 December 2001 relating to honey[5] and in particular in Article 2 thereof, Council Regulation (EC) No 247/2006 of 30 January 2006 laying down specific measures for agriculture in the

---

[4]. OJ L 149, 14.6.1991, p. 1.

[5]. OJ L 10, 12.1.2002, p. 47.

outermost regions of the Union[6] and in particular in Article 14 thereof;
Council Regulation (EC) No 509/2006 of 20 March 2006 on agricultural
products and foodstuffs as traditional specialities guaranteed[7]; Council
Regulation (EC) No 510/2006 of 20 March 2006 on the protection of
geographical indications and designations of origin for agricultural
products and foodstuffs[8]; Council Regulation (EC) No 1234/2007 of 22
October 2007 establishing a common organisation of agricultural markets
and on specific provisions for certain agricultural products (Single CMO
Regulation)[9] and in particular in Part II, Title II, Chapter I, Section I and
in Section Ia, Subsection I thereof; Council Regulation (EC) No 834/2007 of
28 June 2007 on organic production and labelling of organic products[10]; and
Regulation (EC) No 110/2008 of the European Parliament and of the
Council of 15 January 2008 on the definition, description, presentation,
labelling and the protection of geographical indications of spirit drinks[11].

(8) The labelling of agricultural products and foodstuffs should be
subject to the general rules laid down in Directive 2000/13/EC of the
European Parliament and of the Council of 20 March 2000 on the
approximation of the laws of the Member States relating to the labelling,
presentation and advertising of foodstuffs[12], and in particular the
provisions aimed at preventing labelling that may confuse or mislead
consumers.

(9) The Communication from the Commission to the European
Parliament, the Council, the European Economic and Social Committee
and the Committee of the Regions on agricultural product quality policy
identified the achievement of a greater overall coherence and consistency
of agricultural product quality policy as a priority.

(10) The geographical indications scheme for agricultural products
and foodstuffs and the traditional specialities guaranteed scheme have
certain common objectives and provisions.

(11) The Union has for some time been pursuing an approach that
aims to simplify the regulatory framework of the CAP. This approach
should also be applied to regulations in the field of agricultural product
quality policy, without, in so doing, calling into question the specific
characteristics of those products.

(12) Some regulations that form part of the agricultural product
quality policy have been reviewed recently but are not yet fully

---

6.   OJ L 42, 14.2.2006, p. 1.
7.   OJ L 93, 31.3.2006, p. 1
8.   OJ L 93, 31.3.2006, p. 12.
9.   OJ L 299, 16.11.2007, p. 1.
10.   OJ L 189, 20.7.2007, p. 1.
11.   OJ L 39, 13.2.2008, p. 16.
12.   OJ L 109, 6.5.2000, p. 29.

implemented. As a result, they should not be included in this Regulation. However, they may be incorporated at a later stage, once the legislation has been fully implemented.

(13) In the light of the aforementioned considerations, the following provisions should be amalgamated into a single legal framework comprising the new or updated provisions of Regulations (EC) No 509/2006 and (EC) No 510/2006 and those provisions of Regulations (EC) No 509/2006 and (EC) No 510/2006 that are maintained.

(14) In the interests of clarity and transparency, Regulations (EC) No 509/2006 and (EC) No 510/2006 should therefore be repealed and replaced by this Regulation.

(15) The scope of this Regulation should be limited to the agricultural products intended for human consumption listed in Annex I to the Treaty and to a list of products outside the scope of that Annex that are closely linked to agricultural production or to the rural economy.

(16) The rules provided for in this Regulation should apply without affecting existing Union legislation on wines, aromatised wines, spirit drinks, product of organic farming, or outermost regions.

(17) The scope for designations of origin and geographical indications should be limited to products for which an intrinsic link exists between product or foodstuff characteristics and geographical origin. The inclusion in the current scheme of only certain types of chocolate as confectionery products is an anomaly that should be corrected.

(18) The specific objectives of protecting designations of origin and geographical indications are securing a fair return for farmers and producers for the qualities and characteristics of a given product, or of its mode of production, and providing clear information on products with specific characteristics linked to geographical origin, thereby enabling consumers to make more informed purchasing choices.

(19) Ensuring uniform respect throughout the Union for the intellectual property rights related to names protected in the Union is a priority that can be achieved more effectively at Union level.

(20) A Union framework that protects designations of origin and geographical indications by providing for their inclusion on a register facilitates the development of those instruments, since the resulting, more uniform, approach ensures fair competition between the producers of products bearing such indications and enhances the credibility of the products in the consumers' eyes. Provision should be made for the development of designations of origin and geographical indications at Union level and for promoting the creation of mechanisms for their protection in third countries in the framework of the World Trade Organisation (WTO) or multilateral and bilateral agreements, thereby

contributing to the recognition of the quality of products and of their model of production as a factor that adds value.

(21) In the light of the experience gained from the implementation of Council Regulation (EEC) No 2081/92 of 14 July 1992 on the protection of geographical indications and designations of origin for agricultural products and foodstuffs[13] and Regulation (EC) No 510/2006, there is a need to address certain issues, to clarify and simplify some rules and to streamline the procedures of this scheme.

(22) In the light of existing practice, the two different instruments for identifying the link between the product and its geographical origin, namely the protected designation of origin and the protected geographical indication, should be further defined and maintained. Without changing the concept of those instruments, some modifications to the definitions should be adopted in order to better take into account the definition of geographical indications laid down in the Agreement on Trade-Related Aspects of Intellectual Property Rights and to make them simpler and clearer for operators to understand.

(23) An agricultural product or foodstuff bearing such a geographical description should meet certain conditions set out in a specification, such as specific requirements aimed at protecting the natural resources or landscape of the production area or improving the welfare of farm animals.

(24) To qualify for protection in the territories of Member States, designations of origin and geographical indications should be registered only at Union level. With effect from the date of application for such registration at Union level, Member States should be able to grant transitional protection at national level without affecting intra-Union or international trade. The protection afforded by this Regulation upon registration, should be equally available to designations of origin and geographical indications of third countries that meet the corresponding criteria and that are protected in their country of origin.

(25) The registration procedure at Union level should enable any natural or legal person with a legitimate interest from a Member State, other than the Member State of the application, or from a third country, to exercise their rights by notifying their opposition.

(26) Entry in the register of protected designations of origin and protected geographical indications should also provide information to consumers and to those involved in trade.

(27) The Union negotiates international agreements, including those concerning the protection of designations of origin and geographical indications, with its trade partners. In order to facilitate the provision to the public of information about the names so protected, and in particular

---

[13]. OJ L 208, 24.7.1992, p. 1.

to ensure protection and control of the use to which those names are put, the names may be entered in the register of protected designations of origin and protected geographical indications. Unless specifically identified as designations of origin in such international agreements, the names should be entered in the register as protected geographical indications.

(28) In view of their specific nature, special provisions concerning labelling should be adopted in respect of protected designations of origin and protected geographical indications that require producers to use the appropriate Union symbols or indications on packaging. In the case of Union names, the use of such symbols or indications should be made obligatory in order to make this category of products, and the guarantees attached to them, better known to consumers and in order to permit easier identification of these products on the market, thereby facilitating checks. Taking into account the requirements of the WTO, the use of such symbols or indications should be made voluntary for third-country geographical indications and designations of origin.

(29) Protection should be granted to names included in the register with the aim of ensuring that they are used fairly and in order to prevent practices liable to mislead consumers. In addition, the means of ensuring that geographical indications and designations of origin are protected should be clarified, particularly as regards the role of producer groups and competent authorities of Member States.

(30) Provision should be made for specific derogations that permit, for transitional periods, the use of a registered name alongside other names. Those derogations should be simplified and clarified. In certain cases, in order to overcome temporary difficulties and with the long-term objective of ensuring that all producers comply with the specifications, those derogations may be granted for a period of up to 10 years.

(31) The scope of the protection granted under this Regulation should be clarified, in particular with regard to those limitations on registration of new trade marks set out in Directive 2008/95/EC of the European Parliament and of the Council of 22 October 2008 to approximate the laws of the Member States relating to trade marks[14] that conflict with the registration of protected designations of origin and protected geographical indications as is already the case for the registration of new trade marks at Union level. Such clarification is also necessary with regard to the holders of prior rights in intellectual property, in particular those concerning trade marks and homonymous names registered as protected designations of origin or as protected geographical indications.

(32) Protection of designations of origin and geographical indications should be extended to the misuse, imitation and evocation of the registered

---

[14]. OJ L 299, 8.11.2008, p. 25.

names on goods as well as on services in order to ensure a high level of protection and to align that protection with that which applies to the wine sector. When protected designations of origin or protected geographical indications are used as ingredients, the Commission Communication entitled 'Guidelines on the labelling of foodstuffs using protected designations of origin (PDOs) or protected geographical indications (PGIs) as ingredients' should be taken into account.

(33) The names already registered under Regulation (EC) No 510/2006 on 3 January 2013 should continue to be protected under this Regulation and they should be automatically included in the register.

(34) The specific objective of the scheme for traditional specialities guaranteed is to help the producers of traditional products to communicate to consumers the value-adding attributes of their product. However, as only a few names have been registered, the current scheme for traditional specialities guaranteed has failed to realise its potential. Current provisions should therefore be improved, clarified and sharpened in order to make the scheme more understandable, operational and attractive to potential applicants.

(35) The current scheme provides the option to register a name for identification purposes without reservation of the name in the Union. As this option has not been well understood by stakeholders and since the function of identifying traditional products can be better achieved at Member State or regional level in application of the principle of subsidiarity, this option should be discontinued. In the light of experience, the scheme should only deal with the reservation of names across the Union.

(36) To ensure that names of genuine traditional products are registered under the scheme, the criteria and conditions for registration of a name should be adapted, in particular those concerning the definition of 'traditional', which should cover products that have been produced for a significant period of time.

(37) To ensure that traditional specialities guaranteed comply with their specification and are consistent, producers organised into groups should themselves define the product in a specification. The option of registering a name as a traditional speciality guaranteed should be open to third-country producers.

(38) To qualify for reservation, traditional specialities guaranteed should be registered at Union level. The entry in the register should also provide information to consumers and to those involved in the trade.

(39) In order to avoid creating unfair conditions of competition, any producer, including a third-country producer, should be able to use a registered name of a traditional speciality guaranteed, provided that the

product concerned complies with the requirements of the relevant specification and the producer is covered by a system of controls. For traditional specialities guaranteed produced within the Union, the Union symbol should be indicated on the labelling and it should be possible to associate it with the indication 'traditional speciality guaranteed'.

(40) In order to protect registered names from misuse, or from practices that might mislead consumers, their use should be reserved.

(41) For those names already registered under Regulation (EC) No 509/2006 that, on 3 January 2013, would otherwise not be covered by the scope of this Regulation, the terms of use laid down in Regulation (EC) No 509/2006 should continue to apply for a transitional period.

(42) A procedure should be introduced for registering names that are registered without reservation of name pursuant to Regulation (EC) No 509/2006, enabling them to be registered with reservation of name.

(43) Provision should also be made for transitional measures applicable to registration applications received by the Commission before 3 January 2013.

(44) A second tier of quality systems, based on quality terms which add value, which can be communicated on the internal market and which are to be applied voluntarily, should be introduced. Those optional quality terms should refer to specific horizontal characteristics, with regard to one or more categories of products, farming methods or processing attributes which apply in specific areas. The optional quality term 'mountain product' has met the conditions up to now and will add value to the product on the market. In order to facilitate the application of Directive 2000/13/EC where the labelling of foodstuffs may give rise to consumer confusion in relation to optional quality terms, including in particular 'mountain products', the Commission may adopt guidelines.

(45) In order to provide mountain producers with an effective tool to better market their product and to reduce the actual risks of consumer confusion as to the mountain provenance of products in the market place, provision should be made for the definition at Union level of an optional quality term for mountain products. The definition of mountain areas should build on the general classification criteria employed to identify a mountain area in Council Regulation (EC) No 1257/1999 of 17 May 1999 on support for rural development from the European Agricultural Guidance and Guarantee Fund (EAGGF)[15].

(46) The added value of the geographical indications and traditional specialities guaranteed is based on consumer trust. It is only credible if accompanied by effective verification and controls. Those quality schemes should be subject to a monitoring system of official controls, in line with

---

[15.] OJ L 160, 26.6.1999, p. 80.

the principles set out in Regulation (EC) No 882/2004 of the European Parliament and of the Council of 29 April 2004 on official controls performed to ensure the verification of compliance with feed and food law, animal health and animal welfare rules[16], and should include a system of checks at all stages of production, processing and distribution. In order to help Member States to better apply provisions of Regulation (EC) No 882/2004 for the controls of geographical indications and traditional specialities guaranteed, references to the most relevant articles should be mentioned in this Regulation.

(47) To guarantee to the consumer the specific characteristics of geographical indications and traditional specialities guaranteed, operators should be subject to a system that verifies compliance with the product specification.

(48) In order to ensure that they are impartial and effective, the competent authorities should meet a number of operational criteria. Provisions on delegating some competences of performing specific control tasks to control bodies should be envisaged.

(49) European standards (EN standards) developed by the European Committee for Standardisation (CEN) and international standards developed by the International Organisation for Standardisation (ISO) should be used for the accreditation of the control bodies as well as by those bodies for their operations. The accreditation of those bodies should take place in accordance with Regulation (EC) No 765/2008 of the European Parliament and of the Council of 9 July 2008 setting out the requirements for accreditation and market surveillance relating to the marketing of products[17].

(50) Information on control activities for geographical indications and traditional specialities guaranteed should be included in the multiannual national control plans and annual report prepared by the Member States in accordance with Regulation (EC) No 882/2004.

(51) Member States should be authorised to charge a fee to cover the costs incurred.

(52) Existing rules concerning the continued use of names that are generic should be clarified so that generic terms that are similar to or form part of a name or term that is protected or reserved should retain their generic status.

(53) The date for establishing the seniority of a trade mark and of a designation of origin or a geographical indication should be that of the date of application of the trade mark for registration in the Union or in the

---

[16]. OJ L 165, 30.4.2004, p. 1.
[17]. OJ L 218, 13.8.2008, p. 30.

Member States and the date of application for protection of a designation of origin or a geographical indication to the Commission.

(54) The provisions dealing with the refusal or coexistence of a designation of origin or a geographical indication on the ground of conflict with a prior trade mark should continue to apply.

(55) The criteria by which subsequent trade marks should be refused or, if registered, invalidated on the ground that they conflict with a prior designation of origin or geographical indication should correspond to the scope of protection of designation of origin or a geographical indication laid down.

(56) The provisions of systems establishing intellectual property rights, and particularly of those established by the quality scheme for designations of origin and geographical indications or those established under trade mark law, should not be affected by the reservation of names and the establishment of indications and symbols pursuant to the quality schemes for traditional specialities guaranteed and for optional quality terms.

(57) The role of groups should be clarified and recognised. Groups play an essential role in the application process for the registration of names of designations of origin and geographical indications and traditional specialities guaranteed, as well as in the amendment of specifications and cancellation requests. The group can also develop activities related to the surveillance of the enforcement of the protection of the registered names, the compliance of the production with the product specification, the information and promotion of the registered name as well as, in general, any activity aimed at improving the value of the registered names and effectiveness of the quality schemes. Moreover, it should monitor the position of the products on the market. Nevertheless, these activities should not facilitate nor lead to anti-competitive conduct incompatible with Articles 101 and 102 of the Treaty.

(58) To ensure that registered names of designations of origin and geographical indications and traditional specialities guaranteed meet the conditions laid down by this Regulation, applications should be examined by the national authorities of the Member State concerned, in compliance with minimum common provisions, including a national opposition procedure. The Commission should subsequently scrutinise applications to ensure that there are no manifest errors and that Union law and the interests of stakeholders outside the Member State of application have been taken into account.

(59) Registration as designations of origin, geographical indications and traditional specialities guaranteed should be open to names that relate to products originating in third countries and that satisfy the conditions laid down by this Regulation.

(60) The symbols, indications and abbreviations identifying participation in a quality scheme, and the rights therein pertaining to the Union, should be protected in the Union as well as in third countries with the aim of ensuring that they are used on genuine products and that consumers are not misled as to the qualities of products. Furthermore, in order for the protection to be effective, the Commission should have recourse to reasonable budget resources on a centralised basis within the framework of Council Regulation (EC) No 1698/2005 of 20 September 2005 on support for rural development by the European Agricultural Fund for Rural Development (EAFRD)[18] and in accordance with Article 5 of Council Regulation (EC) No 1290/2005 of 21 June 2005 on the financing of the common agricultural policy[19].

(61) The registration procedure for protected designations of origin, protected geographical indications and traditional specialities guaranteed, including the scrutiny and the opposition periods, should be shortened and improved, in particular as regards decision making. The Commission, in certain circumstances acting with the assistance of Member States, should be responsible for decision-making on registration. Procedures should be laid down to allow the amendment of product specifications after registration and the cancellation of registered names, in particular if the product no longer complies with the corresponding product specification or if a name is no longer used in the market place.

(62) In order to facilitate cross-border applications for joint registration of protected designations of origin, protected geographical indications or traditional specialities guaranteed, provision should be made for appropriate procedures.

(63) In order to supplement or amend certain non-essential elements of this Regulation, the power to adopt acts in accordance with Article 290 of the Treaty should be delegated to the Commission in respect of supplementing the list of products set out in Annex I to this Regulation; establishing the restrictions and derogations with regard to the sourcing of feed in the case of a designation of origin; establishing restrictions and derogations with regard to the slaughtering of live animals or with regard to the sourcing of raw materials; laying down rules which limit the information contained in the product specification; establishing the Union symbols; laying down additional transitional rules in order to protect the rights and legitimate interests of producers or stakeholders concerned; laying down further details on the eligibility criteria for the names of traditional specialities guaranteed; laying down detailed rules relating to the criteria for optional quality terms; reserving an additional optional quality term, laying down its conditions of use and amending those

[18]. OJ L 277, 21.10.2005, p. 1.
[19]. OJ L 209, 11.8.2005, p. 1.

conditions; laying down derogations to the use of the term 'mountain product' and establishing the methods of production, and other criteria relevant for the application of that optional quality term, in particular, laying down the conditions under which raw materials or feedstuffs are permitted to come from outside the mountain areas; laying down additional rules for determining the generic status of terms in the Union; laying down rules for determining the use of the name of a plant variety or of an animal breed; defining the rules for carrying out the national objection procedure for joint applications concerning more than one national territory; and for complementing the rules of the application process, the opposition process, the amendment application process and the cancellation process in general. It is of particular importance that the Commission carry out appropriate consultations during its preparatory work, including at expert level. The Commission, when preparing and drawing up delegated acts, should ensure a simultaneous, timely and appropriate transmission of relevant documents to the European Parliament and to the Council.

(64) In order to ensure uniform conditions for the implementation of this Regulation, implementing powers should be conferred on the Commission as regards laying down rules on the form of the product specification; laying down detailed rules on the form and content of the register of protected designations of origin and protected geographical indications; defining the technical characteristics of the Union symbols and indications as well as the rules on their use on products, including the appropriate linguistic versions to be used; granting and extending transitional periods for temporary derogations for use of protected designations of origin and protected geographical indication; laying down detailed rules on the form and content of the register of traditional specialities guaranteed; laying down rules for the protection of traditional specialities guaranteed; laying down all measures relating to forms, procedures and other technical details for the application of Title IV; laying down rules for the use of optional quality terms; laying down rules for the uniform protection of indications, abbreviations and symbols referring to the quality schemes; laying down detailed rules on the procedure, form and presentation of applications for registration and of oppositions; rejecting the application; deciding on the registration of a name if an agreement has not been reached; laying down detailed rules on the procedure, form and presentation of an amendment application; cancelling the registration of a protected designation of origin, a protected geographical indication or a traditional speciality guaranteed; and laying down detailed rules on the procedure and form of the cancellation process and on the presentation of the requests for cancellation. Those powers should be exercised in accordance with Regulation (EU) No 182/2011 of the European Parliament and of the Council of 16 February 2011 laying down the rules and general

principles concerning mechanisms for control by Member States of the Commission's exercise of implementing powers[20].

(65) In respect of establishing and maintaining registers of protected designations of origin, protected geographical indications and traditional specialties guaranteed, recognised under this scheme; defining the means by which the name and address of product certification bodies are to be made public; and registering a name if there is no notice of opposition or no admissible reasoned statement of opposition or in the case there is one the agreement has been reached, the Commission should be empowered to adopt implementing acts without applying Regulation (EU) No 182/2011,

HAVE ADOPTED THIS REGULATION:

TITLE I

GENERAL PROVISIONS

Article 1

Objectives

1.   This Regulation aims to help producers of agricultural products and foodstuffs to communicate the product characteristics and farming attributes of those products and foodstuffs to buyers and consumers, thereby ensuring:

(a) fair competition for farmers and producers of agricultural products and foodstuffs having value-adding characteristics and attributes;

(b) the availability to consumers of reliable information pertaining to such products;

(c) respect for intellectual property rights; and

(d) the integrity of the internal market.

The measures set out in this Regulation are intended to support agricultural and processing activities and the farming systems associated with high quality products, thereby contributing to the achievement of rural development policy objectives.

2.   This Regulation establishes quality schemes which provide the basis for the identification and, where appropriate, protection of names and terms that, in particular, indicate or describe agricultural products with:

(a) value-adding characteristics; or

(b) value-adding attributes as a result of the farming or processing methods used in their production, or of the place of their production or marketing.

---

[20]. OJ L 55, 28.2.2011, p. 13.

Article 2

Scope

1.   This Regulation covers agricultural products intended for human consumption listed in Annex I to the Treaty and other agricultural products and foodstuffs listed in Annex I to this Regulation.

In order to take into account international commitments or new production methods or material, the Commission shall be empowered to adopt delegated acts, in accordance with Article 56, supplementing the list of products set out in Annex I to this Regulation. Such products shall be closely linked to agricultural products or to the rural economy.

2.   This Regulation shall not apply to spirit drinks, aromatised wines or grapevine products as defined in Annex XIb to Regulation (EC) No 1234/2007, with the exception of wine-vinegars.

3.   This Regulation shall apply without prejudice to other specific Union provisions relating to the placing of products on the market and, in particular, to the single common organisation of the markets, and to food labelling.

4.   Directive 98/34/EC of the European Parliament and of the Council of 22 June 1998 laying down a procedure for the provision of information in the field of technical standards and regulations and of rules on Information Society services[21] shall not apply to the quality schemes established by this Regulation.

Article 3

Definitions

For the purposes of this Regulation the following definitions shall apply:

(1)   'quality schemes' means the schemes established under Titles II, III and IV;

(2)   'group' means any association, irrespective of its legal form, mainly composed of producers or processors working with the same product;

(3)   'traditional' means proven usage on the domestic market for a period that allows transmission between generations; this period is to be at least 30 years;

(4)   'labelling' means any words, particulars, trade marks, brand name, pictorial matter or symbol relating to a foodstuff and placed on any packaging, document, notice, label, ring or collar accompanying or referring to such foodstuff;

[21.] OJ L 204, 21.7.1998, p. 37.

(5) 'specific character' in relation to a product means the characteristic production attributes which distinguish a product clearly from other similar products of the same category;

(6) 'generic terms' means the names of products which, although relating to the place, region or country where the product was originally produced or marketed, have become the common name of a product in the Union;

(7) 'production step' means production, processing or preparation;

(8) 'processed products' means foodstuffs resulting from the processing of unprocessed products. Processed products may contain ingredients that are necessary for their manufacture or to give them specific characteristics.

TITLE II

PROTECTED DESIGNATIONS OF ORIGIN AND PROTECTED GEOGRAPHICAL INDICATIONS

Article 4

Objective

A scheme for protected designations of origin and protected geographical indications is established in order to help producers of products linked to a geographical area by:

(a) securing fair returns for the qualities of their products;

(b) ensuring uniform protection of the names as an intellectual property right in the territory of the Union;

(c) providing clear information on the value-adding attributes of the product to consumers.

Article 5

Requirements for designations of origin and geographical indications

1.   For the purpose of this Regulation, 'designation of origin' is a name which identifies a product:

(a) originating in a specific place, region or, in exceptional cases, a country;

(b) whose quality or characteristics are essentially or exclusively due to a particular geographical environment with its inherent natural and human factors; and

(c) the production steps of which all take place in the defined geographical area.

2.   For the purpose of this Regulation, 'geographical indication' is a name which identifies a product:

(a) originating in a specific place, region or country;

(b) whose given quality, reputation or other characteristic is essentially attributable to its geographical origin; and

(c) at least one of the production steps of which take place in the defined geographical area.

3.   Notwithstanding paragraph 1, certain names shall be treated as designations of origin even though the raw materials for the products concerned come from a geographical area larger than, or different from, the defined geographical area, provided that:

(a) the production area of the raw materials is defined;

(b) special conditions for the production of the raw materials exist;

(c) there are control arrangements to ensure that the conditions referred to in point (b) are adhered to; and

(d) the designations of origin in question were recognised as designations of origin in the country of origin before 1 May 2004.

Only live animals, meat and milk may be considered as raw materials for the purposes of this paragraph.

4.   In order to take into account the specific character of production of products of animal origin, the Commission shall be empowered to adopt delegated acts, in accordance with Article 56, concerning restrictions and derogations with regard to the sourcing of feed in the case of a designation of origin.

In addition, in order to take into account the specific character of certain products or areas, the Commission shall be empowered to adopt delegated acts in accordance with Article 56, concerning restrictions and derogations with regard to the slaughtering of live animals or with regard to the sourcing of raw materials.

These restrictions and derogations shall, based on objective criteria, take into account quality or usage and recognised know-how or natural factors.

Article 6

**Generic nature, conflicts with names of plant varieties
and animal breeds, with homonyms and trade marks**

1.   Generic terms shall not be registered as protected designations of origin or protected geographical indications.

2.   A name may not be registered as a designation of origin or geographical indication where it conflicts with a name of a plant variety or

an animal breed and is likely to mislead the consumer as to the true origin of the product.

3.   A name proposed for registration that is wholly or partially homonymous with a name already entered in the register established under Article 11 may not be registered unless there is sufficient distinction in practice between the conditions of local and traditional usage and presentation of the homonym registered subsequently and the name already entered in the register, taking into account the need to ensure equitable treatment of the producers concerned and that consumers are not misled.

A homonymous name which misleads the consumer into believing that products come from another territory shall not be registered even if the name is accurate as far as the actual territory, region or place of origin of the products in question is concerned.

4.   A name proposed for registration as a designation of origin or geographical indication shall not be registered where, in the light of a trade mark's reputation and renown and the length of time it has been used, registration of the name proposed as the designation of origin or geographical indication would be liable to mislead the consumer as to the true identity of the product.

Article 7

Product specification

1.   A protected designation of origin or a protected geographical indication shall comply with a specification which shall include at least:

(a)   the name to be protected as a designation of origin or geographical indication, as it is used, whether in trade or in common language, and only in the languages which are or were historically used to describe the specific product in the defined geographical area;

(b)   a description of the product, including the raw materials, if appropriate, as well as the principal physical, chemical, microbiological or organoleptic characteristics of the product;

(c)   the definition of the geographical area delimited with regard to the link referred to in point (f)(i) or (ii) of this paragraph, and, where appropriate, details indicating compliance with the requirements of Article 5(3);

(d)   evidence that the product originates in the defined geographical area referred to in Article 5(1) or (2);

(e)   a description of the method of obtaining the product and, where appropriate, the authentic and unvarying local methods as well as information concerning packaging, if the applicant group so determines and gives sufficient product-specific justification as to why the packaging must take place in the defined geographical area to safeguard quality, to ensure the origin or to ensure control, taking into account Union law, in particular that on the free movement of goods and the free provision of services;

(f) details establishing the following:

    (i) the link between the quality or characteristics of the product and the geographical environment referred to in Article 5(1); or

    (ii) where appropriate, the link between a given quality, the reputation or other characteristic of the product and the geographical origin referred to in Article 5(2);

(g) the name and address of the authorities or, if available, the name and address of bodies verifying compliance with the provisions of the product specification pursuant to Article 37 and their specific tasks;

(h) any specific labelling rule for the product in question.

2.   In order to ensure that product specifications provide relevant and succinct information, the Commission shall be empowered to adopt delegated acts, in accordance with Article 56, laying down rules which limit the information contained in the specification referred to in paragraph 1 of this Article, where such a limitation is necessary to avoid excessively voluminous applications for registration.

The Commission may adopt implementing acts laying down rules on the form of the specification. Those implementing acts shall be adopted in accordance with the examination procedure referred to in Article 57(2).

Article 8

Content of application for registration

1.   An application for registration of a designation of origin or geographical indication pursuant to Article 49(2) or (5) shall include at least:

(a) the name and address of the applicant group and of the authorities or, if available, bodies verifying compliance with the provisions of the product specification;

(b) the product specification provided for in Article 7;

(c) a single document setting out the following:

    (i) the main points of the product specification: the name, a description of the product, including, where appropriate, specific rules concerning packaging and labelling, and a concise definition of the geographical area;

(ii) a description of the link between the product and the geographical environment or geographical origin referred to in Article 5(1) or (2), as the case may be, including, where appropriate, the specific elements of the product description or production method justifying the link.

An application as referred to in Article 49(5) shall, in addition, include proof that the name of the product is protected in its country of origin.

2.   An application dossier referred to in Article 49(4) shall comprise:

(a)   the name and address of the applicant group;

(b)   the single document referred to in point (c) of paragraph 1 of this Article;

(c)   a declaration by the Member State that it considers that the application lodged by the applicant group and qualifying for the favourable decision meets the conditions of this Regulation and the provisions adopted pursuant thereto;

(d)   the publication reference of the product specification.

Article 9

Transitional national protection

A Member State may, on a transitional basis only, grant protection to a name under this Regulation at national level, with effect from the date on which an application is lodged with the Commission.

Such national protection shall cease on the date on which either a decision on registration under this Regulation is taken or the application is withdrawn.

Where a name is not registered under this Regulation, the consequences of such national protection shall be the sole responsibility of the Member State concerned.

The measures taken by Member States under the first paragraph shall produce effects at national level only, and they shall have no effect on intra-Union or international trade.

Article 10

Grounds for opposition

1.   A reasoned statement of opposition as referred to in Article 51(2) shall be admissible only if it is received by the Commission within the time limit set out in that paragraph and if it:

(a)   shows that the conditions referred to in Article 5 and Article 7(1) are not complied with;

(b) shows that the registration of the name proposed would be contrary to Article 6(2), (3) or (4);

(c) shows that the registration of the name proposed would jeopardise the existence of an entirely or partly identical name or of a trade mark or the existence of products which have been legally on the market for at least five years preceding the date of the publication provided for in point (a) of Article 50(2); or

(d) gives details from which it can be concluded that the name for which registration is requested is a generic term.

2.   The grounds for opposition shall be assessed in relation to the territory of the Union.

Article 11

Register of protected designations of origin and protected geographical indications

1.   The Commission shall adopt implementing acts, without applying the procedure referred to in Article 57(2), establishing and maintaining a publicly accessible updated register of protected designations of origin and protected geographical indications recognised under this scheme.

2.   Geographical indications pertaining to products of third countries that are protected in the Union under an international agreement to which the Union is a contracting party may be entered in the register. Unless specifically identified in the said agreement as protected designations of origin under this Regulation, such names shall be entered in the register as protected geographical indications.

3.   The Commission may adopt implementing acts laying down detailed rules on the form and content of the register. Those implementing acts shall be adopted in accordance with the examination procedure referred to in Article 57(2).

4.   The Commission shall make public and regularly update the list of the international agreements referred to in paragraph 2 as well as the list of geographical indications protected under those agreements.

Article 12

Names, symbols and indications

1.   Protected designations of origin and protected geographical indications may be used by any operator marketing a product conforming to the corresponding specification.

2.   Union symbols designed to publicise protected designations of origin and protected geographical indications shall be established.

3.   In the case of products originating in the Union that are marketed under a protected designation of origin or a protected geographical indication registered in accordance with the procedures laid down in this Regulation, the Union symbols associated with them shall appear on the labelling. In addition, the registered name of the product should appear in the same field of vision. The indications 'protected designation of origin' or 'protected geographical indication' or the corresponding abbreviations 'PDO' or 'PGI' may appear on the labelling.

4.   In addition, the following may also appear on the labelling: depictions of the geographical area of origin, as referred to in Article 5, and text, graphics or symbols referring to the Member State and/or region in which that geographical area of origin is located.

5.   Without prejudice to Directive 2000/13/EC, the collective geographical marks referred to in Article 15 of Directive 2008/95/EC may be used on labels, together with the protected designation of origin or protected geographical indication.

6.   In the case of products originating in third countries marketed under a name entered in the register, the indications referred to in paragraph 3 or the Union symbols associated with them may appear on the labelling.

7.   In order to ensure that the appropriate information is communicated to the consumer, the Commission shall be empowered to adopt delegated acts, in accordance with Article 56, establishing the Union symbols.

The Commission may adopt implementing acts defining the technical characteristics of the Union symbols and indications as well as the rules of their use on the products marketed under a protected designation of origin or a protected geographical indication, including rules concerning the appropriate linguistic versions to be used. Those implementing acts shall be adopted in accordance with the examination procedure referred to in Article 57(2).

Article 13

Protection

1.   Registered names shall be protected against:

(a)   any direct or indirect commercial use of a registered name in respect of products not covered by the registration where those products are comparable to the products registered under that name or where using the name exploits the reputation of the protected name, including when those products are used as an ingredient;

(b) any misuse, imitation or evocation, even if the true origin of the products or services is indicated or if the protected name is translated or accompanied by an expression such as 'style', 'type', 'method', 'as produced in', 'imitation' or similar, including when those products are used as an ingredient;

(c) any other false or misleading indication as to the provenance, origin, nature or essential qualities of the product that is used on the inner or outer packaging, advertising material or documents relating to the product concerned, and the packing of the product in a container liable to convey a false impression as to its origin;

(d) any other practice liable to mislead the consumer as to the true origin of the product.

Where a protected designation of origin or a protected geographical indication contains within it the name of a product which is considered to be generic, the use of that generic name shall not be considered to be contrary to points (a) or (b) of the first subparagraph.

2.   Protected designations of origin and protected geographical indications shall not become generic.

3.   Member States shall take appropriate administrative and judicial steps to prevent or stop the unlawful use of protected designations of origin and protected geographical indications, as referred to in paragraph 1, that are produced or marketed in that Member State.

To that end Member States shall designate the authorities that are responsible for taking these steps in accordance with procedures determined by each individual Member State.

These authorities shall offer adequate guarantees of objectivity and impartiality, and shall have at their disposal the qualified staff and resources necessary to carry out their functions.

Article 14

**Relations between trade marks, designations
of origin and geographical indications**

1.   Where a designation of origin or a geographical indication is registered under this Regulation, the registration of a trade mark the use of which would contravene Article 13(1) and which relates to a product of the same type shall be refused if the application for registration of the trade mark is submitted after the date of submission of the registration application in respect of the designation of origin or the geographical indication to the Commission.

Trade marks registered in breach of the first subparagraph shall be invalidated.

The provisions of this paragraph shall apply notwithstanding the provisions of Directive 2008/95/EC.

2.   Without prejudice to Article 6(4), a trade mark the use of which contravenes Article 13(1) which has been applied for, registered, or established by use if that possibility is provided for by the legislation concerned, in good faith within the territory of the Union, before the date on which the application for protection of the designation of origin or geographical indication is submitted to the Commission, may continue to be used and renewed for that product notwithstanding the registration of a designation of origin or geographical indication, provided that no grounds for its invalidity or revocation exist under Council Regulation (EC) No 207/2009 of 26 February 2009 on the Community trade mark[22] or under Directive 2008/95/EC. In such cases, the use of the protected designation of origin or protected geographical indication shall be permitted as well as use of the relevant trade marks.

Article 15

Transitional periods for use of protected designations of origin and protected geographical indications

1.   Without prejudice to Article 14, the Commission may adopt implementing acts granting a transitional period of up to five years to enable products originating in a Member State or a third country the designation of which consists of or contains a name that contravenes Article 13(1) to continue to use the designation under which it was marketed on condition that an admissible statement of opposition under Article 49(3) or Article 51 shows that:

(a)   the registration of the name would jeopardise the existence of an entirely or partly identical name; or

(b)   such products have been legally marketed with that name in the territory concerned for at least five years preceding the date of the publication provided for point (a) of Article 50(2).

Those implementing acts shall be adopted in accordance with the examination procedure referred to in Article 57(2).

2.   Without prejudice to Article 14, the Commission may adopt implementing acts extending the transitional period mentioned in paragraph 1 of this Article to 15 years in duly justified cases where it is shown that:

(a)   the designation referred to in paragraph 1 of this Article has been in legal use consistently and fairly for at least 25 years before the application for registration was submitted to the Commission;

---

[22] OJ L 78, 24.3.2009, p. 1.

(b)   the purpose of using the designation referred to in paragraph 1 of this Article has not, at any time, been to profit from the reputation of the registered name and it is shown that the consumer has not been nor could have been misled as to the true origin of the product.

Those implementing acts shall be adopted in accordance with the examination procedure referred to in Article 57(2).

3.   When using a designation referred to in paragraphs 1 and 2, the indication of country of origin shall clearly and visibly appear on the labelling.

4.   To overcome temporary difficulties with the long-term objective of ensuring that all producers in the area concerned comply with the specification, a Member State may grant a transitional period of up to 10 years, with effect from the date on which the application is lodged with the Commission, on condition that the operators concerned have legally marketed the products in question, using the names concerned continuously for at least the five years prior to the lodging of the application to the authorities of the Member State and have made that point in the national opposition procedure referred to in Article 49(3).

The first subparagraph shall apply *mutatis mutandis* to a protected geographical indication or protected designation of origin referring to a geographical area situated in a third country, with the exception of the opposition procedure.

Such transitional periods shall be indicated in the application dossier referred to in Article 8(2).

Article 16

Transitional provisions

1.   Names entered in the register provided for in Article 7(6) of Regulation (EC) No 510/2006 shall automatically be entered in the register referred to in Article 11 of this Regulation. The corresponding specifications shall be deemed to be the specifications referred to in Article 7 of this Regulation. Any specific transitional provisions associated with such registrations shall continue to apply.

2.   In order to protect the rights and legitimate interests of producers or stakeholders concerned, the Commission shall be empowered to adopt delegated acts, in accordance with Article 56, concerning additional transitional rules.

3.   This Regulation shall apply without prejudice to any right of coexistence recognised under Regulation (EC) No 510/2006 in respect of designations of origin and geographical indications, on the one hand, and trade marks, on the other.

TITLE III

TRADITIONAL SPECIALITIES GUARANTEED

Article 17

Objective

A scheme for traditional specialities guaranteed is established to safeguard traditional methods of production and recipes by helping producers of traditional product in marketing and communicating the value-adding attributes of their traditional recipes and products to consumers.

Article 18

Criteria

1. A name shall be eligible for registration as a traditional speciality guaranteed where it describes a specific product or foodstuff that:

(a) results from a mode of production, processing or composition corresponding to traditional practice for that product or foodstuff; or

(b) is produced from raw materials or ingredients that are those traditionally used.

2. For a name to be registered as a traditional speciality guaranteed, it shall:

(a) have been traditionally used to refer to the specific product; or

(b) identify the traditional character or specific character of the product.

3. If it is demonstrated in the opposition procedure under Article 51 that the name is also used in another Member State or in a third country, in order to distinguish comparable products or products that share an identical or similar name, the decision on registration taken in accordance with Article 52(3) may provide that the name of the traditional speciality guaranteed is to be accompanied by the claim 'made following the tradition of' immediately followed by the name of a country or a region thereof.

4. A name may not be registered if it refers only to claims of a general nature used for a set of products, or to claims provided for by particular Union legislation.

5. In order to ensure the smooth functioning of the scheme, the Commission shall be empowered to adopt delegated acts, in accordance with Article 56, concerning further details of the eligibility criteria laid down in this Article.

Article 19

Product specification

1. A traditional speciality guaranteed shall comply with a specification which shall comprise:

   (a) the name proposed for registration, in the appropriate language versions;

   (b) a description of the product including its main physical, chemical, microbiological or organoleptic characteristics, showing the product's specific character;

   (c) a description of the production method that the producers must follow, including, where appropriate, the nature and characteristics of the raw materials or ingredients used, and the method by which the product is prepared; and

   (d) the key elements establishing the product's traditional character.

2. In order to ensure that product specifications provide relevant and succinct information, the Commission shall be empowered to adopt delegated acts, in accordance with Article 56, laying down rules which limit the information contained in the specification referred to in paragraph 1 of this Article, where such a limitation is necessary to avoid excessively voluminous applications for registration.

The Commission may adopt implementing acts laying down rules on the form of the specification. Those implementing acts shall be adopted in accordance with the examination procedure referred to in Article 57(2).

Article 20

Content of application for registration

1. An application for registration of a name as a traditional speciality guaranteed referred to in Article 49(2) or (5) shall comprise:

   (a) the name and address of the applicant group;

   (b) the product specification as provided for in Article 19.

2. An application dossier referred to in Article 49(4) shall comprise:

   (a) the elements referred to in paragraph 1 of this Article; and

   (b) a declaration by the Member State that it considers that the application lodged by the group and qualifying for the favourable decision meets the conditions of this Regulation and the provisions adopted pursuant thereto.

Article 21

Grounds for opposition

1.   A reasoned statement of opposition as referred to in Article 51(2) shall be admissible only if it is received by the Commission before expiry of the time limit and if it:

(a)   gives duly substantiated reasons why the proposed registration is incompatible with the terms of this Regulation; or

(b)   shows that use of the name is lawful, renowned and economically significant for similar agricultural products or foodstuffs.

2.   The criteria referred to in point (b) of paragraph 1 shall be assessed in relation to the territory of the Union.

Article 22

Register of traditional specialities guaranteed

1.   The Commission shall adopt implementing acts, without applying the procedure referred to in Article 57(2), establishing and maintaining a publicly accessible updated register of traditional specialties guaranteed recognised under this scheme.

2.   The Commission may adopt implementing acts laying down detailed rules on the form and content of the register. Those implementing acts shall be adopted in accordance with the examination procedure referred to in Article 57(2).

Article 23

Names, symbol and indication

1.   A name registered as a traditional speciality guaranteed may be used by any operator marketing a product that conforms to the corresponding specification.

2.   A Union symbol shall be established in order to publicise the traditional specialities guaranteed.

3.   In the case of the products originating in the Union that are marketed under a traditional speciality guaranteed that is registered in accordance with this Regulation, the symbol referred to in paragraph 2 shall, without prejudice to paragraph 4, appear on the labelling. In addition, the name of the product should appear in the same field of vision. The indication 'traditional speciality guaranteed' or the corresponding abbreviation 'TSG' may also appear on the labelling.

The symbol shall be optional on the labelling of traditional specialities guaranteed which are produced outside the Union.

4.   In order to ensure that the appropriate information is communicated to the consumer, the Commission shall be empowered to

adopt delegated acts, in accordance with Article 56, establishing the Union symbol.

The Commission may adopt implementing acts defining the technical characteristics of the Union symbol and indication, as well as the rules of their use on the products bearing the name of a traditional speciality guaranteed, including as to the appropriate linguistic versions to be used. Those implementing acts shall be adopted in accordance with the examination procedure referred to in Article 57(2).

Article 24

Restriction on use of registered names

1.   Registered names shall be protected against any misuse, imitation or evocation, or against any other practice liable to mislead the consumer.

2.   Member States shall ensure that sales descriptions used at national level do not give rise to confusion with names that are registered.

3.   The Commission may adopt implementing acts laying down rules for the protection of traditional specialities guaranteed. Those implementing acts shall be adopted in accordance with the examination procedure referred to in Article 57(2).

Article 25

Transitional provisions

1.   Names registered in accordance with Article 13(2) of Regulation (EC) No 509/2006 shall be automatically entered in the register referred to in Article 22 of this Regulation. The corresponding specifications shall be deemed to be the specifications referred to in Article 19 of this Regulation. Any specific transitional provisions associated with such registrations shall continue to apply.

2.   Names registered in accordance with the requirements laid down in Article 13(1) of Regulation (EC) No 509/2006, including those registered pursuant to applications referred to in the second subparagraph of Article 58(1) of this Regulation, may continue to be used under the conditions provided for in Regulation (EC) No 509/2006 until 4 January 2023 unless Member States use the procedure set out in Article 26 of this Regulation.

3.   In order to protect the rights and legitimate interests of producers or stakeholders concerned, the Commission shall be empowered to adopt delegated acts, in accordance with Article 56, laying down additional transitional rules.

Article 26

Simplified procedure

1.   At the request of a group, a Member State may submit, no later than 4 January 2016, to the Commission names of traditional specialities guaranteed that are registered in accordance with Article 13(1) of Regulation (EC) No 509/2006 and that comply with this Regulation.

Before submitting a name, the Member State shall initiate an opposition procedure as defined in Article 49(3) and (4).

If it is demonstrated in the course of this procedure that the name is also used in reference to comparable products or products that share an identical or similar name, the name may be complemented by a term identifying its traditional or specific character.

A group from a third country may submit such names to the Commission, either directly or through the authorities of the third country.

2.   The Commission shall publish the names referred to in paragraph 1 together with the specifications for each such name in the *Official Journal of the European Union* within two months from reception.

3.   Articles 51 and 52 shall apply.

4.   Once the opposition procedure has finished, the Commission shall, where appropriate, adjust the entries in the register set out in Article 22. The corresponding specifications shall be deemed to be the specifications referred to in Article 19.

TITLE IV

OPTIONAL QUALITY TERMS

Article 27

Objective

A scheme for optional quality terms is established in order to facilitate the communication within the internal market of the value-adding characteristics or attributes of agricultural products by the producers thereof.

Article 28

National Rules

Member States may maintain national rules on optional quality terms which are not covered by this Regulation, provided that such rules comply with Union law.

Article 29

Optional quality terms

1.   Optional quality terms shall satisfy the following criteria:

(a)   the term relates to a characteristic of one or more categories of products, or to a farming or processing attribute which applies in specific areas;

(b)   the use of the term adds value to the product as compared to products of a similar type; and

(c)   the term has a European dimension.

2.   Optional quality terms that describe technical product qualities with the purpose of putting into effect compulsory marketing standards and are not intended to inform consumers about those product qualities shall be excluded from this scheme.

3.   Optional quality terms shall exclude optional reserved terms which support and complement specific marketing standards determined on a sectoral or product category basis.

4.   In order to take into account the specific character of certain sectors as well as consumer expectations, the Commission shall be empowered to adopt delegated acts, in accordance with Article 56, laying down detailed rules relating to the criteria referred to in paragraph 1 of this Article.

5.   The Commission may adopt implementing acts laying down all measures related to forms, procedures or other technical details, necessary for the application of this Title. Those implementing acts shall be adopted in accordance with the examination procedure referred to in Article 57(2).

6.   When adopting delegated and implementing acts in accordance with paragraphs 4 and 5 of this Article, the Commission shall take account of any relevant international standards.

Article 30

Reservation and amendment

1.   In order to take account of the expectations of consumers, developments in scientific and technical knowledge, the market situation, and developments in marketing standards and in international standards, the Commission shall be empowered to adopt delegated acts, in accordance with Article 56, reserving an additional optional quality term and laying down its conditions of use.

2.   In duly justified cases and in order to take into account the appropriate use of the additional optional quality term, the Commission shall be empowered to adopt delegated acts, in accordance with Article 56,

laying down amendments to the conditions of use referred to in paragraph 1 of this Article.

Article 31

Mountain product

1.   The term 'mountain product' is established as an optional quality term.

This term shall only be used to describe products intended for human consumption listed in Annex I to the Treaty in respect of which:

(a)   both the raw materials and the feedstuffs for farm animals come essentially from mountain areas;

(b)   in the case of processed products, the processing also takes place in mountain areas.

2.   For the purposes of this Article, mountain areas within the Union are those delimited pursuant to Article 18(1) of Regulation (EC) No 1257/1999. For third-country products, mountain areas include areas officially designated as mountain areas by the third country or that meet criteria equivalent to those set out in Article 18(1) of Regulation (EC) No 1257/1999.

3.   In duly justified cases and in order to take into account natural constraints affecting agricultural production in mountain areas, the Commission shall be empowered to adopt delegated acts, in accordance with Article 56, laying down derogations from the conditions of use referred to in paragraph 1 of this Article. In particular, the Commission shall be empowered to adopt a delegated act laying down the conditions under which raw materials or feedstuffs are permitted to come from outside the mountain areas, the conditions under which the processing of products is permitted to take place outside of the mountain areas in a geographical area to be defined, and the definition of that geographical area.

4.   In order to take into account natural constraints affecting agricultural production in mountain areas, the Commission shall be empowered to adopt delegated acts, in accordance with Article 56, concerning the establishment of the methods of production, and other criteria relevant for the application of the optional quality term established in paragraph 1 of this Article.

Article 32

Product of island farming

No later than 4 January 2014 the Commission shall present a report to the European Parliament and to the Council on the case for a new term, 'product of island farming'. The term may only be used to describe the products intended for human consumption that are listed in Annex I to the

Treaty the raw materials of which come from islands. In addition, for the term to be applied to processed products, processing must also take place on islands in cases where this substantially affects the particular characteristics of the final product.

That report shall, if necessary, be accompanied by appropriate legislative proposals to reserve an optional quality term 'product of island farming'.

Article 33

Restrictions on use

1. An optional quality term may only be used to describe products that comply with the corresponding conditions of use.

2. The Commission may adopt implementing acts laying down rules for the use of optional quality terms. Those implementing acts shall be adopted in accordance with the examination procedure referred to in Article 57(2).

Article 34

Monitoring

Member States shall undertake checks, based on a risk analysis, to ensure compliance with the requirements of this Title and, in the event of breach, shall apply appropriate administrative penalties.

TITLE V

COMMON PROVISIONS

CHAPTER I

Official controls of protected designations of origin, protected geographical indications and traditional specialities guaranteed

Article 35

Scope

The provisions of this Chapter shall apply in respect of the quality schemes set out in Title II and Title III.

Article 36

Content of official controls

(Paragraphs 1 and 2 deleted by Regulation 2017/625.)

3. Official controls performed in accordance with Regulation (EU) 2017/625 of the European Parliament and of the Council shall cover:

(a) verification that a product complies with the corresponding product specification; and

(b)   monitoring of the use of registered names to describe product
      placed on the market, in conformity with Article 13 for names
      registered under Title II and in conformity with Article 24 for
      names registered under Title III.

Article 37

Verification of compliance with product specification

1.   In respect of protected designations of origin, protected
geographical indications and traditional specialities guaranteed that
designate products originating within the Union, verification of compliance
with the product specification, before placing the product on the market,
shall be carried out by:

(a)   the competent authorities designated in accordance with Article 4
      of Regulation 2017/625; or

(b)   delegated bodies as defined in Article 3/(5) of Regulation 2017/625.

The costs of such verification of compliance with the specifications may
be borne by the operators that are subject to those controls. The Member
States may also contribute to these costs.

2.   In respect of designations of origin, geographical indications and
traditional specialities guaranteed that designate products originating in
a third country, the verification of compliance with the specifications before
placing the product on the market shall be carried out by:

(a)   one or more of the public authorities designated by the third
      country; and/or

(b)   one or more of the product certification bodies.

3.   The Commission shall make public the name and address of the
authorities and bodies referred to in paragraph 2 of this Article and update
that information periodically.

4.   The Commission may adopt implementing acts, without applying
the procedure referred to in Article 57(2), defining the means by which the
name and address of product certification bodies referred to in paragraph
2 of this Article shall be made public.

Article 38

(Deleted by Regulation 2017/625.)

Article 39

Delegated bodies performing controls in third countries

The delegated bodies performing controls in the third countries
referred to in paragraph 2(b) of Article 37 shall be accredited to the relevant
harmonised standard for "Conformity assessment- Requirements for
bodies certifying products, processes and services". These delegated bodies

may be accredited either by a national accreditation body outside the Union, in accordance with Regulation (EC) No 765/2008, or by an accreditation body outside the Union that is a signatory of a multilateral recognition arrangement under the auspices of the International Accreditation Forum.

Article 40

Planning and reporting of control activities

1.   Member States shall ensure that activities for the control of obligations under this Chapter are specifically included in a separate section within the multi-annual national control plans in accordance with Articles 41, 42 and 43 of Regulation (EC) No 882/2004.

2.   The annual reports concerning the control of the obligations established by this Regulation shall include a separate section comprising the information laid down in Article 44 of Regulation (EC) No 882/2004.

CHAPTER II

Exceptions for certain prior uses

Article 41

Generic terms

1.   Without prejudice to Article 13, this Regulation shall not affect the use of terms that are generic in the Union, even if the generic term is part of a name that is protected under a quality scheme.

2.   To establish whether or not a term has become generic, account shall be taken of all relevant factors, in particular:

(a) the existing situation in areas of consumption;

(b) the relevant national or Union legal acts.

3.   In order to fully protect the rights of interested parties, the Commission shall be empowered to adopt delegated acts, in accordance with Article 56, laying down additional rules for determining the generic status of terms referred to in paragraph 1 of this Article.

Article 42

Plant varieties and animal breeds

1.   This Regulation shall not prevent the placing on the market of products the labelling of which includes a name or term protected or reserved under a quality scheme described in Title II, Title III, or Title IV that contains or comprises the name of a plant variety or animal breed, provided that the following conditions are met:

(a) the product in question comprises or is derived from the variety or breed indicated;

(b) consumers are not misled;

(c) the usage of the name of the variety or breed name constitutes fair competition;

(d) the usage does not exploit the reputation of the protected term; and

(e) in the case of the quality scheme described in Title II, production and marketing of the product had spread beyond its area of origin prior to the date of application for registration of the geographical indication.

2.   In order to further clarify the extent of rights and freedoms of food business operators to use the name of a plant variety or of an animal breed referred to in paragraph 1 of this Article, the Commission shall be empowered to adopt delegated acts, in accordance with Article 56, concerning rules for determining the use of such names.

Article 43

Relation to intellectual property

The quality schemes described in Titles III and IV shall apply without prejudice to Union rules or to those of Member States governing intellectual property, and in particular to those concerning designations of origin and geographical indications and trade marks, and rights granted under those rules.

CHAPTER III

Quality scheme indications and symbols and role of producers

Article 44

Protection of indications and symbols

1.   Indications, abbreviations and symbols referring to the quality schemes may only be used in connection with products produced in conformity with the rules of the quality scheme to which they apply. This applies in particular to the following indications, abbreviations and symbols:

(a) 'protected designation of origin', 'protected geographical indication', 'geographical indication', 'PDO', 'PGI', and the associated symbols, as provided for in Title II;

(b) 'traditional speciality guaranteed', 'TSG', and the associated symbol, as provided for in Title III;

(c) 'mountain product', as provided for in Title IV.

2.   In accordance with Article 5 of Regulation (EC) No 1290/2005, the European Agricultural Fund for Rural Development (EAFRD) may, on the

initiative of the Commission or on its behalf, finance, on a centralised basis, administrative support concerning the development, preparatory work, monitoring, administrative and legal support, legal defence, registration fees, renewal fees, trade mark watching fees, litigation fees and any other related measure required to protect the use of the indications, abbreviations and symbols referring to the quality schemes from misuse, imitation, evocation or any other practice liable to mislead the consumer, within the Union and in third countries.

3.   The Commission shall adopt implementing acts laying down rules for the uniform protection of the indications, abbreviations and symbols referred to in paragraph 1 of this Article. Those implementing acts shall be adopted in accordance with the examination procedure referred to in Article 57(2).

Article 45

Role of groups

1.   Without prejudice to specific provisions on producer organisations and inter-branch organisations as laid down in Regulation (EC) No 1234/2007, a group is entitled to:

(a) contribute to ensuring that the quality, reputation and authenticity of their products are guaranteed on the market by monitoring the use of the name in trade and, if necessary, by informing competent authorities as referred to in Article 36, or any other competent authority within the framework of Article 13(3);

(b) take action to ensure adequate legal protection of the protected designation of origin or protected geographical indication and of the intellectual property rights that are directly connected with them;

(c) develop information and promotion activities aiming at communicating the value-adding attributes of the product to consumers;

(d) develop activities related to ensuring compliance of a product with its specification;

(e) take action to improve the performance of the scheme, including developing economic expertise, carrying out economic analyses, disseminating economic information on the scheme and providing advice to producers;

(f) take measures to enhance the value of products and, where necessary, take steps to prevent or counter any measures which are, or risk being, detrimental to the image of those products.

2.   Member States may encourage the formation and functioning of groups on their territories by administrative means. Moreover, Member States shall communicate to the Commission the name and address of the groups referred to in point 2 of Article 3. The Commission shall make this information public.

Article 46

Right to use the schemes

1.   Member States shall ensure that any operator complying with the rules of a quality scheme set out in Titles II and III is entitled to be covered by the verification of compliance established pursuant to Article 37.

2.   Operators who prepare and store a product marketed under the traditional speciality guaranteed, protected designation of origin or protected geographical indication schemes or who place such products on the market shall also be subject to the controls laid down in Chapter I of this Title.

3.   Member States shall ensure that operators willing to adhere to the rules of a quality scheme set out in Titles III and IV are able to do so and do not face obstacles to participation that are discriminatory or otherwise not objectively founded.

Article 47

Fees

Without prejudice to Regulation (EC) No 882/2004 and in particular the provisions of Chapter VI of Title II thereof, Member States may charge a fee to cover their costs of managing the quality schemes, including those incurred in processing applications, statements of opposition, applications for amendments and requests for cancellations provided for in this Regulation.

CHAPTER IV

Application and registration processes for designations of origin, geographical indications, and traditional specialities guaranteed

Article 48

Scope of application processes

The provisions of this Chapter shall apply in respect of the quality schemes set out in Title II and Title III.

Article 49

Application for registration of names

1.   Applications for registration of names under the quality schemes referred to in Article 48 may only be submitted by groups who work with

the products with the name to be registered. In the case of a 'protected designations of origin' or 'protected geographical indications' name that designates a trans-border geographical area or in the case of a 'traditional specialities guaranteed' name, several groups from different Member States or third countries may lodge a joint application for registration.

A single natural or legal person may be treated as a group where it is shown that both of the following conditions are fulfilled:

(a) the person concerned is the only producer willing to submit an application;

(b) with regard to protected designations of origin and protected geographical indications, the defined geographical area possesses characteristics which differ appreciably from those of neighbouring areas or the characteristics of the product are different from those produced in neighbouring areas.

2.   Where the application under the scheme set out in Title II relates to a geographical area in a Member State, or where an application under the scheme set out in Title III is prepared by a group established in a Member State, the application shall be addressed to the authorities of that Member State.

The Member State shall scrutinise the application by appropriate means in order to check that it is justified and meets the conditions of the respective scheme.

3.   As part of the scrutiny referred to in the second subparagraph of paragraph 2 of this Article, the Member State shall initiate a national opposition procedure that ensures adequate publication of the application and that provides for a reasonable period within which any natural or legal person having a legitimate interest and established or resident on its territory may lodge an opposition to the application.

The Member State shall examine the admissibility of oppositions received under the scheme set out in Title II in the light of the criteria referred to in Article 10(1), or the admissibility of oppositions received under the scheme set out in Title III in the light of the criteria referred to in Article 21(1).

4.   If, after assessment of any opposition received, the Member State considers that the requirements of this Regulation are met, it may take a favourable decision and lodge an application dossier with the Commission. It shall in such case inform the Commission of admissible oppositions received from a natural or legal person that have legally marketed the products in question, using the names concerned continuously for at least five years preceding the date of the publication referred to in paragraph 3.

The Member State shall ensure that its favourable decision is made public and that any natural or legal person having a legitimate interest has an opportunity to appeal.

The Member State shall ensure that the version of the product specification on which its favourable decision is based, is published, and shall provide electronic access to the product specification.

With reference to protected designations of origin and protected geographical indications, the Member State shall also ensure adequate publication of the version of the product specification on which the Commission takes its decision pursuant to Article 50(2).

5.   Where the application under the scheme set out in Title II relates to a geographical area in a third country, or where an application under the scheme set out in Title III is prepared by a group established in a third country, the application shall be lodged with the Commission, either directly or via the authorities of the third country concerned.

6.   The documents referred to in this Article which are sent to the Commission shall be in one of the official languages of the Union.

7.   In order to facilitate the application process, the Commission shall be empowered to adopt delegated acts, in accordance with Article 56, defining the rules for carrying out the national objection procedure for joint applications concerning more than one national territory and complementing the rules of the application process.

The Commission may adopt implementing acts laying down detailed rules on procedures, form and presentation of applications, including for applications concerning more than one national territory. Those implementing acts shall be adopted in accordance with the examination procedure referred to in Article 57(2).

Article 50

Scrutiny by the Commission and publication for opposition

1.   The Commission shall scrutinise by appropriate means any application that it receives pursuant to Article 49, in order to check that it is justified and that it meets the conditions of the respective scheme. This scrutiny should not exceed a period of six months. Where this period is exceeded, the Commission shall indicate in writing to the applicant the reasons for the delay.

The Commission shall, at least each month, make public the list of names for which registration applications have been submitted to it, as well as their date of submission.

2.   Where, based on the scrutiny carried out pursuant to the first subparagraph of paragraph 1, the Commission considers that the

conditions laid down in this Regulation are fulfilled, it shall publish in the *Official Journal of the European Union*:

(a) for applications under the scheme set out in Title II, the single document and the reference to the publication of the product specification;

(b) for applications under the scheme set out in Title III, the specification.

Article 51

Opposition procedure

1. Within three months from the date of publication in the *Official Journal of the European Union*, the authorities of a Member State or of a third country, or a natural or legal person having a legitimate interest and established in a third country may lodge a notice of opposition with the Commission.

Any natural or legal person having a legitimate interest, established or resident in a Member State other than that from which the application was submitted, may lodge a notice of opposition with the Member State in which it is established within a time limit permitting an opposition to be lodged pursuant to the first subparagraph.

A notice of opposition shall contain a declaration that the application might infringe the conditions laid down in this Regulation. A notice of opposition that does not contain this declaration is void.

The Commission shall forward the notice of opposition to the authority or body that lodged the application without delay.

2. If a notice of opposition is lodged with the Commission and is followed within two months by a reasoned statement of opposition, the Commission shall check the admissibility of this reasoned statement of opposition.

3. Within two months after the receipt of an admissible reasoned statement of opposition, the Commission shall invite the authority or person that lodged the opposition and the authority or body that lodged the application to engage in appropriate consultations for a reasonable period that shall not exceed three months.

The authority or person that lodged the opposition and the authority or body that lodged the application shall start such appropriate consultations without undue delay. They shall provide each other with the relevant information to assess whether the application for registration complies with the conditions of this Regulation. If no agreement is reached, this information shall also be provided to the Commission.

At any time during these three months, the Commission may, at the request of the applicant extend the deadline for the consultations by a maximum of three months.

4.   Where, following the appropriate consultations referred to in paragraph 3 of this Article, the details published in accordance with Article 50(2) have been substantially amended, the Commission shall repeat the scrutiny referred to in Article 50.

5.   The notice of opposition, the reasoned statement of opposition and the related documents which are sent to the Commission in accordance with paragraphs 1 to 4 of this Article shall be in one of the official languages of the Union.

6.   In order to establish clear procedures and deadlines for opposition, the Commission shall be empowered to adopt delegated acts, in accordance with Article 56, complementing the rules of the opposition procedure.

The Commission may adopt implementing acts laying down detailed rules on procedures, form and presentation of the oppositions. Those implementing acts shall be adopted in accordance with the examination procedure referred to in Article 57(2).

Article 52

Decision on registration

1.   Where, on the basis of the information available to the Commission from the scrutiny carried out pursuant to the first subparagraph of Article 50(1), the Commission considers that the conditions for registration are not fulfilled, it shall adopt implementing acts rejecting the application. Those implementing acts shall be adopted in accordance with the examination procedure referred to in Article 57(2).

2.   If the Commission receives no notice of opposition or no admissible reasoned statement of opposition under Article 51, it shall adopt implementing acts, without applying the procedure referred to in Article 57(2), registering the name.

3.   If the Commission receives an admissible reasoned statement of opposition, it shall, following the appropriate consultations referred to in Article 51(3), and taking into account the results thereof, either:

   (a)   if an agreement has been reached, register the name by means of implementing acts adopted without applying the procedure referred to in Article 57(2), and, if necessary, amend the information published pursuant to Article 50(2) provided such amendments are not substantial; or

   (b)   if an agreement has not been reached, adopt implementing acts deciding on the registration. Those implementing acts shall be adopted in accordance with the examination procedure referred to in Article 57(2).

4.   Acts of registration and decisions on rejection shall be published in the *Official Journal of the European Union*.

Article 53

Amendment to a product specification

1.   A group having a legitimate interest may apply for approval of an amendment to a product specification.

Applications shall describe and give reasons for the amendments requested.

2.   Where the amendment involves one or more amendments to the specification that are not minor, the amendment application shall follow the procedure laid down in Articles 49 to 52.

However, if the proposed amendments are minor, the Commission shall approve or reject the application. In the event of the approval of amendments implying a modification of the elements referred to in Article 50(2), the Commission shall publish those elements in the *Official Journal of the European Union*.

For an amendment to be regarded as minor in the case of the quality scheme described in Title II, it shall not:

(a)   relate to the essential characteristics of the product;

(b)   alter the link referred to in point (f)(i) or (ii) of Article 7(1);

(c)   include a change to the name, or to any part of the name of the product;

(d)   affect the defined geographical area; or

(e)   represent an increase in restrictions on trade in the product or its raw materials.

For an amendment to be regarded as minor in the case of the quality scheme described in Title III, it shall not:

(a)   relate to the essential characteristics of the product;

(b)   introduce essential changes to the production method; or

(c)   include a change to the name, or to any part of the name of the product.

The scrutiny of the application shall focus on the proposed amendment.

3.   In order to facilitate the administrative process of an amendment application, including where the amendment does not involve any change

to the single document and where it concerns a temporary change in the specification resulting from the imposition of obligatory sanitary or phytosanitary measures by the public authorities, the Commission shall be empowered to adopt delegated acts, in accordance with Article 56, complementing the rules of the amendment application process.

The Commission may adopt implementing acts laying down detailed rules on procedures, form and presentation of an amendment application. Those implementing acts shall be adopted in accordance with the examination procedure referred to in Article 57(2).

Article 54

Cancellation

1.   The Commission may, on its own initiative or at the request of any natural or legal person having a legitimate interest, adopt implementing acts to cancel the registration of a protected designation of origin or of a protected geographical indication or of a traditional speciality guaranteed in the following cases:

(a)   where compliance with the conditions of the specification is not ensured;

(b)   where no product is placed on the market under the traditional speciality guaranteed, the protected designation of origin or the protected geographical indication for at least seven years.

The Commission may, at the request of the producers of product marketed under the registered name, cancel the corresponding registration.

Those implementing acts shall be adopted in accordance with the examination procedure referred to in Article 57(2).

2.   In order to ensure legal certainty that all parties have the opportunity to defend their rights and legitimate interests, the Commission shall be empowered to adopt delegated acts, in accordance with Article 56 complementing the rules regarding the cancellation process.

The Commission may adopt implementing acts laying down detailed rules on procedures and form of the cancellation process, as well as on the presentation of the requests referred to in paragraph 1 of this Article. Those implementing acts shall be adopted in accordance with the examination procedure referred to in Article 57(2).

TITLE VI

PROCEDURAL AND FINAL PROVISIONS

CHAPTER I

Local farming and direct sales

Article 55

Reporting on local farming and direct sales

No later than 4 January 2014 the Commission shall present a report to the European Parliament and to the Council on the case for a new local farming and direct sales labelling scheme to assist producers in marketing their produce locally. That report shall focus on the ability of the farmer to add value to his produce through the new label, and should take into account other criteria, such as the possibilities of reducing carbon emissions and waste through short production and distribution chains.

That report shall, if necessary, be accompanied by appropriate legislative proposals on the creation of a local farming and direct sales labelling scheme.

CHAPTER II

Procedural rules

Article 56

Exercise of the delegation

1.   The power to adopt the delegated acts is conferred on the Commission subject to the conditions laid down in this Article.

2.   The power to adopt delegated acts referred to in the second subparagraph of Article 2(1), Article 5(4), the first subparagraph of Article 7(2), the first subparagraph of Article 12(5), Article 16(2), Article 18(5), the first subparagraph of Article 19(2), the first subparagraph of Article 23(4), Article 25(3), Article 29(4), Article 30, Article 31(3) and (4), Article 41(3), Article 42(2), the first subparagraph of Article 49(7), the first subparagraph of Article 51(6), the first subparagraph of Article 53(3) and the first subparagraph of Article 54(2) shall be conferred on the Commission for a period of five years from 3 January 2013. The Commission shall draw up a report in respect of the delegation of power not later than nine months before the end of the five-year period. The delegation of power shall be tacitly extended for periods of an identical duration, unless the European Parliament or the Council opposes such extension not later than three months before the end of each period.

3.   The delegation of power referred to in the second subparagraph of Article 2(1), Article 5(4), the first subparagraph of Article 7(2), the first subparagraph of Article 12(5), Article 16(2), Article 18(5), the first

subparagraph of Article 19(2), the first subparagraph of Article 23(4), Article 25(3), Article 29(4), Article 30, Article 31(3) and (4), Article 41(3), Article 42(2), the first subparagraph of Article 49(7), the first subparagraph of Article 51(6), the first subparagraph of Article 53(3) and the first subparagraph of Article 54(2) may be revoked at any time by the European Parliament or by the Council. A decision to revoke shall put an end to the delegation of the power specified in that decision. It shall take effect the day following the publication of the decision in the *Official Journal of the European Union* or at a later date specified therein. It shall not affect the validity of any delegated acts already in force.

4.   As soon as it adopts a delegated act, the Commission shall notify it simultaneously to the European Parliament and to the Council.

5.   A delegated act adopted pursuant to the second subparagraph of Article 2(1), Article 5(4), the first subparagraph of Article 7(2), the first subparagraph of Article 12(5), Article 16(2), Article 18(5), the first subparagraph of Article 19(2), the first subparagraph of Article 23(4), Article 25(3), Article 29(4), Article 30, Article 31(3) and (4), Article 41(3), Article 42(2), the first subparagraph of Article 49(7), the first subparagraph of Article 51(6), the first subparagraph of Article 53(3) and the first subparagraph of Article 54(2) shall enter into force only if no objection has been expressed either by the European Parliament or the Council within a period of two months of notification of that act to the European Parliament and the Council or if, before the expiry of that period, the European Parliament and the Council have both informed the Commission that they will not object. That period shall be extended by two months at the initiative of the European Parliament or of the Council.

Article 57

Committee procedure

1.   The Commission shall be assisted by the Agricultural Product Quality Policy Committee. That committee shall be a committee within the meaning of Regulation (EU) No 182/2011.

2.   Where reference is made to this paragraph, Article 5 of Regulation (EU) No 182/2011 shall apply.

Where the committee delivers no opinion, the Commission shall not adopt the draft implementing act and the third subparagraph of Article 5(4) of Regulation (EU) No 182/2011 shall apply.

CHAPTER III

Repeal and final provisions

Article 58

Repeal

1.   Regulations (EC) No 509/2006 and (EC) No 510/2006 are hereby repealed.

However, Article 13 of Regulation (EC) No 509/2006 shall continue to apply in respect of applications concerning products falling outside the scope of Title III of this Regulation, received by the Commission prior to the date of entry into force of this Regulation.

2.   References to the repealed Regulations shall be construed as references to this Regulation and be read in accordance with the correlation table in Annex II to this Regulation.

Article 59

Entry into force

This Regulation shall enter into force on the twentieth day following that of its publication in the *Official Journal of the European Union*.

However, Article 12(3) and Article 23(3) shall apply from 4 January 2016, without prejudice to products already placed on the market before that date.

This Regulation shall be binding in its entirety and directly applicable in all Member States.

Done at Strasbourg, 21 November 2012.

For the European Parliament

The President

M. SCHULZ

For the Council

The President

A. D. MAVROYIANNIS

ANNEX I

AGRICULTURAL PRODUCTS AND FOODSTUFFS
REFERRED TO IN ARTICLE 2(1)

I. Designations of Origin and Geographical indications

— beer,

— chocolate and derived products,

— bread, pastry, cakes, confectionery, biscuits and other baker's wares,

— beverages made from plant extracts,

— pasta,

— salt,

— natural gums and resins,

— mustard paste,

— hay,

— essential oils,

— cork,

— cochineal,

— flowers and ornamental plants,

— cotton,

— wool,

— wicker,

— scutched flax,

— leather,

— fur,

— feather.

II. Traditional specialities guaranteed

— prepared meals,

— beer,

— chocolate and derived products,

— bread, pastry, cakes, confectionery, biscuits and other baker's wares,

— beverages made from plant extracts,

— pasta,

— salt.

ANNEX II

CORRELATION TABLE REFERRED TO IN ARTICLE 58(2)

Regulation (EC) No 509/2006	This Regulation
Article 1(1)	Article 2(1)
Article 1(2)	Article 2(3)
Article 1(3)	Article 2(4)
Article 2(1), point (a)	Article 3, point (5)
Article 2(1), point (b)	Article 3, point (3)
Article 2(1), point (c)	—
Article 2(1), point (d)	Article 3, point (2)
Article 2(2), first to third subparagraph	—
Article 2(2), fourth subparagraph	—
Article 3	Article 22(1)
Article 4(1), first subparagraph	Article 18(1)
Article 4(2)	Article 18(2)
Article 4(3), first subparagraph	—
Article 4(3), second subparagraph	Article 18(4)
Article 5(1)	Article 43
Article 5(2)	Article 42(1)
Article 6(1)	Article 19(1)
Article 6(1), point (a)	Article 19(1), point (a)
Article 6(1), point (b)	Article 19(1), point (b)
Article 6(1), point (c)	Article 19(1), point (c)
Article 6(1), point (d)	—
Article 6(1), point (e)	Article 19(1), point (d)

Regulation (EC) No 509/2006	This Regulation
Article 6(1), point (f)	—
Article 7(1) and (2)	Article 49(1)
Article 7(3), points (a) and (b)	Article 20(1), points (a) and (b)
Article 7(3), point (c)	—
Article 7(3), point (d)	—
Article 7(4)	Article 49(2)
Article 7(5)	Article 49(3)
Article 7(6), points (a), (b) and (c)	Article 49(4)
Article 7(6), point (d)	Article 20(2)
Article 7(7)	Article 49(5)
Article 7(8)	Article 49(6)
Article 8(1)	Article 50(1)
Article 8(2), first subparagraph	Article 50(2), point (b)
Article 8(2), second subparagraph	Article 52(1)
Article 9(1) and (2)	Article 51(1)
Article 9(3)	Article 21(1) and (2)
Article 9(4)	Article 52(2)
Article 9(5)	Article 52(3) and (4)
Article 9(6)	Article 51(5)
Article 10	Article 54
Article 11	Article 53
Article 12	Article 23
Article 13(1)	—
Article 13(2)	—
Article 13(3)	—
Article 14(1)	Article 36(1)
Article 14(2)	Article 46(1)
Article 14(3)	Article 37(3), second subparagraph

Regulation (EC) No 509/2006	This Regulation
Article 15(1)	Article 37(1)
Article 15(2)	Article 37(2)
Article 15(3)	Article 39(2)
Article 15(4)	Article 36(2)
Article 16	—
Article 17(1) and (2)	Article 24(1)
Article 17(3)	Article 24(2)
Article 18	Article 57
Article 19(1), point (a)	—
Article 19(1), point (b)	Article 49(7), second subparagraph
Article 19(1), point (c)	Article 49(7), first subparagraph
Article 19(1), point (d)	Article 22(2)
Article 19(1), point (e)	Article 19(1), point (f)
Article 19(1), point (e)	Article 54(1)
Article 19(1), point (g)	Article 23(4)
Article 19(1), point (h)	—
Article 19(1), point (i)	—
Article 19(2)	Article 25(1)
Article 19(3), point (a)	—
Article 19(3), point (b)	Article 25(2)
Article 20	Article 47
Article 21	Article 58
Article 22	Article 59
Annex I	Annex I (Part II)

Regulation (EC) No 510/2006	This Regulation
Article 1(1)	Article 2(1) and (2)
Article 1(2)	Article 2(3)
Article 1(3)	Article 2(4)
Article 2	Article 5
Article 3(1), first subparagraph	Article 6(1)
Article 3(1), second and third subparagraph	Article 41(1), (2) and (3)
Article 3(2), (3) and (4)	Article 6(2), (3) and (4)
Article 4	Article 7
Article 5(1)	Article 3, point (2), and Article 49(1)
Article 5(2)	Article 49(1)
Article 5(3)	Article 8(1)
Article 5(4)	Article 49(2)
Article 5(5)	Article 49(3)
Article 5(6)	Article 9
Article 5(7)	Article 8(2)
Article 5(8)	—
Article 5(9), first subparagraph	—
Article 5(9), second subparagraph	Article 49(5)
Article 5(10)	Article 49(6)
Article 5(11)	—
Article 6(1), first subparagraph	Article 50(1)
Article 6(2), first subparagraph	Article 50(2), point (a)
Article 6(2), second subparagraph	Article 52(1)
Article 7(1)	Article 51(1), first subparagraph
Article 7(2)	Article 51(1), second subparagraph
Article 7(3)	Article 10
Article 7(4)	Article 52(2) and (4)

Regulation (EC) No 510/2006	This Regulation
Article 7(5)	Article 51(3) and Article 52(3) and (4)
Article 7(6)	Article 11
Article 7(7)	Article 51(5)
Article 8	Article 12
Article 9	Article 53
Article 10(1)	Article 36(1)
Article 10(2)	Article 46(1)
Article 10(3)	Article 37(3), second subparagraph
Article 11(1)	Article 37(1)
Article 11(2)	Article 37(2)
Article 11(3)	Article 39(2)
Article 11(4)	Article 36(2)
Article 12	Article 54
Article 13(1)	Article 13(1)
Article 13(2)	Article 13(2)
Article 13(3)	Article 15(1)
Article 13(4)	Article 15(2)
Article 14	Article 14
Article 15	Article 57
Article 16, point (a)	Article 5(4), second subparagraph
Article 16, point (b)	—
Article 16, point (c)	—
Article 16, point (d)	Article 49(7)
Article 16, point (e)	—
Article 16, point (f)	Article 51(6)
Article 16, point (g)	Article 12(7)
Article 16, point (h)	—
Article 16, point (i)	Article 11(3)

Regulation (EC) No 510/2006	This Regulation
Article 16, point (j)	—
Article 16, point (k)	Article 54(2)
Article 17	Article 16
Article 18	Article 47
Article 19	Article 58
Article 20	Article 59
Annex I and Annex II	Annex I (Part I)

ICANN UNIFORM DOMAIN NAME DISPUTE RESOLUTION POLICY (UDRP)

(As Approved by ICANN on October 24, 1999)

1. <u>Purpose</u>. This Uniform Domain Name Dispute Resolution Policy (the "Policy") has been adopted by the Internet Corporation for Assigned Names and Numbers ("ICANN"), is incorporated by reference into your Registration Agreement, and sets forth the terms and conditions in connection with a dispute between you and any party other than us (the registrar) over the registration and use of an Internet domain name registered by you. Proceedings under Paragraph 4 of this Policy will be conducted according to the Rules for Uniform Domain Name Dispute Resolution Policy (the "Rules of Procedure"), which are available at www. icann.org/udrp/udrp-rules-24oct99.htm, and the selected administrative-dispute-resolution service provider's supplemental rules.

2. <u>Your Representations</u>. By applying to register a domain name, or by asking us to maintain or renew a domain name registration, you hereby represent and warrant to us that (a) the statements that you made in your Registration Agreement are complete and accurate; (b) to your knowledge, the registration of the domain name will not infringe upon or otherwise violate the rights of any third party; (c) you are not registering the domain name for an unlawful purpose; and (d) you will not knowingly use the domain name in violation of any applicable laws or regulations. It is your responsibility to determine whether your domain name registration infringes or violates someone else's rights.

3. <u>Cancellations, Transfers, and Changes</u>. We will cancel, transfer or otherwise make changes to domain name registrations under the following circumstances:

    a. subject to the provisions of Paragraph 8, our receipt of written or appropriate electronic instructions from you or your authorized agent to take such action;

    b. our receipt of an order from a court or arbitral tribunal, in each case of competent jurisdiction, requiring such action; and/or

    c. our receipt of a decision of an Administrative Panel requiring such action in any administrative proceeding to which you were a party and which was conducted under this Policy or a later version of this Policy adopted by ICANN. (See Paragraph 4(i) and (k) below.)

We may also cancel, transfer or otherwise make changes to a domain name registration in accordance with the terms of your Registration Agreement or other legal requirements.

4.   Mandatory Administrative Proceeding.

This Paragraph sets forth the type of disputes for which you are required to submit to a mandatory administrative proceeding. These proceedings will be conducted before one of the administrative-dispute-resolution service providers listed at www.icann.org/udrp/approved-providers.htm (each, a "Provider").

    a.   Applicable Disputes. You are required to submit to a mandatory administrative proceeding in the event that a third party (a "complainant") asserts to the applicable Provider, in compliance with the Rules of Procedure, that

        (i)   your domain name is identical or confusingly similar to a trademark or service mark in which the complainant has rights; and

        (ii)   you have no rights or legitimate interests in respect of the domain name; and

        (iii) your domain name has been registered and is being used in bad faith.

In the administrative proceeding, the complainant must prove that each of these three elements are present.

    b.   Evidence of Registration and Use in Bad Faith. For the purposes of Paragraph 4(a)(iii), the following circumstances, in particular but without limitation, if found by the Panel to be present, shall be evidence of the registration and use of a domain name in bad faith:

        (i)   circumstances indicating that you have registered or you have acquired the domain name primarily for the purpose of selling, renting, or otherwise transferring the domain name registration to the complainant who is the owner of the trademark or service mark or to a competitor of that complainant, for valuable consideration in excess of your documented out-of-pocket costs directly related to the domain name; or

        (ii)   you have registered the domain name in order to prevent the owner of the trademark or service mark from reflecting the mark in a corresponding domain name, provided that you have engaged in a pattern of such conduct; or

(iii) you have registered the domain name primarily for the purpose of disrupting the business of a competitor; or

(iv) by using the domain name, you have intentionally attempted to attract, for commercial gain, Internet users to your web site or other on-line location, by creating a likelihood of confusion with the complainant's mark as to the source, sponsorship, affiliation, or endorsement of your web site or location or of a product or service on your web site or location.

c.   How to Demonstrate Your Rights to and Legitimate Interests in the Domain Name in Responding to a Complaint. When you receive a complaint, you should refer to Paragraph 5 of the Rules of Procedure in determining how your response should be prepared. Any of the following circumstances, in particular but without limitation, if found by the Panel to be proved based on its evaluation of all evidence presented, shall demonstrate your rights or legitimate interests to the domain name for purposes of Paragraph 4(a)(ii):

(i)   before any notice to you of the dispute, your use of, or demonstrable preparations to use, the domain name or a name corresponding to the domain name in connection with a bona fide offering of goods or services; or

(ii) you (as an individual, business, or other organization) have been commonly known by the domain name, even if you have acquired no trademark or service mark rights; or

(iii) you are making a legitimate noncommercial or fair use of the domain name, without intent for commercial gain to misleadingly divert consumers or to tarnish the trademark or service mark at issue.

d.   Selection of Provider. The complainant shall select the Provider from among those approved by ICANN by submitting the complaint to that Provider. The selected Provider will administer the proceeding, except in cases of consolidation as described in Paragraph 4(f).

e.   Initiation of Proceeding and Process and Appointment of Administrative Panel. The Rules of Procedure state the process for initiating and conducting a proceeding and for appointing the panel that will decide the dispute (the "Administrative Panel").

f.   Consolidation. In the event of multiple disputes between you and a complainant, either you or the complainant may petition to consolidate the disputes before a single Administrative Panel. This petition shall be made to the first Administrative Panel appointed to hear a pending dispute between the parties. This

Administrative Panel may consolidate before it any or all such disputes in its sole discretion, provided that the disputes being consolidated are governed by this Policy or a later version of this Policy adopted by ICANN.

g. Fees. All fees charged by a Provider in connection with any dispute before an Administrative Panel pursuant to this Policy shall be paid by the complainant, except in cases where you elect to expand the Administrative Panel from one to three panelists as provided in Paragraph 5(b)(iv) of the Rules of Procedure, in which case all fees will be split evenly by you and the complainant.

h. Our Involvement in Administrative Proceedings. We do not, and will not, participate in the administration or conduct of any proceeding before an Administrative Panel. In addition, we will not be liable as a result of any decisions rendered by the Administrative Panel.

i. Remedies. The remedies available to a complainant pursuant to any proceeding before an Administrative Panel shall be limited to requiring the cancellation of your domain name or the transfer of your domain name registration to the complainant.

j. Notification and Publication. The Provider shall notify us of any decision made by an Administrative Panel with respect to a domain name you have registered with us. All decisions under this Policy will be published in full over the Internet, except when an Administrative Panel determines in an exceptional case to redact portions of its decision.

k. Availability of Court Proceedings. The mandatory administrative proceeding requirements set forth in Paragraph 4 shall not prevent either you or the complainant from submitting the dispute to a court of competent jurisdiction for independent resolution before such mandatory administrative proceeding is commenced or after such proceeding is concluded. If an Administrative Panel decides that your domain name registration should be cancelled or transferred, we will wait ten (10) business days (as observed in the location of our principal office) after we are informed by the applicable Provider of the Administrative Panel's decision before implementing that decision. We will then implement the decision unless we have received from you during that ten (10) business day period official documentation (such as a copy of a complaint, file-stamped by the clerk of the court) that you have commenced a lawsuit against the complainant in a jurisdiction to which the complainant has submitted under Paragraph 3(b)(xiii) of the Rules of Procedure. (In general, that jurisdiction is either the location of our principal office or of your address as shown in our Whois database. See Paragraphs 1 and 3(b)(xiii) of the Rules of Procedure for details.) If we receive such documentation within the ten (10) business day period, we will not implement the Administrative Panel's decision, and we will take no further action, until we receive (i) evidence satisfactory to us of a resolution between the parties; (ii) evidence satisfactory to us that your lawsuit has been dismissed or withdrawn; or (iii) a copy of an order from such court dismissing your lawsuit or ordering that you do not have the right to continue to use your domain name.

5.   All Other Disputes and Litigation. All other disputes between you and any party other than us regarding your domain name registration that are not brought pursuant to the mandatory administrative proceeding provisions of Paragraph 4 shall be resolved between you and such other party through any court, arbitration or other proceeding that may be available.

6.   Our Involvement in Disputes. We will not participate in any way in any dispute between you and any party other than us regarding the registration and use of your domain name. You shall not name us as a party or otherwise include us in any such proceeding. In the event that we are named as a party in any such proceeding, we reserve the right to raise any and all defenses deemed appropriate, and to take any other action necessary to defend ourselves.

7.   Maintaining the Status Quo. We will not cancel, transfer, activate, deactivate, or otherwise change the status of any domain name registration under this Policy except as provided in Paragraph 3 above.

8.   Transfers During a Dispute.

a.   Transfers of a Domain Name to a New Holder. You may not transfer your domain name registration to another holder (i) during a pending administrative proceeding brought pursuant to Paragraph 4 or for a period of fifteen (15) business days (as observed in the location of our principal place of business) after such proceeding is concluded; or (ii) during a pending court proceeding or arbitration commenced regarding your domain name unless the party to whom the domain name registration is being transferred agrees, in writing, to be bound by the decision of the court or arbitrator. We reserve the right to cancel any transfer of a domain name registration to another holder that is made in violation of this subparagraph.

b.   Changing Registrars. You may not transfer your domain name registration to another registrar during a pending administrative proceeding brought pursuant to Paragraph 4 or for a period of fifteen (15) business days (as observed in the location of our principal place of business) after such proceeding is concluded. You may transfer administration of your domain name registration to another registrar during a pending court action or arbitration, provided that the domain name you have registered with us shall continue to be subject to the proceedings commenced against you in accordance with the terms of this Policy. In the event that you transfer a domain name registration to us during the pendency of a court action or arbitration, such dispute shall remain subject to the domain name dispute policy of the registrar from which the domain name registration was transferred.

9.   Policy Modifications. We reserve the right to modify this Policy at any time with the permission of ICANN. We will post our revised Policy at least thirty (30) calendar days before it becomes effective. Unless this Policy has already been invoked by the submission of a complaint to a Provider, in which event the version of the Policy in effect at the time it was invoked will apply to you until the dispute is over, all such changes will be binding upon you with respect to any domain name registration dispute, whether the dispute arose before, on or after the effective date of our change. In the event that you object to a change in this Policy, your sole remedy is to cancel your domain name registration with us, provided that you will not be entitled to a refund of any fees you paid to us. The revised Policy will apply to you until you cancel your domain name registration.